NEW SUNDAY
AND HOLY DAY
LITURGIES

YEAR B

Flor McCarthy is a Salesian priest who has worked as a catechist in second level schools and has extensive parish experience in Ireland and the USA. His other books include *Funeral Liturgies* and *Wedding Liturgies*.

Information about the artists whose work is featured appears on page 6.

New
Sunday and Holy Day
Liturgies

YEAR B

Flor McCarthy

DOMINICAN PUBLICATIONS

First published (1999) by
Dominican Publications
42 Parnell Square
Dublin 1

ISBN 1-871552-71-0

British Library Cataloguing in Publications Data.
A catalogue record for this book is available
from the British Library.

Cover design by David Cooke

Printed in Ireland by
Betaprint, Dublin.

Reprinted   January 2000
July 2002

Contents

Artists Featured

Seán Adamson is an Irish artist. His line drawing 'Resurrection' (page 99) first appeared in *Doctrine and Life*, in March 1967.

Albert Carpentier (see pages 65 and 359) is a Belgian-born Dominican artist who lives and works in Tokyo. His 'Madonna' (page 359) is from a stained glass window in a Dominican convent in Tokyo.

Gerard Kavanagh (see page 33) studied at the National College of Art and Design, Dublin. His painting of Saint Augustine has been acquired for the Irish Augustinians.

Oisín Kelly (1915-1981) was a distinguished sculptor. His most acclaimed public work is the depiction of the Children of Lir for the Graden of Remembrance, Dublin. He did some work for churches, notably Holy Cross, Sligo, and his meditation on the Trinity appears on page 151.

Patrick Pye, painter, stained glass artist and etcher, whose work is reproduced on page 9, is one of Ireland's most distinguished artists, and is widely recognised as the country's foremost religious artist.

Introduction

Fifteen years have passed since the original *Sunday and Holy Day Liturgies* came out. Much to my surprise these works proved very successful. Since then I have done a lot of preaching, reading and reflecting. As a result I have accumulated a lot of new material. The new series gives me the opportunity to share this material with others.

Now, there are three homilies for each occasion, and sometimes additional material besides. The vast bulk of this material is new. Wherever old material is retained, I have tried to improve it. In general, the homilies are shorter and more focused than in the original series. Once again, I rely heavily on stories.

But in preparing a Sunday liturgy don't turn to this book just for the homily. Every part of a liturgy should speak. For this reason I have put a lot of care into the Introduction to the Mass, the Key to the Readings, the Prayer of the Faithful, and the Reflection. The main thing here is to be brief and to the point. We must guard against turning the Mass into a series of mini-homilies.

Even though I have worked and reworked these homilies, they are not put forward as the complete thing. They are put forward as approximations in the hope that the user will take them up, refine them, adapt them, and make them his/her own. In this way they can be kept alive. They are sentenced to death once they are judged definitive.

The series contains one new feature. On most occasions I have added a brief Scripture Note which highlights the theme of the readings or the theological meaning of a particular feast. If no mention is made of the Second Reading it means that I consider what is said in the Key to the Readings to be sufficient. In compiling these notes I am indebted to the works of two scripture scholars in particular, Wilfrid Harrington and the late Raymond Brown.

My thanks to Frs Austin Flannery and Bernard Treacy and to all the staff at Dominican Publications for their help. My thanks also to the many people who have told me how helpful they found the original series.

Flor McCarthy

ADVENT

John the Baptist

PATRICK PYE

First Sunday of Advent

Advent is a time of watchfulness. We are waiting for the final coming of Christ at the end of time. And we are also waiting for his coming to us at the time of our death. Since both times are hidden from us, we should maintain a state of watchfulness so that we are ready to meet the Lord at any moment. [Pause]

Lord Jesus, you call us to be watchful in prayer. Lord, have mercy.

You call us to be active in good works. Christ, have mercy.

You call us to be strong in faith, serene in hope, and constant in love. Lord, have mercy.

HEADINGS FOR READINGS

First Reading (Is 63:16-17; 64:1.3-8). The prophet recalls God's past goodness to his people, and pleads with him to save them from their present sinfulness.

Second Reading (1 Cor 1:3-9). As we await the coming of Christ in glory, the Holy Spirit keeps us steadfast in bearing witness to him.

Gospel (Mk 13:33-37). We need to stay awake at our appointed tasks, because we do not know the hour when the Jesus, our Master, will return.

SCRIPTURE NOTE

The season of Advent prepares us for Christmas. In order to understand the message of Christmas we have to start at the beginning – with the history of salvation. The Advent liturgy relives in a microcosmic way the history of Israel, viewing it through the eyes of Christian faith. It shows that all of that history was pointing and leading towards Jesus. He was the one who fulfilled the messianic prophecies.

As for today's readings – the First is a poem (written by a returned exile) entreating God to come and save his people. It recalls God's past goodness, and candidly acknowledges the ingratitude and sinfulness of his people.

The Second Reading and the Gospel talk about the final coming of Christ, something the early Christians believed was imminent. For the faithful, the Lord's coming is not something to fear. They are urged to live in such a way as to be always ready to meet the Lord. These words are addressed to us now.

HOMILY 1   **The sleep of habit**

Three times in today's Gospel passage Jesus urges his disciples to 'stay awake'. The call to 'stay awake' is meant for us too. It is a very appropriate call for the beginning of the new liturgical year.

They say that the swallows return to the exact same nest each year. They travel all that way to end up in the same locality. What does this tell us about swallows? That they are creatures of habit.

Habit plays a big part in our lives. All of us, except the very young, are to a great degree creatures of habit. It is said that we live the second half of our lives according to the habits acquired during the first half. That will be comforting for those who have formed good habits. But it will be disturbing for those who have formed bad habits.

There is a *positive side* to habit. Repetition is necessary. It is a hard grind and a tough discipline, but it can bear fruit. Athletes have shown us that repetition can produce results. Only thus is a skill mastered. The most perfect actions are effortless, because through dent of habit, they have become second nature to us.

Habits can be life-giving and sustaining. Daily habits and routines can keep people going and help them to get through bad times, when even the smallest of our daily habits becomes meaningful.

Nelson Mandela gives us an example of this. Writing about his time in prison, he says: 'To survive in prison, one must develop ways to take satisfaction in one's daily life. One can feel fulfilled by washing one's clothes, by sweeping a corridor ... '

But there is a *negative side* to habit. There is a lot of repetition in life, especially in work. As a result of doing the same things day in and day out, we get into a rut, and end up doing things merely out of habit. This results in things being done absented-mindedly and in a casual, unthinking manner. There is no real heart or feeling in them. This is sad, and soul-destroying.

Habit can be a great deadener. It can dull our senses, especially our seeing and hearing. It can put us to sleep, so that we are not so much living as merely functioning.

Furthermore, habits can be selfish. Habits are very hard to break, especially bad habits. We can get used to anything, even prison walls. First you hate them, then you get used to them, and then you depend on them.

If you place a frog in a pot of hot water, it will jump right out. But if you put a frog into a pot of cold water that is slowly brought to the boil, the frog will just sit there. Its nervous system is so primitive, it needs a sudden jolt to realise that it is in danger.

Maybe that is the purpose of Advent. It gives us a jolt. It issues a wake-up call to us. It provides us with a chance to start again. We can easily become Christians by habit only. We may be just going through the motions, taking part in rituals that have lost all freshness and meaning. We don't hear the Gospel anymore.

Advent calls us to wake up. To shake off the dust of routine and habit, and to let Christ come alive in our lives once more.

HOMILY 2   **Treasure in vessels of clay**

Today's First Reading ends like this: 'Lord, you are our Father; we are the clay, you are the potter, we are all the work of your hand.' These words humble us because they remind us that we are clay. But they also elevate us because they tell us that God is the potter. Better still. God is our Father, which means we are his children. We have a divine dignity, though we carry this dignity in vessels of clay.

There was a father who had four children. When they were old enough to leave home, he gave each of them a treasure. The treasure was sealed in a simple earthenware jar. Though this surprised them, none of them objected. A treasure was still a treasure.

Justin, the oldest of the four, bore the treasure away with great joy. However, the joy soon wore off. He got tired of having to handle the jar as if it were a piece of rare china. He began to grumble against his father, saying that it was unfair, even cruel, of him to ask him to carry the treasure in such a perishable container.

And yet there were times when he could see reasons for this. Was his father not showing the greatest possible trust in him? If he had put the treasure in an unbreakable container that would not be showing much trust in him. Nevertheless, Justin grew tired and careless. The inevitable happened. He let the jar fall. It got badly cracked, so he put it aside. Ever afterwards he held a grudge against his father.

Anne, the second oldest, went at once and had the jar encased in a metal container. Then she proceeded to encrust the case with precious stones. Every penny she earned, and she earned a great amount, went into this. The jar glittered with diamonds and rubies. She was very proud of it, and availed of every opportunity to show it off in public. However, the result was that the container became her real treasure, and she forgot about the inner treasure.

Brendan, the third oldest, carried the treasure with care and love for a while. But then he began to have doubts about its value. 'How can I be sure that I'm not being deceived?' he asked himself. 'What if there is no treasure in the jar after all?' Falling on hard times, he sold it for a pittance, but afterwards felt guilty for having done so.

Sarah, the youngest of the four, carried the treasure with the utmost care. She had no doubts about its value, so great was her trust in her father. Even though many misfortunes befell her, she never lost heart. She had one real anchor in her life. Not so much the treasure, as the love of her father which the treasure symbolised.

Years went by. Then one day a message came saying that their father was dying and wished to see them. They figured that he wanted them to give an account of what they had done with the treasures he had given them. Justin and Brendan were apprehensive about the encounter. Anne was looking forward to it. Sarah was overcome with sorrow at the prospect of her father's death.

When the meeting took place the father enquired earnestly about the well-being of each of his children. Not as much as a word about the treasures! Finally Anne said, 'Dad, aren't you going to ask us about the treasures?'

'I've already done so,' he replied.

'I don't understand,' said she.

'Why, you are my treasures,' said he.

We are God's children. He loves us with an unconditional love. This should be a solid place to which we return after every failure. We must let ourselves be loved, not for what we have done, but just for being. We are not lumps of clay. We are God's precious children. Happy those who do not doubt this. However, God has given us responsibility for our lives. The way to return his love is to use his great gift in a responsible way.

Three times in today's Gospel passage Jesus tells his disciples to 'stay awake'. The call to 'stay awake' is meant for us too. It is a very appropriate call for the beginning of the new liturgical year. It's an ideal opportunity to wake up to the grandeur of our divine dignity, and to try to live accordingly.

HOMILY 3   **The servants**

In today's Gospel there is a short little parable. It concerns a householder who had a number of servants. Once, before leaving for a trip abroad, he called them together and gave each of them a job to do. He urged them to be responsible saying, 'When I return I want to find you awake.' He singled out the doorkeeper for a special warning.

Christ's story ends there with that warning ringing in our ears. Let us take it a little further, concentrating on the doorkeeper. Perhaps the greatest danger facing him is not so much that he may fall asleep on the job, as that he may grow accustomed to it.

In the beginning he is all excited about the task. He feels honoured that the Boss placed so much trust in him. He loves the uniform. When he puts it on he feels he is somebody. He is conscientious to the point of being scrupulous. It is not so much a job for him as a labour of love.

But time goes by. Opening and closing doors can get very monotonous. The novelty wears off. Slowly but surely the dust of habit accumulates on him and his world. A deadly routine takes over. He is still responsible, still unfailingly at his post. But he is merely going through the motions. The initial love and enthusiasm have evaporated. His heart is no longer in it. When the Master returns he will undoubtedly find him at his post. He will be awake, but he will not be alive. He will be dead, for he has lost his soul.

Habit gradually deadens us and in the end snuffs out all life. We get sunk in ruts of tradition and conformity. We forget we once had dreams. We sit in our armchairs practising idle and musty virtues, passing judgement on everything and everybody.

What happens in ordinary life happens in our Christian life too. We can get into a deadly routine with the result that we are Christians by habit only. We are merely going through the motions. We are taking part in rituals that have lost all freshness and meaning. We don't hear the Gospel anymore. It just goes in one ear and out the other. The face of Christ has vanished from our sight.

So what's the solution? We need to be disturbed from time to time. This is where Advent comes in. Advent issues a great 'wake up' call to us. It provides us with an opportunity to shake off the dust of habit, and to let Christ come alive in our lives once more.

The Lord is coming. He will come to each of us at death, and to the world at the end of time. We don't know the day or the hour of his coming. Any time is the wrong time for the unfaithful servant. But any time is the right time for the faithful servant. The faithful servant doesn't fear the Lord's coming; he welcomes it.

We have to be ready. How? By being alive, alert, responsible servants of the Lord and of one another.

ANOTHER STORY **The gate-keeper**

Once upon a time there was a great kingdom. At the centre of this kingdom stood a magnificent castle. From this castle the kingdom was ruled. At the time our story begins the Blues were in possession of the castle.

Robert was in charge of the main gate leading to the castle. All who wished to enter had to go through him. He wore a blue uniform, which he loved dearly and kept in immaculate condition. He was both intelligent and efficient. And he was as reliable as the gateposts themselves.

Though his job was a very responsible one, it was quite straightforward. Hence, his life, though busy, was tranquil and uncomplicated. He knew exactly what was expected of him. He had his orders. According to those orders, he was to keep out all Non-Blues.

He carried out those orders to the letter. He made not the slightest exception. He listened to no pleas, no matter how heart-rending they might be. He was especially hard on Greens. But where Blues were concerned he was the perfect gentleman, all smiles and graciousness.

Time passed. Then the Greens revolted, overthrew the Blues, and took possession of the castle. The first thing they did was to issue a decree prohibiting all Non-Greens from entering the castle.

What happened to Robert? One might think that his head would have been one of the first to roll. Believe it or not, he retained his job. And he was every bit as faithful to his new bosses as he had been to his old ones. He was rigid in keeping out all Non-Greens, and, according to instructions, was especially hard on Blues. But where Greens were concerned he was the perfect gentleman.

In a sense, then, the revolution scarcely touched him. In fact, there was only one tangible change in his life. He was now wearing a green uniform.

Comment: Robert is a very loyal man. But who or what is he loyal to? In actual fact, he has no morality, no conscience, no loyalties, except perhaps to himself. He has sold his soul. It is people like him who enable despots to carry out their dark deeds. Auschwitz could never have happened without people like Robert. He is a million miles from the kind of servant Jesus had in mind in his parable.

PRAYER OF THE FAITHFUL

President: In a world divided by greed and fear, let us ask God to come to our help and bring us back to him.

Response: Lord, hear us in your love.

Reader(s): For Christians: that their lives may bear witness to the faith they profess with their lips. [Pause] We pray in faith.

For all those who hold positions of trust and responsibility in our society: that they may prove to be good and faithful servants. [Pause] We pray in faith.

For those who do dull and repetitive work. [Pause] We pray in faith.

For al gathered here: that God may awaken our faith from the sleep of habit and routine. [Pause] We pray in faith.

For our dead, those we have loved and those no one remembers: that God may keep them all in his care. [Pause] We pray in faith.

For our own special needs. [Longer pause] We pray in faith.

President: All-powerful God, you are the same yesterday, today, and forever; help us to have confidence in your unchanging love for us, so that we may have the strength to persevere in goodness. We ask this through Christ our Lord.

REFLECTION   **Advent: a time of hope**

It is said that while there is life there is hope.
This has an even deeper meaning in reverse:
while there is hope there is life.

Hope is strength.
Hope sheds light into despairing hearts.
It inspires the will to live.
It is the doctor's most powerful ally.
It is a shield against defeat and failure.
It revives ideals and renews dreams.
As long as there is hope, no situation is impossible.
Advent summons us to wait in joyful hope
for the coming of our Saviour, Jesus Christ.
In the final analysis, he is our hope.

Second Sunday of Advent
PREPARING THE WAY FOR THE LORD

INTRODUCTION AND CONFITEOR

In today's liturgy we hear again the lonely voice of John the Baptist calling us to prepare a way for the Lord. This involves finding time in our busy lives, and space in our busy hearts, for the Lord. Let us offer that time and space to the Lord now so that he can come to us in this Eucharist. [Pause]

One thing the Lord brings us is forgiveness. Let us confess our sins with confidence in his mercy.

HEADINGS FOR READINGS

First Reading (Is 40:1-5.9-11). The people are urged to prepare a way for the Lord who is coming to save them.

Second Reading (2 Pet 3:8-14). If the Lord appears to be slow in coming, it is to give people an opportunity to be ready to meet him when he comes.

Gospel (Mk 1:1-8). John the Baptist urges the people to prepare for the imminent coming of the Saviour.

SCRIPTURE NOTE

The First Reading is a message of hope and consolation addressed to the exiles in Babylon. Humanly speaking, at that time there was little ground for hope. Yet the prophet assures his people that God is about to come to their aid, and will lead them back to their own land in a new exodus. Even though the actual return from exile fell far short of the glowing picture painted here, Isaiah's words point the way to the messianic era.

This leads into the Gospel. Like a new Elijah, John appears in the desert and announces the coming of the redeemer – Jesus, the Christ and Son of

God (two christological titles with which Mark begins his Gospel). Both readings issue a call to repentance: 'Prepare a way for the Lord.'

In the Second Reading Peter is talking about the second coming. The reason for the Lord's delay is to give everybody an opportunity to repent.

HOMILY 1   **The straight path**

One message rings out loud and clear from the readings of today's Mass. We hear it in the First Reading, and it sounds again in the Gospel. That message is: 'Prepare a way for the Lord … make a straight highway for our God … '

A straight road shortens the journey for the traveller. In modern times the bulldozer has straightened out many a winding road, levelled many a mountain, and filled in many a valley. But of course this is not what the prophet is talking about when he says, 'Make a straight highway for the Lord.'

The highway to be made straight is our way of life. It is not the Lord who needs the straight path but we. And it's not so much a straight path we need as a straight attitude. People may be living next door to one another, yet, because of a hostile or unforgiving attitude, they may be unable to travel the few yards that separate them from one another.

Here the word 'straight' stands for honesty and right living. People are sometimes urged to straighten themselves out. We know what that means. To go straight means to reform after having been dishonest or criminal. Crooked, on the other hand, stands for dishonesty, cheating, deceit, and so on. There can be a crooked way of dealing with others, a crooked attitude, a crooked way of living.

We find the path by acting with integrity, treating people fairly, refraining from any form of oppression, not making life more difficult for anyone, sharing with those in need. This is the way to seek God. The prophet Micah put it even more simply when he said, 'This is what God asks of you: That you act justly, love tenderly, and walk humbly with your God.' (Mic 6:8).

How easy things become for the one who walks the straight path – the path of the Lord. But to walk a straight path one needs strength, wisdom, and single-mindedness.

How crooked the path of the one who is devious. How dark the path of the one who lies and cheats. It may be downhill, but the vision is diminishing. The right path, on the other hand, is an ascending one. The ever-expanding view compensates for the difficulty of the climb.

If there is some crooked attitude, or some crooked way of behaving, or some crooked relationship that needs to be straighten out, let us try to do so. Then we will truly be preparing a way for the Lord to come to us, and to come to others through us.

Fortunately everything doesn't depend on our efforts. The Lord can come in spite of us, just as the dawn comes. However, let us ask the Lord to take the blindness from our eyes, the weakness from our wills, and the hardness from our hearts, so that the world may be flooded by the grace of his coming.

HOMILY 2   **John the Baptist**

A man went out for a walk on a cold but bright winter's morning. The sun had just come up and was scattering light to the four corners of the sky. As he walked along he noticed that the moon too was in the sky. But it was so pale compared to the sun that it was barely visible. An hour or so ago, it was a bright and beautiful creature, and dominated the sky. Now it looked like a beggar, and had been pushed into the background. It was like a candle made redundant by electric light. But as the man looked at it, it suddenly occurred to him that it was this ragged creature whose faithful light had seen people through the darkness of the night.

The moon reminds us of the Old Testament prophets, and perhaps especially of John the Baptist. The prophets had kept alive the hopes of the people during the long night of expectation, when it seemed that the dawn would never come. It was thanks to them that the flame never went out.

John was the last and greatest of those selfless and courageous individuals who prepared the people for the coming of the Messiah. He worked hard to bring his own light to the people. For a while he dominated the scene, and enjoyed great popularity. But he was always conscious of the fact that a greater light was coming, a light he himself was not destined to walk in.

When that light appeared in the person of Jesus, John knew that his task was done. He didn't hinder or seek to delay the advent of the new light. On the contrary, he welcomed it, facilitated it, encouraged it. He pointed Jesus out to the people, and acknowledged that Jesus was far greater than himself. He was only the moon; Jesus was the sun. Then John stepped aside and allowed Jesus to shine, knowing that it meant obscurity for himself. That took greatness. Jesus recognised the greatness of John and acknowledged the debt he owed to him.

To make way, or even just to make room, for another person calls for humility and generosity. Indeed, it calls for a kind of dying to self. To retire from high office is to die a little, even more than a little. Some people, even great and holy people, spoil things and damage their cause by holding on too long to the reins of power.

Parents spend the best years of their lives preparing the way for their children, in the sense of opening them to life. But there comes a time when they have to withdraw so that their children can come into their own. Having given life to their children, parents must allow them to live that life.

All of us are tempted to hug the limelight. We often, inadvertently perhaps, dominate others and relegate them to the shadows. As a result people feel oppressed, and a lot of light is lost to the world. We must try to shine to the best of our ability, while being careful not to block the path for others. And we must be conscious of the debt we owe to others who prepared the way for us.

We can even make the same mistake with God. We act as if it was our work that matters. We make too much of ourselves. Whereas it may be a question of getting ourselves out of the way and allowing God to take over.

Christ opened the way to salvation for all of us. We must strive to walk in his light and avoid being a source of darkness to anyone. The only way to find peace and happiness is to forget ourselves and love others.

HOMILY 3   **God is faithful**

In today's Gospel we hear the voice of John the Baptist announcing the good news that the long-awaited saviour was about to arrive. He urges the people to 'prepare a way for the Lord.'

The Israelites had lived on God's promise: first of a land, then of a saviour. This is not to say that they didn't sometimes forget it in good times, and doubt it in bad times. And they knew a lot of bad times, the worst being the slavery in Egypt and the years of wandering in the desert. What sustained them during all those bad times was the belief that God would not abandon them, or forget the promise he had made to them.

One of the great things Advent does is remind us of God's faithful love for his people, and how his promise was fulfilled in Jesus. The Scripture readings are full of reminders of God's fidelity. 'The grass withers, the flower fades, but the word of our God remains for ever.' (Tuesday, Week 2). 'The mountains may depart, the hills be shaken, but my love for you will never leave you, and my covenant of peace with you will never be shaken.' (Thursday Week 3). Today's First Reading is a joyful proclamation of God's faithful love. [Maybe quote a little from it.]

These messages of reassurance are addressed to us also. We too are living by God's promise. A Christian is someone who is journeying in faith towards the promised land of eternal glory. What sustains the Christian is the belief that God is faithful to his word and true to his promise.

But like the Israelites of old we too can forget God's promise. There are lots of voices calling us in other directions. The most obvious ones are those that come from outside us. There are the strident, hate-filled voices of demagogues and bigots calling us to racism, discrimination, bigotry

... There are the voices of the newspapers, the radio, the television, which entertain us, inform us, distract us ... And of course there are the persuasive voices of the commercials calling us to self-indulgence.

But some of the voices that call to us come from inside ourselves. The inner voices may not be so loud, but they are even more dangerous because they are so insidious and persistent.

But God too is calling us. God's voice is perhaps the smallest and loneliest voice of all. It can so easily be drowned out in the torrent of words, and in the din of daily life. God's voice is not to be heard in the midst of the crowd, but rather in quiet, solitary places.

God is faithful. God is true to his word. God keeps his promises.

We sometimes make God's fidelity conditional on our behaviour. It's as if we believe God won't come to us unless we prove ourselves worthy. But if we were worthy, he wouldn't need to come at all. He comes because we are sinners, sinners in need of redemption.

In the lovely words of the *Benedictus*, God comes to free us from our sins, and to deliver us from the power of evil. He comes to rid us of fear, and to enable us to live in holiness and justice all the days of our lives. He comes to give light to us when we are in darkness and the shadows of death surround us. He comes to guide our feet into the way of peace.

[The first Eucharist Prayer of Reconciliation would reinforce the message of this homily.]

PRAYER OF THE FAITHFUL

President: Let us pray that we may so prepare a way for the Lord that the world may be flooded with the grace of his coming.

Response: Lord hear our prayer.

Reader(s): That those who minister to the flock of Christ may seek out the lost, bandage the wounded, and make the weak strong. [Pause] We pray to the Lord.

That political leaders may strive to level the mountains of injustice and fill in the valleys of poverty, and so bring about a just society. [Pause] We pray to the Lord.

That those in high positions may give opportunities to those below them to use their talents and gifts. [Pause] We pray to the Lord.

That Christ may come with his truth to guide those who have lost their way in life. [Pause] We pray to the Lord.

That the light of Christ may shine on those who live in the shadow of death. [Pause] We pray to the Lord.

That we may create a time and a space for God in our lives. [Pause] We pray to the Lord.

That God may grant our own special needs. [Longer pause] We pray to the Lord.

President: Almighty and ever-living God, your love surpasses all that we ask or deserve; open for us the treasures of your goodness, and grant us more even than we dare ask. We make our prayer through Christ our Lord.

REFLECTION   **Lonely voices**

> The voice of John the Baptist was a lonely voice
> which many of his contemporaries ignored.
> There are many lonely voices in our world.
> Somewhere at this moment a child is crying –
> crying for love or maybe simply for bread.
> Somewhere a young person is crying –
> crying for a listening ear or an understanding heart.
> Somewhere an old person is crying –
> crying for a visit or a word from his/her children.
> There are a thousand unheard cries in our world,
> coming from the victims of injustice and neglect.
> Lord, help us to listen to these voices.
> Above all, help us to listen to your voice,
> whispering to us in the wilderness of our hearts,
> telling us that we are loved by you,
> and that we are to love one another.

Third Sunday of Advent

INTRODUCTION AND CONFITEOR

John the Baptist said to his contemporaries: 'There stands among you one whom you know not.' He was referring to Jesus, who was present among the people unbeknownst to them. Jesus is present among us as we gather to celebrate the Eucharist. [Pause]

Lord Jesus, you bring liberty to captives. Lord, have mercy.
You bring good news to the poor. Christ, have mercy.
You bind up hearts that are broken. Lord, have mercy.

HEADINGS FOR READINGS

First Reading (Is 61:1-2.10-11). The writer declares that he has been sent by God to usher in the age of salvation. Jesus used this prophecy to announce the programme of his own ministry.

Second Reading (1 Thess 5:16-24). St Paul tells the Thessalonians how they ought to live as they await the second coming of Christ.

Gospel (Jn 1:6-8.19-28). John the Baptist declares that he is not the Saviour. His task is to prepare the way for the Saviour, who is already among the people, though they do not recognise him.

SCRIPTURE NOTE

In the First Reading, the writer (a post-exilic prophet) declares that he has been sent by God to usher in the age of salvation for Jerusalem and all God's people. Jesus used this prophecy to announce the programme of his own ministry.

The subject of the Gospel is the same as that of last Sunday: the witness of John the Baptist to Jesus. John summons all to faith in Jesus. He declares that he himself is not the light, and tells the people that unbeknownst to them the light (Jesus) is already present among them.

In the Second Reading Paul takes a very practical line, telling the Thessalonians how they should live as they await the second coming of Christ.

HOMILY 1   **Witnesses for the light**

John the Baptist had a central role to play in the coming of the Saviour. His role, as today's Gospel puts it, was to be 'a witness to speak for the light.' The light in question was Jesus.

John proved to be a courageous and effective witness. He was a strong personality and a man of principle. He didn't go in for a life of comfort. He lived not in a palace but in the desert. His lifestyle, as well as his personal integrity, lent credence to his words. He was a living example of what he preached. And when his task was done, he moved aside to make way for Jesus.

Jesus still needs witnesses. Fortunately there still are people who witness faithfully and at no little personal cost. (The following example is from *The Tablet*, May 1998).

A priest tells how a few years ago he made a visit to China. While there he met an elderly couple who were both doctors. They had studied together at medical school, fallen in love and married. She was a Catholic, he was not. She wanted to convince him that he should join the Church, but he did not wish to be baptised. A short time later she had a child.

During one of China's political movements, the husband, along with several other intellectuals, was arrested and sent to a labour camp. The separation was very difficult for the wife, who had to work long hours at the hospital during the day and care for her son at night. In addition to her loneliness, she was under pressure from the Government to divorce her husband and to renounce her religion, so that she could gain political advantages. But she refused. Every night after she returned home, she and her son knelt down to pray and ask strength from God to endure the difficulties.

At the end of the 1970s, she heard that her husband and other intellectuals were to be allowed come home. When the day came, she and her son went to the railway station, where they were the only family members on the platform to welcome the men. Unable to endure the long separation, all the other women had divorced and remarried. Deeply moved, her husband took instruction and was later baptised.

That woman bore witness to the light just as truly as John the Baptist did. Now it's our turn. For many people in the world today Christ has become a very dim and distant figure. The words of today's Gospel are literally true: 'There stands one among you whom you know not.' Christ still needs witnesses, people who can effectively make him present to other people.

We can't be a witness for the light if we are living in darkness. We have to be living in the light. A good life is a strong and effective witness, and in itself is a proclamation of the Gospel. When religious practice is divorced from life a vital element is missing. But when religious practice leads to deeds, a very effective witness is given. No witness reaches our contemporaries as persuasively as the witness of those who do what Jesus commanded.

Without the witness of Christians the face of Christ, already blurred, will continue to fade from our world. He will continue to stand among us, unknown and unrecognised. And hearts will remain broken, and people will remain imprisoned in darkness, and the good news will not be preached to the poor.

The task is not one for the individual Christian only but for the Christian community as a whole. It is easier to witness to Christ as a member of a supportive community.

HOMILY 2   **The meaning of salvation**

One of the key words in our religion is the word 'salvation'. The theme of salvation dominates today's readings. But what do we mean by 'salvation'?

This world is full of wonder, riches and beauty. Nevertheless, it is also a broken world, full of poverty and wounds. It is a world which needs and longs for salvation. But what kind of salvation are we talking about?

In the past there was a tendency to see salvation in a purely spiritual sense – as the salvation of the soul from sin and eternal damnation. Moreover, it tended to be understood in a very individualistic and selfish way – I save my own soul, and more or less forget about the salvation of others. Also it was seen too often as something which really only happened in the next world.

[23]

Today, while we are more conscious of our common destiny, there is a tendency to go to the opposite extreme. Salvation is seen in a purely secular sense – as salvation from want, suffering, oppression. And it is seen as being concerned with this world only. Salvation is seen in purely political, economic and social terms. But there are nations that are economically and socially advanced where many vices and excesses exist.

The biblical idea of salvation is a much deeper and richer one. The Bible calls people to something much larger than the struggle for political or economic rights. It is a struggle against all the forces of death wherever they are manifest – a struggle for life in the fullest sense. 'It is not a question of saving the soul at the hour of death but the person in living history.' (Oscar Romero).

In the Bible, salvation embraces the idea of salvation from the ills of body and soul. The salvation of the individual cannot be seen except in relation to the salvation of others. And, of course, it includes salvation from death, and so is not limited to this world.

We see this understanding of salvation fulfilled in Jesus. 'The spirit of the Lord has been given to me ... He has sent me to bring good news to the poor, to bind up hearts that are broken; to proclaim liberty to captives, freedom for those in prison; to proclaim a year of favour from the Lord.' These lovely words are taken from today's First Reading. Jesus used them to announce the programme of his own ministry (Lk 4:18-21).

While he took care of his own needs, Jesus spent himself in ministering to his brothers and sisters, especially the poorest and most wounded among them. He cared not just for their souls but also for their bodies. And he announced to them the good news of the Kingdom of Heaven. Salvation begins here, but its full blossoming is in the hereafter.

While we work for a better world for ourselves and others, we must not put all our hopes in this world, or in human efforts. Our ultimate hope of complete salvation lies in Jesus, the One who was sent into the world by the Father. Blessed are we if we do not lose faith in him.

HOMILY 3   **A hidden God**

John the Baptist said to the people: 'There stands one among you whom you know not.' The one of whom he spoke was Jesus. God is often referred to as a 'hidden' God. In this respect God might be compared to a biographer. The job of the biographer is to tell the story while staying in the background. A good biographer is everywhere present but nowhere visible. God is everywhere present in his creation but nowhere visible.

There is a story about a man who came home one day to find his little daughter crying bitterly. He asked her what the matter was. She said that she had been playing at hide-and-seek with her friends. But when it was her turn to hide, she had hid so well that they had given up looking for her and had gone off to play another game. She waited and waited for them to find her, but they failed to do so. When she finally came out of her hiding place she found herself all alone.

Perhaps God sometimes feels lonely. He has hidden himself so successfully in his creation that some people are unable to find him. And eventually they give up looking for him, and go off in other directions.

Even when his Son came on earth, for most of his life he went unrecognised. Even when he did come into the public sphere, not everyone believed in him. As John the Baptist said, 'There stands among you – unknown to you – the one who is coming after me.' And in the prologue to his Gospel John the Evangelist said sadly, 'He was in the world that had its being through him, and the world did not know him.'

Here is where Christmas comes to our aid. At Christmas we are filled with wonder at the nearness of God. In the incarnation God is perfectly hidden and perfectly revealed. In Jesus, God comes to us clothed in our humanity. To see him is to see the Father (Jn 14:9).

Before the coming of Jesus, God was seen as distant and remote, not really concerned about us and our sufferings. Worse still, he was seen as a judge or a spy, ready to pounce and punish. But since the coming of Jesus we no longer see God as someone remote. We see God as someone who is very close to us, and who is concerned about each of us, because we are his children.

Jesus reveals God as a loving, compassionate, forgiving Father. A God who is not far away from us, but who lives among us, and who is passionately interested in us. A God whose concern is not to judge and condemn, but to heal and to save. A God who is especially close to the weak, the poor, and the overburdened.

God is like a spring within us from which we can drink and refresh ourselves. To know God in this way is a cause of great joy. This is the joy announced to the shepherds at the first Christmas, and which is announced to us now.

PRAYER OF THE FAITHFUL

President: Let us pray that the light of God's salvation may shine on us and on our world.

Response: Lord, graciously hear us.

Reader(s): For all Christians: may they cause the light of Christ's love and mercy to shine brightly in the world. [Pause] Lord, hear us.

For world leaders: that God may bless and unite them in their work for a better world. [Pause] Lord, hear us.

For all those people, especially our parents, who sacrificed themselves for us. [Pause] Lord, hear us.

For those who are sorrowful or lonely: that they may experience the presence of Christ. [Pause] Lord, hear us.

For all gathered here: that we may live our lives to the full in this world while having our hearts set on eternal glory. [Pause] Lord, hear us.

For the dead: that God may bring them into the light of everlasting life. [Pause] Lord, hear us.

For our own special needs. [Longer pause] Lord, hear us.

President: Lord our God, you know our weakness. May we reach out with joy to grasp your hand, and walk more readily in your ways. We ask this through Christ our Lord.

REFLECTION   **Joy and pleasure**

There is a world of difference between joy and pleasure.
Pleasure can be planned. Joy can't be planned;
it comes unexpectedly, and is all the sweeter for that.
Pleasure is immediate. Joy often comes later,
and the sweetest joy of all is that which follows pain.
Pleasure comes from saying 'yes' to ourselves.
Joy comes from saying 'no' to ourselves.
Pleasure is like a flare in the night:
it brightens things up for a while, but when it's over,
we feel darker and emptier than ever.
Joy, on the other hand, is like a bright fire in the hearth;
even when it dies down, it leaves a warm glow behind it.

Fourth Sunday of Advent

INTRODUCTION AND CONFITEOR

As the birth of a child draws near, attention focuses on the mother. Since we are nearing the celebration of the birth of Christ, it is no surprise to find that Mary is at the centre of today's Gospel. Mary's only concern was to do the will of God. She will help us to do it also. [Pause]

Lord Jesus, you free us from fear, and guide our feet into the way of peace. Lord, have mercy.

Lord Jesus, you enable us to serve God in holiness and justice all the days of our lives. Christ, have mercy.

Lord Jesus, you give light to us when we walk in darkness and in the shadow of death. Lord, have mercy.

HEADINGS FOR READINGS

First Reading (2 Sam 7:1-5.8-11.16) David wants to build a house for God. But instead God promises to build an everlasting dynasty for him.

Second Reading (Rom 16:25-27). God's plan of salvation for Jews and Gentiles has come to fulfilment in Christ.

Gospel (Lk 1:26-38). God's promise to David was fulfilled in Jesus.

SCRIPTURE NOTE

Now that David was king of a united country, with Jerusalem as the capital, he set about building a house (temple) for the Lord. (First Reading). But the Lord pre-empted David's plan. Instead it is the Lord who will build a dynasty for David, a dynasty that will last for ever. When Jerusalem was destroyed in 587 BC it seemed that the promise would not be fulfilled. Still, the hope remained that a Messiah would come from the house of David.

The expectation was fulfilled when Gabriel announced to Mary that she was to be the mother of the Redeemer, who, through Joseph, would be of the line of David. Gabriel's words echo the words of God's promise to David.

In the Second Reading Paul says that the promises made in Old Testament times have been fulfilled in the person and life of Jesus.

HOMILY 1   **Saying yes to God**

Today many seek fulfilment and happiness through 'doing their own thing'. It's what *I* want that matters. They believe that happiness lies in having no commitments, no one to answer to, no one whose needs or problems will ever tie us down.

It is, of course, good and necessary to find and do that which deep down we feel we are called to do. Nevertheless, human nature being what it is, we have to be on our guard. There can be a lot of selfishness in the 'do your own thing' approach. It often means taking the easiest path in the belief that this is where freedom and happiness lie. But this approach is more likely to lead to slavery and unhappiness.

Here is an important truth: freedom, happiness, and fulfilment are more likely to be found *in the acceptance of duty*. However, for this to happen, a grim acceptance of duty is not good enough. It has to be a loving acceptance of duty. The more difficult the task to which we devote ourselves out of love, the more it will exalt us.

In this Mary gives us a great example. She didn't say to the angel, 'Sorry, but I have my own plans. I want to do my own thing.' She said, 'It's not what I want, but what God wants that matters. Let what God wants be done to me.'

Mary made a complete gift of herself to God, and accepted the task he gave her. Even though she didn't understand all the implications of it, she trusted that God would give her all the help she needed.

In effect she was saying, 'I don't know what all this means, but I trust that good things will happen.' She trusted so deeply in God that she was open to all possibilities. She gave up control over her future and let God define her life.

Life imposes a lot of duties on us. Besides duties to ourselves, there are duties to others, and duties to God. Where would the world be if everyone just thought of themselves, and insisted on doing their own thing, seeking their own freedom, happiness, and fulfilment independent of others and of God?

Those who accept duty as Mary did, may not find happiness and fulfilment in the eyes of the world, but they certainly will find it in eyes of God. And deep down they will know it.

The greatest grace in life is when what we have to do is what we want to do.

HOMILY 2   **A leap of trust**

The setting: a southern town in America. A father lived with his young son and daughter. His wife had died. He was strict with the children but good to them, and they loved him. He was an upright man and an excellent lawyer. However, he made himself very unpopular in the town by opting to defend a black man who was accused of murder – the town was rife with discrimination against black people.

At the end of the street lived an elderly woman, who spent her afternoons sitting in her front garden. She gave out to the lawyer's two children as they passed on their way to and from school. The kids were very hurt by the names she called their father.

One evening the son decided he had taken enough. He jumped over her garden wall and destroyed some of her flowers. Then he ran home. Later his father said, 'Son, you shouldn't have done that.'

'But I did it for you,' the son protested.

'She's a very sick woman. Now go down and apologise to her.'

Reluctantly the son did so. The woman asked him if he would read to her for an hour each evening. He was horrified at the thought, but when his father insisted that he must say Yes to the old lady he agreed to do so. So each evening the boy, accompanied by his little sister, went and read for the old lady. After about an hour she would get a violent fit of trembling. The children would leave and a nurse took over. However, as the weeks went by, the fits became less frequent.

Then one evening their father told them that the old lady had just died. They thought 'thank God' but did not say it. But then the father told them that several years previously a doctor had prescribed painkilling drugs for her and she had become addicted to them. But when she was told she hadn't long to live, she decided that she would try to kick the habit before she died. The fits they saw her getting were withdrawal symptoms.

'And did she succeed?' the kids asked earnestly.

'She did,' the father answered. 'Just before she died she told me that she would never have succeeded if you hadn't read to her. She wanted me to thank you.'

The kids were very moved on hearing this, and said, 'If only we had known what she was going through, we would have been nicer to her.'

'It doesn't matter,' the father said. 'The main thing is you did what I asked you to do. You are good children. I'm proud of you.'

The two children didn't realise the full significance of the task their father asked them to do. Nevertheless, they did it in a spirit of love and obedience.

Often in life we can't see the full meaning of what we do. Sometimes this meaning is completely hidden from us, as it was from the two children. In such a case it becomes very difficult to go on, especially if the task is disagreeable, or those for whom we do it are ungrateful.

In today's Gospel we see how Mary consented to become the mother of the Redeemer. But when she said Yes to God, she didn't realise the full implications of what she was agreeing to? She had no idea that at his birth every door would be closed in her face. That shortly after his birth she would be a refugee in a foreign country. That some thirty-three years later she would see him executed as a criminal.

Mary didn't just say her Yes once. She had to confirm that original Yes many times during her life. Without Mary's obedience to God we would not have a Redeemer.

Each of us has said Yes when we have undertaken commitments and responsibilities. When we said our original Yes, we took a leap in the dark, for we didn't know the full implications of what we were undertaking. This is gradually revealed to us as we go along. Hence, we too have to confirm our original Yes, not once but many times, and ask God to help us to remain faithful.

Just as the children asked questions, Mary asked questions. Faith is not blind. It is beyond reason but not against it. But having asked questions, the answers to which can never fully satisfy us, we have to let God be God. We have to bow to the mystery.

HOMILY 3   **The first Crib**

The appearance of the crib in our churches is a sure sign that Christmas is near. Once there was a parish which had a beautiful crib. The parishioners, who for the most part were white and well-off, were very proud of it.

Mary was depicted as a handsome young maiden with snow-white hands. Joseph was a strong man with a serene expression on his face. The smiling child had the face of an angel. The shepherds were dressed in the garb of gentlemen. All the figures of course were white. The background consisted of low hills with a gorgeous castle perched on the summit of one of them. The star-strewn sky completed the idyllic picture.

Then a new parish priest was appointed to the parish. One of the first things he did was to change the crib. Mary and Joseph and the infant Jesus were now coloured. As were the shepherds. The backdrop consisted of a shanty town with row after row of impoverished shacks. The whole scene spoke of poverty and marginalisation. The devout parishioners took an instant dislike to it. They insisted that their traditional crib be put back.

When we look at the crib, everything seems so pretty, so peaceful, so orderly. Not a cry is heard from the child, not a sound from the donkey or the oxen, not a smell of any kind. The straw is clean. The coloured but subdued lights add a surreal quality to the whole scene. With our inward ear we hear the singing of the angels, and with our inward eye we see the star which led the Magi to Bethlehem.

This is pretty, and we may want to believe it. But we know it's not real. It's not true. It's a false picture. Everything wasn't as neat and tidy and pretty as that. The first Christmas was as full of hurry and worry as our Christmas is. It was full of uncertainty, disappointment, and fear. It was no picnic for Mary and Joseph. It was more like an ordeal, perhaps even a nightmare.

They had just completed a long journey. They arrived in Bethlehem poor, unknown, and without influence of any kind. They were unable to find accommodation. When the time came for Mary to gave birth to Jesus, there were no doctors or nurses on stand by.

It's easy to move away from the poverty of the original crib.

We have a tendency to pretty up the Christmas story. But in doing that we remove it from us. We empty it of much of the meaning it carries for us.

It was St Francis of Assisi who assembled the first crib in a cave on an Italian hillside in the year 1223. His aim was to make the Christmas story come alive for the people of the locality. His idea was to show them how close it was to them and their lives.

And it seems that he succeeded. On Christmas eve the friars and the people assembled with candles and torches around the crib. Francis spoke to the people, who were mostly farmers and shepherds, about God's Son coming among us to teach us that we too are children of God, and that as such we have an eternal destiny.

The shepherds and farmers got the message: God had time for simple folks like them. At the end of the vigil they all returned to their homes, full of peace and joy, feeling very close to God and to one another.

PRAYER OF THE FAITHFUL – 1

President: God seems to be very near us and especially loving towards us at Christmas time. Therefore, it is easier to come to him with our needs.

Response: Lord, graciously hear us.

Reader(s): For the Pope and the bishops: that they may guide the people of God not only by word but also by example. [Pause] Lord, hear us.

For all who hold public office: that they may bring a spirit of self-sacrifice to the performance of their duties. [Pause] Lord, hear us.

For those who are addicted to alcohol or drugs: that they may recognise their problem and seek help. [Pause] Lord, hear us.

For those who for whatever reason are not looking forward to Christmas. [Pause] Lord, hear us.

For all gathered here: that each of us may strive to imitate Mary in her obedience to God. [Pause] Lord hear us.

For this congregation: that the coming of Christ may strengthen our faith in God's love for us, and help us to love one another. [Pause] Lord, hear us.

For our own special needs. [Longer pause] Lord, hear us.

President: Lord our God, take pity on our weakness. May your Son at his coming dispel the darkness of our hearts and of our world. We make this prayer through the same Christ our Lord.

PRAYER OF THE FAITHFUL – 2

President: Let us pray that the world may be flooded with the grace of the Lord's coming.

Response Come, Lord Jesus.

Reader(s): Come into our hearts. *Response*
Come into our homes. *Response*
Come to those who are lonely. *Response*
Come to those who are fearful. *Response*
Come to those who are sick. *Response*
Come to those who are poor. *Response*
Come to those who are grieving. *Response*
Come to those who have no faith. *Response*
Come to those who have no hope. *Response*
Come to those who have no love. *Response*
Come to the victims of violence. *Response*
Come to those in the grip of addiction. *Response*
Come to those in prison. *Response*
Come to us in our needs at Christmas. [Pause] *Response*

President: Lord our God, take pity on our weakness. May your Son at his coming dispel the darkness of our hearts and of our world. We make this prayer through the same Christ our Lord.

REFLECTION **Lonely at Christmas**

You sometimes hear people say,
'I always find Christmas Day a lonely day.'
I think what they are really saying is:
'*I* always feel lonely on Christmas day.'
Loneliness is caused chiefly by two things:
absence and emptiness.
Let us spare a thought, a prayer, and maybe a visit
for someone who will spend Christmas alone.
And if while spending Christmas in the midst of others,
we still feel lonely, let us not be alarmed.
Our hearts are always longing for something more,
or rather, for Someone else.
In every human heart there is an empty chamber
waiting for a guest. That guest is God.

CHRISTMAS SEASON

'A Heavenly Host Singing, and Praising God'

GERARD KAVANAGH

Christmas

Welcome to this Christmas Mass. At Christmas we feel that God is very close to us and very loving towards us. At the same time we feel a closeness to one another. All this happens because God's Son became one of us. He has brought God near us, and brought us near one another. [Pause]

Let us now invoke the help of our Lord and Saviour.

Lord Jesus, you are mighty God and Prince of peace. Lord, have mercy.

You are Son of God and Son of Mary. Christ, have mercy.

You are Word made flesh and splendour of the Father. Lord, have mercy.

HEADINGS FOR READINGS

Midnight Mass

First Reading (Is 9:1-7). This prophecy about the coming of a saviour-child, who will rescue his people from oppression, is fulfilled in Jesus.

Second Reading (Tit 2:11-14). St Paul reminds us what is expected of us if we are to enjoy the salvation won for us by Jesus.

Gospel (Lk 2:1-14). This tells about the birth of Jesus, and how the news of his birth was brought by angels to shepherds.

Dawn Mass

First Reading (Is 62:11-12). The joy of the exiles returning from Babylon is a foretaste of the joy Christians experience at the birth of Jesus.

Second Reading (Tit 3:4-7)). We did nothing to merit the birth of Jesus; rather, God sent his Son out of compassion for us.

Gospel (Lk 2:15-20). With Mary we are invited to ponder on the deeper meaning of the birth of Jesus so that, with the shepherds, we may be moved to glorify and praise God.

Day Mass

First Reading(Is 52:7-10). This great hymn of exultation at the return of the exiles from Babylon is also a poem of joy for our redemption.

Second Reading (Heb 1:1-6). The whole history of God's dealings with his people in the past was a preparation for the coming of his Son at a particular moment in history.

Gospel (Jn 1:1-18). This is a great hymn to the Word of God, the source of all life, whose coming among us makes us children of God.

SCRIPTURE NOTE

Luke's account of the birth of Jesus forms the Gospel for the first two Masses of Christmas. The story reflects the faith of the post-resurrection Church. The same titles that Peter attributes to the risen Jesus, 'Lord and

Messiah' (Acts 2:36), are now applied to the newborn child by the angels. Luke's chief concern is theological. Every detail in the story serves this purpose. This is not to say that there is no historical basis for what he recounts.

Luke gives the birth of Jesus a solemn setting. He is also hinting at the cosmic significance of the event. Unwittingly Augustus becomes an instrument of the Lord by ensuring that Jesus (the Messiah) was born in the town of David. His rejection at the inn anticipates his rejection by the Jewish people as a whole. Mary is shown to be a caring mother, wrapping the child in swaddling clothes and laying him in a manger-cradle. Her loving care reflects God's care.

Since Jesus was born in poverty, it is fitting that the news of his birth was first announced to simple shepherds. This also reflects Jesus' concern (and Luke's) for the poor and the lowly. The faith of shepherds serves as a model for future believers, and their joy anticipates the blessings that will come to those who accept Jesus as the Saviour sent by God.

For the third Mass of Christmas the prologue of John's Gospel is used. This brings out the fullest meaning of what the feast reveals. Here John reaches back even before creation and identifies the new-born child as the Word of God. Eternally present with God, the Word brings life and light to the world. To those who accept him he gives the power to become children of God. [For a note on John's prologue, see Second Sunday of Christmas.]

HOMILY 1   **Christ, the Light of the World**

This homily, with its own Prayer of the Faithful, is perhaps best suited for Midnight Mass.

It may come as a surprise to some to learn that the actual date of Christ's birth is unknown. December 25 was chosen by Rome around the year 300 AD. Why this particular date?

In olden times, before artificial light was invented, the season of winter was long, and dark, and dreary. And all of this was due to the fact that the sun had gone away. However, the people knew that at a certain point the sun began to come back, and things changed for the better. So they had a feast to celebrate this fact. It was known as the feast of the Unconquerable Sun (*Sol Invictus*).

To counter this pagan feast the Church chose December 25, which is close to the winter solstice, to celebrate the birth of Christ. Instead of worshipping the Sun-God, people were encouraged to worship Christ, the Son of God. The Church saw the coming of Jesus as fulfilling the prophecy of Isaiah: 'The people that lived in darkness have seen a great light;' Jesus described his mission in similar terms when he said: 'I am the light of the world.'

December is the darkest month of the year (in the northern hemisphere). It's a time when we appreciate the value of light. Christmas means the coming of God's light into the darkness of our world. This night is made radiant by the light of Christ. The liturgy is filled with references to light and to the glory of God. Someone described Christmas as a pool of light in the inky darkness of winter.

How dark the world would be if the light of Christ had never shone. The Russian writer, Dostoevsky, put it like this: 'While we are on earth, we grope in the dark, and, but for the precious image of Christ before us, we would lose our way completely and perish.'

The teaching of Christ was truly a source of light to all who accepted him. But it was above all through his deeds and encounters with people that his luminous goodness manifested itself. Countless people came to him in darkness and went away bathed in light.

Christ's light was not lit in Bethlehem once and then extinguished. Unlike the sun, Christ's light knows no setting. It continues to shine for all who believe in him and follow him. The light of Christ is a persistent light, and has the power to draw people to its shining. It's not an illusory comfort, or a false reassurance that all is well when this is clearly not the case. It shines in the midst of devastation, disaster and upheaval. The Gospel is a persistent and defiant light, which no darkness can overpower.

Christ's light comes as a friend. It brings healing not hurt, freedom not oppression, life not death. Those who follow him will always have the light of life. He teaches us who we are and what our destiny is. We are children of God, destined for eternal life. May the Lord in his goodness give us a taste of that joy which the shepherds experienced when the light of God's glory shone around them on that first Christmas night..

PRAYER OF THE FAITHFUL

President: Christ is the light of the world. With his light shining on us tonight, let us pray for those who are in any kind of the darkness.
Response: Lord, let your light shine on them tonight.

Red candles are brought up in procession – one for each prayer. After each intercession, the candle is placed on or near the altar.

Reader(s): We pray for the homeless. **R.**
We pray for the hungry. **R.**
We pray for the lonely. **R.**
We pray for those who live in the midst of war and upheaval. **R.**
We pray for prisoners. **R.**
We pray for the sick. **R.**
We pray for those who are away from home tonight. **R.**

We pray for those who have been bereaved. **R.**

We pray for those who have died. **R.**

For our own special needs. [Pause] **R.**

President: God of love and mercy, may your Son scatter the darkness of the world, and make this night radiant with his light. We ask this prayer through the same Christ our Lord.

HOMILY 2   **The miracle of Christmas**

Whether we are conscious of it or not, our lives are linked together. As the poet, John Donne, said: 'No man is an island; each is a part of the continent.' Yet the world is full of division. We are divided by class, race, creed, nationality ... Just what is it then that unites us?

Sometimes when a tragedy happens in a community, all of a sudden the barriers come down. For a few moments, there are no strangers, no rich people, no poor people, no Christians, no Moslems, no Jews. Just brothers and sisters in the same boat, helping one another to get through.

The Russian writer, Dostoyevsky, spent four years in a Siberian prison. It was a bleak experience which brought him into contact with some truly desperate men. Yet in his book, *Memoirs from the House of the Dead*, he gives a moving account of what Christmas Day meant to these men.

He tells us that on Christmas Day the mood of the prisoners was very touching. They felt that they were not altogether outcasts, lost souls, pieces of flotsam. They felt like human beings, and that they had bonds with one another and with all the world. Christmas Day took them out of themselves. Even the most frugal among them thought it their duty to be open-handed on a day like this.

Christmas affects us too. It achieves a great levelling off. Nobody can feel superior to another on this day. Neither should anybody feel inferior. It puts an end to all elitism.

It's not that Christmas reduces us all to the same common denominator, as happens when people share the same hospital ward or prison cell. No, Christmas achieves this levelling off, not by lowering us all, but by lifting us all up. Just as a rising tide lifts all the boats in the harbour, so Christmas lifts all of us. It's as if we are placed on a high plateau.

Christmas gathers us all together in a great universal fellowship in the name of Christ. On this day we experience the brotherhood and sister-hood of all human beings. Christ turns a foreigner into a neighbour, a stranger into a brother. This is the miracle of Christmas.

On Christmas Day we feel at one with everyone. We feel a desire to reach out to others. Christmas Day takes us out of our narrow world and breaks our selfish habits. It enables us to see selfishness and prejudice for what they are. We are put in touch with our common humanity, with our shared fears and hopes.

In this way Christmas brings about a wonderful happiness. But it's a disturbing happiness, because it turns upside down many of the priorities we live by. Normally we seek happiness by looking to ourselves, and by accumulating material things. But Christmas shows us that it is by coming together, by opening our hearts to one another that we find happiness. Happiness is to be sought in community and sharing rather than in individualism and hoarding.

When we are praised or win an award we experience joy. This joy springs from the fact that we feel we are better or smarter than others. But such joy is temporary. True joy springs from a feeling of being the same as others – weak and fragile and mortal. It's the joy of belonging to the human race. It's the joy of being with others as a friend, a companion, a fellow traveller on the road of life.

This is the joy of Christmas: God becomes like us, God becomes one with us. Jesus is Emmanuel, God-with-us. He made himself our friend, our brother, our companion on the road to God's kingdom. By becoming one with us, he has taken away the distance between the human and the divine. He makes us one with God.

On this day the world becomes a friendlier place. It shines with meaning and hope. On this day we are given a sense of a living bond with another world, with the other world. And all this because of the 'great joy' that was announced to the shepherds, and that is now announced to us: 'Today a saviour has been born to you; he is Christ the Lord.'

HOMILY 3   **The joy of believing**

We may be tempted to envy the shepherds because they saw the Christ Child with their own eyes, and touched him with their hands. Faith was easy for them. And we are convinced that it would be easy for us too if only we could see Christ in person as they did.

Yes, the shepherds had the advantage of seeing Christ with their own eyes. But did that make faith any easier for them? I don't think so. If they believed their eyes, they would have been deceived, for God is not immediately visible and knowable. Christ is knowable as the Son of God only by faith, and faith is a gift of God.

Given this, the people who actually saw Christ probably found it harder to believe. For what did they see? They did not and could not have seen God. They saw a human being ostensibly like themselves. Which means they too had to make an act of faith.

Yet if we are to believe in Christ we must see him somehow. But just how can people like us see Christ? What must we do in order to believe? At best we are disciples at second hand. For the disciple at second hand, things are harder in some ways, but easier in others.

Things are harder because twenty centuries have gone by since Jesus walked the earth. A lot of dust has gathered. The light has dimmed. But on the positive side, the notion that the Son of God came down on earth has become 'naturalised' over time, and so in some ways has become easier to believe. In reality, all disciples are essentially equal – all have to make the leap of faith.

The shepherds said to one another, 'Let us go to Bethlehem and see this thing that has happened, which the Lord has made known to us.' In Bethlehem they 'found Mary and Joseph, and the baby lying in the manger.' Yet they returned to their flocks 'glorifying and praising God for all they had heard and seen.' You could say that they came on foot, and went away on wings. That's what faith does. It lightens and sweetens our being in the world.

Joy is an authentic sign of the truth of Christianity. This joy springs first of all from the goodness of God in himself. Then from his goodness in his dealings with us. Life is unintelligible and unbearable without God. When people allowed themselves to get disconnect from God an enormous loss results. An enormous vacuum occurs.

Happy those who taste the joy of believing, the rapture of faith in God, the ecstasy of heeding the divine invitation and clasping his outstretched hand. At Christmas we are filled with wonder at the nearness of God. Somebody is watching over us. Somebody is watching out for us. If God is with us who can be against? By our presence here we have, in a sense, made the journey to Bethlehem. We have heard the message of the angels to the shepherds.

May the Lord help us to make the leap of faith so that we may experience some of the 'great joy' announced to the shepherds. This will give us new heart as we journey towards the heavenly Bethlehem, where we shall see him face to face, not as an infant, but in his glory.

HOMILY 4   **The Word was made flesh**

Once upon a time there was a little boy who was given the gift of a tin soldier for Christmas. For a while it made him happy. But then he thought that it would be fun if the soldier came to life. Suppose he could really bring him to life. Imagine turning a tin soldier into a real little person. It would involve turning the tin into flesh.

But then the boy wondered how the tin soldier would take to such a change. Suppose the tin soldier didn't like it? Suppose he didn't like the idea of becoming flesh, because to become flesh would leave him open to all kinds of hurt, and of course to the greatest hurt of all – death. No, the boy didn't think the tin soldier would want that. He would think you were killing him, and would do everything to prevent it.

But this is like what happened in the Incarnation. Jesus, the Son of God, became flesh like us. Not only that. He became a baby, and before that, a foetus inside a woman's body.

There you have the Incarnation. That's the pattern of redemption. God entered our world on our terms. He wanted to feel the pain of our humanity. Here was no safe remoteness. Here was closeness, here was involvement at the deepest level. Now we have a God who understands us when we speak to him about our pain.

In the Hindu tradition, Krishna and Rama are regarded as incarnations of God. But they are not described as having suffered and died. God does not really become man. He only appears in human form. Behind this earthly appearance, he remains purely divine and unaffected by human vicissitudes. But in the Incarnation God made himself present to us in the life of One who walked on this earth.

When the Son of God came on earth, he clothed himself in the cloak of our weak, fragile, mortal humanity. By so doing he has shown us that there is nothing fundamentally wrong with that humanity. In that humanity he lived, suffered, and died. And by rising from the dead, he clothed our mortal humanity with immortality. The result for us is that, though we are made of flesh, we have a divine dignity. But we carry this priceless treasure in a vessel of clay.

As we look at Jesus today, we thank him for joining us where we are, for becoming one of us, for becoming one with us. He does so in order to raise us up. He humbled himself to share in our humanity so that we might share in his divinity. This is 'the great joy' announced to the shepherds. Let us open our hearts to receive it.

HOMILY 5   **Christ is with us**

Once a group of young people were discussing the meaning of Christmas. In the group was an older woman whom they tended to ignore. However, when finally she got a chance to speak, they were deeply moved by what she had to say.

She spoke from the heart. She told them that she was dreading the approach of Christmas. She was an only child. Her parents were dead. She had no aunts or uncles. No close relatives. She was the last of her family. She had friends with whom she exchanged cards and gifts at Christmas. But none of them ever thought of inviting her to their home on Christmas Day.

How did she spend Christmas Day? On her own, though she is by no means a recluse. After an early Mass she goes out to help in some voluntary work. Then she comes back, cooks dinner, and eats it on her own. She switches on the TV, but TV is no substitute for having someone with you.

She cries a lot. She just can't help it. Towards evening, she goes for a walk. But on Christmas evening it's lonely out of doors too. The streets and parks are almost deserted. All doors are closed. She tries the door of her local church but it too is firmly locked. There seems to be no room in any inn for her. So she has no choice but to head back home. Back home, the loneliness closes in again.

But then came the best part of her story. She told how in the midst of her loneliness and tears she feels very close to Christ. She feels close to his sufferings. She realises that in a very real sense he was an outsider at the first Christmas – there was no room for him at the inn. And even though her tears continue to fall, she feels an inner happiness that is impossible to describe or explain. Why? Because Christ gives a meaning to her loneliness and pain. He came to share our lives, to help us carry our burdens, and to walk the road of life with us. That is the meaning of Christmas.

For this woman many of the trimmings of Christmas were missing. But she had the essence. Christ was with her.

Christ is present with us too. Not as a vague memory of a person who lived long ago, but as a real, life-giving presence that transforms us and the way we see our lives. He doesn't enable us to escape from the human condition. He doesn't spare us all strife, all the uncertainty, all the suffering and all the doubt. He doesn't offer us a religion without the Cross.

Christ came to show solidarity with us. He comes to show us where the journey of life is leading, and accompanies us on that road. He gives us hope, meaning, love, support, but we still have to carry those burdens, suffer those losses and illnesses. But it's not the same since he came among us and shares them with us.

PRAYER OF THE FAITHFUL

President: Jesus is Emmanuel, God-with-us. Let us then with confidence place our requests before the Father.

Response: Lord, hear us in your love.

Reader(s): That the coming of Christ may help Christians to walk in the light of hope and love. [Pause] We pray in hope.

That the birth of the Prince of Peace may spread understanding and unity among all peoples throughout the world. [Pause] We pray in hope.

That Christ who took on himself our human weakness, may be the eyes of the blind, the strength of the weak, the friend of the lonely. [Pause] We pray in hope.

That the coming of Christ may fill our hearts with joy, and make us heralds of his Gospel as it did the shepherds. [Pause] We pray in hope.

That our own needs on this special night (day) may be blessed before God. [Longer pause] We pray in hope.

President: Father of mercy, Christ your Son made this day (night) radiant with his light. May we come to share in his divine life who came on earth to share our human lives. We ask this through the same Christ our Lord.

SIGN OF PEACE

Lord Jesus Christ, at your birth the angels sang: 'Glory to God in the highest, and peace to his people on earth.' Grant that we who have heard the message of the angels may enjoy the peace and unity of your kingdom, where you live for ever and ever.

REFLECTION   **The greatness of our humanity**

Sometimes people expect something extraordinary,
or even miraculous to happen at Christmas.
But when Christ came on earth,
he came clothed, not in the extraordinary,
but in the ordinary.
He came dressed in the cloak
of our weak, fragile, mortal humanity.
'They wrapped the baby in swaddling clothes,
and laid him in a manger.'
Like an acorn that falls to earth, silently and unheralded,
in a remote corner of the forest,
and which grows into a great oak tree,
so from these lowly origins Jesus grew up
to show us the greatness of our humanity.

Feast of the Holy Family

INTRODUCTION AND CONFITEOR

On this feast we think of the Holy Family. But we also think of our own families. And we think of the human family, and of the family of the Church. Sadly, all of our families are wounded by sin and division. We ask God to heal these wounds and divisions. [Pause]

Lord Jesus, you came to reconcile us to one another and to the Father. Lord, have mercy.

Lord Jesus, you heal the wounds of sin and division. Christ, have mercy.

Lord Jesus, you intercede for us with the Father. Lord, have mercy.

HEADINGS FOR READINGS

First Reading (Gen 15:1-6; 21:1-3). God promises the childless Abraham an heir and innumerable descendants.

Second Reading (Heb 11:8.11-12.17-19). This stresses the faith of Abraham and Sarah, and how God's promise to them was fulfilled.

(The First and Second Readings from Year A may be used as alternatives).

Gospel (Lk 2:22-40). This tells us about the presentation of the child Jesus in the temple, and also provides us with a glimpse of his life at Nazareth.

HOMILY 1   **Reflecting on the Scripture Readings**

This homily is a brief commentary on the Scripture readings for the feast of the Holy Family.

First Reading: This stresses the giftedness of Isaac. In Old Testament times childlessness was seen as a curse. But Christians no longer so regard it. Though childlessness is a cause of great sadness, it must not be seen as a punishment from God.

Abraham was sad and worried because he had no heir. But God promised him an heir, and, through that heir, numerous descendants. In fact, through him all the nations of the world would receive a blessing, because it was from his descendants that Christ came.

Children truly are a blessing. What is the best inheritance parents can leave to their children? It is not money or material things. It is rather the experience of being loved. If this is missing, no amount of money will make up for it.

Second Reading: This stresses the great faith of Abraham and Sarah. They put their trust in God and were not disappointed. Husbands and wives today need great faith. When a man and a woman get married, they make a life-long commitment to one another. To be faithful to such a commitment is never easy. But it is easier for those who believe in God, and who turn to him for help in time of need.

Happy are those couples who have faith in God, because God is totally reliable. And if the couple have children, they will seek God's guidance so as to bring them up rightly. They will also strive to pass their faith on to their children, a faith that will be nourished by family prayer.

Gospel: The events surrounding the conception and birth of Jesus marked him out as a special child with a unique destiny. He was the one through whom the promise to Abraham would be fulfilled. He would be the hope and comfort of Israel, and a light for the nations. But the Gospel also talks about the rejection of Jesus, a rejection which would cause a sword of sorrow to pierce Mary's heart. Parents share in the joys and sorrows of their children. And *vice versa*.

There is no reason to believe that Mary and Joseph had a clear understanding of either the full identity or the great destiny of the Child Jesus. Nevertheless, in welcoming him into their lives, and in bringing him up in faith and love, they played their part in helping him to realise his destiny. The Gospel shows that at Nazareth they provided the kind of atmosphere in which he was able to grow to maturity.

Every child is a gift from God. And every child has a unique destiny. But that destiny is hidden from the parents. They wonder what will become of their children. Naturally they want the best for them. But all they can do is launch them on their way. Having given them life, they must allow them the freedom to live that life. Above all, they must be careful not to obstruct God's plans for them.

Parents should pray that God will guide their children in the choices they make. All of us need God's guidance if we are to achieve what God wants us to achieve.

Ideally a family is a little community of love. The atmosphere in the home is all important. The atmosphere is determined by the quality of the relationships. Parents and children contribute to the making of that atmosphere.

Family life is very challenging. It can't be only about receiving; it must also be about giving. Family ties enrich us but also tie us down. They involve ties of duty and love.

HOMILY 2   **The Holy Family**

We call Jesus' family *the Holy Family*, and rightly so. But perhaps we have an idealised picture of it: angels whispering in the ears of Mary and Joseph telling them what to do in moments of doubt, warning them in times of danger, and so on. It's as if they never had a doubt, never had to agonise over a decision. So how can the Holy Family become a model for our families?

Moreover, we tend to see the home at Nazareth as a place where perfect harmony and complete understanding always reigned. It's as if Jesus, Mary, and Joseph lived on a sunlit island, cut off from the storms of the world.

We are not told much about the life of the Holy Family in the Gospels. All we get are some glimpses. But these glimpses are enough to show how unreal the above picture is. We see that the Holy Family had more than its share of troubles.

For instance, when the time came for Jesus to be born, Joseph and Mary could find no accommodation. And their joy at his birth was short-lived, because he immediately became a target for Herod's murderers. So they had to take the Child and flee to a foreign country, where they discovered what it was like to be aliens.

Back in their own country, they had to find a place where they could begin life all over again. So they settled in Nazareth. When Jesus was twelve, during a visit to Jerusalem, he got lost. Joseph and Mary sought him with fear and sorrow in their hearts.

During his public life Mary didn't always understand what Jesus was doing. She feared that he was being taken over by the crowds. On one occasion she made a vain attempt to rescue him. Later she saw the tide turn against him and the net of authority close around him. Finally came the ignominy of the crucifixion, when a sword of sorrow pierced her heart, and a real spear pierced the heart of her Son.

In view of all this, no one can claim that the Holy Family lived a sheltered and trouble-free life. Our families too are visited by sorrow, misunderstandings, and problems of one kind or another. Because the Holy Family knew sorrow, trouble and pain it can serve as a model for us.

There is no such thing as a perfect family. Every family goes through rough times. Every family has to make sacrifices. Wherever human beings are living under the one roof misunderstandings and conflicts occur. All of us are wounded by sin. What is important is how we deal with these problems, and how we resolve these conflicts.

The Holy Family had to struggle and to make sacrifices. But these are precisely the things which form a bond between people. People are closer to one another in hard times than in good times. There is nothing like shared hardships to create a bond between people. There is more depth to relationships that have weathered some storms.

Holiness is the fruit of sacrifice and struggle. Ideally there is no place like home. But there is no such place as an ideal home.

HOMILY 3   **The meaning of home**

Every year there is an exhibition in Dublin called 'The Ideal Homes Exhibition'. But it's not so much about homes as about the places in which people live, and the furnishing of those places. It should really be called 'The ideal *houses* exhibition'.

There is a big difference between a house and a home. A house is where people keep their furniture and belongings. A home is where people live together. Sadly, it seems that some homes are meant more for the security and convenience of the furniture than for the people who live in them.

Some homes are so neat and tidy that they are not fit to be lived in – if you know what I mean. To look at them you'd never suspect that people lived there. They are more like museums than homes. On the other hand, other homes remind you of a well-thumbed book. It's obvious that people live in them, people who know how to relax and to enjoy themselves.

To have a home is not just to have a house. It is to have a set of familiar surroundings, habits, routines, and neighbours. It is to have roots. It is to have a clear and unmistakable identity. It is to have a set of close ties with people who accept us for what we are, and who give us a sense of belonging. These are the things that constitute that unique feeling – the feeling of being at home.

People put a lot of effort and money into building a good house. And one can understand why. But perhaps there is a danger of neglecting the more important thing – building a home, that is, a little community of love.

The atmosphere in the home is far more important than the quality and quantity of the furnishings. The atmosphere is determined by the quality of the relationships.

Jesus too needed a home in which to grow up. Mary and Joseph provided that home for him at Nazareth. By their love for him and for one another, Mary and Joseph created the atmosphere in which he thrived. But the Holy Family didn't have an easy life, as the Gospel shows us. During the early years they suffered the fate of homeless refugees.

The family is very fragile in our times. It is under many stresses and difficulties. Yet, in spite of everything, many parents make enormous sacrifices for their children. All such parents can draw inspiration from the example of Mary and Joseph.

Ideally home is the place to which we can always return, and be sure of a welcome. It is a place where we taste on earth the joy and peace of the place God has for us in heaven. Ideally there is no place like home. But there is no such place as an ideal home.

A STORY

Sometimes the value of a thing is seen best through its absence. This is certainly true in the case of family.

There is something broken in Johnny – something in his mind or heart. He grew up in a large urban area. He was only seven when his father left. His mother did the best she could, but it wasn't good enough. When at nine Johnny was sent to his granny's to make room at home he felt rejected.

He was in trouble from the age of ten – fighting, mitching from school, shop-lifting, and so on. At fourteen he was into house-breaking. Next it was on to joy-riding in stolen cars. Soon he was well known in the juvenile court. He was sent to a reform school for six months, but when he came out he went back to his old ways.

Then he was sent to a lock-up centre. Here he had a team of professionals looking after him, all experts in fixing up broken kids. There was a doctor, a nurse, a psychiatrist, a welfare officer, a house father and mother … It cost the state a staggering £70,000 annually to keep him there.

Will all those experts succeed in fixing Johnny? It's possible but far from certain. And just think of it. All those experts could be got rid of in the morning. Their work could be done, and done far more effectively, by just two people: a man and a woman. Not the Six Million Dollar Man and the Bionic Woman either. Just two very ordinary people – two parents.

If Johnny had two parents who loved him and cared for him in the first place, he would never have got broken, and he would never have needed all those experts. The story shows what a splendid job parents do – when they do it. Of all experts they are the most necessary. To succeed at their job, they don't need letters after their names. All they need is a loving heart. Love is to a child what sunshine is to a flower.

The family is vital for our well-being as individuals and for the well-being of society as a whole. It is in the family that we acquire the skills of relationship. It is there we learn to handle the inevitable conflicts that occur within any human group. It is there we first take the risk of giving and receiving love. It is the birthplace of the moral sense. It is there, as children, that we discover who we are and develop a sense of personal worth. Of all the influences upon us, the family is by far the most powerful. Its effects stay with us for a lifetime. No family is perfect, but no better place for raising children has been devised.

PRAYER OF THE FAITHFUL

President: God is the Father of the human family. Let us pray to him for the well-being of all families.

Response: Lord, hear our prayer.

Reader(s): For the human family: that all the different races may realise that they form one family under God. [Pause] Let us pray to the Lord.

For our leaders and legislators: that they may do everything possible to protect the family as the most important unit in society. [Pause] Let us pray to the Lord.

For broken families and families in hardship: that they may find support. [Pause] Let us pray to the Lord.

For all parents: that they may love their children warmly, yet not possessively. [Pause] Let us pray to the Lord.

For children: that they may play their part in making the home a peaceful and happy place. [Pause] Let us pray to the Lord.

For our deceased relatives and friends: that they may enjoy the peace of God's eternal home. [Pause] Let us pray to the Lord.

For the needs of our own family. [Longer pause] Let us pray to the Lord.

President: God of power and love, grant us in all our tasks your help, in all our doubts your guidance, in all our weaknesses your strength, in all our sorrows your consolation, and in all our dangers your protection. We ask this through Christ our Lord.

REFLECTION   **Children**

> Your children are not your children.
> They come through you but not from you.
> And though they are with you,
> yet they belong not to you.
> You may give them your love but not your thoughts,
> for they have their own thoughts.
> You may house their bodies but not their souls,
> for their souls dwell in the house of tomorrow,
> which you cannot visit, not even in your dreams.
> You may strive to be like them,
> but seek not to make them like you.
> For life goes not backward nor tarries with yesterday.
> You are the bows from which your children
> as living arrows are sent forth.

Kahlil Gibran

Second Sunday after Christmas
HE LIVED AMONG US

INTRODUCTION AND CONFITEOR

Today's liturgy assures us that God never abandons his people but is always present with them. God is close to us too. This should be a source of comfort and strength to us, especially in times of difficulty. [Pause]

Let us ask God's forgiveness and help as we confess our sins to him and to one another.

HEADINGS FOR READINGS

First Reading (Eccles 24:1-2.8-12). This is a poem in praise of wisdom, a wisdom that has pitched her tent among God's people.

Second Reading (Eph 1:3-6.15-18). This reading introduces the theme of God's plan of salvation, a plan which is centred in Christ and realised through him.

Gospel (Jn 1:1-18). This is a great hymn to the Word of God, the source of all life, whose coming among us makes us children of God.

SCRIPTURE NOTE

The Gospel consists of the prologue to John's Gospel. Here John introduces the main themes that will be developed in his Gospel – life, light, darkness, truth, witness, glory, the world. It cannot be fully understood until the Gospel as a whole has been read.

Through a summary of history, the prologue shows that from the dawn of creation God has been with humans, and in spite of darkness and ignorance, has invited them to knowledge of and intimacy with himself. But in Jesus something infinitely better is offered to us.

According to John, the Son descends from heaven to our level, and ascends back to heaven bringing us up with him to the divine level. The prologue describes the Son in heaven and the descent; the Gospel describes the Son walking among us and his final elevation and return to the Father.

The first part (vv. 1-11) presents the Son as the Word. Eternally present with God, the Word brings life and light to the world. Sadly, the world, and even his own people, rejected him. This negative response is something that recurs throughout John's Gospel.

The second part (vv. 12-18) notes a more positive response. The Word becomes one of us and lives among us. To those who accept him he gives the power to become children of God.

HOMILY 1   **Power to become children of God**

God entered into a covenant with Israel as a result of which Israel became God's *people*. But through Jesus God offers us something even better. Through Jesus we have become God's *family*. In the words of St John: 'He gave us the power to become children of God.'

This is a most wonderful statement. God has entered into a new and more intimate relationship with us. Now we have become part of his family. We have become his sons and daughters. We are heirs, joint heirs with Christ, to the Kingdom of Heaven. But it's possible to forget who we are, and the splendid destiny that is ours.

Once there was a king whose son committed a serious offence, and ran away from home. There he was separated from everything and everybody he loved. He suffered cold, hunger, loneliness, and poverty. But there was one light in his dark life – the hope that one day he would be able to go back to his father's house. So he waited.

But the years slipped by. As they did his condition deteriorated. Eventually he lost all sense of his identity. He forgot that he was a prince, and that he could return to his father's house. He was now a broken-down man, reduced to suffering and needs. He had lost everything. A person who loses everything, frequently loses himself too.

Meanwhile the king was hoping and praying that his son would come back home. But when he didn't, he sent a messenger to invite him to come back, to remind him that all was forgiven. It took the messenger a long time to track him down. When he found him, he couldn't believe how low he had sunk. Nevertheless, he delivered the message and waited for the prince's reply. But instead of asking for an escort back home, the young man asked only for some money to buy a bottle of cheap wine.

Yes, it's possible to get disconnected from God, and to forget who we are. It grieves the heart of God when his children become estranged from him and from one another. But Christmas is a big help here. Christmas gives us an opportunity to reconnect ourselves with God if we feel we have become disconnected from him. At Christmas we experience the closeness of God. God is not some remote and uncaring figure. God is our heavenly Father, who is close to us, and to whom we are important and precious.

Christmas reminds us of who we are, and what our destiny is. We are not specks of dust or grains of sand. We are sons and daughters of the King. We are heirs to an eternal inheritance.

Of course, our connection with God makes demands on us – we have to live a life that is in keeping with our dignity. But an inner peace springs from being connected with the God who is love.

HOMILY 2 **The Word was made flesh and lived among us**

Once there was a journalist by the name of Alexander whose country was engaged in a bitter war. He decided to write an extended article about the war. In order to do so he went to the front, because he wanted to see for himself what it was like for the soldiers on the ground.

At the front he spared himself nothing. Not once but several times he went into the thick of battle. He spent his nights making careful notes of all he had witnessed during the day. After about a month at the front he decided he had seen enough. So he headed back to his office in the city.

It took a lot of hard work to get the long article into shape. When it was finished he showed it to his editor who was highly pleased with it. It was given centre-page prominence and spread over five days. It created a big stir among the readers. Alexander was purring with self-satisfaction.

But then one day out of the blue came a letter. It was from a soldier who had served at the front but who was now hospitalised with a serious leg wound. In his letter the soldier said:

'I know you meant well. Nevertheless, what you did, praiseworthy though it was, does not entitle you to speak on our behalf. There is an unbridgeable gap between the bravest correspondent and the ordinary soldier. As a journalist you were not part of the force. You were not subject to military discipline. No one would charge you with desertion if you ran away.

'If you really and truly want to understand what it is like for us, you would have to join the unit, fight with it, not knowing if you will live or die, or if your comrades will live or die.'

Even though Alexander knew the soldier was speaking the truth, he was deeply hurt by the letter. If he really wanted to be an authentic spokesman for the soldiers, there was only one way to do it – become a soldier himself. The big question was: good and brave man though he was, was he capable of so big a risk?

But in the Incarnation this is precisely what God did in Jesus. In the words of St John: 'The Word was made flesh, and lived among us.'

Jesus became one of us. He didn't drop in, say 'hello', and disappear again. No. He came and lived among us.

Jesus was not passing through like a tourist. He joined the human family and lived among us. He knows what it is like to be human, what makes us weep, what makes us fall and stumble and somehow rise and go on again. He assumed our fragile, perishable humanity, in order to show us what our humanity is capable of.

Because of the incarnation God is present to us in a way that we can relate to, for Jesus in like us in all things but sin. He is a brother to us. He has made us children of God. From his fullness we have all received. And we should be willing to share with others the love that God has so generously shared with us in Christ.

HOMILY 3   **Emmanuel, God with us**

St Anthony's is home to a small number of endangered boys. The boys have had to be removed from their own homes, or have run away from those homes, because of difficult situations. Not surprisingly, they are not the easiest of kids to deal with. The home is staffed by qualified social workers, who, in the circumstances, do a very good job. They work shifts and do not live in the home.

Brother Aidan also works for those boys. But unlike the paid staff, he lives on the premises. It is his home too. He tries to be both a father figure and an elder brother to the youths. It's not the easiest or quietest place to live. But Aidan likes it. And the fact that he lives on the premises makes a big difference to the kids.

Aidan tells how one day he met one of the kids on the street. The kid greeted him warmly and in the course of a chat said,

'You're different, Brother Aidan. The staff go home every evening. But you live with us.'

Brother Aidan knows all the youths by name. He eats and drinks with them, listens to their stories, lets them know with words, handshakes, and hugs that he truly loves them.

Presence is very important. It is especially important in the lives of young people. It is a sign of interest. No matter how many things we provide for children, they cannot take the place of our presence with them.

Our presence with others is the deepest expression of our love for them.

Christmas is a time when we give gifts and send cards to people. True love, however, goes beyond the giving of gifts. It requires the giving of oneself. People want us to share their lives – their hopes and frustrations, their joys and sorrows. It is not easy to be present like that. It calls for time, humility and love.

This is what God did for us in the Incarnation: 'The Word became flesh, he lived among us.' And he came among us, not to judge us, but to save us. In Jesus' own words, he came 'that we might have life, and have it to the full.'

God has made himself present to us in the life of one who walked on this earth, and who is like us in all things but sin. This is the essence of the Good News. It should be a cause of great joy for us – a joy that springs from the goodness of God in himself, and the goodness he has shown in his dealings with us.

Let us sit for a moment to reflect on the mystery of God's love for us. [Pause for reflection].

ANOTHER STORY   **The gift of presence**

Maximilian Kolbe, a Franciscan priest, was arrested by the Gestapo in February 1941. In May of that year he was transferred to Auschwitz. There he quickly won himself a reputation for dedication to the needs of his fellow prisoners.

Towards the end of July a prisoner escaped from the camp. The camp commander was furious and declared that ten of his companions should die in his place. He lined up the prisoners and went down the line picking out ten men at random. The tenth man to be chosen broke down and pleaded for mercy, saying that he had a wife and young family to support back home. At this point Maximilian Kolbe stepped forward and offered to take his place. After some hesitation the commander agreed, and the substitution was made.

The ten prisoners were left to starve to death in an underground bunker as a deterrent to would-be escapers. In the days that followed, the guards watched through a peep-hole the agony of the dying men. They saw the men gathered around Fr Kolbe. At times they could be seen joking, at other times praying and singing hymns. Fourteen days went by. One by one they died. Last to die was Fr Kolbe. On the night of August 14th he was still alive. A guard put an end to his agony by forcibly administering a lethal injection of carbolic acid to him.

The man whose place Kolbe took survived the camps. Later he stated, 'At first I felt terrible at the thought of letting another man die in my place. But then I realised that he had done this, not so much to save my life, as to be with the other nine in their last terrible agony. His nearness to them in those dreadful last hours was worth more than a lifetime of preaching.'

True love goes beyond the giving of gifts. It requires the giving of oneself. Maximilian Kolbe might have given those men advice and encouragement. He might have visited them in their death cell. But his presence with them was worth more than anything else, even though he wasn't able to save them from their cruel fate.

What Kolbe did was an astonishing act of love. In the prologue to his Gospel St John says, 'The Word was made flesh, and lived among us.' This is a great mystery of love. In Jesus, the only Son of the Father, we have a Brother who loves us to the extent that he came among us and shared our lives to the full. Not only did he share our lives, but he also shared our death.

St John goes on to say, 'From his fullness we have all received.' We should be willing to share with others the love we have received so generously.

PRAYER OF THE FAITHFUL

President: In his great love for us, God has pitched his tent among us. Therefore, let us bring our needs before him with confidence.

Response: Lord, hear our prayer.

Reader(s): For the shepherds of the Church: that they may be selfless ministers of the Gospel. [Pause] Let us pray to the Lord.

For all Christians: that they may give an example to the world of unselfish love. [Pause] Let us pray to the Lord.

For government leaders: that God may bless them with the gifts of wisdom and integrity. [Pause] Let us pray to the Lord.

For all those who suffer in any way: that they may experience the presence of Christ. [Pause] Let us pray to the Lord.

For all gathered here: that we may never forget the great dignity we enjoy, and the great destiny that is ours, as children of God. [Pause] Let us pray to the Lord.

For our own special needs. [Longer pause] Let us pray to the Lord.

President: Father, your Son came to bring us hope. May we always to be aware of his saving presence among us. We ask this through the same Christ our Lord.

PRAYER/REFLECTION   **Prayer for the new year**

Lord, grant us in all our tasks your help,
in all our doubts your guidance,
in all our weaknesses your strength,
in all our dangers your protection,

and in all our sorrows your consolation.
Give us the kind of faith
that will enable us to live out joyfully
the mystery of our fragile human condition,
which sees us suspended between earth and heaven,
between time and eternity,
between nothingness and infinity. Amen.

Epiphany of the Lord
SEARCHING FOR THE KING

INTRODUCTION AND CONFITEOR

The great thing about the Magi was their faith. Even though they were outsiders (Gentiles), they recognised Christ as the Saviour of the world. They are models of faith for us. Let us ask the Lord to increase our faith so that we may recognise his presence in this Eucharist, and welcome him with joy into our hearts. [Pause]

Lord Jesus, you are mighty God and Prince of peace. Lord, have mercy.

Lord Jesus, you are Son of God and Son of Mary. Christ, have mercy.

Lord Jesus, you are Word made flesh and splendour of the Father. Lord, have mercy.

HEADINGS FOR READINGS

First Reading (Is 60:1-6). The prophet cheers the exiles who returned from Babylon with a vision of a restored city. The prophecy is fulfilled in Christ and in the new Israel, the Church.

Second Reading (Eph 3:2-3.5-6). God invites Jew and Gentile to share on an equal footing the salvation brought by Christ.

Gospel (Mt 2:1-12). Three Gentiles came from a far country to pay homage to the Christ-child, while the Jewish leaders rejected him.

SCRIPTURE NOTE

God revealed himself to the Jews through the Scriptures, and to the Gentiles through nature. Since the Magi were Gentiles, Matthew shows them receiving a revelation through astrology. The story highlights the paradox of how the Jews who have the Scriptures reject Jesus, while Gentiles come and, with the help of the Scriptures, find and adore him. For Matthew the story of the Magi becomes an anticipation of the fate of the Good News of salvation, a fate that he knew in the aftermath of the resurrection.

There is little to be gained by speculating where the Magi came from and what exactly the star was. The star was only the means by which a great mystery was revealed – the revelation of Christ as the Saviour of the Gentiles too.

The Second Reading expresses the theological meaning of the feast: God invites Jew and Gentile to share on an equal footing the benefits of the salvation brought by Christ. The feast shows that election by God is not a privilege for some but a hope for all.

HOMILY 1   **Learning from the Magi**

The picture many people have of how the Magi came to Bethlehem goes somewhat like this. They saw a bright star in the eastern sky and began to follow it. The star guided them unerringly, first to Jerusalem, where it temporarily disappeared, and then to Bethlehem where they found the Child Jesus. Put like that, it sounds very simple and very exciting.

But how true is this picture? If we read the Gospel account carefully we will see that it is quite false. In the Gospel it says that they saw the star 'as it rose'. It says nothing about the star guiding them. What this suggests is that the star was no more than a sign that something unusual had happened, or, more precisely, that someone special had been born.

The next time the star is mentioned is when they were on the road to Bethlehem, that is, as they neared the end of their journey. The text says: 'There in front of them was the star they had seen rising.' From this we conclude that in between they travelled in darkness, and had to ask and seek and enquire.

Their journey was neither simple nor easy. They encountered difficulties, doubts and dangers. Yet, in spite of these they persevered in their quest, and were rewarded when they finally found Christ.

This is why their story has such relevance for us. Like them we too are on a journey. When we start out on some road (whether it be following the Christian vocation, or following some other vocation or profession), we too are attracted by something bright – an ideal or vision or hope. But this initial 'star' does not remain for ever in our sky. It grows dim. Clouds get in the way and deprive us of its light.

And we must expect to encounter difficulties and doubts. Some people think they are losing their faith when they experience doubt. We must not be surprised when this happens. We must imitate the Magi. We must not be too proud to ask for guidance. We must believe that the darkness will pass, and once again we will see the initial star beckoning to us.

The Magi can serve as models for us on our faith journey. They were single-minded. They refused to be put off by difficulties and hardships. When they found Christ they offered him gold, frankincense and myrrh. This shows what happens to those who find Christ. Their hearts are awakened and burst into life. When we find Christ and offer our love to him, he will help us to open up the treasures of goodness that lie buried inside us, so that we can offer 'gifts' to our brothers and sisters, especially those who are poor as Christ was.

Having worshipped Christ, the Magi 'returned to their own country by another route'. This suggests not just a new geographical route, but a new mentality. Having met Christ and heard his Gospel, we too will travel through life by a different route. We will have different attitudes, different values, different goals. It is impossible to encounter Christ without it affecting the way we live our lives.

HOMILY 2   **They opened their treasures**

Once the people of a very poor parish set their hearts on acquiring an expensive set of figures for their Christmas crib. They worked hard to scrape together the money to buy the figures which were made of rare porcelain. Eventually they had their crib. And were they proud of it!

The church was left open all Christmas Day so that people could visit the crib. In the evening the parish priest went out to lock up. Before doing so he looked in at the crib. To his consternation he discovered that the baby Jesus was missing. He wondered how anyone could stoop so low as to steal baby Jesus.

As he stood there he spotted a little girl with a small pram entering the church. She made straight for the crib. Then she took the baby Jesus out of the pram and lovingly put him back where he belonged – right in front of Mary and Joseph and the adoring donkey and oxen. Before leaving she knelt and said a prayer in front of the crib.

As she was on her way out the parish priest stopped her and asked her what she was doing with the baby Jesus. She told him that before Christmas she had prayed to baby Jesus for a pram. She promised him that if she got the pram, he would have the first ride in it. As she had got her pram, she was keeping her side of the bargain.

This little story shows the power of Christmas. Christmas evokes generosity in people, especially children. To look at the poverty of the infant King of the Universe causes us to open our hearts. By coming in weakness, God's Son evokes in us a feeling of compassion, thereby bringing our hearts to life.

It was the poverty of the child Jesus that evoked that lovely act of generosity in the little girl. It was the poverty of Jesus that caused the Magi to open our treasures of gold, frankincense, and myrrh, and lay them before him.

It has always been the poor who have had to pay homage to the rich – through labour, payment of taxes, and so on. But in the visit of the Magi to the Christ-child, we see a reversal of the established order of things. It was only the first of many radical changes Christ would bring about.

Instead of being impoverished, the Magi were enriched. It is through giving that we are enriched, because, through giving, we discover our own riches.

The poverty of Jesus is a challenge to us too. It gives us an opportunity to open our hearts. To open one's heart is to begin to live. Jesus no longer needs our gifts. But other people may. He wants us to share ourselves with one another. And we too will find ourselves enriched if, as a result of knowing Jesus, we are able to open the treasures of our hearts and share with others.

HOMILY 3   **Searching for the King**

There is a legend that says there were not three but four Magi. The name of the fourth was Artaban. He too saw the star and decided to follow it, taking with him a sapphire, a ruby, and a pearl as gifts for the new King. His three friends, Caspar, Melchior and Balthasar were waiting for him at an agreed spot. However, on the way there he came upon a man lying wounded by the roadside. He brought the man to an inn and had him taken care of.

When he finally got to the agreed meeting place he found that his friends had left. Needing a camel and supplies to get across the desert, he sold the sapphire to buy them. When he reached Bethlehem, once again he was too late. Joseph and Mary had taken the baby and fled into Egypt to escape Herod's killers.

In the house where he was staying there was a year-old baby boy. The mother feared for the life of her child. One evening soldiers came to the door. Artaban went out to meet them. With the ruby he bribed the captain not to enter, and the child was saved. The mother was overjoyed. Artaban, however, was sad because now he had only the pearl left as a gift for the King.

During the years that followed he searched in many places for the King. But he always seemed to be late. Some thirty years later he came to Jerusalem. He was now old and weary and dispirited. A number of crucifixions were taking place the very day he arrived. He was horrified to hear that Jesus was among those who were being executed. He hurried towards the hill of execution. Perhaps with the pearl he could save his life.

However, on his way to Calvary he met a girl who was fleeing from a band of soldiers. The girl's father had incurred large debts, and she was being sold into slavery. Artaban took out his pearl, gave it to the soldiers, and the girl was allowed to go. But now he had to face his King empty-handed.

Just then the sky began to get dark. An earthquake shook the ground. Houses began to rock. Roof tiles began to fly. One of them hit Artaban on the head. Mortally wounded he struggled onwards. But he died before reaching the hill of execution. He never quite succeeded in catching up with his King.

Yet in a sense Artaban always had his King. All those years he had carried him in his mind and heart. The King had inspired in him deeds of love and generosity, and had illuminated all his journeying with meaning and hope.

Artaban had found his God, because the person who is genuinely searching for God has already found him. Artaban is a model of faith. Those who believe in and love Jesus are changed; they act and live differently. [A moment of reflection might follow].

PRAYER OF THE FAITHFUL

President: Let us pray that the light of the Lord's salvation may reach the ends of the earth.

Response: Lord, hear us in your love.

Reader(s): For all Christians: that their lives may bear witness to the faith they profess with their lips. [Pause] We pray in faith.

For all the human family: that Christ's light may shine for all people to see. [Pause] We pray in faith.

For those who are still searching: that God may open their eyes to see, their minds to understand, and their hearts to love. [Pause] We pray in faith.

For our departed relatives and friends: that having ended their earthly pilgrimage they may see the face of God in glory. [Pause] We pray in faith.

For God's blessing on our own needs. [Longer pause] We pray in faith.

President: Almighty and eternal God, today you revealed your Son as the light of all peoples. May we follow him faithfully, and come to the light that shines for ever. We make this and all our prayers through Christ our Lord.

REFLECTION   **The Star of Bethlehem**

Gordon Wilson's daughter was killed by a bomb in Enniskillen on Remembrance Day 1987. Instead of calling for revenge, he forgave her killers and began a campaign for peace and reconciliation. He said:

'I am a very ordinary sort of man.

I have few personal ambitions and no political aspirations.

I just want to live and let live.

Life has been kind to me in the main,

and I have tried to live by the Good Book.

I do not profess to be a good man, but I aim to be.

I would like to leave the world a better place than I found it,
but I have no exaggerated ideas of my ability to do so.
I have hitched my wagon to a star,
a star of hope, the star of Bethlehem.'

Baptism of the Lord

INTRODUCTION AND CONFITEOR

We celebrate birthdays with a lot of fuss. But never our baptism. Yet this is our birthday as Christians. In today's liturgy we celebrate the baptism of Jesus. In celebrating his baptism we celebrate our own baptism too, and renew its grace within us. [Pause]

Lord, in baptism the Father made us his children and his favour rested on us. Lord, have mercy.

In baptism you made us your brothers and sisters. Christ, have mercy.

In baptism the Holy Spirit descended upon us to help us to live as your disciples. Lord, have mercy.

HEADINGS FOR READINGS

First Reading (Is 55:1-11). Here the prophet invites all to the rich banquet of life God provides for his people. In baptism we share in the life of God.

Second Reading (1 Jn 5:1-9). Faith in Jesus leads us to love one another and gives us the ability to overcome evil. Jesus' baptism and death bear witness to his identity.

(*Note* The readings from Year A can be used as alternatives).

Gospel (Mk 1:7-11). This tells how Jesus was baptised by John the Baptist in the river Jordan, and the signs that accompanied his baptism.

SCRIPTURE NOTE

In his account of Jesus' baptism, Mark's main concern is with Jesus' identity. The heavenly voice, 'You are my beloved Son,' echoes Psalm 2:7, a psalm used for the coronation of the kings from the house of David, and thus points to Jesus as the Messiah. The words 'with you I am well pleased,' echo Isaiah 42:1, pointing to Jesus as the Isaian Servant who is to bear the infirmities of many. Thus Mark reveals Jesus as royal Messiah and Suffering Servant.

HOMILY 1   **Decisive moments in life**

Many people experience moments which prove to be decisive turning points in their life. They reach a cross-roads where they are confronted with radically different choices. They are forced to make a fundamental decision after which their life will never be the same again.

It may be a moment of illumination for the mind. If that grace is responded to, people are lifted out of themselves, and start out on a new path. If it is not responded to, the opportunity may be gone forever. Shakespeare put it like this:

> There is a tide in the affairs of men
> Which taken at the flood, leads on to fortune;
> Omitted, all the voyage of their life
> Is bound in shallows and miseries.

This moment of decision can be thrust upon a person like a bolt out of the blue. This happened to the Dubliner, Matt Talbot. He was drinking himself to death. One day he was standing outside a pub, begging the price of a drink from people he considered his friends. But they passed him by. Suddenly the scales fell from his eyes. He saw that he was destroying himself, and he made a decision to give up drink, and to try, with the help of God, to become a saint.

Or this moment may come upon a person gradually, as happened to Mother Teresa. She was working for well-off girls in a convent school in Calcutta. But meanwhile she was becoming more and more uneasy about the fact that poor people were lying uncared for on the streets just outside the convent walls. One day she left her convent and went to work among the poor. Her name became a byword for devotion to the abandoned.

Jesus too knew such moments in his life. Today's Gospel shows us one of the most decisive of these – his baptism by John in the Jordan. This was a turning point in his life.

Prior to this he had lived the comparatively quiet and secure life of a village carpenter in Nazareth. But all the while he had been hearing a call to something more important. Then his cousin John began his work of preaching and baptising people. Suddenly Jesus left his old life and opted for a new one – that of a spiritual teacher and healer to his brothers and sisters.

From that moment on his life would never be the same. He found himself and his real vocation. All his hidden qualities of care and love, which had been growing quietly like wheat in a field, now manifested themselves and were given full expression.

Most of us have known moments that have proved turning points in our lives. However, the direction our lives have taken may not be the result of some major decision, but of a series of little decisions. From time to time we need to look at the direction our lives have taken. If we are not happy with the way things are going then we should try to change them. Perhaps we are stuck in a rut. In which case we should try to get ourselves out of it.

At baptism we were pointed in a very specific direction. God wants us to have life, life in abundance (see First Reading). In baptism we share in the life of God. In baptism we became disciples of Jesus. We are to called to fight against evil, and to love one another (Second Reading).

The ultimate question for a Christian is: Am I being true to the direction in which I was pointed at baptism?

HOMILY 2   **Ripe for the call**

Alpine flowers bloom almost at the very first touch of the spring sun. They are able to respond so quickly because they have been growing quietly under the crust of snow, and are just waiting for the door to be opened in order to burst out. They are ripe for the call of spring, ripe to grow and blossom.

Jesus had lived for thirty years at Nazareth. Why did he wait so long? Was he merely idling his life away? Nothing could be further from the truth. A vocation requires a period of apprenticeship and formation. The profound experiences that shape a person's character, the things that make him what he is, take time. People must be willing to serve an apprenticeship.

Jesus first of all lived a real and true life. He began by doing before he started to preach to others. He made sure his own garden was blooming before he set out to show others what to do with their gardens.

During the thirty years he spent there, Jesus had been growing quietly, growing in wisdom and grace. He has been pictured as a gentle boy, somehow different and apart, with an perpetually watchful air about him. Thirty years is a long time. However, it is better to have a relatively long time of preparation than to start before one is ready. During the quiet seasons Jesus had grown to maturity.

The call when it finally came was no stranger to him. It was always in him, but he couldn't hurry it. He couldn't have done it earlier. The future has to enter into us long before it happens. 'When destiny comes to a man from within, from his innermost being, it makes him strong, it makes him a god.' (Hermann Hesse).

It was a call to the service of his brothers and sisters. Jesus was ripe for this call. And the moment was ripe. John had started a movement of conversion, of turning towards God. A tide was flowing.

We too need to ripen. Not to be ripe is to be unable to respond properly. To give things to people before they are ripe for them is a waste. We have to wait for the natural season.

We learn patience from looking at nature. Nature takes its time. We see the slowness of the unfolding bulbs. The fruit that misses a single stage in its ripening process never attains maturity.

We too are called to grow in wisdom and grace. It took Jesus thirty years to reach maturity and to acquire wisdom. It will take us a lifetime to grow, to mature, and to ripen as human beings and children of God.

May God give us the patience and strength to nurture into ripeness the seeds he sowed in us on the day of our spiritual birth, the day of our baptism.

HOMILY 3   **Identifying with sinners**

Mahatma Gandhi was not a Christian, yet he was one of the most Christlike men of this century. Albert Einstein said of him, 'Generations to come will find it hard to believe that such a man as he ever walked upon this earth.'

Gandhi was a staunch opponent of India's iniquitous caste system. He referred to it as 'a blot on the soul of India.' He especially abhorred the treatment meted out to the untouchables – those who belong to no caste. They were barred from entering the temples. In towns and cities they were confined to the slums and allowed to perform only the most menial jobs. In the country they were forbidden the use of the wells.

On his journeys through India Gandhi was warmly welcomed by the people. When he entered a village the head of the village would invite him to stay in his house for the night, where he would be assured of a bath, good food, and a decent night's rest. But Gandhi politely refused the offer. He asked, 'Where are your untouchables? I will stay with them.' And he did, even though his action shocked the village leaders.

Gandhi went among the untouchables in their hovels on the outskirts of the village. And they welcomed him with open arms. He touched them. He ate with them and played with their children. He once said, 'I have no wish to be reborn. But if this should happen, then I want to be reborn among the untouchables, so that I might succeed in liberating them and myself from their wretched condition.'

Gandhi went out of his way to identify with the untouchables. When Jesus joined the queue of sinners waiting to be baptised by John, it was a mighty act of identification. He was identifying with the kind of people he came to save, namely, sinners. Not just sinners, but the poor and the downtrodden, which at that time constituted the overwhelming majority of the population of Palestine. He was in effect saying to them, 'I'm on your side.'

What Jesus did that day at the Jordan was to serve as a model for his public ministry. He would not keep himself apart from sinners. He would not wait for them to come to him. He would seek them out and befriend them.

Jesus didn't stand apart or put himself above the sinners he came to save. He placed himself among them. He joined them where they were. He was even accused of being a sinner, and was treated as a sinner.

What motivated him was compassion. He was God's servant sent to bring good news to the poor. And God was well pleased with him and with the mission on which he was about to embark. In this way Jesus shows his love for us.

Though completely sinless, Jesus took our sinful condition on himself. He doesn't stand apart from us, but has placed himself beside us as an older Brother. He reveals to us that we are God's precious children. He wants to lead us out from our wretched condition of sin and death. He wants us to have life here and hereafter.

PRAYER OF THE FAITHFUL

President: Let us bring our needs before God who sent his Son to lead us out from sin and death.

Response: Lord, hear our prayer.

Reader(s): For all Christians: that they may strive to live up to the call they received at baptism to follow Christ. [Pause] Let us pray to the Lord.

For our political and civil leaders: that they may see truly and act rightly. [Pause] Let us pray to the Lord.

For those who are faced with difficult and important decisions. [Pause] Let us pray to the Lord.

For those who have strayed from the path of the faith. [Pause] Let us pray to the Lord.

For all gathered here: that we may have the strength to persevere in the right choices we have made, and the courage to correct the wrong ones. [Pause] Let us pray to the Lord.

For our own special needs. [Longer pause] Let us pray to the Lord.

President: Father, you sent your Son into the world to show us the way to you. Help us to follow him with courage and steadfastness, so that we may reach the glory you have prepared for us. We ask this through the same Christ our Lord.

REFLECTION   **Finding one's work**

I think it is a great blessing when people find their work.
I often feel that I am as rich as Croesus, not in money,
but rich because I have found my work.
In that work I have something
to which I can devote myself heart and soul,

and which gives meaning and inspiration to my life.
Even though I have lots of difficulties,
and there are many gloomy days in my life,
I count myself among the fortunate.
This is not the road on which one perishes.
This is a powerful stream that will bear me safely to port.

Vincent Van Gogh

LENT & PASSION (PALM) SUNDAY

'Crucifixion'

ALBERT CARPENTIER, O.P.

First Sunday of Lent

INTRODUCTION AND CONFITEOR

Each of us is involved in a constant struggle against temptation. We see from the Gospel that Jesus too was tempted. Hence, he understands our weakness in the face of temptation. And because he was victorious over temptation, he can help us. Let us then approach him with confidence, asking for the help we need to overcome our temptations. [Pause]

Lord Jesus, you strengthen us when we are weak. Lord, have mercy.

You lift us up when we fall. Christ, have mercy.

You seek us out when we are lost. Lord, have mercy.

HEADINGS FOR READINGS

First Reading (Gen 9:8-15). This tells of the friendship-agreement (covenant) which God established with Noah and his descendants after the Flood.

Second Reading (1 Pet 3 :18-22). The waters of the Flood of Noah's time were a type of the waters of baptism by which we are saved.

Gospel (Mk 1:12-15). After his baptism Jesus spent forty days in the desert, during which time he was tempted by Satan.

SCRIPTURE NOTE

The First Reading introduces the theme of covenant. In it we are told of the first in a series of patriarchal covenants which serve as a preparation for the covenant at Sinai. That in turn prepared the way for the new covenant God formed with humanity in Christ.

In the Gospel we hear of Jesus' victorious struggle against evil. Mark makes no reference to the fast of Jesus. In this first struggle Jesus is not God-forsaken as he will be at his last (15:34).

Like Noah, the Christian is saved by passage through water – the waters of baptism- (Second Reading). It is through our baptism that we enter into the new covenant relationship with God, and that Christ's victory over sin and death is communicated to us.

HOMILY 1   **Like us in all things but sin**

Janet Frame is a New Zealand novelist. During her early years she suffered from mental illness and just escaped being forced to have a lobotomy. Eventually she went to a hospital in England for treatment. There she was fortunate to meet a very understanding doctor who helped her to recover. In what way was this doctor different from the many other doctors she had met? She says:

I was grateful that my doctor was someone who was not afraid to acknowledge and voice the awful thought that he belonged, after all, to the human race, and that there was nothing he could do about it, and pretending to be a god could never change it.

In that hospital the management had wisely included doctors who were themselves handicapped by disabilities. These doctors were more easily able to communicate with their patients.

Compassion is not learned without suffering. Unless we have suffered we don't really understand what compassion is, nor can we comfort someone who is suffering. Unless we have cried we can't dry the tears of others. Unless we have walked in darkness we can't help wanderers to find their way. When we have suffered we can become pathfinders for others.

In the Gospel we see that Jesus was tempted. The Letter to the Hebrews says that Jesus was made 'completely like his brothers [and sisters]. In him we have a high priest who can feel our weaknesses with us; for he was tempted in every way that we are, though he is without sin.' (Heb 2:17-18).

Jesus can identify with us. He is like us in all things and ways, sin excepted. He was tempted as we are. He was not immune to suffering, to hurt, to disappointment ... He deigned to taste of human triumph, of failure, and of death. He rejected none of our joys; he only rejected sin. This is the most profound mystery of God's love.

Jesus was wholly human, but that doesn't mean that he was merely human. The fact that he was 'without sin' did not imply any lack of humanness. Sin is not an intrinsic ingredient of humanity. Quite the contrary. Sin is a fall from humanity. But otherwise he shared our weakness and our temptations.

Because he himself has been through temptation Jesus understands us and is able to help us. Hence, we can approach him with confidence, knowing that we will have mercy from him and find grace in our time of need.

HOMILY 2   **Tempted by the Good**

Insects and flies are lured by the scent of the sweet. Many times they discover that following a sweet scent can lead to a life of imprisonment or worse. Unable to resist the lure of the scent, they crawl far into a flower only to get so steeped in pollen that they can't get out.

You might think this could never happen with us humans. We are too smart to fall for that. The sad fact is that we do allow it to happen. Like the bees we are lured by the scent of the sweet.

The popular meaning of temptation is enticing a person to do wrong. When we think of temptations, we immediately think of bad things. However, it is not only evil which can lead us astray. Good can do so just as effectively. In fact, all temptation comes under the guise of good. And the strength of a temptation is in proportion to the attractiveness of the goal.

It is not only when the path is hard and strewn with obstacles that we fail to reach the goal, but also when it is easy and littered with attractions. In the latter case we are tempted to dally along the way. We allow ourselves to get side-tracked, so that before we know it, we've forgotten our goal and wasted our strength. Earthly food dulls the appetite for heavenly food. There are no shortage of examples of this in the Gospels.

On one occasion Jesus invited a rich young man to become his disciple, but he refused. It wasn't evil which caused him to refuse – he had done no evil. It was something which is good in itself – wealth.

When Jesus went to the house of Martha and Mary, Martha was too busy to listen to him. It wasn't something bad which kept her from listening to him. It was something good, even praiseworthy – the details of hospitality.

Jesus told a story about guests who refused an invitation to a banquet. In refusing they were not acting from bad motives, but from perfectly good ones. One man wanted to inspect a piece of land he had bought. Another wanted to try out some oxen he had bought. And a third was newly married. However, though their reasons for staying away were perfectly good, the effect was the same as if they had been perfectly vile – they allowed the banquet to pass them by.

In his parable of the sower, Jesus said that some of the seed was choked by thorns. What did these 'thorns' consist of? 'The worries and cares of this world and the lure of riches.' Again, things not evil in themselves.

What are we to deduce from all of this? That we may have as much to fear from the good as from the bad. After all, when we see something which is manifestly evil, we are more likely to be repelled than attracted by it. But when we see something which is manifestly good, we are likely to be attracted by it. Hence, it poses more danger. 'Set a bird's wings with gold and it will never fly.' (Rabindranath Tagore).

The things that tempt us to abandon our goal are not always bad. More often than not they are good, and that is what makes it so hard to resist them. The most painful choices are often between the good and the best.

The devil doesn't appear as a repulsive character. He appears as an attractive, ingratiating, charming character, even a friend. He appears to have your best interests at heart – as when he offered Jesus bread and all the kingdoms of the world. We need wisdom and strength to be able to resist temptations, especially those that come under the guise of good.

HOMILY 3   **Reforming one's life**

Once a king was walking through the streets of the capital city when he came upon a beggar, who immediately asked him for money. The king didn't give him any money. Instead he invited him to visit him in his palace. The beggar took up the king's offer.

On the appointed day he made his way to the royal palace, and was duly ushered into the king's presence. However, as he came into the king's presence, he became acutely conscious of his rags and felt ashamed of them. They were an eloquent symbol of the wretchedness of his life.

The king, an exceptionally kind man, received him warmly, took pity on him, and among other things gave him a new suit of clothes. However, a few days later the beggar was back begging on the streets dressed in his old rags.

Why did he give up the new suit? Because he knew that to wear it would mean that he would have to live a new life. It would mean giving up the life of a beggar. This he was not prepared to do. It wasn't that the new life didn't appeal to him. It did. It was just that he knew that a change of life would be slow, painful and uncertain. In other words, he was too steeped in habit to change.

Habit plays a big part in our lives. It is said that we live the second half of our lives according to the habits acquired during the first half. That will bring comfort to those who have formed good habits. But it's quite a terrifying prospect for those who have formed bad habits.

Lent touches something in us all. The sight of Jesus fasting and praying in the desert moves us. But it also forces us to look at our lives. It challenges us to improve ourselves. But often our efforts at renewal do not go deep enough. If we want a new garment, we must caste aside the old one. The wearing of a new garment will involve a new way of living.

If we wish to change the outer aspects of our lives we must first change the inner attitudes of our minds. Change requires the substituting of new habits for old ones. It calls us to command ourselves and make ourselves do what needs to be done. The change of heart to which Lent calls us can be accomplished most of all through the power of prayer.

Even though repentance and prayer are always appropriate, they are especially appropriate during Lent. There is such a thing as a moment of grace. Lent is a great window of opportunity. It is the Church's 'holy spring'. During it, the catechumens were prepared for baptism, for their rebirth in Christ. It was a time of penance and effort. But it was also a time of great joy. It was like springtime. As we progress towards Easter the sun gets brighter and warmer.

What do we have to do? In a nutshell: turn from power to love; be kind; act justly, and walk humbly with God. May the Lord help us to let go of the rags of sin, so that he may clothe us in newness of life.

PRAYER OF THE FAITHFUL

President: Let us now bring our needs before God, who guides us when we stray and raises us up when we fall.

Response: Create a new spirit within us, O Lord.

Reader(s): For all Christians: that they may have a spirit of self-denial, and be moved to help those in need. [Pause] Let us pray to the Lord.

For the Church: that it may nourish the faith of its members with the word of God. [Pause] Let us pray to the Lord.

For political leaders: that they may resist the temptation to seek their own honour and glory, and seek rather to serve the people. [Pause] Let us pray to the Lord.

For the grace to be victorious over our temptations. [Pause] Let us pray to the Lord.

For all gathered here: that this holy season may help us to deepen our commitment to Christ and to the Gospel. [Pause] Let us pray to the Lord.

For our own special needs. [Longer pause] Let us pray to the Lord.

President: Lord, grant us in all our tasks your help, in all our doubts your guidance, in all our temptations your strength, in all our sorrows your consolation, and in all our dangers your protection. We ask this through Christ our Lord.

REFLECTION   **Lent: springtime of the spirit**

Each year the trees give us a lesson in renewal.
First the bud, then the blossom, and finally the shoot.
Spring dresses the trees in a new robe,
and makes them young again.
But this is possible only because in autumn
they let go of their old leaves,
and in between endured a period of nakedness.
Lent is in the springtime of the spirit.
Lord, help us not to be afraid to let go of old habits,
and to face our spiritual poverty,
in order that you may renew us, and so at Easter
we will feel young again in our discipleship.

Second Sunday of Lent

THE TRANSFIGURATION

INTRODUCTION AND CONFITEOR

On Mount Tabor Jesus' disciples got a glimpse of the glory that was his as the Son of God. It was a wonderful experience for them, so much so that Peter exclaimed, 'Lord, it is good for us to here.' And it is good for us to be here this morning (evening), because here we get a glimpse of our own glory, for we too are children of God. [Pause]

Lord, here you forgive our sins are forgiven and enable us to forgive one another. Lord, have mercy.

You strengthen our faith and deepen our hope. Christ, have mercy.

Word of God, you nourish us with the bread of eternal life. Lord, have mercy.

HEADINGS FOR READINGS

First Reading (Gen 22:1-2.9-13.15-18). This reading shows how complete was Abraham's obedience to God.

Second Reading (Rom 8:31-34). Since God is on our side, we can face anything.

Gospel (Mk 9:2-10). On Mount Tabor three apostles of Jesus got a glimpse of the glory that was his as the Son of God.

SCRIPTURE NOTE

The transfiguration is an epiphany story. Epiphany stories are common in ancient writing about holy people. In these stories, the veil which separates the invisible from the visible world, and the future from the present, is removed for a moment, and the truth is revealed. This is the earliest epiphany story about Jesus, older than the voice at his baptism, and older than the manifestation of Jesus to the Magi.

It is no longer possible to say what happened on the mountain. The first and chief significance of the event was for Jesus himself. It was meant to confirm him in the course he had taken. But it also benefited the apostles, and it is this that Mark emphasises. In the transfigured Jesus they got a glimpse of the glory of the risen Lord. Even so, they would not understand until Jesus had risen from the dead.

On the mountain Elijah and Moses appeared to them. Moses represented the law, Elijah the prophets. Thus Jesus is seen as bringing the law and the prophets to fulfilment.

The First Reading shows the depth of Abraham's faith in God. Living among the Canaanites who practised human sacrifice, we see his agonising effort to do what he thought God wanted of him. Abraham's great faith was rewarded.

The Second Reading is obviously linked to the First Reading. It shows us the depth of God's love for us. God did not even spare his own Son, but gave him up for us.

HOMILY 1   **What Mount Tabor meant for Jesus**

The film *Dead Man Walking* tells the story of a nun (Sr Helen Prejean) as she accompanies a man (Robert) during the months leading up to his execution in Louisiana. Noticing how Robert tried to win the confidence of one of the wardens, who was a kind and fatherly figure, Sr Helen reflected:

> Robert never really had a father. (His father spent 27 of his 53 years in prison). It makes me think of my own father. It has to be one of life's most precious feelings to know that your dad is proud of you. I was my daddy's scholar, his scribe who kept the travel diary on family vacations. He always had a special tone in his voice when he introduced me to friends and colleagues: 'And this is my little daughter, Helen.' In the presence of strangers I would fall silent, standing close against him, my hand holding on tightly to his. Afterwards I would squeeze his hand tighter than ever and teem once more with chatter and questions. A child can sail to the moon with that feeling of security from a father.

This may help us to understand something of what the Tabor experience meant for Jesus. It came at a very difficult time in his life, a time of uncertainty and fear of the future. He was headed for Jerusalem, where he sensed that the same fate awaited him as befell all the prophets – a violent death. Naturally he recoiled from such a fate. In order to reflect on it and pray about it, he climbed to the top of Mount Tabor.

We don't know exactly what happened on the mountain. But it seems that he had an intense experience of the presence of God. He heard those marvellous words: 'You are my beloved Son.' On Tabor Jesus felt himself comforted and affirmed. He knew that his Father was pleased with him, and would give him the strength to face a dark and threatening future. With God on his side, he could face anything.

At times life can become dark for all of us. There are a lot of voices which say to us: 'You're good, but only if you're successful, or if you're good, or if you're popular.' But there is a still small voice which whispers to us in our hearts: 'You are my beloved son/daughter.' This is the voice we need to pay attention to. We must recognise that we are God's beloved children, and try to live our lives by the light of this truth.

Jean Vanier has set up communities for the mentally handicapped. He tells how in one of those communities there is a man called Pierre who has a mental handicap. One day somebody asked Pierre, 'Do you like praying?'

'Yes,' he answered.

'And what do you do when you pray?' the questioner asked.

'I listen,' Pierre answered.

'And what does God say to you?'

'He says, "Pierre, you are my beloved son".'

HOMILY 2   **Sacrifice of Isaac**

The story of God asking Abraham to sacrifice his son Isaac is a strange story. In truth, it is a shocking story. What we find most disturbing is the image of God that comes across.

However, we must try to understand what the story is meant to convey. It has something very important to teach us. As a story, it is a very clever one. It sets out in the opposite direction to that in which it hopes to leave the listener. It starts out by seeming to say that God approves of human sacrifice, and even on occasion demands it. But its object is to show the exact opposite. It tries to show us that human sacrifice is in fact abhorrent to God.

And it does this very well. What God appears to ask of Abraham is so cruel and unjust that it makes us want to cry out, 'Stop! This is wrong. This is terrible!' We are revolted by the idea of the elderly Abraham being asked by God to sacrifice his son Isaac. Our sense of revulsion is heightened by the special burden of hope that rested on Isaac's youthful shoulders – the fulfilment of the promise that Abraham would have numerous descendants.

The aim of the story is to evoke horror at the idea of God demanding the sacrifice of human beings. Abraham lived among the Canaanites who practised human sacrifice. He must somehow have got the idea that God was demanding this deed of him. But God showed him otherwise. This story was meant to put an end to human sacrifice to God.

Why did God test Abraham? So that the world would know that if anyone tells us, 'I am committing murder in the name of God,' we'll know that he's a liar. That is the unanimous opinion of the Orthodox Jewish tradition.

Sadly, killing in the name of God has been widely practised down the ages. Even in our own day there are people who kill for religious beliefs, and who think that in doing so they are honouring God. Yigal Amir who shot Yitzhak Rabin in October 1995 was a Jewish religious fundamentalist. The Palestinian suicide bombers, who from time to time have struck at Israel, killing innocent men, women and children, were Muslim fundamentalists. Paul Hill, who killed a doctor and his bodyguard outside a Florida abortion clinic in 1994, was a former Presbyterian minister. These are but a few examples.

God does not want us to mete out hurt for hurt, pain for pain, life for life. The pages of history are stained with the blood spilled by people who see themselves as 'God's avengers'. Kings and heads of states have killed, claiming God's authority and God's blessing on their dark deeds.

One thing the story shows clearly is the depth of Abraham's faith. He was prepared to sacrifice what was dearest to him. His extraordinary faith was rewarded in an extraordinary way. No wonder we call him 'our father in faith'.

The story condemns the idea of honouring God by taking a life. But Jesus introduced something that is a lot more challenging: the idea of honouring God by *giving our lives* in the service of God and others. He set the example himself. God didn't demand his life from him. He gave it up freely in the service of his brothers and sisters. 'Giving our lives' doesn't necessarily mean dying. It means spending our lives for others.

HOMILY 3   **God is on our side**

St Paul tells us that God is on our side. Therefore, neither suffering nor tragedy nor death should separate us from the love of God, a love which we have seen in Christ.

Maya Angelu, the American poet and author, is a wise woman and a spiritual one too. She tells how one day she had a religious awakening. It happened in a very simple manner. She was in her twenties and had just moved to San Francisco. She says that at that time she was an acting agnostic. It wasn't that she had stopped believing in God; it was just that God didn't seem to be around the neighbourhoods she frequented. Then a voice teacher introduced her to a book entitled *Lessons in Truth*. She tells how one day the teacher asked her to read to him from the book:

> I was twenty-four, very erudite, very worldly. He asked me to read a section which ended with the words: 'God loves me.' I read the piece and closed the book, and the teacher said, 'Read it again.' I pointedly opened the book, and sarcastically read, 'God loves me.' He said, 'Again.' After about the seventh repetition I began to sense that there might be truth in the statement, that there was a possibility that God really did love me. Yes, me, Maya Angelou.
>
> Suddenly I began to cry at the grandness of it all. I knew that if God loved me, then I could do wonderful things, I could try great things, learn anything, achieve anything. For what could stand against me when God was with me, since any person with God constitutes the majority.

For Maya Angelu, though she believed, God seemed very remote and unreal. It is only when she become convinced that God loved her that God became real for her. Then that belief energised her. Suddenly she felt that she could do anything, face anything, since God loved her and was with her.

Jesus had just begun his journey to Jerusalem. Up to this time he had been working mostly in Galilee. Even there, the area where he had grown up, he had met a lot of opposition from the religious leaders. But in going to Jerusalem he sensed that a violent death awaited him there. Naturally he recoiled from such a fate. It seems that it was to reflect on this and to pray about it, that he climbed to the top of Mount Tabor.

Jesus had a marvellous experience on that mountain. He heard those wonderful words: 'You are my beloved Son; I am pleased with you.' In other words, he knew that God loved him. This assurance would give him the strength to face the future whatever it held.

Our problem is that as soon as we run into trouble our faith fails us. We think that God has abandoned us. But if we pray we will come to realise that God has not abandoned us, but is present in our suffering.

At all times, but especially in times of difficulty, we should remember what St Paul says: 'God is on our side.' And with God on our side, we can face anything.

To know that nothing can separate us from the love of God is our strength in times of weakness and our hope in times of adversity. In the face of pain, all we have to do is abandon ourselves to his care.

Like Jesus on Tabor, we too can experience rare moments of light and joy. We get glimpses of the promised land towards which we are travelling in faith. In his love for us, God allows us to taste on earth the joys of the world to come.

ANOTHER STORY

One day a king assembled his courtiers. He handed the minister a glowing pearl and asked, 'What would you say this is worth?' 'More gold than a hundred donkeys could carry,' the minister replied. 'Break it,' the king ordered. 'Sir, how could I waste your resources like that?' The king presented him with a robe of honour for his answer and took back the pearl.

Then he gave the pearl to the chamberlain asking, 'What would it sell for?' 'Half a kingdom,' the chamberlain replied. 'Break it,' the king ordered. 'Sir, my hand could not move to do such a thing.' The king rewarded him with a robe of honour and an increase in his salary. And so it went with each of the royal courtiers. One by one they imitated the minister and the chamberlain and received new wealth.

Then the pearl was given to Abdul. 'Can you say how splendid this is?' 'It's more than I can say.' 'Break it this second into tiny pieces.' Abdul immediately took two stones and crushed the pearl to powder with them. The court assembly screamed at the recklessness of Abdul, 'How could you do that?' And Abdul replied, 'What the king says is worth more than any pearl. I honour the king, not some coloured stone.'

The courtiers immediately fell to their knees and put their foreheads on the ground. Their sighs for forgiveness went up like a cloud of smoke. The king gestured to his executioners as though to say, 'Take out this trash.'

But Abdul sprang forward. 'Your mercy makes them bow like this.

Give them their lives. Look at their heads against the floor. Whoever bows down like they are bowing down will not rise up in his old self again.' And the king had mercy on them.

The story reminds us of the story of Abraham. (First Reading). However, the story should not be pushed too far. It is only making a point about the centrality of obedience to God for anyone with faith. However, God is not honoured by a fanatical obedience which is completely blind. Besides, God will never ask anyone to do something that is intrinsically evil, or that goes against one of his commandments.

Abraham passed the test, and his faith was rewarded with the benefits of the covenant. His heroic example is the standard against which we measure our puny faith.

PRAYER OF THE FAITHFUL

President: God is on our side. Therefore let us bring our needs before him, confident that we will receive a sympathetic hearing.

Response: Lord, hear our prayer.

Reader(s): For the followers of Christ: that they may never choose the cheap and passing things, and so let go the things that last for ever. [Pause] We pray to the Lord.

For our political leaders: that they may never take the easy way and so abandon the right way. [Pause] We pray to the Lord.

For those who are finding life difficult. [Pause] We pray to the Lord.

For all gathered here: that we may be convinced that God is on our side in good times and in bad, in joy and in sorrow. [Pause] We pray to the Lord.

For all gathered here: that we may never forget that sweat is the price of all great things, and that without the cross there can be no crown. [Pause] We pray to the Lord.

For our own special needs. [Longer pause] We pray to the Lord.

President: Merciful God, give us a love for what you command and a longing for what you promise, so that amid this world's changes, our hearts may be set on the world of lasting joy. We ask this through Christ our Lord.

REFLECTION   **Mountains**

Jesus often went into the hills to pray.
He preached his most famous sermon from a hilltop.
He was transfigured on Mount Tabor,
died on Mount Calvary,
and ascended to heaven from Mount Olivet.
It seems that he loved hills and mountains.
Why was this?

Was it because he grew up among the hills of Galilee?
Or was it because heights enlarge our vision
and cause our spirit to soar?
Lift us up, strong Son of God, that we may see further.
Strengthen our faith that we may see beyond the horizon.
And when the valley closes us in,
help us to remember the view from the hilltop.

Third Sunday of Lent
CLEANSING OF THE TEMPLE

INTRODUCTION AND CONFITEOR

We are gathered in the house of God, which is supposed to be a house of prayer and worship. It is only we who can make of this church a true house of prayer. Let us reflect for a moment on the attitude we bring to our worship this morning (evening). [Pause]

Jesus, who is present among us, helps us to worship the Father in spirit and in truth.

Lord Jesus, you help us to worship in a spirit of humility and sincerity. Lord, have mercy.

You help us to worship in a spirit of deep reverence. Christ, have mercy.

You help us to worship as members of a community reconciled in love. Lord, have mercy.

HEADINGS FOR READINGS

First Reading (Ex 20:1-17). The ten commandments are a map of life for a people that has a special relationship with God.

Second Reading (1 Cor 1:22-25). Paul preached a crucified Christ. To some the idea made no sense. To others it was a sign of the wisdom and power of God.

Gospel (Jn 2:13-25). By chasing the money changers and sellers of sacrificial animals out of the Temple, Jesus passed judgement on the Jewish system of worship.

SCRIPTURE NOTE

Jesus' action in cleansing the temple was a protest against the commercialisation of religion and the desecration of the Temple. But it went deeper. It was a symbolic action, in the fashion of an Old Testament prophet (see Jer 7:11; Mal 3.1), through which he passed judgement on the Jewish sacrificial system. He was declaring that temple worship, with its ritual and animal sacrifices, was irrelevant and could do nothing to bring people to God. He was replacing sacrificial worship with spiritual worship.

He was also protesting at the way religion had become narrow, nationalistic, and exclusive. Israel had failed to fulfil her universal mission to humankind. It was God's intention that the Temple should be a house of prayer 'for all nations'. But the Temple remained the jealously-guarded preserve of Israel. No Gentile dared venture, under threat of penalty and death, beyond what was known as the 'court of the Gentiles'. Jesus declared that salvation was not just for the Jews, but for all peoples.

The First Reading is one of the two versions of the Decalogue. (The other is Deut 5:6-21). The Ten Commandments are a map of life for a people who enjoy a special relationship with God. They were to be seen as a gift, not a burden. However, Christians must not live by the Ten Commandments but by the 'law' of Jesus. He brought in a new and more exacting law- the law of love. He effectively reduced the commandments to two: love of God and love of neighbour.

HOMILY 1   **Righteous anger**

The Gospel scene depicts an angry Jesus with a whip in his hand. This image of Jesus doesn't sit well with the traditional image of a meek and smiling Jesus. It seems to be so out of character with what we know of Jesus from the rest of the Gospels that we might be tempted to dismiss it. It would be a mistake to dismiss it. It shows us that there was another side to Jesus' character. Of course Jesus was gentle. But that doesn't mean he was weak. When the occasion demanded it he could be very strong and very assertive.

Still, it comes as a shock to see Jesus not just angry, but furious. And to see him resort to what looks like a form of violence. We may have been taught that all anger is sinful. But in itself anger is just a feeling, and as such is neither good nor bad morally.

It's true that anger is a dangerous thing and can result in us saying or doing things we later regret. But anger can also be a good thing. It can spur us to put right something that is blatantly wrong. There are times when we ought to be angry. An unjust situation should make us angry. Anger can be an expression of love.

We have to look at the things that make us angry. It is said that you can measure the size of a person's soul by the size of the things that make him angry. Most of our anger is motivated by self-interest and we get angry about petty things.

A man lived on the outskirts of a village. About thirty feet from his house, a large lime tree grew. The tree was something of a village landmark. However, it was getting old. It was clearly only a matter of time before it came crashing down. Every time there was a storm, the man feared for his house and his life. One day, unable to bear the strain any longer, he cut the tree down. He felt sure that the villagers would understand. But he was wrong.

'Shame on you for cutting down such a splendid tree,' said one.

'You've deprived the village of part of its heritage,' said another.

It's amazing how worked up people get when their own interests are threatened, however marginally. But how few get worked up when it's their neighbour's interests that are threatened.

Jesus didn't get angry on his own account. His anger resulted from his love of God and of his neighbour. His action in the temple has been seen as a protest against the commercialisation of religion and the desecration of the temple. But it went deeper than that.

Firstly, he was protesting that Israel had failed to fulfil her universal mission to humankind. Religion had become narrow, nationalistic, and exclusive. The Temple, which was meant to be a house of prayer 'for all nations', remained the jealously-guarded preserve of Israel. Jesus was doing away with the notion of exclusiveness. Salvation was not just for the Jews, but for all peoples.

Secondly, he was attacking the very nature of Jewish worship. The whole temple worship with its ritual and animal sacrifices was irrelevant and could do nothing to bring people to God. He was replacing sacrificial worship with spiritual worship. Worship demands a lot more of us than the offering of things to God and the performance of certain rituals. What God wants above all is the worship of our lives.

May the Lord help us to make this house a house of prayer, joy, and unity. And may what we do here help us to give God the worship of our lives.

HOMILY 2   **Keeping the Commandments**

Once there was a very sincere man who wished to live a holy life. So he went to his rabbi to seek his advice. The rabbi congratulated him on his ambition, then asked, 'How have you been faring so far?'

'Quite well, I think,' the man replied.

'When you say well what do you mean?' the rabbi asked.

'I haven't broken any of the commandments,' the man replied. 'I haven't taken the Lord's name in vain. I haven't profaned the Sabbath day. I haven't dishonoured my father or mother. I haven't killed anyone. I haven't been unfaithful to my wife. I haven't stolen. I haven't borne false witness against anyone. And I haven't coveted my neighbour's wife or goods.'

'I see,' said the rabbi. 'So you haven't broken any of the commandments.'

'That's right,' the man replied with pride.

'But have you kept the commandments?' the rabbi asked.

'What do you mean?' said the man.

'I mean have you honoured God's holy name? Have you kept holy the Sabbath day? Have you loved and honoured your parents? Have you sought to preserve and defend life? When last did you tell your wife that you loved her? Have you shared your goods with the poor? Have you defended the good name of anyone? When last did you put yourself out to help a neighbour?'

The man was taken aback. But to his credit he went away and reflected on what the rabbi had said. He realised that up to this he had been merely intent on avoiding wrong-doing. It's surprising how many people think this is the highest criterion of virtue. But the rabbi offered him a new vision of goodness – not merely to avoid evil, but to do good. Up to now he had a negative concept of goodness. Now the rabbi was offering him a positive concept of goodness. He had given him a new and better compass to guide him, a new and more challenging path to follow.

We must be careful not to make the mistake that man made. We must not approach the commandments in a negative way because this leads to doing the bare minimum. We must approach them in a positive way.

And we must keep them in the right spirit. Our obedience must be motivated not by fear but by love. We don't keep the commandments *so that* God will love us; we keep the commandments *because* God loves us.

Jesus brought in a new and more exacting law – *the law of love*. Far from contradicting or abolishing the old law, the new law goes beyond it, and so brings it to perfection. He said that all of God's laws could be reduced to two: love of God and love of neighbour. In truth, there is only one law – the law of love.

HOMILY 3   **The new decalogue**

The purpose of God's law is not to constrain us, but to show us how to live. God's law is a light for our steps and a lamp for our path. The Ten Commandments were good. But Christ's teaching goes much farther. The person who is content with the old law is like someone who is still going around in candlelight after the advent of electricity.

In what follows we take a look at The Ten Commandments in the light of Christ's teaching. [Two voices could be used.]

Old: Listen Israel! I am the Lord your God who brought you out of the land of Egypt, out of the house of slavery.

New: Listen followers of Christ, new people of God! I am the Lord your God who brought you out of darkness into the light. The effects of the light are seen in goodness, right living and truth.

Once you were slaves to sin and wrong-doing. Now you are to live in the freedom of the children of God.

Old: I am the Lord your God; you shall not have strange gods before me.

New: I am the Lord your God. I am not a strange and distant God. I am your friend and counsellor. Beware of idols. Idols will betray you. Money is the most common idol of all. You cannot serve God and money.

Old: You shall not take the name of the Lord your God in vain.

New: From now on I want you to call me by a new name. Call me 'Father'. Pronounce this name not in fear but in love. Invoke it in praise, in thanks, as well as in making your needs known to me. Your names are written on the palm of my hand.

Old: Remember to keep holy the Sabbath day.

New: Remember that all days belong to the Lord and are to be made holy. But let the first day of the week, Sunday, be special. This is the day Jesus, your Brother, broke the chains of death and rose in triumph from the grave. This day should remind you that you are a people on pilgrimage to the promised land of eternal life. The peace and rest of the Sabbath are a foretaste of the joy to come.

Old: Honour your father and your mother.

New: Love your father and mother, those precious souls through whom you were invited to the banquet of life. Befriend them when they are lonely. Comfort them when they are sick. Take care of them when they get old and feeble.

Old: Thou shalt not kill.

New: You must not hurt another person in any way. Be compassionate as your Father is compassionate. Do not judge, and you will not be judged. Do not condemn, and you will not be condemned. Love your enemies. Do good to those who hate you. Bless those who curse you. Pray for those who speak evil against you. Thus you will show that you are true children of God.

Old: Thou shalt not commit adultery.

New: Love your marriage partner as you would your other self. Physical fidelity is a great thing, but fidelity of the heart is even better.

Old: Thou shalt not steal.

New: There are many ways of stealing. If you pile up and hoard goods that you do not need, while at the same time your neighbour is in need – that is a form of stealing. The goods of the earth were meant for all of God's children. So I say to you: give to those in need. Share your bread with the hungry. Clothe the naked. Open your heart to the lonely and the homeless, and God's light will shine on you.

Old: Thou shalt not bear false witness against thy neighbour.

New: Be a light to your neighbour, not a source of darkness. Let your words build up, support and comfort your neighbour. If you can find nothing good to say about your neighbour, then remain silent.

Old: Thou shalt not covet thy neighbour's wife.

New: You can commit adultery in thought and desire as well as in deed.

Adultery is in the heart – in the desire to possess. Strive, therefore, to keep your heart pure.

Old: Thou shalt not covet thy neighbour's goods.

New: I say to you: do not covet any goods at all. Do not lay up treasures here on earth. Strive, rather, to make yourselves rich in the sight of God. If you covet anything that is your neighbour's, let it be his kindness of heart and gentleness of manner.

Conclusion: Obey these commandments not out of fear but out of love. And if you find ten too many to remember, you can reduce them to two: Love God with all your heart and all your soul; love your neighbour as yourself.

PRAYER OF THE FAITHFUL

President: Let us turn to God and place our needs before him.

Response: Lord, graciously hear us.

Reader(s): For all Christians: that their houses of worship may truly be houses of prayer. [Pause] Lord, hear us.

For our society: that the commandments of God may be to it what road signs are to travellers. [Pause] Lord, hear us.

For those who are walking in the darkness of error and sin: that they may discover the light of Christ's truth and love. [Pause] Lord, hear us.

For ourselves: that we may see the body as a temple of the Holy Spirit. [Pause] Lord, hear us.

For our own special needs. [Longer pause] Lord, hear us.

President: Almighty and ever-living God, strengthen our faith. May we do with loving hearts what you ask of us. We make these prayers through Christ our Lord.

PRAYER / REFLECTION   **The house of God**

The following prayer was found written
over the door of a church:
'Lord, make the door of this house
wide enough to receive
all who need human love and fellowship,
narrow enough to shut out
all envy, pride, and strife.
Make its threshold smooth enough
to be no stumbling block to children,
nor to straying feet.
Make this house a house of prayer
and a gateway to your kingdom.'

Fourth Sunday of Lent
ACCEPTING OR REJECTING THE LIGHT

INTRODUCTION AND CONFITEOR

St John says that when the light of Christ came into the world some people rejected it. Why? Because their deeds were evil. Light stands for truth and goodness. Alas, we ourselves do not always welcome the light. [Pause]

Lord Jesus, you help us to walk in the light of truth. Lord, have mercy.

You help us to walk in the light of goodness. Christ, have mercy.

You help us to walk in hope towards the light that never fades. Lord, have mercy.

HEADING FOR READINGS

First Reading(2 Chron 36:14-16.19-23). Because of their sins God allowed his people to be exiled to Babylon. But his mercy is seen in their home-coming.

Second Reading (Eph 2:4-10). It is not through our own efforts that we are saved, but through the love and mercy of God.

Gospel (Jn 3:14-21). In his love for us, God sent his Son into the world, not to condemn us, but to save us.

SCRIPTURE NOTE

The First Reading shows how God remained faithful to his people in spite of their infidelities. God's promises were not nullified by the sins of his people. It was because of their sins that God allowed his people to be exiled to Babylon. But his mercy is seen in their home-coming.

This leads into the Gospel. God's love and mercy are seen in the fact that he sent his Son to save us. Jesus came into the world as a light. Sadly, some preferred darkness to the light, thus sealing their own condemnation. Judgement is not passed by God; people judge themselves by their response to the light.

The reading from Ephesians stresses the enormity of the love God has shown us in Christ. It makes it clear that we owe our salvation, not to our own efforts, but to the goodness of God.

HOMILY 1   **God loved the world so much**

'God loved the world so much that he gave his only Son, so that everyone who believes in him may not be lost but may have eternal life.' We hear these marvellous words in today's Gospel. They are a good summary of the Good News.

The first thing to note is that it is God who took the initiative in our salvation. Sometimes the impression has been given that God had first of all to be pacified before he would forgive us. We have been presented with a picture of God as stern, angry, and unforgiving. Jesus, on the other hand, was presented as being kind, gentle and forgiving. By his death Jesus changed God's attitude towards us. But this passage shows that it was God who sent his Son to us. It was God who took the first step.

God chose the approach of love, not of power. God acts not for his own sake but for our sake. God is not an absolute monarch who is not happy until he has reduced his creatures to abject obedience. Rather, God is the Father who is not happy until all his wandering children have come home.

This passage also shows how all-inclusive is God's love. His love is not directed at one nation only, nor is it only for the good. It is directed at all nations, to the children of light and to the children of darkness.

But the passage also talks about judgement and condemnation. If God's approach is so loving, how can it include judgement and condemnation? How can condemnation be reconciled with love? Condemnation does not follow from God's action but from people's response. God condemns no one. People condemn themselves by adopting a negative attitude. God sent us a light. If people get lost it is because they haven't accepted the light. The fault is not God's but ours.

A visitor was once being shown around an art gallery. The gallery contained some beautiful paintings, which were universally acknowledged to be masterpieces. At the end of the tour the visitor said, 'I don't think much of these old pictures.' To which his guide replied, 'My good man, these pictures are no longer on trial. But those who look at them are.'

The man's reaction was not a judgement on the pictures but on his own pitiful appreciation of art. In the same way those who prefer darkness to light have condemned themselves.

Evil people hate the light because it reveals themselves to themselves. They hate goodness because it reveals their badness; they hate industry because it reveals their laziness. They will destroy the light, the goodness, the love, in order to avoid the pain of self-discovery.

It's terrible to reject the light, to reject God's offer of love. But how sweet to walk in the light of his love. Our part in the process of redemption is to accept the gift in all humility, and try to respond in kind. We are able to love God because God loved us first.

HOMILY 2   **Coming out into the light**

St John says, 'Whoever does what is true [good], comes out into the light.' Coming to the light is conditional on doing the truth. It's not the one who speculates about the truth but the one who *does* the truth who comes to the light. The shortest journey to the light is by doing the good. But we don't always act like this in practice.

Normally what we do is we try to achieve a state of inner peace, and *then* do the peaceful deed. We try to attain a state of joy and gratitude, and *then* do the joyful and grateful thing. But often we have to do the opposite. We have to perform a peaceful act in order to achieve inner peace. We have to do the joyful or grateful deed in order to experience inner joy and gratitude. In the same way, if we are in darkness, and we do the good deed, then most certainly the light will shine for us. The following true story beautifully illustrates this.

In the Lithuanian city of Kovno there lived a Jewish professor. Though he had been an agnostic all his life, the professor began to be more and more troubled by the sad, neglected condition of the Jewish graveyard in the city. Since the holocaust of Jews by the Nazis and the harassment of them by the Soviets, no one had taken care of their graves. So, out of the goodness of his heart, the professor himself decided to do so.

Whether or not he was aware that tending graves is a *mitzvah*, that is, a traditional good deed, we do not know. In any case, the good man acquired a spade, a sickle and a shears, and began the job of making the graveyard worthy of those buried in it. At first he was on his own, but as the weeks went by other Jews joined him in the work. Most of these were once observant Jews but had become agnostics like the professor. Eventually there were some two hundred of them, all doing the true thing. As they worked a beautiful thing happened. Their Jewish faith came alight in them. Practically all of them became observant Jews once more.

Anyone who does wrong, hates the light and avoids it. But those who do good, love the light and come out into it. How many of our deeds are done in the light? How many of them could bare the scrutiny of the light?

We have to accept that there is darkness in our lives and in our world. We have to recognise that darkness and learn how to live in relationship with it. It is futile to wait for the darkness to go away. We wish it would. But we have to accept that it is here, and will always be here.

What we mustn't do is call the darkness light. When we do that we get trapped by it. When we call it darkness we can learn how to live so that the darkness does not overcome us. When everything is permissible we have failed to distinguish between light and dark.

People who have come to know the love and joy of God do not deny the darkness, but they choose not to live in it. They trust in the light that shines in the darkness, and know that a little light can dispel a lot of darkness. And the light of Christ is such that no darkness can overpower it. If we do the good thing, then the light will shine for us.

HOMILY 3   **Nicodemus**

Nicodemus is at the centre of today's Gospel. Even though he appears only three times in the Gospel Story (all three appearances occur in John), he is a very interesting character. He was a Pharisee, and a member of the Sanhedrin – the supreme court of the Jews.

The first time Nicodemus appears is in the Gospel passage we've just read. We are told that he was impressed by the teaching and deeds of Jesus. It was clear to him that the hand of God was in them. So he came to see Jesus, but did so under cover of darkness, which suggests that he didn't want to be seen. But we shouldn't be too hard on him on this account. Given the fact that he was a Pharisee, it was a wonder he came at all. Jesus honoured him with a long interview.

By the time Nicodemus puts in his second appearance, opposition to Jesus had hardened. By now the Pharisees had made up their minds to kill him, and were ready to do so without even giving him a trial. But Nicodemus intervened, declaring that Jesus should at least be given a fair hearing as the law demanded (Jn 7:51). This was a more public involvement with Jesus. And the third and last time Nicodemus appears is at the burial of Jesus. It was he who provided a large quantity of expensive spices for his burial (Jn 19:39).

What can we deduce about Nicodemus from these three brief appearances? The first appearance shows that he was an open-minded man, and a genuine seeker of the truth. The second appearance shows that he was a fair-minded man, when he insisted that Jesus should not be condemned without a trial. And the third appearance shows that he was a wealthy man, but also a generous and compassionate one.

All of these qualities we can admire and copy with profit. But what Nicodemus seems to have been unable to do was come straight out and make a full and public act of faith in Jesus. He doesn't seem to have had the courage to come out of the darkness and choose decisively for the light. We are left with the picture of a decent man, who could have been a great man. A mediocre person – neither a great saint nor a great sinner.

Reflecting on Nicodemus should challenge us to come out from the shadows, and not to be afraid or ashamed to profess openly our faith in Jesus, and to be ready to pay whatever price is required for doing so.

Those who believe will not be lost, but will have eternal life. But it is not simply a matter of believing, but of living according to that belief.

ANOTHER APPROACH   **Attitude to the Light**

The coming of light ought to be good news for those living in darkness. However, this is not always the case. The Simon Community run night-shelters for down-and-outs. Each night volunteers bring soup and sandwiches to those who for one reason or another do not want to come to the shelters. They go looking for them in derelict buildings and such places. The most important aid they take with them is a torch, because often there is no light where the down-and-outs live.

Most of the down-and-outs receive the volunteers as friends. But some refuse to have anything to do with them. The volunteers can tell at once which group they are dealing with by their reaction to the light. Some welcome the light. Others fear it. You could say that the light judges them, in the sense that it shows up the darkness in their lives – the darkness of alcoholism, misery, hopelessness, crime ... But it does not come to judge them. It comes as a friend, to brighten up their lives, to comfort them. It's advent means the arrival of friends.

That's how it was with the coming of Christ's light. Christ did not come to judge people but to save them. He came bearing a light – the light of truth, goodness, salvation from sin. Some welcomed his light. But others rejected it because it showed up the evil in their lives.

There is darkness in each of us. We need to let the light of Christ shine into that darkness whatever form it takes. But there is goodness in us too. We are also attracted to the light. We should trust this goodness and try to follow it.

Perhaps the greatest danger facing us is that we might settle for a kind of twilight existence. We never decisively declare for the light. We never totally opt for the dark, but we do dabble in it. The result is a mediocre person – neither a great saint nor a great sinner, a person incapable of either great cowardice or great courage. Those who are in darkness may one day see the light and welcome it. But the twilighters? Who can teach them the glory of the light?

Those who follow Christ's light fully and generously will find that their lives will be lit up by his grace, peace, love and freedom.

PRAYER OF THE FAITHFUL

President: God sent his Son into the world so that we might have life through him. Let us pray to him with confidence for our own needs, and the needs of the Church and the world.

Response: Lord, hear us in your love.

Reader(s): For the followers of Christ: that they may walk in the light of truth and goodness. [Pause] We pray in faith.

For all those holding public office: that the light of truth and justice may shine in their words and actions. [Pause] We pray in faith.

For the sick, the lonely, and those who are on a wrong course: that the light of Christ may shine gently on them. [Pause] We pray in faith.

For ourselves: that the words of Christ may be a lamp for our steps and a light for our path. [Pause] We pray in faith.

For all our departed brothers and sisters: that God's eternal light may shine brightly on them. [Pause] We pray in faith.

For our own special needs. [Longer pause] We pray in faith.

President: God of love and mercy, you call us to walk in the light Christ your Son brought into our world of shadows. Free us from darkness and keep us in the radiance of truth. We ask this through the same Christ our Lord.

REFLECTION   **The light of Christ**

In Christ there is no trace of darkness.
His light shows up the darkness in us.
His truth shows up our lies.
His integrity shows up our falseness.
His generosity shows up our selfishness.
His peace shows up our conflicts.
His openness to others shows how closed we are.
However, we should not be afraid of his light.
Rather, we should rejoice in it.
Compared to his light other lights
are mere flares in the night or candles in the wind.
Christ, radiant Light of the world,
guide our steps in the way of truth and goodness,
and lead us through the gloom of this world
to the kingdom of unfailing light.

Fifth Sunday of Lent
THE SEED MUST DIE

INTRODUCTION AND CONFITEOR

A grain of wheat has to die in order to bear fruit. We too have to die to ourselves in order to live more fully as human beings and children of God. This dying to self is a gradual thing and happens in very ordinary ways. [Pause]

The Lord, who died for us, gives us courage strength and love.

HEADINGS FOR READINGS

First Reading (Jer 31:31-34). The prophet Jeremiah tells a shattered people that God has not forsaken them, but will soon make a new and more intimate covenant with them.

Second Reading (Heb 5:7-9). Through his obedience and suffering Christ became the source of eternal life for us.

Gospel (Jn 12:20-33). In his death Jesus will be glorified and this will bring life to those who follow him.

SCRIPTURE NOTE

The First Reading talks about a new covenant between God and his people. This new covenant was brought about through the death of Jesus: 'This cup is the new covenant in my blood' (Lk 22:20).

In the Gospel Jesus talks about his imminent death. It shows the very real disquiet with which he approached it. But it also stresses that what was to take place was within the purposes of God. Jesus uses the example of a grain of wheat dying in order to yield a harvest, thereby suggesting that his own death will bear much fruit.

John has no account of the agony in garden in his Gospel. The nearest he gets to it is when he reports Jesus as saying, 'My soul is troubled.' And in the words, 'Should I ask the Father to save me from this hour?' we catch an unmistakable echo of his prayer in Gethsemane (Mk 14:36).

We catch a similar echo in the Second Reading: 'He learned to obey through suffering.' This reading also stresses the fruitfulness of Jesus' death: he became the source of eternal life for all who obey him.

HOMILY 1   **Human vulnerability**

Some people insist that their hero must never show any sign of weakness, never display hesitation or doubt or uncertainty or fear. The hero must at all times and in all circumstances be strong, brave and unflinching. But real heroes are not like that.

To take just one example. Martin Luther King was the leader of civil rights movement in America – a difficult task which he undertook reluctantly. It brought him hardships, insults, imprisonment, and threats to his life. In the end it claimed his life – he was assassinated.

During that struggle he knew many low moments. He tells how one night he reached rock bottom. His home had been bombed. As a result he felt he could not go on. He was tired of the insults and injuries. In this state of exhaustion and despair, he threw himself on his knees before God, and prayed:

'Lord, I have taken a stand for what I believe is right. But now I'm afraid. The people are looking to me for leadership. If I stand before them without strength and courage, they too will falter. But I'm at the end of my powers. I have nothing left. I can't face it any longer.'

He says that at that moment he experienced the presence of God in a way he had never before experienced it. That experience enabled him to continue the struggle.

Martin Luther King is no less a hero because he showed that he wasn't made of stone. Heroes who never show weakness or vulnerability are simply not believable. Nor are they of much use to us as models. We can't identify with them or imitate them. When, on the other hand, we meet someone who is hesitant, reluctant and fearful, we find that person much more believable. This element of reluctance is of the essence of the matter. The saint or martyr who seeks his fate with eagerness never rings true. We love to see the man behind the hero.

The Lord himself didn't go to his death with any kind of assurance. He had his lowest moment in the garden of Gethsemane when his soul was so deeply troubled that he said, 'My soul is ready to die with sorrow.' St John has no account of the agony in garden in his Gospel. But we catch an echo of it in today's Gospel where Jesus says, 'My soul is troubled.'

In some respects the agony in the garden is the most comforting part of the Gospel because it shows Jesus at his most human. Hitherto, he had gone resolutely to his fate. But now that the dreadful moment has come, he was so distressed that his sweat fell to the ground like drops of blood. He did not contemplate suffering and death with a stoical calm. He was appalled at the prospect. From where did he get the strength to face it? From prayer, and therefore from God. Someone defined courage like this: 'Courage is fear that has said its prayers.'

One would not be human if one didn't feel fear when danger threatens. Courage is not never feeling afraid; it is feeling afraid and going on in spite of it. 'A person without fear is no hero; the person who overcomes fear is.' (Solzhenitsyn).

Jesus' agony in the garden gives us comfort and hope in our low moments. There is no need to pretend that we are made of granite. We must not hide our weakness and fear. Like Jesus we must turn to God in heartfelt prayer. And we must also seek human comforting as Jesus did when he asked Peter, James and John to watch and pray with him.

HOMILY 2   **Losing and gaining life**

Few sights are as beautiful as that of a field filled with young stalks of wheat. To watch them swaying in the wind and dancing in the sun brings joy to the heart. But how strange is the process by which these stalks come into being.

The grain of wheat has to be buried in the cold damp earth as in a tomb. Then it has to die. If it didn't die, no new life would come forth. But when it dies, from the grave of the old grain, a shoot of new wheat miraculously springs forth. It's an amazing paradox – life coming from death.

Just as the grain of wheat has to die in order to bear fruit, so we must die to self if we are to live fully and fruitfully, and realise our full potential as human beings and children of God.

Death is part of life. We are born to die, to die that we may live more fully; born to die a little each day to selfishness, to pretence, and to sin. Every time we pass from one stage of life to another, something in us dies and something new is born. We taste death in moments of loneliness, rejection, sorrow, disappointment, and failure. We are dying before our time when we live in bitterness, in hatred, and in isolation. Each day we are creating our own death by the way we live.

When Jesus says, 'Anyone who loves his life loses it; anyone who hates his life in this world will keep it,' he is not telling us to hate ourselves or our lives. We have to learn to love ourselves. God wants us to be merciful with ourselves. Nobody can love us if we do not love ourselves. Unless we love ourselves we won't be able to love anyone else. Of course, we have to distinguish between true love of self and selfishness.

To forget self, to transcend self – that is what it means to lose oneself, to deny self, to die to self. It is when we forget ourselves that we are most free and most happy. It is in getting out of ourselves, in dedicating ourselves to causes beyond ourselves, that we grow and bear fruit. We may live longer if we take things easy, if we sit at the fire and husband life. We will exist longer. But will we live longer?

. What a poor world it would be if everyone put their own personal safety, security, and selfish advancement first and last – if no one was prepared to go beyond themselves. It is always because people have been prepared to die to self-interest that the most precious things humanity possesses have been born.

Jesus gave us an example. He gave his life in the service of his heavenly Father and of us. But he didn't find it easy. When the actual moment of death arrived, he was filled with fear.

Jesus' life wasn't taken from him. He gave it – gave it out of love of God and of us. To love is to accept that one might die another kind of death, before one dies one's own. The way of love is the way of the cross, but the way of the cross leads to the resurrection.

Those who die to self will find the moment of actual death easy. The hour of death will become an hour of glory. It is by dying that we are born to eternal life.

HOMILY 3   **His finest hour**

Stephen Roche was one of Ireland's greatest cyclists. His finest hour came on the day he won the Tour de France in 1987. However, when we think of a person's finest hour we think of it in very worldly terms. We see it as an hour of triumph and glory. And we tend to speak of it in a rather glib way. We concentrate solely on the hour of glory. We forget the many other hours that made the hour of glory possible, hours of blood, sweat and tears. The glory cannot be separated from the pain. The pain then is part of the joy now.

Jesus too spoke about 'his hour'. He spoke about it several times during his public ministry. But he always spoke of it as not having yet come. However, in today's Gospel passage he speaks of it as having come at last. What kind of hour had he in mind? The hour in question was the hour of his death. It was an hour of supreme self-giving in which he made a complete sacrifice of himself for us.

From a worldly point of view that hour was an hour of failure. Worse, it was an hour of shame and humiliation. But by raising him from the dead, God turned it into an hour of triumph for Jesus, and an hour of grace for us. This was Jesus' finest hour. This was the hour when all that he had come to do on earth was accomplished. All his life had led him to it and prepared him for it.

The lowest point proves to be a turning point. This is a great paradox. The lowest, darkest, and most painful hour in the life of a seed is the hour in which it dies. Yet this is precisely the hour in which new life is born.

It is the same with ourselves. Our lowest moments can prove to be turning points. Moments of great worldly success soon fade and often leave people empty inside. On the other hand, moments of darkness, weakness, and failure can prove to be moments of great change and growth – as for instance when an alcoholic hits rock bottom and, by the grace of God, manages to turn his/her life around.

Reflecting on what for Jesus was his finest hour will help us to evaluate our lives differently. Looking back on our lives we will see that the incidents which seemed to be great failures were the incidents which shaped the lives we have now. The things that hurt us and the things which helped us cannot be separated from each other.

To survive the low moment requires a special kind of faith. It involves sowing in tears. It would be unbearable unless there was a quiet hope mixed with our sadness: the hope that after the years of struggle will come the harvest. This can't be seen at the time. It can be seen only in retrospect.

Van Gogh said: 'Painting requires a lot of faith because one cannot prove at the outset that it will succeed. In the first years of hard struggling it may even be a sowing of tears. But we shall check them, because in the far distance we have a quiet hope of the harvest.'

It's not just painting that requires a lot of faith; life requires a lot of faith, because it often involves sowing in sadness, in darkness, and sometimes almost in despair. But if we sow the good, we will reap a harvest, and reap it in joy, a joy made all the sweeter by the pain endured during the sowing. The Psalmist says, 'Those who are sowing in tears will sing when they reap. They go out full of tears, carrying seed for the sowing; they come back full of song, carrying their sheaves' (Ps 126:5-6).

In the end good triumphs. Life triumphs. God has the last word.

ANOTHER APPROACH   **The story of a grain of wheat**

I'm about as small as you can get. I'm only a grain of wheat, but I have a story to tell. Please listen, because it's your story too.

All during the dark cold winter I lay in a barn, warm, dry and safe. Yet I felt unfulfilled. I felt I was not really living. I felt I was born for some great purpose. But what that purpose was I had no idea, and I felt sure there would be suffering involved in it. Little did I know how much.

Then one spring day the farmer took me and a sackful of others out of the barn and scattered us on the soil which had been freshly ploughed. Then he harrowed us into the ground. Suddenly I found myself buried in the cold, dark, damp soil. I had gone from a barn to a tomb. How could he be so cruel?

Days passed, if you could call them days. And still there wasn't the slightest sign of growth. Instead, to my horror, I saw that I was beginning to decay. Still, miraculously, I was alive. A tiny pulse continued to beat deep inside me. But I felt that I was losing the battle, even the will to live. The fact that I continued to live was due to the prompting of some mysterious outside force.

Meanwhile, unknown to me, things were happening in the great world above. Nature was about to come to my rescue. The earth was beginning to thaw out. Rainwater sank slowly down and soaked into me, or what remained of me. Then things began to happen fast. My once tough husk, now ravaged by decay, first began to soften, then to swell. Suddenly it burst open and out came a tiny shoot.

'It's happening,' I cried out deliriously. 'I'm not going to die after all. I'm going to be born.'

And born I was. I shot up, a sturdy shoot that soon turned into a tall stalk. The sun shone warmly on me and the wind passed over me like a blessing. I was growing and ripening. I was no longer a single grain, but a whole host of them, clinging to the top of a tall stalk. I would give life, I would quench hunger. All the pain and uncertainty was worth it.

There is a huge paradox in all of this. A paradox is defined as a seemingly absurd or self-contradictory statement which is nevertheless true. A grain of wheat has to die if it is to bear fruit. And a single grain of wheat can produce as many as seventy grains. Jesus went on to say that there is a sense in which we too must die if we are to bear fruit.

PRAYER OF THE FAITHFUL

President: Jesus turned to the Father in his hour of need. Let us now turn to God with all our needs.

Response: Lord, hear our prayer.

Reader(s): For Christians: that they may not be afraid to suffer in living the Gospel. [Pause] We pray to the Lord.

For all those who hold positions of responsibility: that they may set aside personal ambition and work unselfishly for the good of others.

[Pause] We pray to the Lord.

For the sick and the suffering: that they may unite their sufferings to the sufferings of Christ. [Pause] We pray to the Lord.

For ourselves: that in facing our own trials, we may draw strength from the example of Christ. [Pause] We pray to the Lord.

For our own personal needs. [Longer pause] We pray to the Lord.

President: All-powerful God, our source of life, you know our weakness. May we reach out with joy to grasp your hand, and so walk more readily in your ways. We make this prayer through the same Christ our Lord.

REFLECTION **A grain of wheat must die**

Each of us is like a grain of wheat planted by God.
Just as a grain of wheat must die so as to produce a harvest,
so we must die to self in order to bear the fruits of love.
This dying to self is a gradual process
and happens in little ways.
Every act of humility involves dying to pride.
Every act of courage involves dying to cowardice.
Every act of kindness involves dying to cruelty.
Every act of love involves dying to selfishness.
Thus the false self dies, and the true self,
made in God's image, is born and nurtured.
It is by giving that we receive;
it is by forgiving that we are forgiven;
it is by dying that we are born to eternal life.

Passion (Palm) Sunday

The solemn procession with palms is the traditional start of this, the first liturgy of Holy Week, the most solemn week in the Church's year. When the procession reaches the church, Mass begins with the Collect. If there is no procession then Mass could begin as below.

SIMPLE INTRODUCTION

This week, all over the world, Christians will be celebrating the great mystery of Christ's love for us.

'Greater love no man has than he who lays down his life for his friends.' This is the week Christ lived out the truth of these words. He took on himself our sins and the sins of all the world. [Pause]

Lord Jesus, you were pierced for our faults and crushed for our sins. Lord, have mercy.

Lord Jesus, you bore our sufferings and sorrows. Christ, have mercy.

Lord Jesus, through your wounds we are healed. Lord, have mercy.

HEADINGS FOR READINGS

Gospel for Procession (Mk 11:1-10). Jesus enters Jerusalem as a humble king and gentle Messiah, and is greeted joyfully by his disciples.

First Reading (Is 50:4-7). The prophet suffers in carrying out his mission, but is sustained by the firm belief that God will not abandon him. We think of Jesus as we listen to this reading .

Second Reading (Phil 2:6-11). Because Jesus took on himself our human condition, and accepted death on a cross, the Father has raised him up and made him Lord of heaven and earth.

Gospel (Mk 14:1-15:47). St Mark stresses the crude trial and shocking details of Jesus' suffering.

SCRIPTURE NOTE

The final act in the drama of Jesus has come. The Son of Man must suffer many things. In his account of the Passion, Mark stresses the crude trial and shocking details of Jesus' suffering. He has Jesus die in total isolation – deserted by his disciples, taunted by his enemies, derided by those who hung with him, and, worst of all, abandoned by God.

The rending of the curtain of the temple signifies that the privilege of Israel has ended; henceforth access to the divine presence is open to all. The reply to the question which has dominated Mark's Gospel (Who, then, is this?) is found in the words of the centurion: 'Truly, this man was the Son of God.'

HOMILY 1   **What the passion meant for Jesus**

For three years Jesus had gone from village to village doing good, teaching and healing. Everywhere he went he was surrounded by crowds of people who listened to him, and sought things from him. It had been an incredibly full and active three years. Yet during all that time he had been in control. He came and went more or less as he pleased.

But when he was handed over to his enemies in the garden of Gethsemane (handed over by one of his own), all this came to an end. It represented a turning point in his ministry. From then on he began to undergo suffering. And that's when his *passion* began. From that moment on he was no longer in control of what was happening. Things were now done *to* him rather than *by* him.

[95]

Thus he was arrested, put in prison, led before Caiphas, Herod and Pilate, interrogated, scourged, crowned with thorns, given a cross to carry, stripped of his clothes, nailed to the cross, mocked ... and finally he died. Jesus fulfilled his mission not only by what he did, but also and more especially by what was done to him – by his passion. We have to be very clear about one thing: the Father didn't throw him to the wolves. Jesus died voluntarily. He gave his life.

Much of our lives are determined more by what is done to us than by what we do: in a very real sense this is our passion. It is this passion, if we can genuinely accept it, as well as our actions, that leads to salvation.

It is important to realise the extent to which we are acted upon. As children we are 'at the mercy' of adults. As we move through life there is fate, betrayal, bad-luck, illness of one kind or another, loss of friendships, failure in relationships, disappointments with spouses and children, the death of loved ones, the drudgery of the workplace, and so on.

Of course, there are joyful moments and periods of peace too. But the reality is that there are many things which are outside our control. They are all part of what it means to be human. We do however have a choice in how we respond to what life throws at us. It can make us or break us.

Jesus survived as himself, strong, pure, good. Who would we be, if loss, or crisis, or the depredations of time were to take away from us the trappings of success, of self-importance, even personality itself?

The Passion Story shows how Jesus responded to what was done to him. He absorbed all the violence, transformed it, and returned it as love and forgiveness. This is the victory of love over all the powers of destruction. There was nothing but love in him. Even when they nailed his hands and feet, he was loving. It helps to think about that when we are going through hard times.

HOMILY 2   **He bore our sins**

It was early November and the leaves from the trees that lined the streets lay scattered on the ground. Each household was expected to gather its own leaves into plastic bags for removal by the refuse collectors. That at least was the idea. Now – using the leaves as a symbol of sin – let's see how things worked out.

A few people didn't bother at all. They saw the leaves fall and cover lawn, flower beds, and driveway. They saw them begin to rot and foul the air with their stench. But they walked over them every day as if they never existed. There are people for whom there is no such thing as sin. Herod was one of these.

One man swept the leaves off his lawn and driveway out onto the street. There they became an unsightly mess and created a hazard for drivers. But he couldn't care less. Let someone else clean up the mess. He reminds us of those who blame others for their sins. Pilate, the soldiers, and the crowd would fit into this category.

Most people took care of their own leaves, but wouldn't dream of taking a leaf off a neighbour's lawn. That was his territory and his responsibility. These stand for the people who accept responsibility for their own sins. Peter is an example.

Finally there was one remarkable man. He not only collected the leaves off his own lawn, but collected leaves off the street also. And he did so quietly and without complaining. He reminds us a little of Christ, who died for the sins of all. What makes Christ unique is the fact that he alone was sinless.

Holy Week is not a week to hide behind other people. We must accept responsibility for our own sins. If we acknowledge our sins we have nothing to fear, for Christ came to take them away. Then we can try to feel at least some responsibility for the sins of our neighbours and of the world in general. No man or woman is an island. Each of us is part of the mainland of humanity.

HOMILY 3   **Attitude to suffering**

There's no point in being sentimental about suffering. People can get so hurt that they become bitter and will not be redeemed. 'Too long a sacrifice can make a stone of the heart' (W.B. Yeats).

Yet suffering can be an opportunity. It's not a question of idealising it, but of confronting it with hope. The value of suffering does not lie in the pain of it, but in what the sufferer makes of it. Suffering can purify one's soul and transform one's character. Pain can bear fruit. Pain is an indispensable part in our becoming truly human, that is, people of compassion and maturity.

We must not see suffering as a punishment from God. God punishes no one. God allows us to suffer, yes, but only because good can come from it. Our pain can bring us closer to him. In it we experience his power and love.

It is a great comfort to us to know that Christ, the Innocent and Sinless One, has gone down the road of suffering before us, and gone down it to the end. On the cross he gathered up all human pain and made it his own.

During the communist era, the poet, Irina Ratushinkaya, spent some time in Russia's bleak labour camps. She says, 'The best way to retain your humanity in the camps was to care more about another's pain than your own.' Compassion is not learned without suffering.

We see how, in the midst of his Passion, Christ cared about others – about the women of Jerusalem who sympathised with him, about the thief, and of course about his mother. There was nothing but love in him.

Even when they nailed his hands and feet, he went on loving.

Jesus didn't die to save us from suffering. He died to teach us how to suffer. Though the road of suffering is narrow and difficult, it is not the same since Christ travelled it. A bright light illuminates it. Those who link their sufferings to those of Christ become a source of blessings for the entire community, and will share Christ's Easter glory.

PRAYER OF THE FAITHFUL

President: God the Father did not spare his own Son but gave him up to death on our behalf. Therefore, we can place our needs before him with great confidence.

Response: Lord, hear us in your love.

Reader(s): For the Christian community: that Christ may heal the wounds caused by sin and division. [Pause] We pray in faith.

For world leaders: that they may exercise their office in a way that promotes justice and peace. [Pause] We pray in faith.

For those who are suffering: that they may draw strength from the passion of Christ. [Pause] We pray in faith.

For those who see their loved ones suffer but can't do anything about it: that they may draw strength from the example of Mary standing at the foot of her Son's cross on Calvary. [Pause] We pray in faith.

For our own special needs. [Longer pause] We pray in faith.

President: Heavenly Father, we see your love for us in the sufferings and death of your Son. Help us to respond to your love by loving one another. We ask this through Christ our Lord.

REFLECTION   **Death of the Good Shepherd**

Jesus said: 'I am the good shepherd;
the good shepherd lays down his life for his sheep.'
Jesus did not have to suffer and die.
He had a choice.
He chose to suffer and die because he cared
about the flock God had entrusted to him.
What Jesus wants from us is not our suffering,
but a life of love and service.
Such a life will inevitably bring suffering.
But Jesus supports all those who follow him
down the road of faithful love and generous service.

EASTERTIDE

'Resurrection'

SEÁN ADAMSON

Easter Sunday

INTRODUCTION AND CONFITEOR

For Christians, Easter is the greatest feast of all. This is the day Jesus, our Brother, broke the chains of death and rose in triumph from the grave. This is truly the 'Day of the Lord.' But it is our day too, for Jesus shares with us the fruits of his victory. Let us open our hearts to the joy of this great day. [Pause]

Lord Jesus, on this holy day you drive away all evil. Lord, have mercy.

On this holy day you wash away all guilt, and restore lost innocence. Christ, have mercy.

On this holy day you bring joy to all who mourn. Lord, have mercy.

HEADINGS FOR READINGS

First Reading (Acts 10:34.37-43). This is part of an early sermon of Peter.

Second Reading (Col 3:1-4). Through our Baptism we already share in the risen life of Christ, though in a hidden and mysterious way.

Alternative Second Reading (1 Cor 5:6-8). Christians are to celebrate Easter (the new Passover) by getting rid of old attitudes and living in sincerity and truth.

Gospel (Jn 20:1-9). On discovering that Jesus' tomb is empty, the disciples begin to grasp what the Scriptures had foretold, namely, that he would rise from the dead.

SCRIPTURE NOTE

The reading from Acts is part of an early sermon of Peter. In it he summarises the ministry of Jesus, which culminated in his death. But it didn't end there; God raised him to life, allowing him to be seen by certain witnesses, Peter among them. He goes on to declare that Jesus is the one all the prophets spoke about (the Messiah). All who believe in him will have their sins forgiven.

The Gospel tells about the discovery of the empty tomb. The empty tomb (with the discarded linen cloths) in itself is not a direct proof of the resurrection. Nevertheless, it was the first step towards establishing the truth that Jesus had escaped the bonds of death, and prepared the disciples to encounter the Risen Lord.

Many readings in the Easter cycle instruct the newly baptised on the Christian way of life. Today's Second Reading and its alternative are good examples. Thus the Easter season provides us with an opportunity to reflect on what it means to be baptised members of Christ's Body.

HOMILY 1   **Renewal of baptismal promises**

On this day it is customary to renew our baptismal promises. The ceremony should be done in as solemn a manner as possible. In which case, only the briefest homily would be required. Each member of the congregation should have a lighted candle.

Priest: On this day we celebrate Christ's great victory over death. Christ, our Brother, has broken the chains of death, and wants to share his victory with us. The power of his resurrection enables us to live in the joy and freedom of the children of God.

Which of us would not wish to share in so great a victory? We can do so if we believe in Christ and follow him. This, after all, is what we promised at Baptism.

Hence, it is fitting that on this great day we should renew our baptismal promises, and commit ourselves once more to follow Christ, our risen Lord. At the same time we renew our belief in the great truths of the faith.

Response to each question: I do.

Priest: Christ has revealed to us that God is a kind and loving Father, who cares about each of us. Do you believe in God the Father, and in his love for you?

The modern world sets many idols before us: comforts, possessions, pleasures ... Do you reject these false gods?

Do you believe in Jesus, the Son of God, who died for us and rose again, so that we might rise to newness of life?

Do you believe that he lives on among us as our Companion and Friend on the road of life?

Do you reject Satan, the spirit of evil?

Satan tempts us with false and empty promises: that material things can fully satisfy us; that happiness consists in easy and comfortable living; that all that matters in life is to be popular and successful. Do you reject these empty promises?

Do you believe in the Holy Spirit, the Spirit of love and forgiveness, the Spirit of joy and goodness, the Spirit of gentleness and peace?

Do you believe that the Holy Spirit lives within you, consoling, guiding and strengthening you?

Do you believe that each person has a tremendous dignity as a human being and a child of God?

Do you believe that human life is sacred from the first moment to the last?

Do you believe that, in spite of differences of race, politics, creed, and colour, human beings are equal in dignity and form one family under God?

Do you believe in the Church in which we become brothers and sisters in Christ, and through which the Gospel is preached to the world?

Do you believe that as followers of Christ, we are called to be his witnesses in the world?

Do you believe that Mary, the Mother of Jesus, is also our Mother, and the Mother of the Christian community?

Do you believe in the everlasting life Christ won for us through his life, death, and resurrection?

The priest now blesses the people with holy water. As he does so he may say: 'May the Lord bless you and keep you faithful.' Meanwhile each one should pray silently for the grace to be faithful to Christ.

Priest: All-powerful and ever-living God, we thank you that in a world which is full of false trails and false promises, you sent your Son to teach us the truth about ourselves, about life, and about you. Help us to follow him faithfully so that one day we may share in his Easter victory in that kingdom where sadness and death will be no more. We ask this through the same Christ our Lord.

HOMILY 2   **The joy of Easter**

How great must have been the joy the apostles experienced on Easter Day. The following story should help us to catch a little of the flavour of their joy.

A Russian Cossack had two sons, Peter and Gregory, in the First World War. One day he got a letter from the front. Being unable to read, he handed it to his daughter. It was from Gregory's commanding officer and began like this: 'I regret to have to inform you that your son Gregory was killed in action on July 10th. Gregory was an excellent soldier and died the death of the brave. You have every reason to be proud of him ... etc.'

The effect of this news on the father was immediate and alarming. He seemed to wilt visibly. In a matter of days he aged, turning grey almost overnight. His memory began to fail and even his mind was affected. He began to drink to excess.

He kept the letter under the icon in the kitchen. Each day he would take it down and ask his daughter to read it to him once more. But as soon as she began: 'I regret to inform you that ... ' he would take it from her and put it away again. After the local priest had offered a Requiem for his son he felt a little better.

Twelve days went by like this. On the thirteenth day a second letter arrived from the front. It said that his son wasn't dead after all! He had been wounded and left for dead on the battlefield. Next morning he had come to and crawled four miles back to his own lines, dragging a wounded officer with him. He was to be raised to the rank of corporal, and had been awarded the Cross of St George in recognition of his bravery. Right now he was recovering from his wounds in hospital, and they could expect him home soon.

On hearing this the father was a sight to see. Scalded with joy, he grabbed the letter and went into the village with it. He stopped everyone he met, forcing everyone to read it. 'My son is alive!' he exclaimed. 'He's been awarded St George's Cross for bravery!'

This should give us some idea of the joy the disciples experienced that first Easter. But there are differences too. The Cossack's son hadn't actually died. Jesus had died. The disciples had witnessed his death with their own eyes. And now the tomb was empty and Jesus had been seen alive! We must remember, however, that the resurrection was not a return to earthly life – Jesus rose to a new life beyond death.

Their joy bubbled over. Jesus, their leader and friend, had broken the chains of death through the power of God. Death, the last and greatest enemy, had been overcome in him.

The joy of the apostles is meant to be ours too. It does not immediately remove from us the fear of death, for we still have to go through it. But it was by going through it that Jesus overcame it. So it is for us who believe in him.

Without Easter the story of Jesus would have been little better than a flare in the night. Darkness would still have had the last word. But with the resurrection we know that the darkness did not have the last word. Let us not be afraid to bask in the bright light the risen Christ has brought into our world of darkness and death.

We should never allow anything to so fill us with sorrow that we forget the joy of Easter, the joy of Christ risen from the dead.

HOMILY 3 **Victory already won**

We can't appreciate the greatness of Jesus' resurrection unless we acknowledge the full reality of his death. Jesus died in darkness. But he trusted enough in God to face the darkness, and to wait for the resurrection. His leap of faith was not in vain. The Father raised him up. The Scriptures and the early Church seldom said, 'Jesus rose from the dead.' What they said was, 'God raised Jesus from the dead.' Jesus too had to make that leap of faith which we will one day be called upon to make.

Jesus entered the dark kingdom of death, and emerged victorious. He has won *his* victory – he has conquered death. But that victory has to work its way through and become a reality in us, his disciples. His victory was won in *our* nature. If the battle had not been fought and won in our nature, we would be incapable of profiting from his victory, we would still be under the power of death.

The resurrection itself was never in doubt – God cannot die. But the surprise and gift of Easter is that the resurrection is for us too. Jesus has been raised in our flesh and blood. It is our death that has been defeated.

As we go on in life, we become increasingly conscious of our mortality and the inevitable journey towards death. Death constitutes a huge challenge to our faith, for we see beyond death only as through a darkened glass. But on this day we breathe the pure air of everlasting life.

The forces of darkness may seem overwhelming, but the victory is already won. We must trust that victory, and not live as if death still dominated us.

To be a Christian is to be a person of hope because of what happened on the third day. But Christian hope is not a superficial optimism based on a refusal to look at the facts. Rather, it is a deep trust in God.

Good Friday, day of darkness and death, comes to everyone. So does Holy Saturday, that day of emptiness and sorrow. On such days it's hard to believe. But Easter Sunday, day of life and joy, will come as surely as the dawn. Death, the last enemy, has been overcome.

May the Lord in his goodness open our minds and hearts so that we may believe the good news of his victory over death. In his love for us, God draws us outwards into the unknown, the beyond, the infinite, the eternal. We go forward more confidently and hopefully because Jesus our Brother has gone ahead of us.

PRAYER OF THE FAITHFUL

President: Christ, the Morning Star, came back from the dead, and now sheds his peaceful light on the world. With his light shining on us, let us pray with confidence for all our needs.

Response: Lord, graciously hear us.

Reader(s): For all believers: that they may be messengers of joy and hope to a world filled with sadness and despair. [Pause] Lord, hear us.

For government leaders: that they may strive to end the conflicts which divide the world. [Pause] Lord, hear us.

For prisoners: that the Lord who broke the chains of death may bring them comfort and hope. [Pause] Lord, hear us.

For those who have no hope of eternal life: that they may hear and believe the Good News of Christ's victory over death. [Pause] Lord, hear us.

For all who mourn: that Christ, who experienced the anguish of death, may console them. [Pause] Lord, hear us.

For our own special needs. [Longer pause] Lord, hear us.

President: God of mercy, the power of this holy day drives away all evil, washes away all guilt, restores lost innocence, and brings joy to those who mourn. May we who celebrate the resurrection of your Son experience its power in our lives and in our world. We ask this through the same Christ our Lord.

PRAYER FOR PEACE

Lord Jesus Christ, on Easter Day you appeared to your frightened and disheartened disciples, and said to them: 'Peace be with you'. Then you showed them your wounded hands and side, and they were filled with joy. Grant that we who have heard the message of Easter may enjoy the peace and unity of your kingdom where you live for ever and ever.

REFLECTION 1 **Moments of death and resurrection**

As we go through life we all experience little deaths.
We get a foretaste of death when we live
in bitterness, loneliness, sadness and despair.
In times like these the world closes in on us,
and we seem to have one foot in the grave.
But we also experience little resurrections.
When we know love, acceptance, and forgiveness;
when we open our hearts to others and to life,
the world opens up and we emerge from the tomb.
Lord, may the splendour of your resurrection
scatter the shadows of death,
and enable us to walk in radiant hope
towards the kingdom where there are
no more shattered hopes or broken dreams.

REFLECTION 3

A description of an Easter ceremony in Russia under communism when it was dangerous to be a believer:

'Someone at the back of the church lit a candle,
a single point of light not able to pierce the darkness.
Then there was another, and another.
Swiftly the flame was passed from one to another.
In less than a minute the church was a blaze of light.
Each candle lit up the face behind it,
a face marked with suffering.
But now that suffering turned into joy,
because of the certain knowledge that the Lord has risen.
These people do not debate the resurrection.
They have experienced it in their lives.
They have not persevered the faith in hostile surroundings;
it has preserved them.'
Lord, may your Easter light shine on us this day,
and chase the shadows of the night of death away.

Second Sunday of Easter

INTRODUCTION AND CONFITEOR

Faith is the most precious thing in the world. But it is exposed to the harsh winds of doubt which blow through the modern world. Here on Sunday we ought to experience a strengthening of our faith. [Pause]

Lord, you strengthen our faith by your presence among us. Lord, have mercy.

Lord, you strengthen our faith by your steadfast love for us. Christ, have mercy.

Lord, you nourish our faith with the word of God and the food of the Eucharist. Lord, have mercy.

HEADINGS FOR READINGS

First Reading (Acts 4:32-35). This reading gives us a picture of the how the first Christians lived community.

Second Reading (1 Jn 5:1-6). Christians are children of God, and show their love for God by keeping his commandments.

Gospel (Jn 20:19-31). When he touched the wounds of the risen Jesus, Thomas' doubt was turned into faith.

SCRIPTURE NOTE

The reading from Acts gives a picture of a Christian community that is ideally faithful to the Gospel. It is a community of shared faith and shared possessions.

In the Gospel Jesus appears to his apostles, showing them his wounds and bestowing peace on them. Then he entrusts his mission to them, giving them the gift of the Spirit and the power to forgive sin. Thomas's profession of faith, 'My Lord and my God', is the supreme christological statement of John's Gospel. Originally John's Gospel ended where to-day's passage ends.

The Second Reading stresses the Christian vocation to love. Through faith in Jesus Christ, Christians have become children of God. They will show their love for God by keeping his commandments. And if they love God, they will surely love their fellow Christians, because they too are children of God. Keeping the commandments is not difficult because through baptism they share in Christ's victory over the powers of evil.

HOMILY 1   **Touching is believing**

When we are feeling good we are quite happy to let others come near us.

But when we are in pain we tend to cut ourselves off from others. No one wants to have a sore spot touched. We want it left alone. While this is understandable, it is a mistake. How can healing happen if we will not allow our wounds to be seen and touched?

A priest was going from the United States to Latin America. On the plane he found himself sitting beside a woman from Peru. The woman told him how she was returning home with her mother who had undergone three operations in the United States. 'Is your mother feeling better now?' he asked. 'Oh yes,' the woman replied. 'She's completely cured. All her family will be waiting at the airport to welcome her back.'

Then the woman asked him why he was going south. He told her that he was a priest and was going there to do missionary work. On hearing that he was a priest her face changed dramatically. She leaned over, took him by the arm, and whispered in an agonised voice, 'Oh Father, mother has cancer, and there is no hope for her.'

Why did that woman feel she had to keep up the pretence that all was well? Why did she have to hide, not only the mortal physical wounds of her mother, but her own emotional wounds as well? Surely they were not things to be ashamed of? Her own wounds were caused by love. Only when she discovered that the man beside was a priest, that is, someone from whom she might expect sympathy and comfort, did she come out with the truth, allowing herself to touch and be touched.

Now let us consider the case of the man who is at the centre of today's Gospel – Thomas. After the death of Jesus he fled from the company of the other apostles. Thus he missed the first appearance of the risen Lord. However, he was there for the next appearance. It's interesting to see how Jesus dealt with him.

The first thing Jesus did was to show him his own wounds. Jesus felt no need to hide his wounds for they were the proof of his love. They were the mortal wounds the Good Shepherd suffered in defending his flock from the wolf. He invited Thomas to touch those wounds.

But in truth, Thomas was the wounded one. He was wounded by grief, loneliness, doubt and despair. In his pain he wanted to be alone. Even though his wounds were invisible, they were very real. But Jesus was able to see them. It was he who touched Thomas' wounds, and so made him whole and well again. It was by touching and being touched that Thomas was healed of his unbelief as well as of his other wounds.

It is by showing our wounds, by touching and being touched, that we are healed. The human heart is healed only by the presence of another human being who understands human pain.

The world today is full of Doubting Thomases. They will not come to believe unless they can touch Jesus' wounds and see the radiance of his face. This can happen only if he is seen to be alive in his followers.

HOMILY 2   **What is essential is invisible**

'Unless I see, unless I touch, I will not believe' – so said Thomas. It sounds very reasonable and very logical. It represents the rational approach so much in vogue today. Today the opinion prevails that everything can be rationally explained. If something is obscure, all we have to do is shed a ray of scientific light on it and it will become clear.

Of course we must be guided by reason, but we must also listen to the imagination and the heart. There are aspects of life which cannot be understood by purely rational means. Science isn't everything.

To adopt Thomas' approach would be to condemn ourselves to living in a purely material world. But some of the most important ingredients of life can neither be seen nor touched. There is a layer of reality which eludes the senses but which, nevertheless, is absolutely real. The visible world is only part of a greater world which includes invisible realities from which it draws its chief significance. As the Little Prince said, 'What is essential is invisible.'

Seeing and hearing can be crutches which prevent us from thinking, feeling, and imagining. Often the handicapped have more feeling and more perception than the so-called normal. Vision, insight, understanding, perception, have little to do with seeing. Many people prefer facts to vision. 'It is necessary sometimes to believe in something a little in order to see it.' (Van Gogh).

When a person knows something, really knows it, deep down in his heart, he doesn't have to argue about it or prove it. He just knows it, and that's enough. We are no longer sufficiently aware of the importance of what we cannot know intellectually, and which we must know in other ways.

Nevertheless, we can sympathise with Thomas. He was merely echoing the human cry for certainty. However, here on earth there is no absolute certainty about God and spiritual realities. We have to be content with 'seeing a dim reflection in a mirror'. We are not looking through an open door but peering through a chink. This chink is big enough to let the light in, but not so big as to eliminate the wonder and the mystery.

Too much light or too little light and we are blind. 'There is enough light for those who want to see, and enough darkness for those of a contrary disposition.' (Pascal)

Rationalists approach God and religion as something that can be understood and explained; mystics approach God as something mysterious that can neither be understood nor explained but only experienced. Faith takes us where our senses cannot go. But which is the stronger: faith without doubts, or faith that contends with doubt?

HOMILY 3   **Community life**

The most visible and immediate impact of the teaching of Jesus on his followers was on their attitude to property. We see this in the reading from Acts. No one felt justified in keeping for his own exclusive use what he did not need, when others lacked necessities. They shared their goods with one another. Those that had much had nothing left over, and those that had little had no want.

They lived as a community. Firstly, it was a community of prayer and worship. Secondly, it was a community in which the members loved and cared for one another. The celebration of the Eucharist was at the centre of their worship of God and service of one another.

The preaching of the message was undertaken by the group of disciples. Even though this was sometimes done individually, there was always the group, the community, the little fraternity to return to for companionship and support.

Even on a human level we have a deep need for community. Loneliness is a major complaint today. We also need community as Christians. We need a support system to sustain our faith, hope and love. We need a community, or small group, in order to be able to survive. But our parishes have become so large and so anonymous.

In his book, *Small Christian Communities*, Jim O'Halloran tells the following story about a young woman from Nairobi called Sylvia. She says:

When I left school I would say that I had the faith. I lived on the outskirts of Nairobi, and every Sunday I travelled by bus to the centre of the city where I attended Mass at the Holy Family Basilica. But the basilica was very big and I knew hardly anyone. I felt alone. Then going home one Sunday and feeling a bit depressed, I said to myself, I don't have a spiritual friend in the whole world.

However, soon afterwards I came across a small Christian community in my own area and became a member. With that everything changed. In the community I didn't simply hear about love, as in the basilica, I actually tasted the sweetness of togetherness. And little by little I grew spiritually, made good friends, and was able to take part in work for my neighbourhood. I blossomed as a person. No longer am I that girl who travelled alone into Nairobi, was lost in the big church, and returned home sad.

Here we see the fruits of community, of bonding, sharing, togetherness. God doesn't mean us to do it alone. So we shouldn't be afraid to immerse ourselves in a supportive community. Perhaps what we need is a network of little faith-sharing groups in which people can have a sense of community and comradeship. These groups would be connected to parishes.

The parish needs the small group as a leaven to keep it from stagnating. The small group needs the parish to keep it from becoming narrow and inward-looking.

One of the greatest mistakes Thomas made was to cut himself off from the other apostles, that is, from the community. In his doubt and grief he walked alone. It was only when he rejoined the community that he encountered the risen Jesus, and so found faith again.

To be a believer, or just a spiritual person, in today's world can be a lonely business. With the help of the community we are able to resolve our doubts and sustain our faith. Community is an essential part of Christian witness.

PRAYER OF THE FAITHFUL

President: As members of a believing and caring community, let us now bring our needs before God whose love has no end.

Response: Lord, hear our prayer.

Reader(s): For the Church: that through its ministry people may experience the presence of Christ. [Pause] We pray to the Lord.

For those who govern our country: that they may exercise their office with justice and compassion. [Pause] We pray to the Lord.

For those who are wounded emotionally or physically: that they may be delivered from pain and distress. [Pause] We pray to the Lord.

For those of weak faith or no faith. [Pause] We pray to the Lord.

For this community: that we may be able to live in freedom, peace and joy. [Pause] We pray to the Lord.

For our deceased relatives and friends: that the Lord may receive them into the kingdom of his glory. [Pause] We pray to the Lord.

For our own special needs. [Longer pause] We pray to the Lord.

President: God of love and mercy, you give strength to the weary, and new courage to those who have lost heart. Hear the prayers of all who call on you in any trouble, so that they may have the joy of receiving your help in their need. We ask this through Christ our Lord.

REFLECTION   **The first Christians**

Defending the Christians before the Emperor Hadrian, Aristides, a non-Christian, said of them:

'These Christians love one another.
They never fail to help widows.
They save orphans from those who would hurt them.
If a man has something,
he gives freely to the man who has nothing.
If they see a stranger, Christians take him into their homes

and treat him as a brother.
And if they hear that one of them is in jail,
or persecuted for professing the name of their redeemer,
they all give him what he needs.
If it is possible, they bail him out.
If one of them is poor and there isn't enough food to go around, they
    fast several days to give him the food he needs.
We are dealing with a new kind of person.
There is something divine in them.'

Third Sunday of Easter

INTRODUCTION AND CONFITEOR

In the Gospel we find the apostles gathered behind closed doors, wounded in heart and in spirit. But Jesus appears to them, gives them his peace, and breathes new life into them. He does the same for us. Let us open ourselves to the gifts the risen Lord wants to give us. [Pause]

Lord Jesus, you banish our doubts with the gift of faith. Lord, have mercy.

You calm our fears with the gift of peace. Christ, have mercy.

You heal our wounds with your love, and rekindle our hopes with your victory over death. Lord, have mercy.

HEADINGS FOR READINGS

First Reading (Acts 3:13-15.17-19). This reading is an early explanation of the Passion and an example of the early witness to the resurrection.

Second Reading (1 Jn 2:1-5). We show that we know God by keeping his commandments. But when we fail, Christ intercedes for us with the Father.

Gospel (Lk 24:35-48). Jesus appears to the apostles, and commissions them to preach the Gospel to all nations.

SCRIPTURE NOTE

In the First Reading Peter shows great courage when he confronts the people with their part in the death of Jesus. However, he goes on to excuse them on the grounds that they acted in ignorance. In this he may have been inspired by the dying prayer of Jesus: 'Father, forgive them, they know not what they do.' He urges them to repent, assuring them that if they do, their sins will be forgiven.

In the Gospel Luke's primary interest is to show that the risen Jesus is the same person the apostles had known prior to the crucifixion. He emphasises the reality of Jesus' bodily resurrection, but makes it clear that the resurrection is not a return to earthly life – Jesus has risen to a new life beyond death.

It was only by combining various passages from the prophets that the early Christians came to accept the idea that a suffering Messiah was part of God's plan of salvation. So Luke has the risen Lord showing the apostles how the Scriptures had foretold that the Christ would suffer and so enter into his glory. Jesus also gives them a mission – the proclamation of repentance and forgiveness of sins.

In the Second Reading John says that authentic love is proved by obedience to the commandments. Anticipating that the Christian will sin, he reminds us that we have in Jesus an advocate who will plead our cause.

One theme occurs in all three readings: forgiveness is available to those who repent and believe in Jesus as their Saviour. This has great relevance for us. A lot of ugly crimes are committed today, not all of which can be put down to ignorance. But if there is forgiveness for those who killed Jesus, then surely there is forgiveness for those who do these things. The task of preachers of the word is to assure people that God's forgiveness is available to them, thus enabling them to make a fresh start.

HOMILY 1   **Breaking through**

On Easter Sunday evening the apostles were gathered in the upper room with the doors locked. The room was haunted by absence, and was full of bitter-sweet memories for them. It was here the Master had washed their feet and celebrated the Last Supper with them. But it was here too that they had sworn loyalty to him, a loyalty which didn't even see the night through.

The apostles were wounded individually – by fear, doubt, guilt, grief and despair. But they were also wounded collectively because their unity was broken: two of their number were absent – one was dead (Judas), the other (Thomas) was going through a crisis of faith. Like all people in pain, they had erected a barrier around themselves.

Jesus didn't wait for them to come to him. He came to them, while they were still fearful and guilt-ridden (because of their cowardice and betrayal). In one bold move he broke through that barrier, and stood among them. He didn't blame them or even scold them for failing him. There was no blame, no recrimination. He knew how they were feeling, so he didn't rub salt into their wounds. Instead, he brought them something they desperately needed. He said to them, 'Peace be with you.' He said it not once but twice, to make sure it sank in. In receiving his peace, they received his forgiveness.

Suddenly the greatness and wonder of it struck them: death had been overcome, evil had been overcome, their sins and betrayal had been overcome. Good had triumphed, love had triumphed, life had triumphed. The humble Jesus had triumphed over all the evil forces that had been arrayed against him. A fresh start was possible. As a result they were filled with joy.

Jesus' approach was so gentle. There was no harshness in him. The humble Jesus, who triumphed over death, gave courage to his crushed apostles, healed their wounds, renewed their hope, gave them life, and empowered them. From utter collapse and failure, something totally and utterly new arose. The result was that they not only believed in him, but also in themselves. What a joy to be fully known and fully loved at the same time.

Easter doesn't take away our pain or remove our fears. But it does introduce a new element into our lives. It gives a meaning to our pain. It lights it up with hope. All is different because Jesus is alive and speaks his words of peace to us as he spoke them to the apostles. When we fail under trial and temptation we can draw encouragement from the story of Jesus' own disciples, all of whom failed during the passion.

Therefore, there is a quiet joy among us and a deep sense of peace because we know that life is stronger than death.

HOMILY 2   **The wounds of love**

There was a man who was very attached to his father, who had been a labourer all his life. When the father died the son was grief-stricken. As he stood quietly gazing down into the coffin in which he was laid out, he was particularly struck by his father's hands. Even small things can reveal the essence of a person's life. Later he said:

'I will never forget those magnificently weathered old hands. They told the story of a countryman's life in the eloquent language of wrinkles, veins, old scars and new. My father's hands always bore some fresh scratch or cut as adornment, the result of his latest tangle with a scrap of wire, a rusted pipe, a stubborn root. In death they did not disappoint even in that small and valuable particular.

'It is not given to sons to know everything about their fathers, but I have those hands in my memory to supply evidence of the obligations he met, the sweat he gave, the honest deeds he performed. By looking at those hands you could read the better part of the old man's heart.'

Jesus said to the apostles: 'Look at my hands and feet ... Touch me and see for yourselves ... ' He said the same thing to Thomas: 'See my wounded hands and side. Cease doubting and believe.'

One might have expected the risen body of Jesus to be whole and without blemish. Yet, not only is his body still scarred, but it is those very scars which help the disciples to recognise him. Those scars were the wounds caused by humiliation, torture, and crucifixion. Jesus showed his wounds to the apostles. Why his wounds? Firstly, those wounds show that the risen Jesus is the same person who was crucified. Secondly, because those wounds were the proof of his love.

Those who care about others pick up a lot of wounds as they go through life. Perhaps there are no great wounds but only a multiplicity of little ones – a host of scratches, wrinkles and welts. Yet these are only the visible wounds.

What about the myriad of invisible wounds: the furrows left on the mind and the soul by hardship, worry and anxiety? And those piercing ones which affect that most sensitive part of us – the heart – things like disappointments, ingratitude, betrayal. Emotional hurt hits you in the gut, and can be harder to deal with than physical hurt.

But these wounds are not things to be ashamed of. They are the proof of our love. Will anyone see these wounds and come to believe in our love because of them? Even if no one else sees them, God sees them, and he is proud of us, for he sees that we resemble his Son. We must not look at a person's achievements only, but at his/her wounds and scars.

Jesus didn't hide his wounds for they were the proof of his love. They were the mortal wounds the Good Shepherd suffered in defending his flock from the wolf. He invited the apostles to touch those wounds. It was by touching and being touched that they were healed of their unbelief. His wounds give us hope in our wounds.

Jesus didn't become embittered because of his wounds. Neither should we. Having brought peace and healing to the apostles, Jesus commissioned them to go and bring the good news to others. Jesus wants us to be witnesses to his resurrection. A sad, embittered person is a poor witness.

HOMILY 3   **Rebirth of a dream**

There was a train driver who drove his train up and down the same line every day. There was this lovely little cottage set in a short distance from the track. Its white walls shone in the sun. In front of it grew the most gorgeous roses he had ever seen. It was like something one imagines exists only in picture postcards. He soon fell in love with it.

One afternoon as he was passing he saw a little girl playing on the front lawn. She waved to him as the train swept past. He hooted the horn in response. The same thing happened next afternoon. Thus began an innocent and beautiful friendship between him and the child. Every afternoon she waved to him, and he hooted the horn in response. Sometimes the girl was joined by her mother, and they both waved. It made him very happy, and also made the monotonous journey seem short.

Years passed. The child grew up. Only occasionally now was she there to wave to him. Nevertheless, the bond that had been forged over the years was still intact. Then he retired and went to live a distance away. But he could not get the cottage and his two friends out of his mind. So one day he decided to visit them.

When he got there things were very different from what he had imagined. The walls of the cottage were not nearly as white as he had thought. The roses were not as beautiful as they seemed. But the biggest disappointment of all came when he met the woman and her daughter.

They were polite to him when he told them who he was. They led him into a gloomy parlour where they chatted over tea. But he felt out of place. So he left as soon as he could politely do so. He felt empty. His dream-world had dissolved. The friendship which had given so much meaning to his life was shattered.

We feel sorry for that train driver. Yet it was his own fault. He had been living in a dream-world. He had been pursuing an illusion.

Many people pursue illusions. The apostles did. For three years they had been pursuing the illusion of a glorious Messiah who could not suffer. When Jesus was crucified the illusion was exposed and their world fell apart. Their reaction was to cut themselves off behind closed doors.

It was only when Jesus appeared to them and opened their minds to a new truth that their collapsed dream was reborn. What was this new truth? That it was precisely through his suffering and death that he had come into glory. It took some time for this to sink in, but when it did, they knew that even death had not succeeded in breaking the bond that had been forged between him and them over three years.

The resurrection means that Jesus lives and we too can encounter him in faith. We encounter him especially in 'the breaking of bread', that is, in the Eucharist. He will not insulate us from reality. But he will be with us where we are, helping to give meaning and beauty to our lives, especially to the painful and dark parts. And like the apostles we too are commissioned to bring the good news to others.

ADDITIONAL MATERIAL

The resurrection of Jesus is the crowning truth of our Christian faith. The empty tomb in itself is not a direct proof of the resurrection. Nevertheless, it was the first step towards establishing the truth that Jesus had escaped the bonds of death, and prepared the disciples to encounter the risen Lord.

The shock caused by his death was such that the disciples were slow to believe in the news of the resurrection. Even when faced with the reality of the risen Jesus, they still doubted, thinking they were seeing a ghost. Hence, the theory that the resurrection was produced by the faith (or credulity) of the apostles does not hold up. On the contrary, their faith in the resurrection was born from the direct experience of the risen Jesus.

It is crucial to affirm the bodily resurrection of Jesus. This is different from the belief (shared by other faiths) that the human spirit is in some way 'naturally' eternal and continues after the death of the body. The body dies and the soul is released into new life. Nowhere does the Bible teach this.

The Christian belief is that the body will share in the triumph of the resurrection. The resurrection stories keep stressing that Jesus rose with his body: the tomb is empty, the apostles touched him, he eats with them and walks with them.

All the stories stress he is the same person, yet somehow changed, and therefore not immediately recognisable. This is an effective way of making the point that resurrection is not a return to earthly life as before; Jesus has risen to a new life beyond death, a life with God. He is the same, yet transformed.

He was not a resurrected corpse, but had a body not subject to the human boundaries of time and space. It was a body marked with signs of his previous life (the wounds), but also a body that was different from the flesh and bones that were nailed to the cross. It was a body no longer subject to the ordinary laws of nature. He is not as he was; but he is who he was.

The bodily resurrection of Jesus is the most profound basis for the Christian attitude towards the human body. We take care of the bodies of the hungry, the sick, because we know they are destined to share in the resurrection of Jesus.

This is the message of true Christian humanism. It invites humanity not to become something else, but to be more authentically what it already is.

PRAYER OF THE FAITHFUL

President: Let us bring our prayers before him who has been raised from the dead and now intercedes for us with the Father.

Response: Stay with us, Lord.

Reader(s): For all Christians: that they may preach the Gospel by their words and deeds. [Pause] We pray to the Lord.

For the leaders of our country: that they may fulfil their responsibilities worthily and well. [Pause] We pray to the Lord.

For those who have suffered a bereavement or disappointment: that the Lord may turn their sorrow into joy. [Pause] We pray to the Lord.

For the sick: that God may renew their strength. [Pause] We pray to the Lord.

For the those who have died: that the radiance of Christ's risen glory may shine on them. [Pause] We pray to the Lord.

For our own special needs. [Longer pause] We pray to the Lord.

President: Lord Jesus, don't walk ahead of us, we may not follow; don't walk behind us, we may not lead; just walk beside us and be our friend. We make all our prayers to the Father through you, Christ our Lord.

REFLECTION   **The wounds of love**

Those who care about others pick up a lot of wounds.
There may be no great wounds,
only a multiplicity of little ones—
a host of scratches, wrinkles and welts.
But there can also be a lot of invisible wounds:
the furrows left on the mind and the heart
by hardship, worry and anxiety,
disappointments, ingratitude, and betrayal.
These wounds are not things to be ashamed of.
They are badges of honour.
They are the proof of our love.
Jesus didn't hide his wounds.
Neither should we.
By his wounds we are healed.

FOURTH SUNDAY OF EASTER
THE GOOD SHEPHERD AND THE HIRELING

INTRODUCTION AND CONFITEOR

Of all the images we have of Jesus, one of the loveliest is that of the Good Shepherd. It was Jesus himself who used it. How well do we trust and how closely do we follow the Good Shepherd? [Pause]

Lord Jesus, you are our Shepherd with whom we want for nothing. Lord, have mercy.

You guide us along the path of eternal life. Christ, have mercy.

You are with us even if we have to walk through the valley of darkness. Lord, have mercy.

HEADINGS FOR READINGS

First Reading (Acts 4:8-12). Peter tells the Jewish leaders that Jesus is the one and only Saviour.

Second Reading (1 Jn 3:1-2). In his love for us God has made us his children. In the next life we shall see him as he is.

Gospel (Jn 10:11-18). Unlike the hireling, Jesus, the Good Shepherd, is ready to give his life for his sheep.

SCRIPTURE NOTE

From the earliest days the apostles encountered hostility from the Jewish leaders just as Jesus himself had. Even so, the First Reading shows Peter fearlessly proclaiming the resurrection of Jesus. He asserts that the stone they rejected (Jesus) has become the cornerstone of a new building. The risen Jesus is the one and only Saviour.

The Gospel presents Jesus as the good shepherd who knows his sheep intimately and is known by them. Unlike the hireling, he is willing to die to protect his sheep.

In the Second Reading John talks about the wonderful love God has shown for us by making us his children. Our future state will be like that of the glorified Jesus. This reading invites us to rejoice in our status as God's adopted children.

If there is a theme in all three readings perhaps it is this: the great love God has shown us in what he has done for us in Jesus, the Good Shepherd and our one and only Saviour.

HOMILY 1   **Finding one's work**

A huge amount of our lives is taken up with work. Hence, the way we regard our work is of the greatest importance. If our work has meaning, it becomes a blessing. But if it has no meaning, or little meaning, it becomes almost a curse.

It has been said that the first of our problems is to find the work we are meant to do in this world. Vincent van Gogh spent many years trying to find out what he wanted to do with his life. Finally, after much searching, he discovered that he wanted to be a painter. From that day on his life changed. It wasn't that it suddenly became easy. The opposite would be nearer the truth. It was just that, whereas up to this his life was going nowhere, now it was going somewhere definite. He said:

> I often feel that I am as rich as Croesus, not in money, however. I am rich because I have found in my work something to which I can devote myself heart and soul, and which gives meaning and inspiration to my life. I think it is a very great blessing when people find their work.
>
> If at times I feel rising within me the desire for a life of ease, I go back fondly to a life of hardship. This is not the road on which one perishes. Rather, this is a powerful stream that will bear me safely to port.

What's the difference between the good shepherd and the hireling? It is the contrasting attitudes they bring to the work of shepherding. The hireling does it because he has to. For him it's just a job; his heart is not in it. The good shepherd does it because he wants to. His heart is in it.

People like the good shepherd are very fortunate people. They have found a real treasure. They haven't just found a work; they have found a *vocation* in life. They have an occupation into which they can put their hearts, and which affords an outlet for the talents that are in them.

Even though their work may be difficult and unspectacular, it glows with meaning because it is a labour of love. Even though their lives may contain many difficulties and hardships, deep down they are contented. We must never equate a happy life with an easy life. The harder the task to which we give ourselves for love's sake, the more it will exalt us.

Happy those who have found their work, no matter how humble that work is. They are saved from half-heartedness, and from the tragedy of only half-living their lives. That work brings out the best in them. It's no exaggeration to say that for them it becomes the road to salvation.

Jesus found his work. It consisted in being a good shepherd to the Father's flock. Two characteristics mark the relationship between the good shepherd and his sheep. First, he cares about his sheep to the point where he is willing to die to defend them. And Jesus did give his life for his sheep. He died voluntarily. Second, he knows his sheep and they know him. Good leaders know their own, and their own know them. There is a closeness between the leader and the led. Without this, leadership easily becomes oppressive.

Needless to say, we are not sheep. As St John reminds us: we are God's children, and God wants us to have life and hereafter.

HOMILY 2   **A sense of vocation**

Today's Gospel is about caring or not caring. The hireling doesn't know or care about the sheep. The good shepherd knows his sheep, and cares about them to the point that he is willing to die to defend them. Caring is costly and risky. Carers are very special people.

Today there is a lot of concern about care-giver burnout, and rightly so. However, burn-out is not always the result of too much work. It is more likely to result from a sense of futility. People can work long hours as long as they feel that their work is making a difference. But if they feel that their efforts are being wasted, that no matter how long and hard they work, it won't make any difference, then they will experience a feeling of weariness and exhaustion.

The thing to consider is not so much whether the work is difficult in itself, but whether it has a purpose. What really saps one's energy is giving oneself puroselessly. Purposeful giving is not as apt to deplete one's energy.

To have a work which absorbs one gives a person tremendous strength and energy. Alexander Solzhenitsyn spent several years in a Siberian labour camp. The thing which most helped him to survive was his writing. In his monumental work, *The Gulag Archipelago,* he says:

> Sometimes in a sullen work party with machine-gunners barking around me, lines and images crowded in so urgently that I felt myself borne through the air, overleaping the column in my hurry to reach the work compound and find a corner to write. At such moments I was both free and happy.
>
> I went on writing. In winter in the warming-up shack, in spring and summer on the scaffolding at the building site; in the interval between two barrowloads of mortar I would put my bit of paper on the bricks and write down with a pencil stub the verses which had rushed into my head while I was slapping on the last hodful. I was searched, and counted, and herded over the steppe. I sat in the mess hall over the ritual gruel sometimes not even noticing its taste, deaf to those around me – feeling my way about my verses and trimming them to fit like bricks in a wall.

To have a work which absorbs one is a great blessing. But to have a sense of vocation is an even greater blessing. In fact, it is one of the greatest blessings in life. Jesus had it to a degree we will never equal. On one occasion he said to his apostles, 'I have a food of which you know nothing. My food is to do the will of the one who sent me, and to complete his work' (Jn 4:33-34). And we see it even more clearly in today's Gospel where he talks about himself as the good shepherd.

Unlike the hireling, the good shepherd loves his work. To him shepherding is a vocation. It doesn't mean that his life is easier than that of the hireling. In fact, his life is more difficult because he works harder and cares more about the sheep than the hireling does. But his life is more satisfying. His work nourishes him.

Love is a marvellous source of strength and energy. Love makes a person brave. Where genuine love is present no sacrifice is too great. Love conquers all difficulties. If we love, and the energy will be given to us.

Today is often referred to a 'vocations' Sunday. For Christians, all vocations are vocations to love.

HOMILY 3   **Working with love**

The performance of a duty, even the faithful performance of such, can result in a withering of the heart when one is not motivated by love.

Two people can be doing the exact same work, even working side by side, and yet bring contrasting attitudes to it. One loves his work and has made a total gift of himself to it. He takes pride in what he's doing and puts a part of his soul into it. The other hates his work, and is at best only half-hearted. For him it's only a job. The only thing that concerns him is the pay packet.

Jesus gives us a good example of this in his parable of the hireling and the good shepherd. What a contrast there is between them. For the hireling, minding the sheep is just a job. He's in it only for the wages. He doesn't know the sheep or care about them. The sheep suffer as a result.

For the good shepherd minding the sheep is not just a job. It is a way of life, a vocation. He knows his sheep, and cares about them to the point that he is prepared to risk his life to save them. The sheep thrive as a result.

What makes the good shepherd so different from the hireling is the fact that he loves his work. He is interested in it, and dedicated to it. This doesn't make it any easier. If anything it makes it harder because he does it more thoroughly. But it enables him to bring all his energies to it. If you love what you do, the energy will be given to you. Not only does the work benefit, but the worker benefits too – it brings out the best in one. To work like this is to be free.

Most of us are hirelings, in the sense that we do not work for ourselves. But that doesn't mean that we have to have the mentality of the hireling. Just because a person demands adequate remunerated for his work, doesn't mean that he is the kind of hireling Jesus was talking about. He doesn't have to bring the attitude of the hireling to his work. He doesn't have to do it just for the pay. He can still bring the attitude of the good shepherd to his work.

We have a right to a decent wage. Apart from other considerations, it is good for one's dignity. But as Christians we ought to try to see our work, whatever it happens to be, as a service to others. If we do, then we are being good shepherds. We have left the ranks of the hirelings. We are members of a sacred band – those who perform needful but irksome tasks in a spirit of service. Honest toil makes a person's bread taste sweet.

The hireling works under the severest handicap of all – his heart is not in his work. It is possible to go through ones entire life with the mentality of a hireling. The loss hardly bears thinking about. Something corrosive happens to the soul of those who stop caring about the quality of their work, and are just going through the motions.

'If you feel no love, leave people alone. Occupy yourself instead with things' (Tolstoy).

ADDITIONAL MATERIAL   **Attitudes to work**

Some years ago an American journalist (Studs Terkel) did a survey to try to find out how people felt about their work. Armed with a tape recorder he went around the country interviewing people. His findings were that the overwhelming majority of people are unhappy with what they are doing. And work begins when you don't like what you're doing.

However, not liking one's work is nothing new. In the old days miners, railroad labourers, cotton pickers, sweatshop workers didn't like what they did. Conditions were very bad in those days. The workers worked long hours and were poorly paid. Yet even though people didn't like their work they never dreamed of questioning it. They were content to have a job that put bread on the table for their family.

But today people are asking questions. They want more from work than a wage. They want the work to have some meaning. They want to get some feeling of fulfilment out of doing it. They don't want to be regarded as mere cogs in a machine.

Their deepest ache comes from the need for recognition. A workman told Terkel how he would like to see a skyscraper with a plaque bearing the names of all the workers who put it up, not just those of the architect and the builder. 'Who built the pyramids?' he asks. 'We don't know the names of those guys. All we know is the name of Pharaoh.'

A check-out girl in a supermarket describes herself as 'nothing'. A refuse collector sees himself as a horse pulling a wagon.

On the other hand, those who like their work know who they are. They feel needed and useful. Tommy loves being a fireman because it gives him a chance to help people. The chemist feels close to the people who come in and out of her shop.

Terkel's book leaves us pondering this thought: if people find their work to be empty, what do they find their lives to be? Where does all this leave the unemployed, and what can we say to them?

PRAYER OF THE FAITHFUL

President: St John reminds us that we are God's children. Let us bring our needs before God, confident that he will listen to us because we are his children.

Response: Lord, hear our prayer.

Reader(s): For the leaders of the Church: that they may be true shepherds to the flock of Christ. [Pause] Let us pray to the Lord.

For those who make our laws and who apply them: that the Lord may bless them with the gifts of wisdom and compassion. [Pause] Let us pray to the Lord.

For those who feel that nobody cares about them. [Pause] Let us pray to the Lord.

For our lapsed brothers and sisters: that they may find their way back to the flock Christ nourishes. [Pause] Let us pray to the Lord.

For those whose work is hard and unrewarding. [Pause] Let us pray to the Lord.

For artists, craftspeople, and musicians: that their work may bring joy and inspiration into the lives of others. [Pause] Let us pray to the Lord.

For all gathered here: that we may see our work as a service to others, and put our hearts into it. [Pause] Let us pray to the Lord.

For ourselves: that we may be people who care about those around us, and so imitate the love of the Good Shepherd. [Pause] Let us pray to the Lord.

For the unemployed: that they may not lose heart. [Pause] Let us pray to the Lord.

For our own special needs. [Longer pause] Let us pray to the Lord.

President: God of compassion, grant that we may never doubt the love of Christ, the Good Shepherd, and show our gratitude by loving one another. We ask this through the same Christ our Lord.

REFLECTION   **Working with love**

All work is empty save when done with love.
And what is it to work with love?
It is to weave the cloth with threads drawn from your heart,
even as if your beloved were to wear that cloth.
It is to build a house with affection,
even as if your beloved were to dwell in that house.
If you cannot work with love but only with distaste,
it is better that you should leave your work,
and sit at the gate of the temple
and take alms from those who work with joy.
For if you bake bread with indifference,
you bake a bitter bread that feeds but half of man's hunger.
And if you grudge the crushing of the grapes,
your grudge distils a poison in the wine.
Work is love made visible.   *Kahlil Gibran*

Fifth Sunday of the Year
THE VINE AND THE BRANCHES

INTRODUCTION AND CONFITEOR

There is no such thing as a solitary Christian. Every Christian is linked to Christ and to all other Christians. This is clear from the words of Jesus: 'I am the vine, you are the branches.' Alas, often we ignore and hurt others, and live only for ourselves. [Pause]

Lord, you are the vine, we are the branches. Lord, have mercy.

You unite us with yourself and one another to make our lives fruitful. Christ, have mercy.

You call us to have your words abide in us. Lord, have mercy.

HEADINGS FOR READINGS

First Reading (Acts 9:26-31). This tells us about some of the trials Paul endured after his conversion.

Second Reading (1 Jn 3:18-24). Here John is reflecting on Christ's commandment of love.

Gospel (Jn 15:1-8). Jesus uses the image of a vine and its branches to illustrate how close are the ties that bind him to his disciples.

SCRIPTURE NOTE

The First Reading tells how, three years after his conversion, Paul went up to Jerusalem. In spite of being introduced by Barnabas, such was the hostility he encountered that he had to be smuggled out of the city. The fact that Paul took all these trials in his stride shows the depth of his faith in Jesus.

In the Gospel we have the lovely image of the vine and the branches. Here Jesus stresses the unity that exists between him and his disciples. Vine and branches need each other. The vine cannot bear fruit without the branches. And the branches can have no life if separated from the vine. The branches need to be pruned (by trials) in order to be fruitful. (Paul is a good example.)

The Second Reading tells us what we have to do in order to be at rights with God. We have to believe in his Son, Jesus, and love one another as he told us. Active charity is what distinguishes true Christians from those who are such in name only. (This is what makes them fruitful branches of Christ, the true vine.)

HOMILY 1   **The hour of departure**

In order to understand a statement fully we need to know the context in which it is was made. This is perhaps especially true of the statements of Jesus which are recorded in the Gospel. The statement in today's Gospel – 'I am the vine, you are the branches' – is a beautiful image of unity and closeness. When we look at the context in which Jesus spoke these words, I think we will appreciate the beauty of this image all the more.

Jesus spoke these words to his apostles towards the end of the last supper, or, more likely, on the way to the garden of Gethsemane. In any event, he spoke them a short time before his death.

It was a night when everything seemed to be breaking up, falling apart, ending. It was a night when all of the disciples would abandon him; when their leader would deny him publicly, and another of their company would betray him. Yet this was the night he chose to speak about unity and togetherness.

At first it seems a strange time to talk about unity. But on reflection we see that it was a natural and most appropriate time. This was the hour of departure. The hour of departure causes us to focus on essentials. It is at such an hour that we really appreciate our native place and especially our friends.

In the Dingle peninsula, in Co. Kerry, there is a rock known as the Rock of Tears, *Carraig na nDeoir*. It is at a bend on the road to Dingle. It was here that emigrants from the Blasket Islands and Slea Head paused for a while and wept. From here they caught a last glimpse of the home they were leaving and would never see again. Beyond this bend the road stretched to Dingle, to Cobh, and to the ships that would carry them into exile.

At the hour of departure, Jesus felt very close to his apostles. And he let them know this. He also wanted them close to him. He foresaw that they would abandon him later that night. He foresaw that Peter would deny him and that Judas would betray him. Betrayal is a terribly thing. Few if any relationships can survive it. Yet Jesus also foresaw that in spite of these upheavals, their unity would survive.

The apostles learned a lot about their own weakness and cowardice when confronted with the demands of unity and solidarity. But they learned even more about Jesus. They learned that he loved them in and through their weakness. If they should ever get separated from him, it would not be because he had cut them off. Far from being ended by the events of that night, their bond with Jesus was strengthened.

It is through facing struggle, failure, danger, and sacrifice that unity grows and deepens. There is more depth to a relationship that has weathered some storms.

HOMILY 2   **The vine and the branches**

Christ wrote no books. He left no buildings or monuments behind. Yet he did something far greater and more necessary, though less ostentatious – he built a community. That was his 'monument'.

He said to his apostles, 'I am the vine, you are the branches.' This was the image he used in talking about the community he had founded. It is a simple but profound illustration of unity, closeness and interdependence.

In spring the branches of the vine teem with life in the form of leaves and blossoms. In autumn they are loaded with grapes. But they have this life, and are able to produce this fruit, only because they are connected to the vine. Cut off from the vine, they would not only become barren, but quickly wither and die. Just as the branches need the vine, so we need

Christ. Separated from him, we have no life and are unable to bear fruit.

But the vine also needs the branches – it is the branches that produce the fruit. Which means that Christ also needs us. We are his branches. Vine and branches need each other. Together they form a unity. From this we can see how great is the trust he has placed in us. We may feel inadequate. But we must remember that the vine is sturdy and full of life.

Christ depends on us to produce fruit in the world. There is a big difference between successfulness and fruitfulness. Success comes from strength, control and respectability. Success brings rewards and sometimes fame as well. Fruitfulness, however, often comes from weakness and vulnerability, and frequently goes unrecognised and unrewarded.

Christ didn't ask us to be successful, but to be fruitful. Each of us has some gift. By developing, using, and sharing that gift with others, we become fruitful. The world is waiting for fruit. What is important is to love. God will make our love fruitful, whether we see that fruitfulness or not.

During the winter months the branches are pruned. Pruning is a painful process for a fruit tree. The pruner rids it of suckers and excess shoots which use up a lot of energy but produce no fruit. The aim of this surgery is not to inflict pain, but to help the tree to produce more and better fruit.

We, the branches of the True Vine, need some pruning too. There is much that is useless and perhaps harmful in our lives, which saps our energy, and diminishes our spiritual fruitfulness. If Christ prunes us through trials it is only to make us more fruitful. Pruned by suffering, a person produces the fruit of understanding and compassion.

HOMILY 3   **Our need of community**

Often it takes a common danger to bring people close to one another. People can travel side by side for years, each locked up in his or her silent world, or exchanging words that carry no real significance, until danger strikes. Then they stand shoulder to shoulder. They discover that they belong to the same family. They wax and bloom in the recognition of each other as fellow human beings. They become loyal comrades. They truly encounter one another.

Happiness is not to be found in possessions or even in achievements, but in the warmth of human relationships. Often our individual interests and concerns imprison us within walls and cut us off from others. It is only the grasp of a warm and friendly hand that sets us free from this prison of our own making.

The evening before he died Jesus ate a very special meal with his friends – the Passover meal. Danger lurked in every corner. It was hard to tell who could be trusted. He felt this more keenly than they did. In this hour of darkness and danger, Jesus felt closer than ever to his apostles. To show them how he felt about them he got down on his knees and washed their feet. Then he spoke to them about love—about the love he had for them and the love they should have for one another.

On the way to the garden he found the ideal symbol for the bond he felt with them. Stopping by a vine he said, 'I am the vine, you are the branches. If you remain attached to me, you will produce much fruit. But if you cut yourselves off from me, you will wither and die.' Even as he spoke one of their number, Judas, had already cut himself off. What a barren end he came to.

This is how Jesus felt. This is how he wanted it to be between him and his disciples. This is the way he wants it to be between him and us. He is the vine, we are the branches. We should not wait for danger to threaten before we experience this reality. It should be the climate in which we live.

This also meets the human need for a supportive community. There is much loneliness in the world. People today are crying out for recognition. They want to be noticed, not in a showy way, or because they have money or status, but just because they are human beings. The greatest need of all is the need to be loved. But often we pass one another by without the slightest sign of recognition. People can come to church and leave again without meeting anyone. Is that right?

The world is crying out for community. There should be no such thing as a solitary Christian. The fruit which Christ desires from us is primarily that of unity among ourselves. By this all will know that we are living branches of the Vine – by the bond that exists between us and the care we show for one another.

ADDITIONAL MATERIAL

Many today ask, 'Why should I go to church? Why can't I just worship God in my own way? Surely religion is about my personal relationship with God?'

From the earliest times, following Jesus was never just a private, personal matter. Christians came together to live in community, to profess their faith in Jesus Christ, to witness to his resurrection, and live by his teachings. The profound reason for this is given to us by Christ himself, when he said, 'I am the vine, you are the branches.'

The vine and its branches are one. There is a mutual interdependence of branch and vine, and branch with branch. To say, 'I will follow Jesus but not the Church,' is to separate Jesus from the Church, to cut off the branches from the vine.

The first disciples of Jesus had seen him, eaten with him, and spoken with him after his resurrection. As a consequence they had a deep sense of connectedness with him, a connectedness from which they drew great strength. Jesus had chosen them. He had made them his friends, and sent them out to bear fruit, the fruit of love.

By this all will know that we are living branches of the Vine – by the bond that exists between us and the care we show for one another.

PRAYER OF THE FAITHFUL

President: Christ wanted his followers to be united with him and with one another. Let us pray for the gift of unity.

Response: Lord, hear us in your love.

Reader(s): For the Church: that it may be a true community, producing the fruits of love. [Pause] We pray in faith.

For our civil leaders: that they may help to create a society in which all can enjoy the fruits of freedom and justice. [Pause] We pray in faith.

For those who are cut off from human companionship, especially shut-ins and outcasts. [Pause] We pray in faith.

For those who feel that their lives are barren and empty. [Pause] We pray in faith.

For this community: that as we meet around the Lord's table, he may strengthen our unity and deepen our faith. [Pause] We pray in faith.

For our own special needs. [Longer pause] We pray in faith.

President: Lord our God, in a world of injustice, indifference and unrest, may we be conscious of our calling to produce the fruits of justice, love and peace. We ask this through Christ our Lord.

PRAYER FOR PEACE

Lord Jesus Christ, you said to your apostles, 'I am the vine, you are the branches. Separated from me you can do nothing; united with me you will bear much fruit.' Strengthen the bonds that unite us with you and with one another so that we may enjoy the peace and unity of your kingdom where you live for ever and ever.

PRAYER/REFLECTION   **The vine and the branches**

Lord, you said:
'I am the vine, you are the branches.
Separated from me you can do nothing,
but united with me you will bear much fruit.'
Thank you, Lord, for the bond you formed with us.
And thank you for the bond that exists among us
because of our union with you.
Thanks to this bond we have invisible riches
to share with one another.
Grant that we may never be separated from you,

so that we may produce in the world
the fruits of faith, hope, and love.

Sixth Sunday of Easter
NO GREATER LOVE

INTRODUCTION AND CONFITEOR

The Gospel of today's Mass reminds us of the commandment Christ left
his disciples: 'Love one another as I have loved you.' It was God who first
loved us. As we call to mind God's love for us in Christ, let us also call to
mind that our response to that love is to love one another. [Pause]

Let us ask forgiveness from God and from one another for our failure
to live Christ's commandment of love.

I confess ...

HEADINGS FOR READINGS

First Reading (Acts 10:25-26.34-35.44-48). The baptism of Cornelius, the
first pagan to receive the grace of baptism, shows that God's salvation is
offered to all.

Second Reading (1 Jn 4:7-10). This contains what is probably the most
important statement ever made about God.

Gospel (Jn 15:9-17). Jesus leaves his friends the supreme commandment
of love.

SCRIPTURE NOTE

The first Christian community had been exclusively Jewish. Now comes
a turning point – the reception of the first Gentiles. Cornelius was the
first pagan to receive the grace of baptism. The reading from Acts tells of
his baptism, and shows that God's salvation is offered to all.

In the Gospel Jesus talks about the love that binds him to the Father,
and the love that should bind the disciples to him and to one another.
Jesus' love is modelled on that of the Father. The disciples should model
themselves on the Son: as he has observed the Father's commandments,
so they should observe his. Obedience arises out of love, and obedience
is love. Now he is going to give them the supreme proof of his love –
giving his life for them. He has chosen them and sent them into the world
to bear fruit – the fruit of love.

In the Second Reading John says that Christians must love one another because love comes from God. Love is of God's essence. God has
shown his love for us by sending his Son into the world so that we might

have life through him. Loving is the only way we can really know God and share in God's life.

HOMILY 1 **God is love**

Once there was a young man who was having doubts about the existence of God. So one day he paid a visit to a monk who had a reputation for holiness. He asked the monk, 'Do you believe in God?'

'Yes, I do,' the monk answered.

'On what evidence do you believe?' the young man asked.

'I believe in God because I know him,' came the reply. 'I experience the presence of God within me every day.'

'But how is that possible?' the youth asked.

'When we love, we experience God, and doubt vanishes like early morning mist before the sun,' replied the monk.

The youth thought about this for a while, then asked, 'How can I achieve this kind of certainty?'

'By acts of love,' came the reply. 'Try to love your neighbours; love them actively and unceasingly. As you learn to love them more and more, you will become more and more convinced of the existence of God and the immortality of the soul. This has been tested. This is the true way.'

The monk was only echoing the words of St John: 'My dear friends, let us love one another, because love is from God; everyone who loves is born of God and knows God. Whoever does not love does not know God, for God is love' (Second Reading).

Love is a precondition for a true understanding of life and especially of God. As Father Zosima says in Dostoevsky's *The Brothers Karamazov*: 'You must love all that God has created, both his entire world and each single tiny sandgrain of it. If you love all things, you will also attain the divine mystery that is in all things.' Van Gogh said something similar: 'The best way to know God is to love many things. Love a friend, a wife, something, and you will be on the right way to knowing about God.'

Love is the best teacher we have. But it does not come of its own accord. It is dearly bought. It often demands many years of persevering toil before a person can reach the point where he or she is able to love.

There is a big gap between knowing God and loving God. Not to love is not to know God. But when we love, the gap is closed. To love is to know God. Where love is, God is; where God is, love is. To know is not to prove, or to explain.

Hate is a bad thing. It's bad to hate anything. It is a good thing to love something, even a rosebush. 'For myself I am contented to be a small gardener who loves his plants' (Van Gogh).

Because we are made in God's image, each of us has an innate capacity for love. However, for this to happen the heart has to be right. If only the heart was right we could give so much more. But, alas, the heart is sometimes cold and unwelcoming, sometimes empty, and sometimes broken. We shouldn't be surprised at this. All it says is that we have a heart of flesh, not one of stone. But we have to heal the wounds of the heart in order to be able to produce the fruits of love.

The image of God is at its best and brightest in us when we love.

HOMILY 2   **Where love is, God is**

In a certain village in the Swiss Alps there is a small church which has been used by generations of worshippers. Even though it is no work of art, the local people have always had a special affection for it. What is it that makes it so beautiful in the eyes of the people? It is the story of how it came to be built on that particular spot. The story goes like this.

Two brothers worked a family farm, sharing the produce and profit. One was married, the other wasn't. The climate was harsh with the result that grain was sometimes scarce.

One day the single brother said to himself, 'It's not fair that we should share the produce equally. I'm alone, but my brother has a family to support.' So every now and then he would go out at night, take a sack of grain from his own barn, quietly cross the field between their houses, and place it in his brother's bin.

Meanwhile, his brother had a similar idea, and said, 'It's not right that we should share the produce equally. I have a family to support me but my brother is all alone.' So every now and then he would go at night, take a sack of grain from his barn, and quietly place it in his brother's bin.

This went on for a number of years. Each brother was puzzled how his supply of grain never dwindled. Then one night they bumped into each other in the dark. When they realised what had been happening, they dropped their sacks, and embraced each other. Suddenly a voice from heaven said: 'Here I will build my church. For where people meet in love, there my presence shall dwell.'

What's the purpose of life if not to love? William Blake put it like this: 'We are put on earth a little space that we may learn to bear the beams of love.'

But we cannot give love unless we have first received it. A radiator cannot give out heat unless it has first received heat. This was true of Jesus too. He said to his disciples, 'As the Father has loved me, so I have loved you.' The love he shared so generously with his disciples and with the people at large was the love he had received from the Father, and from Mary, Joseph and others too.

It is not a sign of weakness to admit one's need of love. We should acknowledge and be grateful for the love we have received. As far as God's love is concerned, we don't have to earn it. It is God who first loved us. God loves us, not because we are good, but because he is good. Our very existence is a sign of God's love. All we have to do is receive it, and then try to share it with others.

Love is well-being. It makes life fruitful. To refuse to love is to begin to die. To love is to begin to live. Few get the opportunity of showing their love for others by dying for them. But all have the opportunity to live for others.

Love is costly. To love is to accept that we might die another death before we die our own. The way of love is the way of the cross, and it is only through the cross that we come to the resurrection. There is nothing terrible about suffering a bit on earth if it has taught us how to love.

There is a prayer which goes like this: 'Lord, don't let me die yet, because I haven't loved enough.' It's a prayer we would do well to make our own.

HOMILY 3   **Love sets us free**

Every afternoon as they came home from school the children played in the Giant's garden. It was a lovely garden, with soft green grass and fragrant flowers. Twelve apple trees grew there, which in spring broke out in lovely blossoms, and in autumn were laden with large red apples.

Once the Giant went away for seven years. He returned home on a winter's day to find the local children playing in the garden. He got very angry. 'Get out of here!' he cried. 'The garden is mine. No one plays in it but me.'

He chased them out and put up a big sign on the gate which said: TRESPASSERS WILL BE PROSECUTED. Now the children had nowhere to play except on the dusty road. They used to wander around the high walls sadly.

Spring came, and all over the land there were lovely blossoms and the birds sang happily. Only in the Giant's garden it was still winter. There no green leaf or blade of grass or flower appeared. There the birds refused to sing. Snow covered the grass with a white cloak, and frost painted the trees silver. Then they invited the north wind to stay with them, and he was glad to come. And they invited the hail, and he too came.

'I cannot understand why spring is so late in coming,' said the Giant, as he sat by the window and looked out at his cold, white garden. 'I hope there will be a change in the weather soon.' But the spring never came, nor the summer. Autumn came and gave fruit to every garden but none to his.

The following year he awoke one morning to find that the hail had stopped dancing, and the north wind had ceased blowing. A lovely perfume came to him. 'I believe that spring has come at last,' he said. He jumped out of bed, looked out the window, and saw a wonderful sight.

Through a little hole in the garden wall the children had crept in and were sitting in the branches of the trees. And the trees were so glad to have them back that they covered themselves in blossoms.

The Giant quietly entered the garden and with a broad smile on his face approached the children. Then in a kind voice he said to them, 'It's your garden now.' He knocked down the wall. When the people were going to the market they saw the Giant playing with their children in the most beautiful garden they had ever seen.

Oscar Wilde's beautiful story is a commentary on Christ's command-ment of love. When we refuse to love, we build a wall around ourselves. But we ourselves are the first to suffer. We condemn ourselves to a winter of loneliness and unhappiness.

But when we love, the wall falls down. We open ourselves to others. And we ourselves are the first to benefit. We experience a springtime of friendship, goodwill, peace and joy.

Love bestows many benefits on the one who loves. One of the greatest of these is the gift of joy. Jesus said to his apostles, 'If you keep my com-mandments you will remain in my love, just as I have kept my Father's commandments and remain in his love. I have told you this so that my own joy may be in you and your joy be complete.'

Jesus talks about love and joy in the same breath. This is because they are intimately connected. Joy is the fruit of love. Joy is an over-flowing heart. The amount of joy we have is in proportion to the amount of love we share with others. If then we are not as joyful as we might be, perhaps it is telling us something.

ANOTHER STORY   **Greater love no man has**

Mary and Kathy were good friends and shared a flat at the top of a three-storey building. When Kathy was struck down by pneumonia she be-lieved she was doomed to die, and refused to take food or drink. Mary called the doctor for her.

When the doctor left, Mary went into Kathy's bedroom, and found her lying in bed looking out the window. In a low voice she was counting backwards: '50, 49, 48, 47 ... ' Mary looked out the window to see what her friend was counting. The only thing to be seen was the brick wall which constituted the gable end of the house next door. An old ivy plant was attached to the wall. The cold wind had already stripped it of most of its leaves.

'What are you counting?' Mary asked.

'The leaves on the ivy plant,' Kathy answered. 'A few days ago there were hundreds of leaves on it. Now there are only a few left. I'll die when the last leaf falls.'

Mary tried in vain to talk this nonsense out of her head. Now in the basement flat lived an old artist by the name of Benson. As an artist he was a total failure. He drank to excess but still talked about the master-piece he would one day paint. Mary went and told him about her friend's condition. 'Leave it to me,' Benson said.

That evening when Mary visited Kathy she found her asleep.

Before closing the curtain she looked out the window. A cold wind was blowing and a steady rain was falling. When she entered Kathy's room next morning she found her awake and staring hard at the drawn curtain. 'Open it,' Kathy whispered. Mary obeyed. To her surprise, there was still one leaf left on the ivy. 'It's the last one,' said Kathy sadly. 'It will surely fall today, and I will die at the same time.'

The day wore on and still the lone leaf clung to the branch. With the coming on of night the wind and rain returned. At dawn on the second morning Kathy again asked for the curtain to be pulled back. The ivy leaf was still there! She looked at it in silence for some time. Then she said, 'I've been wrong. I've been selfish. Something has made that leaf stay there to show me how wrong I was. Please bring me a little soup.'

On the third day the doctor declared her out of danger. That afternoon Mary entered Kathy's room to find her sitting up in bed knitting. 'Kathy,' she began slowly, 'I've something to tell you.' 'What is it?' Kathy enquired. 'Benson died this morning. He had been sick only two days. Yesterday morning the caretaker found him in his room in great pain. His clothes were soaked through. They found a lantern, still lighting and some scat-tered brushes, and a palette with fresh paint on it. And look – look out the window at the last leaf. Did you never ask yourself why it didn't move with the wind? Benson painted it there the night the last leaf fell.'

So, in a sense, Benson did paint his masterpiece after all. His life may have been a failure in every other way, but this act of love redeemed every-thing.

PRAYER OF THE FAITHFUL

President: Everyone who loves is born of God and knows God, because God is love. Let our prayers be an expression of our love for one another.

Response: Lord, hear us in your love.

Reader(s): For all Christians: that they may be known by their love. [Pause] We pray in faith.

For those who govern the nations of the world: that they may strive to rid the world of hatred and fear. [Pause] We pray in faith.

For husbands and wives: that in spite of difficulties their love may endure. [Pause] We pray in faith.

For those who have known little love in their lives and who practise even less. [Pause] We pray in faith.

For all gathered here: that we may show love in little ways, especially towards those we meet every day. [Pause] We pray in faith.

For our own needs. [Longer pause] We pray in faith.

President: Heavenly Father, your Son commanded us to love one another, and set us an example by laying down his life for his friends. Help us to follow his way of love so that we may taste the joy that only he can give us, a joy no one can take from us. We ask this through the same Christ our Lord.

PRAYER FOR PEACE

Lord Jesus Christ, you said to your apostles: 'A new commandment I give you: love one another, as I have loved you.' Touch our hearts so that we may be able to love, and thus we will enjoy the peace and unity of your kingdom where you live for ever and ever.

REFLECTION   **The wounded heart**

If only the heart was right
we could give so much more.
But, alas, the heart is often empty.
It is often cold and unwelcoming.
It is often hard and unyielding.
It is often weighed down with worry.
It is often sad and lonely.
It is often in darkness.
It is often wounded.
And it is sometimes broken.
We have to heal the wounds of the heart
in order to be able to love.
Lord, touch our hearts and heal them,
so that we may be able to bear the fruits of love. Amen.

The Ascension of the Lord

INTRODUCTION AND CONFITEOR

Today we celebrate the Ascension of Jesus into heaven. It is not a day for narrowness and sadness. It is a day for openness and joy. It is a day for renewing our hope in the goal towards which the Lord is leading us, namely, a place in his kingdom. [Pause]

Our sins prevent us from walking freely and joyfully towards Jesus' kingdom. Let us confess them humbly and trustingly.

HEADINGS FOR READINGS

First Reading (Acts 1:1-11). This describes the ascension of Jesus into heaven, and his promise to send the Holy Spirit to his disciples.

Second Reading (Eph 1:17-23). Here Paul describes the meaning of the ascension: God raised Jesus above all earthly powers, and made him head of the Church and Lord of creation.

Gospel (Mk 16:15-20). Before ascending to his Father, Jesus commissions his apostles to preach the Gospel to the whole world.

SCRIPTURE NOTE

The reading from Acts describes the ascension of Jesus. It also shows how Jesus, now in the glorious presence of his Father, continues to act through the Holy Spirit and through his followers.

The Gospel is concerned with the Lord's ascension and the missionary charge he gave his apostles. The preaching of the apostles was to have the same effect as the preaching of Jesus. The reference to picking up snakes and drinking poison is not be taken literally. According to the Middle Eastern mentality hyperbole is an accepted way of making a point – through the power of Jesus the apostles will triumph over all evils.

The apostles are to challenge people of all times and places either to believe or reject the Gospel. The statement that equates belief in Christ with salvation and disbelief with condemnation, can't be preached as bluntly as that. Today unbelief springs from many factors, not least from the poor witness given by those who claim to believe in Jesus.

The theological meaning of the feast is expressed in the Second Reading: God has glorified Jesus, raising him above all earthly powers, and making him head of the Church and Lord of creation.

The ascension of Jesus is his liberation from all restrictions of time and space. It does not represent his removal from the earth, but his constant presence everywhere on earth.

HOMILY 1   **Witnessing to the Lord**

Before leaving his apostles Jesus commissioned them to preach the Gospel to the whole world. In order to help them carry out that mission he promised to send them the Holy Spirit. On Pentecost day he fulfilled that promise.

Today the task of preaching the Gospel to the world depends on us. It's a great privilege but a daunting task. However, we also can rely on the help of the Holy Spirit. The best way to preach the Gospel is by living a Christian life. A question each of us might ask ourselves is this: If it were a crime to be a Christian, and I was put on trial, would enough evidence be found in my life to convict me?

Christopher was a practising Christian. Never missed church on Sunday. He and his family lived in a comfortable house in a fashionable part of town. With good health, and a secure, well-paying job, he was happy and satisfied.

However, one thing bothered him. It concerned his next-door neighbour. The man was a professed atheist, and never darkened the door of a church. As a Christian, Christopher felt it was his responsibility to try to convert him. But how was he to do it? On a number of occasions, in talking with him, he had brought up the subject of religion, doing so as delicately as he could. Alas, he had got nowhere.

Then one day he got an inspiration. If only he could get his neighbour to read the Gospel, that would surely do the trick. Who could fail to be moved by the Gospel? The only problem was how to get a copy of the Gospel to him. He couldn't very well knock on the man's door and hand him a copy. That was more likely to put him off. He would have to be more subtle in his approach. So what did he do? He posted a paperback copy of the Gospel to him anonymously.

Having done this, he waited to see what would happen. Days went by and nothing happened. There wasn't the slightest indication from next door that the man had seen the light. About two weeks later, Christopher's wife had occasion to visit their neighbour. When she came back she said to her husband, 'You know that copy of the Gospels you sent him?'

'Yes.'

'It's in the refuse bin.'

Christopher was indignant. It was not right to throw the Good Book into the refuse bin. He went next door, picking up the copy of the Gospel as he passed the refuse bin.

'I hope I'm not intruding,' he said to his neighbour. 'But I found this in your refuse bin. You know, if only you'd read it, you might find God.'

'But I do read it,' came the surprising reply. 'I read it every day.'

'I don't understand,' said Christopher.

'You are a Christian, aren't you?'

'Why, yes.'

'Well, I've been reading your life every day for the past ten years.' End of story.

There's a little poem that goes like this:

I am my neighbour's Bible; he reads me when we meet.
Today he reads me in my house, tomorrow in the street.
He may a relative, or friend, or slight acquaintance be;
He may not even known my name, yet he is reading me.

HOMILY 2   **Making disciples**

Once upon a time a spiritual leader called six of his disciples to him and said, 'Go out and make disciples.' And the six set off at once. Time passed and, one by one, they returned.

The first came back with five hundred disciples.

'How did you manage to gain so many?' the leader asked.

'I went around among the poorer sections of the people,' the disciple answered. 'There I found great poverty, suffering and want. I promised them that we would take care of all their needs.'

'I see,' said the leader.

The second came back with four hundred disciples.

'And what approach did you use?' the leader asked.

'I told them about heaven and the great reward that is waiting there for the followers of our way,' was the reply.

'I see,' said the leader.

The third came back with three hundred disciples.

'What approach did you use?' the leader asked.

'I pulled no punches,' this disciple replied. 'I told them they would all go to hell unless they followed our way. They were still not entirely convinced until I worked a miracle. I cursed a mad dog and it dropped dead. That convinced them.'

'I see,' said the leader.

The fourth came back with two hundred disciples.

'What approach did you use?' the leader asked.

'I decided to go around among the simple and uneducated. I convinced them with arguments. I blinded them with knowledge.'

'I see,' said the leader.

The fifth came back with one hundred disciples.

'And what approach did you use?' asked the leader.

'I went among the young,' the disciple replied. 'I told them about our way. Then I simply commanded them, and this is the result. They were standing around, waiting for a leader. If I hadn't got to them, some false messiah would have got to them and exploited them.'

'I see,' said the leader.

Finally, after a long delay, the sixth returned with only a dozen disciples. 'What kept you so long?' the leader asked.

'I wasn't able to sow the seed at once,' he replied. 'There is no point in sowing the seed in the middle of winter. You have to wait for the snow to melt and the ground to soften. So I waited. As I waited I befriended them, trying to give them an example of our way by the kind of life I lived.

'While I was sharing their lives I discovered that freedom was very important to them. To deprive them of this would be to undermine their dignity and greatly to devalue their consent. I also learned something else about them. I learned that they are a very generous people and not afraid of sacrifice. I told them about the cost of discipleship, but I stressed the good they could do for others and for God as disciples. They seemed impressed. However, when the crunch came, only twelve agreed to come with me.'

The leader commended the last disciple.

Five appealed to the weakness and fears of the people. It's easy to play on people's fear and manipulate them. But this is to interfere with their freedom, and so to damage their consent. The sixth man appealed to their strengths. He befriended them and tried to win them over by example.

That is what Christianity does. This is a slower and more difficult method, but in the end those who will be converted will have deeper roots, and will be more committed in following the way.

HOMILY 3   **A new and wider vision**

Jesus is presented as ascending to heaven from the top of Mount Olivet. A mountain is a place of vision. On a mountain top we feel somehow closer to God. Indeed, we feel we are in the presence of God.

A story is told about a man who had lived all his life in a clearing in the forest. The clearing was only about 100 yards across and was hemmed in by trees. The man's world was extremely enclosed. He had very little concept of space or distance. In such a world even comparatively small objects can appear larger than life because of one's nearness to them.

One day an explorer took him out of the forest and led him up to the top of a high mountain. He couldn't get over the wide open spaces that existed beyond the forest, the immensity of the sky, and the vastness of the horizon. He was amazed at discovering that a world existed in which there were no trees and very little vegetation. He was like a little child in his excitement. He was so happy that he wanted to remain up there.

But of course he had to go back down to his small, enclosed, narrow world. However, he never forgot his visit to the mountain top. It had a wonderful effect on him. It helped him to take a broader view of life, especially when things were becoming too much for him and the world was closing in on him.

When the time came for Jesus to leave this world, he took his apostles up to the top of the Mount of Olives. He was returning to the Father. He was going to glory. As he ascended he directed their eyes upwards, towards the place where he was going.

But he also pointed their eyes outwards. He showed them that there was a great world out there waiting to hear the Gospel. He gave them the task of bringing the Gospel to that vast world, and promised to send them the Holy Spirit to equip them for that task.

The apostles liked it on the hill, so much so that they wanted to remain there. But a voice called them back to reality: 'Men of Galilee, why do you stand here looking up into the heavens?' Even though they had to go back down into the real world, their lives would never be the same.

This feast is as much about us as about Jesus. His ascension shows us where the goal of our earthly journey lies. It is a goal and a destiny which defies even our imagination. It gives us a new and wider vision. It pushes out our horizons beyond the boundaries of this world. It gives an eternal dimension to our lives.

Jesus went back to the source, the Alpha and the Omega. This is the meaning of his Ascension. It is not a journey into outer space, but a journey home. His Ascension does not represent his removal from the earth, but his constant presence everywhere on earth. During his earthly ministry he could only be in one place at a time. But now that he is united with God, he is present wherever God is present; and that is everywhere.

We live in the hope that the words of Jesus will come true for us: 'Where I am, you too shall be.' Meanwhile we have a task to do: to preach the Gospel and to be his witnesses in the world.

PRAYER OF THE FAITHFUL

President: Jesus sits at the right hand of the Father in glory. Let us bring our prayers to the Father knowing that Jesus is interceding for us.

Response: Lord, hear our prayer.

Reader(s): For all the followers of Jesus: that they may rise above the things that enslave them. [Pause] Let us pray to the Lord.

For the human family: that people may see the world as their common home. [Pause] Let us pray to the Lord.

For those who have no faith and whose horizons are limited to this world. [Pause] Let us pray to the Lord.

For those who are troubled: that they may be able to rise above their problems and worries. [Pause] Let us pray to the Lord.

For all gathered here: that our lives may bear witness to the faith we profess with our lips. [Pause] Let us pray to the Lord.

For our deceased relatives and friends, and for all the faithful departed: that the Lord may receive them into the kingdom of his glory. [Pause] Let us pray to the Lord.

For our own special needs. [Longer pause] Let us pray to the Lord.

President: Lord, you are now exalted at the right hand of the Father. Help us to follow the path you traced out for us, so that we may one day be where you now are, living and reigning with the Father and the Holy Spirit, one God for ever and ever.

REFLECTION   **Instruments of the Lord**

'Go, preach the Gospel to all nations.'
This was the farewell command of Christ.
He has no body now on earth but ours.

He has no hands but ours to raise up the fallen.
No feet but ours to seek out the lost.
No eyes but ours to see the silent tears of the suffering.
No ears but ours to listen to the lonely.
No tongue but ours to speak a word of comfort to the sad.
No heart but ours to love the unloved.
Lord, take pity on us, your timid and fearful disciples;
give us the courage to witness to you in the world,
and so the Gospel will be preached,
and people will find their way into your kingdom.

Seventh Sunday of Easter
WAITING FOR THE SPIRIT

INTRODUCTION AND CONFITEOR

We are gathered here in the Lord's name. We are doing what he asked his apostles to do: waiting in prayer for the coming of the Holy Spirit. Without the Spirit the apostles were like a sail boat without the wind. We too need the Spirit in order to be able to follow Christ whole-heartedly. [Pause]

> Lord Jesus, you put a steadfast spirit within us. Lord, have mercy.
> You give us again the joy of your help. Christ, have mercy.
> With a spirit of fervour you sustain us. Lord, have mercy.

HEADINGS FOR READINGS

First Reading (Acts 1:15-17. 20-26). This reading tells us how Matthias was chosen to fill the gap left by the defection of Judas.

Second Reading (1 Jn 4:11-16). Since God has loved us, we too must love one another.

Gospel (Jn 17:11-19). Jesus prays for his present and future disciples who are to carry on his work in the world.

SCRIPTURE NOTE

The reading from Acts tells of the choice of Matthias as the replacement for Judas. Jesus had chosen twelve apostles to be the nucleus of the new Israel (the Church). Just as the Jews traced their roots back to the twelve sons of Jacob, so the new Israel is rooted in the twelve apostles. This explains why it was so important to choose a substitute for Judas.

In the Gospel we have part of Jesus' solemn prayer at the Last Supper. Here he prays for his disciples whom he is leaving behind to carry on his work.

The Second Reading talks of the centrality of love in the life of a Christian. First of all, there is God's love for us, the proof of which is seen in the fact that he sent his Son to be our Saviour. Then there is our love for one another. Anyone who lives in love lives in God, because God is love.

HOMILY 1   **Jesus' prayer for his disciples**

In the Gospel we have part of Jesus' solemn prayer at the Last Supper. Here he prays for his disciples whom he is leaving behind to carry on his work. Just as Jesus was sent into the world by the Father, so the disciples were being sent into the world by Jesus. They are to bring his word to others. During the Last Supper, knowing that he was soon to leave them, Jesus prayed to his heavenly Father for them. In praying for them, he also prayed for us. What kind of things did he pray for?

He prayed that they would remain *faithful:* 'Keep those whom you have given me true to your name.' Our task is not to be successful; only to be faithful.

He prayed for *unity* among them: 'May they be one, as you and I are one.' Disunity among the disciples of Jesus is a blight on their witness.

He prayed that they might be *preserved in the truth:* ''May they be consecrated in the truth.' The truth here is the truth that Jesus is the revelation of the unseen God.

And he prayed that they might be *victorious over evil:* 'I do not ask you to remove them from the world, but to protect them from the evil one.' The disciples are being sent to challenge the world to turn from darkness to light. In bearing witness, they must be prepared to suffer the world's hate.

So he prayed for faithfulness, unity, truth, and victory over evil.

He foresaw that life would be difficult for them. But he did not pray that they might be spared trials and sufferings, but that they might remain faithful in spite of them. He did not offer a release from problems but the strength to cope with them.

It is wrong to blame our troubles on God. God is with us in our trials. It is to him we turn in our troubles, for comfort, strength, patience and hope.

This is how Jesus prayed for his apostles, and how we too should pray. We pray not to be spared trials, but that God will help us to cope with whatever trials life sends us.

HOMILY 2   **As long as we love one another**

A man arrived at the gate of heaven where he was met by St Peter and the Devil's Advocate. They both began to examine his record.

'He wasn't a very ambitious person,' said the DA. 'He was far too careless and happy-go-lucky. He could have done a lot better for himself.'

'Yes,' said Peter. 'He could have made a lot of money. But I see here that he was a good neighbour, always ready to give a helping hand.'

'If you ask me,' said the DA, 'he was too generous for his own good. People regarded him as a soft touch, even a bit of a fool.'

'Maybe he was a bit over-generous. And it's true that people did take advantage of him now and then. But that's no sin,' said Peter.

'Oh, he had his sins too,' the DA hastened to add. 'He could blow his fuse from time to time, and when he did, he could use some choice language.'

To which Peter replied, 'But I see that he held no grudges or resentments. He regarded hatred as a kind of poison. Any kind of revenge was anathema to him.'

'But he wasn't a very religious man,' the DA insisted. 'By no stretch of the imagination could he be called a holy man. And surely no one can enter heaven without being holy.'

'True, but what does it mean to be holy?' Peter countered. 'It's clear to me that we are dealing with a man who was incapable of hurting another person, a compassionate man who was scrupulously honest in all his dealings. I'm going to let him in.'

'Wait a minute!' cried the DA. 'I'm not finished. He had other faults which I was coming to.'

'I don't want to hear any more about his faults,' said Peter curtly. 'I'm interested only in one thing: the kind of person he was. He was a loving man. That's what's important. That's enough.'

With that he let him in.

St John tells us that God is love. (Second Reading). It was God who first loved us. God doesn't love us because we are good; God loves us because he is good. And because God loves us, we are to love one another. We show our love for God by loving one another.

It was St Peter who said, 'Love covers a multitude of sins.' When he denied Jesus, Jesus didn't cut him off. He went on loving him. And what did he ask of Peter in return? 'Take care of my sheep.' In other words, to prove his love by caring for his brothers and sisters in the community.

The Christian life is not a pursuit of virtues leading to the perfection of love, but a process which begins with love and grows to perfection from this beginning. 'The biggest disease in the world today is lack of love' (Mother Teresa). Love is everything. Love demands the best of us and brings out the best in us.

HOMILY 3   **Choosing a replacement for Judas**

The American writer, Tobias Wolff, tells how when he was in the army he had two friends. One of them became a thief and was thrown out of the army. The other deserted. And Wolff reflects:

> L. was thrown out of the army for being a thief. It must seem unbeliev-
> able that this happened to him, unbelievable and unfair. He didn't set
> out to become a thief. And H. didn't set out to be a deserter. Nor did I
> set out to be what I am, either – a conscientious man, a responsible
> man, maybe even what you'd call a good man – I hope so.

The writer's concern is to show how a bad person is made out of human material that might have become something else.

The First Reading is very much concerned with two apostles – Peter
and Judas. Both were chosen by Jesus, yet how different were their fates.

I'm quite sure that Judas didn't set out to become a thief and a traitor.
Nor did God predestine him to play that role. He became a traitor through
the choices he made. Judas too had a dream. But something went wrong.
What exactly that was we'll never know. Like all evil-doers, he is an
enigma. 'We don't understand good, so how can we hope or presume to
understand evil?' (Alan Paton).

But Judas was not a demon. He was made from human material that
might have become something very different.

Just how, and at what point, were the seeds sown that would later
cause him to become a traitor? The only thing we can say with confidence is that he didn't suddenly fall from grace. There must have been a
gradual slipping, a gradual dimming of the light, a gradual loss of faith.
The first step then as now was usually of no seeming consequence – just
one of those 'small acts of cowardice' with which all of the terrible things
of the world begin.

But Peter too failed the Lord. However, there is a huge difference between what Peter did and what Judas did. Judas knew what he was doing. His betrayal was a planned thing, and was carried out in a cold,
calculating manner. Peter's denial was not a planned thing. It was a spur
of the moment thing, and was the result of weakness rather than malice.
Besides, he repented.

Few people are bad but many are weak. A person doesn't fall because
he is weak but because he thinks he is strong. Before people attain greatness, they must descend to lowliness. Peter has been called a stumbling
saint. He is a great consolation to us.

In choosing a replacement for Judas the apostolic community realised
they were picking someone who would be a leader in the community.
What qualities did they look for? Basically two.

First of all: faithfulness. He would have to be someone who had been
there from the start – not some recent 'blow-in'. This was an exterior thing,
something they could judge for themselves.

Secondly: integrity of heart. This is an interior thing, something which

God alone can judge. Hence the need for prayer. Matthias was the man they chose.

The Lord calls each of us to be a witness to his resurrection, that is, to prove to the world by the way we live that he is alive. Not just alive in the world, but alive in us. The Holy Spirit will help us to be like Matthias: people of integrity, who follow the Lord through thick and thin.

PRAYER OF THE FAITHFUL

President: Each Pentecost renews the grace of Pentecost in us and in the Church. Therefore, let us pray for the coming of the Holy Spirit.

Response: Come, Holy Spirit.

Reader(s): For the Church: that the Holy Spirit may renew its life. [Pause] Let us pray.

For all rulers and government leaders: that the Holy Spirit may help them to be wise and just. [Pause] Let us pray.

For those who suffer persecution for the name of Christ: that the Holy Spirit may give them strength and courage. [Pause] Let us pray.

For this community: that the Holy Spirit may keep us rooted in faith, hope and love. [Pause] Let us pray.

For our own special needs. [Longer pause] Let us pray.

President: Lord God, dispose us to receive the Holy Spirit, and may his coming breathe new life into us. We ask this through Christ our Lord.

REFLECTION   **The transformation**

As I passed the cherry tree in February,
it had a bare and forlorn look about it.
It contained not a shred of beauty.
In fact, it required no small act of faith
to believe that it was still alive.
I passed the tree again in April.
When I look at it now I could scarcely believe my eyes,
so great was the transformation it had undergone.
It was now decked out in a robe of brilliant blossoms.
From where had all this beauty come?
It had come from within the tree itself.
On looking at it back in February,
when it was still in the grip of winter,
who could have believed that it contained all this?
Sometimes we write off people as having no possibilities.
Every human being is a well of possibilities.
If in some people these possibilities
haven't yet manifested themselves,
all it means is that for them spring hasn't yet come.

Pentecost Sunday

INTRODUCTION AND CONFITEOR

Pentecost saw the birth of a new community, the Church. This is the day the apostles left the upper room, where they had been hiding for fear of the Jews, and went out fearlessly to preach the Gospel to the world. They could not have done this if they had not received 'power from on high', that is, the Holy Spirit. We too need the Holy Spirit in order to live as Christians. [Pause]

Lord Jesus, you send the Holy Spirit to heal the wounds caused by sin and division. Lord, have mercy.

You send the Holy Spirit to bind us together in ties of love. Christ, have mercy.

You send the Holy Spirit to guide us into the fullness of truth. Lord, have mercy .

HEADINGS FOR READINGS

First Reading (Acts 2:1-11). Luke describes the descent of the Holy Spirit on the apostles, and the effect it had on them.

Second Reading (1 Cor 12:3-7.12-13). The Holy Spirit gives different gifts to different people, for the good of the Church, the Body of Christ.

Gospel (Jn 20:19-23). The risen Jesus gives the gift of the Holy Spirit to his disciples and inaugurates the mission of the Church.

SCRIPTURE NOTE

Luke has the giving of the Spirit happening on the feast of Pentecost. Jewish tradition saw Pentecost as the feast of the giving of the Law on Mount Sinai. According to a legend a mighty wind turned to fire and a voice proclaimed the Law. In a further refinement, the fire split into seventy tongues of fire corresponding to the seventy nations of the world: the law was proclaimed, not only to Israel, but to all humankind.

Luke exploits this tradition. He, too, has the mighty wind and tongues of fire coming upon the group of disciples. But for Luke the universal proclamation was not that of the Law, but of the Good News, a proclamation that has undone the sentence of Babel and re-united the scattered nations.

In his Gospel John has the giving of the Spirit happening on Easter Day. However, we must avoid any impression of a two-fold initial solemn bestowal of the Spirit. Luke and John are saying the same thing: the risen Lord gives the gift of the Spirit, and inaugurates the mission of the

Church. That they differ in their dating is due to theological concerns.

A new community is born

Once upon a time a group of powerful people set out to build a tower that would reach to heaven. They assembled architects, masons, and an army of labourers. They brought in a huge supply of the finest granite and cement. The organisers were of one mind and spoke the same language. The plans were drawn up, and the project got underway.

However, there was trouble from the word go. The bosses were interested in one thing only – their own glory. The tower was to be a monument to them. There was jealousy among the architects, each of whom wanted to leave his mark on the tower. There was a rash of strikes. There were numerous accidents.

The workers had bitter quarrels over politics and nationalities. Materials were constantly disappearing. Costs mounted. The banks began to kick up. Sponsors withdrew their support. Mistrust was rampant. The builders no longer spoke the same language. The tower was abandoned.

This is a modern version of the story of the Towel of Babel. The tower is a symbol of man's attempts to create on earth a paradise without any recourse to God. After they had eaten the forbidden fruit, God sent forth the man and the woman from Paradise. But what did they do? They undertook to build a Paradise of their own, from which they endeavoured to banish God. But what kind of Paradise is it?

The effort is still going on. We have massive highways, supersonic planes, nuclear power stations, manned space flights. Yet we cannot live at peace with one another.

Pentecost is meant to be a reversal of what happened at Babel. We have a group of people who came together, ordinary people with little faith in their own abilities, but great faith in God. They set out to build a 'tower' of a different kind. This tower took the form of a new community, a spiritual stairway to heaven.

On Pentecost Day the apostles set out to build this new community. They spoke a new language – the language of love and co-operation, a language all people of good will understand. It shines in the face and is felt in the clasp of a hand.

Today is the anniversary of this great happening. It is the birthday of the Church, the community of the followers of Jesus. On this day, thanks to the coming of the Holy Spirit, the infant Church took its first steps. It is made up not of saints but of sinners. Down the ages it has had its share of problems and setbacks. But it is still being built.

Part of it is assembled here today. We assemble here not as rivals but as friends. Factors which normally divide people – such as class, colour, age, wealth – count for nothing here. Here we are one family under God.

At Pentecost God reversed the disaster of Babel which divided and confused the unity of the human family. The Holy Spirit makes known to all peoples the one true God, and so creates from the many languages of people one voice to profess one faith.

This is the wonderful thing that began on Pentecost Sunday. We not only find shelter in this tower, but are also builders of it.

HOMILY 2 **Birthday gifts**

Americans are notoriously extravagant when it comes to birthday celebrations. Even though it was only his second birthday, Simon got over twenty presents. When the time came for him to open them, he sat on the floor and began to tear off the fancy wrappings. Once he had opened a gift, he examined it for a few seconds, then threw it aside and went on to the next. Instead of feeling happy for him, one felt sorry for him. He didn't need all those presents. He was being smothered with things when all he really wanted and needed was a little loving.

Pentecost is the birthday of the Church. On that day the apostles received the gifts of the Holy Spirit. But this doesn't mean they were like children receiving birthday gifts. The Holy Spirit didn't give the apostles any *things*. The Spirit did not bring them anything, or give them anything they did not already have.

Take the example of spring. Spring doesn't give anything to the trees. All it does is help to bring out what is already within them in a germinal state. So it was with the apostles. What the Holy Spirit did was awaken them to the gifts that God had already given them. And what resulted was a marvellous sharing of their gifts – for the benefit of the infant Christian community.

Gifts are not given just for our own use. They are meant to be shared (see Second Reading). Often people allow their gifts to lie idle. They may have great potential for goodness, but that potential is not released. To develop a gift calls for patience and self-discipline. But it leads to growth and joy. A tree is never more alive that when teeming with blossoms or with fruit.

The action of the Spirit is mysterious, but it's not magic. What is called for on our part is openness, willingness and effort. Fear, selfishness, laziness, apathy – all these lead to stagnation. What the Holy Spirit did for the apostles was to imbue them with courage and boldness so that they were able to overcome their fear and timidity. From being a group of people, huddled together in fear of each other and of the world at large, they became people with a mission and a message for the world – the Good News of Jesus Christ. After the coming of the Spirit they became living witnesses for Christ.

The Holy Spirit has been given to us too. Just as spring enables the trees to blossom and grow, so the Holy Spirit enables us to be fruitful disciples of the Lord.

HOMILY 3   **Small beginnings**

Great events often begin in small and hidden ways. Things which begin with a splash often peter out, whereas those which begin quietly put down deep roots, grow steadily, and survive to produce fruit, fruit that lasts.

Today the Catholic Church contains close to one billion members – not to mention the millions of Christians belonging to other denominations. They are scattered all over the world, and come from every tribe and race and tongue. Anyone who has been to Lourdes or Rome has got the feeling of belonging to something great. This is a wonderful experience. You feel buoyed up, supported, and carried along.

Today is the birthday of the Church. How simply it all began. The Church was born in frailty and weakness. It had no property, no buildings, no money. Its only resource was people, and there weren't many of those. As they waited for the coming of the Spirit, all the followers of Jesus were able to fit into one room. They knew each other's names. The Church was very small then. But they had spirit, and were united in prayer and charity. The Church is sustained, not by organisational structures and membership statistics, but by its prophets, martyrs and saints.

While it's nice to belong to something big, it can be a drawback too. In fact, people are put off by the large. When an organisation becomes big there is a loss of closeness, of intimacy, and of a sense of belonging. The individual tends to get lost, and may feel like a mere cog in a huge impersonal machine.

The Church should never forget its humble origins. If it does, it will not value the importance of the small. We need to experience the Church as small. We need to belong to a specific community. We need a sense of closeness, and of belonging. A sense of interdependence and of mutual service, such as Paul talks about (Second Reading).

In this gathering, in this very church, this very day, we have all we need to experience what the apostles experienced. Though we have no pomp or grandeur, we have the essentials. Here the Church is stripped down to essentials. Here we have the simplicity of the Gospel – a group of disciples listening to the Word of God and receiving the broken bread in memory of Jesus. And, of course, we have the Holy Spirit. It is the Holy Spirit who binds us together and helps us to witness to Christ in the world.

PRAYER OF THE FAITHFUL

President: Let us pray that the Holy Spirit may descend on us, on our

Church, and on our world.

Response: Spirit of the living God, fall afresh on us.

Reader(s): For the Christian community: that the Holy Spirit may bless it with the gifts of unity and peace. [Pause] Let us pray.

For the world community: that it may enjoy the gifts of freedom, justice, and peace. [Pause] Let us pray.

For those who have cut themselves off from the Church. [Pause] Let us pray.

For all gathered here: that with the help of the Holy Spirit our lives may bear witness to the faith we profess with our lips. [Pause] Let us pray.

For our own special needs. [Longer pause] Let us pray.

President: God of power and love, may the Holy Spirit enlighten our minds, purify our hearts, and strengthen our wills, so that we may give effective witness to our Christian faith. We ask this through Christ our Lord.

REFLECTION **Be guided by the Spirit of God**

Do not let yourselves be guided
by the spirit of self-indulgence.
Look at the legacy self-indulgence produces:
bad temper, fighting, jealousy, cruelty, meanness,
revenge, fornication, idolatry, and drunkenness.
These are ugly things, and make life miserable.
Rather, let yourself be guided by the Spirit of God.
Look at the legacy the Spirit brings:
love, joy, peace, patience, kindness,
goodness, faithfulness, gentleness and self-control.
These are beautiful things, and make life joyful.
They are a foretaste of the joy of heaven.
Spirit of the living God, fall afresh on us.

FEASTS OF THE LORD

'The strong name of the Trinity ... '
OISÍN KELLY

Trinity Sunday

We are celebrating the feast of the Blessed Trinity. We begin and end the Eucharist with the names of the Father, the Son, and the Spirit on our lips. The Trinity is a mystery to be celebrated with childlike love and trust. Our celebration of the Eucharist should deepen our relationship with the Blessed Trinity. [Pause]

Lord Jesus, you have revealed the Father to us as a God of love. Lord, have mercy.

You yourself have become a Brother to us. Christ, have mercy.

You have sent the Holy Spirit to be our Counsellor. Lord, have mercy.

HEADINGS FOR READINGS

First Reading (Deut 4:32-34.39-40). Moses reminds the people of the close and loving relationship God established with them, and of the obligations and blessings that flow from such a relationship.

Second Reading (Rom 8:14-17). Through the in-dwelling of the Holy Spirit, we have become children of God and co-heirs with Christ his Son.

Gospel (Mt 28:16-20). In his last appearance to his apostles, Jesus commissions them to preach the Gospel to all peoples, and promises to be with them to the end of time.

SCRIPTURE NOTE

The First Reading talks about the power and glory of God, who nonetheless, entered into a close and loving relationship with his people, Israel, and of the obligations and blessings that flow from such a relationship. This reading stresses the oneness of God.

In the Second Reading this relationship is taken deeper; we are not just members of God's people, but members of God's family. We are God's children. The Holy Spirit dwells within us and has made us co-heirs with the Son. This reading makes clear reference to the three persons in God.

The Gospel also makes reference to the three persons of the Blessed Trinity. Jesus, who has total power over the whole universe, now empowers his apostles to preach the Gospel to the whole world. The all-powerful Son of God promises to be with them (and by implication with us) until the end of time. The mission of the Church is to help all people to know the Father, the Son, and the Holy Spirit.

HOMILY 1   **I will be with you always**

Sometimes all a carer can do for someone who is suffering is just to be present. But this can be vital because it provides the sufferer with a steady companionship. To know that there is someone there who cares, makes the world of difference. It saves the sufferer from the feeling of being abandoned.

Jesus commissioned his apostles to preach the Gospel to all nations, saying that he would be with them always. That's all he promised them. Simply, 'I'll be with you always … to the end of time.' There were no other assurances. Just, 'Trust in me. I'll be with you always.'

But this was the most important assurance he could have given them. Even though it didn't guarantee them a trouble-free life, or even success; they knew that as long as Jesus was with them, they would have the courage and strength to face whatever difficulties lay ahead.

A sense of the presence of Jesus with us doesn't change the world for us, but it can give us the courage to face it. We don't ask God to change the world to make life easier for us. We ask him only to assure us that he will be with us as we face some difficult situation. God's closeness shields us against a sense of abandonment and despair.

The *Credo* of the righteous in biblical tradition is their unswerving belief in God's presence with them. God never abandons the upright, but his reward is in the life-to-come.

Down the ages, the followers of Jesus haven't always behaved as Christians should. There have been bitter quarrels among them, with the result that today we have not one Christian Church, but several Christian Churches. Yet, in spite of the failings of his followers, and many terrible persecutions, the Gospel has come down to us across two thousand years. The explanation for this surely lies in the promise of Jesus: 'I will be with you always, to the very end of time.'

God is always with us. But we are not always with God. Our busy lives cause us to get disconnected from God. When get disconnected from God, an enormous loss occurs. We should deliberately cultivate a sense of the presence of God, and nourish it through prayer.

God is with us as Father, Son and Holy Spirit. And when we are with God we are also with one another.

> When you are with everyone but me, you are with no one. When you are with no one but me, you are with everyone (Rumi).

HOMILY 2   **Belief in God**

The following prayer was found on the body of a young soldier, killed in action during World War I.

> Look, God, I've never spoken to you before, but now I just want to say 'hello'. They told me you didn't exist, and like a fool I believed them. But last night I looked up at the sky from a shell hole. When I saw the beauty of the stars, and thought how big the universe is, I knew they

were telling me a lie.

I wonder if you will shake hands with me when we meet? Somehow I feel you will understand all my failures. Strange how I had to come to this horrible place to get to know you. What was I doing before this?

There isn't much more to say, but I'm sure glad I got to know you today. I feel the zero hour will soon be here. This is going to be a horrible fight. Who knows but I may come to your house tonight.

I'm crying! Fancy me crying! I never thought this could happen to me. I have to go now. Strange, since I met you, I'm no longer afraid to die.

It was sad that the young soldier got to know God so late. But better late than never, as they say. When we allow ourselves to get disconnected from God, an enormous loss occurs. The author, Salman Rushdie, said, 'When I was young, I was religious in an unthinking way. Now I am not, but I am conscious of a space where God was.'

When people get disconnected from God the fault does not lie with God. The First Reading shows how God entered into a close and loving relationship with his people. In the Second Reading this relationship becomes even more intimate. We are not just members of God's people; we are his children, members of his family. While this kinship carries obligations, the blessings that flow from it are enormous. We are co-heirs with the Son to the kingdom of heaven.

It's lonely not knowing God. People seek security in wealth, possessions, connections, and so on. But God is the ultimate refuge. Those who surrender to God, begin to taste the peace that passes all understanding. Human beings cannot be happy unless they are virtuous, and they can't be virtuous without God.

Jesus has lifted the veil on the mystery of God. We are no longer far away. We have been brought into the family of God. We have a Father who cares about us, a Brother who died for us, and a Comforter who guides us along the path of life eternal.

HOMILY 3   **A window into the beyond**

A man was confined to a prison cell. His only view of the outside world was through a small window high up on the wall. At first he hated his confinement, and despised the miserable view he had of the outside world, which was the only world he believed in.

But time passed, and that little window became his friend. True, it offered only tiny morsels of life - a wisp of cloud, a free-flying bird, a passing plane, a falling leaf, a raindrop, a snowflake ... But he realised that this was not such a bad thing. It forced him to concentrate on the particular, and to make much of little. He was amazed at discovering how much life there can be in a small sample. 'Through a chink too wide there comes in no wonder' (Patrick Kavanagh).

At times the view from the window was shallow and opaque. The world seemed to end at the window. But at other times the window opened onto a blue and empty sky. Then it gave access to infinity, and he felt awakening within him transcendent longings he never knew were there. Thus, the little window helped him to appreciate the things of heaven as well as the things of earth.

Eventually he was released. Of course he gained by being released. Now everything was available to him. But there was a tendency to see everything in general and nothing in particular. And he lost too. In the cell he had a transcendent dimension to his life. The 'beyond' was very important to him. He grew to love the feeling that there was another world greater by far than this one. Now he feared that this feeling, this longing, submerged by triviality, would go back to sleep, or die of neglect.

Faith provides us with a window into the beyond. It gives us access to another world – the world of the eternal, the world of God. But our pre-occupation with the here-and-now can deprive us of 'the beyond', can draw a curtain over the window. However, though we may bury our transcendent longings we can't extinguish them.

When we allow ourselves to get disconnected from God, an enormous loss occurs. The author, Salman Rushdie, said, 'When I was young, I was religious in an unthinking way. Now I am not, but I am conscious of a space where God was.'

For us too there is a desire to possess something beyond the world we know, beyond ourselves, even beyond our power of imagining. This is where our faith comes in.

God is Father, Son and Holy Spirit. In God the Father we have a Father who cares deeply about us. In Jesus we have a Brother who died for us, and who has promised to remain with us always. And in the Holy Spirit, we have a Comforter, who guides us to the kingdom of eternity.

PRAYER OF THE FAITHFUL

President: The Lord looks lovingly on those who revere him and who hope in his love. Our prayers are an expression of our trust in his love.

Response: Lord, hear us in your love.

Reader(s): For all Christians: that they may be effective witnesses to the love of God. [Pause] Let us pray to the Lord.

For all rulers: that God may grant them wisdom in their efforts to make the world a better place for everyone. [Pause] Let us pray to the Lord.

For those who have no belief in God: that they may discover signs of his love in their lives. [Pause] Let us pray to the Lord.

For ourselves: that we may always have a sense of the presence of God with us in good times and in bad. [Pause] Let us pray to the Lord.

For our own special needs. [Longer pause] Let us pray to the Lord.

President: Father, source of all life, be our guide when we stray, our strength when we are weak, and our comforter when we grow discouraged. We ask this through your Son, our Lord Jesus Christ, who lives and reigns with you and the Holy Spirit, one God for ever and ever.

PRAYER/REFLECTION

O Great Spirit, whose voice I hear in the winds.
and whose breath gives life to the world, hear me.
I come to you as one of your many children.
I am small and weak; I need your strength and your wisdom.
Make my eyes ever behold the red and purple sunset.
Make my hands respect the things you have made,
and my ears sharp to hear your voice.
Make me wise so that I may know
the things you have taught your children,
the lessons you have hidden in every leaf and rock.
Make me strong, so that I may not be superior to other people, but
    able to fight my greatest enemy, which is myself.
Make me ever ready to come to you with straight eyes,
so that when life fades as the fading sunset,
my spirit may come to you without shame.

Prayer of a native American

The Body and Blood of Christ

INTRODUCTION AND CONFITEOR

This is the feast of *Corpus Christi* - the Body of Christ. St Paul continually reminds us that we are the Body of Christ. When we gather here the Body of Christ becomes visible. As we prepare to celebrate the Eucharist, we call to mind how important it is that we should be reconciled with one another. [Pause]

We ask God's forgiveness for our sins and the grace to be reconciled with one another.

Lord Jesus, you reconcile us to one another and to the Father. Lord, have mercy.

You heal the wounds of sin and division. Christ, have mercy.

You plead for us at the right hand of the Father. Lord, have mercy.

HEADINGS FOR READINGS

First Reading (Ex 24:3-8). This reading describes the solemn ratification by Moses and the people of the covenant God made with them on Mount Sinai.

Second Reading (Heb 9:11-15). Through the redeeming work of Christ, God has entered into a new and eternal covenant with his people.

Gospel (Mk 14:12-16.22-26). This describes the preparation and the celebration of the Passover meal Jesus ate with his disciples the night before he died.

SCRIPTURE NOTE

The theme of covenant dominates all three readings. The reading from Exodus describes the ratification of the Sinai covenant between God and Israel. The covenant was sealed with the blood of animals. Blood is a symbol of life which belongs exclusively to God. The sprinkling of the people with blood symbolises the fact that God is sharing his life with them.

Jesus established a new covenant. Like the old covenant, it too was sealed with blood, except now it is not the blood of animals but his own blood. A new rite (the Eucharist) was instituted which would be a perpetual reminder of the intimate bond that now exists between God and his people. In the Eucharist Jesus shares his life with us.

By the sacrificial death of Christ, the supreme high priest, God has entered into a new and eternal covenant with his people (Second Reading).

HOMILY 1   **The new covenant**

After the story of creation, the story of God's covenant with Abraham is the key moment in the Old Testament. The story of our redemption begins here. From this point on the Bible becomes the story of God's relationship with his people. It is summed up in a formula which is repeated many times in the Old Testament: 'You shall be my people, and I will be your God'

A covenant is not like the relationship which exists between trading partners – that is strictly a business arrangement. A covenant is more like that which exists between a husband and wife. In fact, this is exactly how some of the prophets described it: they compared the covenant between God and his people to a marriage relationship. For his part, God is always faithful; his love is unchanging. Sadly, the people weren't always faithful.

In order to love and be loved, God has to give us freedom to choose. The covenant between God and humanity has to be more than a matter of an almighty God laying down the Law. In that case God would have our obedience but not our love. It has to be an agreement freely entered into between two free parties.

In today's First Reading we see how Moses ratified the covenant before the people entered the promised land. But the people did not keep the covenant. They fell into idolatry. Even then God did not abandon them. Again and again he offered a covenant to them, and through the prophets taught them to hope for salvation.

And in the fullness of time God sent his Son to be our Saviour. Through him God established a new and everlasting covenant with us. Jesus sealed the covenant anew in his own blood. Jesus is the head of the new People of God. The land to which he is leading us is not some piece of earthly land, but the land of eternal life. Through him we have a closer bond than ever with God. We are not just God's people; we are God's sons and daughters; we are God's family.

In and through Christ, God has formed a bond with us, a bond that can never be broken. This is what we are celebrating when we celebrate the Eucharist. The Eucharist is a perpetual reminder of the intimate bond we enjoy with God, thanks to the saving death of Jesus.

As a community we are in covenant with a God who is always faithful to us. We are invited to live in a way that is consistent with such a relationship. We are not called to be successful, only to be faithful.

HOMILY 2   **Retelling the story**

On a hill near Cape Town, South Africa, just below the famed Table Mountain, a gun is fired every day at noon. The hill is known as Signal Hill. The firing of the gun once served a beautiful purpose. It signalled that a ship, on its way to or from India, had arrived in the harbour with a cargo of goods, and was in need of supplies of food and fresh water. A beautiful exchange resulted. There was receiving and giving.

But that was a long time ago. The purpose no longer exists. Yet the gun is still fired dutifully every day. However, the firing is now little more than an empty ritual. Once it had a beautiful meaning. Now the meaning has gone out of it. Most of the local people ignore it. Visitors are told, 'If you hear a loud bang at mid-day, don't worry. It's only the gun going off.'

However the ritual still has one thing going for it. Most people know the story behind it. If that story were to be lost, then the ritual would become poorer still.

The Eucharist celebrates a wonderful event – the gift which Jesus made of his life on our behalf. Every time we celebrate the Eucharist we tell that story again. But like anything that is repeated over and over again, there is a danger that it may become just a ritual.

In the Eucharist Jesus nourishes us with the bread of life. But it's not meant to be one-way traffic. Having received from Jesus, we are expected to give something in return – not to him but to one another. Often the Eucharist doesn't produce the effect it is meant to produce – unselfish giving of oneself in the service of others.

We keep giving out the bread and the cup, 'This is my body, given for you ... This is my blood, poured out for you.' Yet it seems to have little effect on people. We don't see a people who pour out their lives in the service of others. The people who eat the bread and drink the cup every day often are living self-centred lives.

For the Hebrews, remembering was not a mere recalling. It was the making present to each generation of the saving events of the past. In the same way, the Eucharist is no mere making present of Christ's body and blood, but is a proclamation and a memorial of his life-giving death.

The Eucharist is the heart of everything. But it can never be separated from the washing of the feet. The two realities are linked – being in communion with Jesus so that we can be in communion with others.

It would be a pity if the Eucharist became just a ritual, an empty ritual. Jesus gives himself to us here, so that we in our turn may give ourselves to others.

HOMILY 3 ·   **Companions**

It is necessary to be alone sometimes, for the soul requires solitude in order to maintain its individuality. But we couldn't live like that. We'd go mad. The fact is: we are remarkably dependent on one another. We need other people in our lives – for support, affirmation, encouragement, companionship. They nourish and sustain us in a hundred different ways. And of course we nourish them also.

Today people are schooled in individualism with the result that they find community difficult. There is a lot of loneliness in the world today. Many people are crying out for a friend, for a companion, for a sense of belonging.

The word 'companion' is a lovely word. It comes from two Latin words: *cum* which means with, and *panis* which means bread. So a 'companion' literally means someone with whom I share bread. It's not everyone that you enjoy a meal with. Not everyone that you invite in for a cup of tea. There has to be a bond. And that bond is deepened by the sharing of food and drink

When people invite us to their table they offer us more than food. They offer us trust, welcome and friendship. We feel honoured. The talk is as much a part of the fare as the food. Afterwards we feel nourished, not only in body, but also in heart and spirit.

The Eucharist is the meal that we share in the Lord's memory and at his command. By inviting us to partake of the sacred food of the Eucharist, Jesus makes us his companions and friends. And in doing so we ought to become companions and friends to one another. But does this happen?

Nowadays a person could come to Mass in a car, and go away afterwards without making contact with anyone. Can such a person say that he has really and truly been to Mass? We've met God, but have we met our fellow Christians, our neighbours? The two realities are linked – being in communion with Jesus so that we can be in communion with one another.

A person could be broken and no one would know, no one would care. Building community is not that hard. It just takes ordinary friendliness. The first step is to become acquainted.

If we were able to go into the room where Jesus ate the Last Supper with his apostles, we would immediately get that sense of bonding. Here was a group of companions sitting around a table sharing a meal. In our churches sometimes people sit as far apart as possible. Why is this? There seems to be a reluctance to meet each other. And if we don't meet, we can't share with one another. What we give to one another here we get back a hundredfold. But if we give nothing we will get nothing.

We need Christ – that's obvious. But we also need one another. To be a believer, or just a spiritual person, in today's world can be a lonely business. Here is where the community comes in. We are a community of believers whose common faith strengthens the faith of each individual.

The first Christians supported one another. They forgave each other's offences, shared their possessions, and fostered the spirit of community. Sharing creates a bond, and bonding leads to sharing. The Eucharist was at the centre of everything. It was this that bound them together and enabled them to offer a loving service to one another.

PRAYER OF THE FAITHFUL

President: Gathered in love around the table of the Lord, we lay before him our own needs and the needs of the community.

Response: Lord, hear our prayer.

Reader(s): For the Church: that it may be a sign of unity and an instrument of peace in a world torn asunder by war and divisions. [Pause] Let us pray to the Lord.

For government leaders: that God may grant them the gifts of unity, love, and peace. [Pause] Let us pray to the Lord.

For the sick, the lonely, and the unloved: that in their pain they may know God's comforting. [Pause] Let us pray to the Lord.

For this congregation: that as we meet around the Lord's table, he may strengthen our unity and deepen our faith. [Pause] Let us pray to the Lord.

For our departed relatives and friends, who partook of the Eucharist: that they may now enjoy the banquet of eternal life in heaven. [Pause] Let us pray to the Lord.

For our own special needs. [Longer pause] Let us pray to the Lord.

President: Heavenly Father, may our celebration of Christ's farewell meal of love mould us into a caring community. We ask this through the same Christ our Lord.

PRAYER/REFLECTION **Before the Blessed Sacrament**

Outside the church the noisy traffic flows past.
People rush hither and thither.
But I have left that world behind
and I am here before you, Lord.
I do not exclude my brothers and sisters.
I bring them with me,
for I know that they are equally dear to you.
I have nothing. Yet I know that because I have you,
I have everything.
I close my mind and open my heart, and so I am at peace.
Here I experience my true worth, which consists,
not in my possessions or achievements,
but in knowing that I am loved by you.

SUNDAYS OF THE YEAR

Mark the Evangelist
TRADITIONAL

Second Sunday of the Year
GOD'S CALL

In the Gospel we will hear Jesus say to his first two disciples, 'Come and see.' They accepted his invitation and had an encounter with him which changed their lives. Each time we celebrate the Eucharist we have an opportunity to encounter the Lord. Let us prepare ourselves for this encounter. [Pause]

Jesus is the Lamb of God who takes away the sins of the world. Let us confess our sins with humility, confident of his mercy.

HEADINGS FOR READINGS

First Reading (1 Sam 3:3-10.19). The prophet Samuel played a very important role in the history of Israel. Here we have the story of his call by God.

Second Reading (1 Cor 6:13-15.17-20). Paul tells us that our bodies are temples of the Holy Spirit, and we must use them, not for sin, but for the glory of God.

Gospel (Jn 1:35-42). Here we have John's account of the call of the first disciples.

SCRIPTURE NOTE

Even though this is the year of Mark, we begin with a reading from John. The Second Sunday of Ordinary Time respects an old liturgical theme of celebrating different epiphanies or manifestations of Jesus. John shows us a gradual recognition of who Jesus is – through the testimony of John the Baptist and the confession of the first disciples. Here John the Baptist calls Jesus 'the Lamb of God,' and Andrew calls him 'the Messiah'.

The main theme of the readings, however, is that of call and response. In the First Reading we have the call of Samuel, who played a big part in the building up of Israel. His call marked the beginning of a new era. It was through him that Israel got its first kings. This paves the way for the Gospel story of the call of the first disciples – Andrew, John and Peter. The call of Peter is highlighted because of the important role he played in the first community. In the two readings we are dealing with a unique and specific call, what is more commonly called a vocation.

HOMILY 1   **A significant encounter**

During the course of our lives we have lots of encounters with people. Most of these turn out to be of little significance, and are soon forgotten.

You could meet some people every day, but never get close to them.

Surface meets surface. You could talk to some people for hours, even years, without feeling that you had ever revealed your true self to them. You could live for years in the same community as people and never get to know them, or talk about the deeper things of life with them. Some contacts with others throw us back on ourselves poorer than when we left. This is one of the great sadnesses of life.

But other encounters turn out to be of great significance; they enrich our lives and sometimes change them utterly. You may have just one meeting with someone, and an immediate bond is formed. You are able to reveal yourself in a true and clear light. This is one of the most delightful and rewarding things in life.

When a friendship is born there is no tangible change in one's life – just an awareness that one's life is different, and that one's capacity to love and care has miraculously been enlarged without any effort on one's own part.

It is wrong to think that love comes from long companionship and persevering courtship. According to Kahlil Gibran, 'Love is the offspring of spiritual affinity, and unless that affinity is created in a moment, it will not be created in years or even generations.'

Many significant encounters appear to happen by accident. Some people will tell you that this was how they met their marriage partner: the circumstances of that first encounter are never forgotten. Once we come to love or hate someone, we remember almost every detail of that first encounter.

This helps us in understanding the importance of that first meeting between Jesus and three of the men who later became his apostles – Peter, Andrew and John. It's clear that they had a wonderful encounter. Years later when John came to write his Gospel he could remember the exact time of day in which the encounter took place – it was about the tenth hour (four o'clock in the afternoon).

One meeting with Jesus, and they were captivated by him. He gave them as much time as they wanted. They found him warm, friendly, welcoming. They knew they had met a remarkable person, and a rare friendship was born.

They felt totally at peace in his presence. Through their contact with him they began to discover themselves. Because of the kind of person he was, they got a vision of what they themselves might become.

There is a huge difference between power and influence. Those who wield power over us oppress us, trying to turn us into slaves or copies of themselves. Those who exercise influence on us do not try to convert us, or change us, or mould us. They offer us the space in which we can find ourselves and our own way. Jesus didn't exercise power over his disciples. But he had a profound influence on them. That encounter changed forever the lives of Peter, Andrew and John.

We can't encounter Jesus in the flesh. But we can encounter him spiritually in faith as a Friend, a Brother, and a Saviour. Not to know Jesus is not to have discovered what Christianity is about. Christianity involves a warm, close relationship with Jesus.

Jesus is for ever passing by. He is always available to those who are sincerely looking for him. But he never forces himself on anyone. To those who are interested in knowing more, he says what he said to John and Andrew: 'Come and see.'

Of course it is not a once-and-for-all encounter, but a growing relationship with him that we are talking about.

HOMILY 2   God's call

Samuel had been born in response to a mother's prayer. To show her thankfulness, his mother dedicated him to the Lord. He had been brought up by the priest Eli at the sanctuary of Shiloh.

Then one day he heard a voice calling him. Even though it is described as being an outside voice, it may well have been inside himself. Voices can be very dangerous. People have done dreadful things while claiming that a voice told them to do them. Hence, the need for discernment. The youthful Samuel didn't know what to make of the voice. So he sought the guidance of the elderly Eli.

Eventually, convinced that it truly was the voice of God that was calling him, Samuel responded, 'Speak, Lord, your servant is listening.' That was how he received the call to be a prophet. He played a big part in the building up of Israel. He was the instrument through whom Israel got its first kings.

In the Gospel we have St John's version of the call of Jesus' first disciples – Andrew, John and Peter. The call of Peter is highlighted because he had an important role in the first community. Their call came about in a much more down-to-earth way. It came through John the Baptist and the invitation of Jesus himself.

Who knows in what way a person's fate (call) makes itself heard. We might conclude from the story of Samuel's call that we must hear God's voice calling clearly if we are supposed to do a particular thing. But it's obvious that choosing a vocation depends on many things.

In the two readings we are dealing with a unique and specific call, what is more commonly called a vocation. Samuel is being called to the role of prophet, and Andrew and the others to discipleship. The initiative is always with God. The 'call' is always his. And every call demands a response.

Great events often begin very simply. This was how Jesus began his mission. He looked for a little band of kindred souls, and demanded total commitment from them. And got it.

God calls us too, in many ways and at many different levels. He called us into life. Throughout out lives God continues to call us to a life worthy of our dignity as his children. At death God will call us from this life into eternal life.

God's call can take many forms, and be fulfilled in different ways. It is not likely to be as dramatic as was the call of Samuel, or as 'real' as that of the first apostles. Yet God speaks to us in the depths of our heart, calling us to intimacy with himself, and to be his co-workers in the world. Rather than a voice, his call is more a tug at our hearts, which we feel at quiet and reflective moments in our lives. Sometimes this may make itself felt in a very forceful way. But most times it is likely to be as gentle as a breeze.

The call of Samuel and the call of the first disciples are both relevant for our lives. Just as Samuel was called by God to the task of being a prophet, so each of us is called to do some specific work for God in the world. And the call of the disciples applies to us too, because at our baptism we were called to discipleship.

Every vocation is worthy of honour. And every vocation is a call to the fullness of love.

HOMILY 3   **Temples of the Holy Spirit**

No religion takes the body as seriously as does the Christian religion. The body is not seen as the enemy of the spirit, or as a prison of the spirit. Through Christ's birth, life, death and resurrection, the human body has become part of the life of God. There is no place in Christianity for contempt of the body. But neither is there a place for worship of the body.

We are God's creatures. Our body is the work of God. That is reason enough for respecting it and caring for it. But St Paul gives us a further and deeper reason for respecting the body. He says, 'Your body is the temple of the Holy Spirit.'

Today there is a cult of the body, especially in modelling and advertising – a cult of the body apart from the person. It is the body that counts, not the person. And it is always a young and beautiful body. Needless to say, this is not what St Paul is talking about. This is not respect. This is more like exploitation.

Today there is also huge interest in physical fitness and physical health. While this is to be welcomed, it should be kept in perspective. Care of the body shouldn't result in neglect of the soul. Bodily health shouldn't be sought at the expense of health of soul.

The Church respects the body from the beginning of life right to the end, from that of a tiny infant to that of an elderly person. At Baptism it pours water over the body of the child. It anoints it not once but twice. It adorns it with a white robe. At the end of life it again anoints and blesses the body of the Christian. Even when life has gone out of it, it still considers it sacred. The Church buries it in consecrated ground. And when cremation occurs it urges that the ashes be treated with respect.

This is because the Church regards the body as a temple in which the Holy Spirit dwells. Moreover, in the incarnation Jesus took on a body like ours. He lived, suffered, and died in our flesh. And he rose from the dead and was glorified in our flesh. This is another reason for respecting the body: it is destined for eternal glory. 'God will raise up these mortal bodies and make them like his own in glory' (St Paul).

We don't show respect for our bodies by sins of the flesh, or by over-indulgence in food or drink. Having more respect for our bodies would go a long way towards reducing social problems such as addiction, the spread of AIDS, and teen-age pregnancies.

Once in a small town in Poland a young boy stood watching a gypsy as he drank from a well in the town square. After drinking, the man stood there, gazing down into the well, as though looking at someone. He was a giant of a man but had a friendly face. So the boy approached him and asked, 'Who lives down there?'

'God does,' answered the gypsy.

'Can I see him?'

'Sure you can,' said the gypsy.

Then he took the boy into his arms, lifting him up so that he could see down into the well. All the boy could see, however, was his own reflection in the water.

'But that's only me,' he cried in disappointment. 'All I see is me.'

'Ah,' replied the gypsy, 'now you know where God lives. He lives in you.'

ANOTHER STORY

Sr Sheila, a member of the Sisters of Charity of the Incarnate Word, is based in Houston, Texas. She is involved in a beautiful but demanding ministry. She works in a hospice. She says she loves her ministry. And if you watch her in action you can easily believe this. How did she come to this ministry?

She says she felt called to it from an early age. Indeed, the first stirrings of her vocation came at the age of twelve. Confined to bed in the local district hospital (in Co. Kerry), she had lots of time to consider the 'happenings' around her. There were twelve beds in her ward and people moved in and out at will.

In the corner of the ward was an elderly woman. During the day she never ate the food served, and no one stopped by her bed to visit. At night when the lights dimmed, and the ward became deathly quiet, with a faint, quivering voice she would call, 'Sheila, Sheila, come.' Sheila got out of bed and tiptoed to her bedside. The woman smiled at her and said, 'Water, water.' From a plastic cup with a spout Sheila dropped water in her mouth, pulled the blankets over her shoulders and quietly returned to bed. This was repeated two or three more times during the night. No other words were exchanged.

These visits went on for many nights, and Sheila always returned to bed wondering, 'Whose grandmother is she, and why is she all alone?'

Awakening one morning and doing her usual early checking on the old lady, Sheila was shocked to find only starched white linens on her bed. Her name was never mentioned in the ward again. For days Sheila was angry with the nurses and doctors who worked on the ward. She often found herself saying, 'No one should die alone like that. She could have called me.'

Two years later, without warning, her dad died. He died on a cold Sunday afternoon in February while trying to get turf for some strangers who came to their door. Her first reaction was, 'At least he was not alone in a hospital bed!' Later she discovered that he had been alone, and in pain. Then she wished he had been some place where at least he could have been given some water, as no one should die alone.

In was in this way that the seeds of her vocation were planted in Sheila's heart, and how she eventually found herself working in hospice care. She says, 'The hospice journey is short in terms of calendar days, six months or less. But being a companion to those who are aware of the shortness of life is truly a privilege. Being at the bedside is being on holy ground. No two deaths are alike. The goal of the hospice is to make the body sufficiently comfortable so that the works of living and dying can happen.'

PRAYER OF THE FAITHFUL

President: Let us pray that as individuals and as a Church we may be open to the call of God.

Response: Lord, graciously hear us.

Reader(s): For the Church: that it may enable people to hear the call of God and help them to answer it with generosity. [Pause] Lord, hear us.

For Christians: that they may always be conscious of the call they received in baptism to be disciples of Christ. [Pause] Lord, hear us.

For our civil leaders: that they may promote justice and unity in society. [Pause] Lord, hear us.

For those who have received the call to serve God in the priesthood and/or religious life. [Pause] Lord, hear us.

For all gathered here: that we may deepen our own relationship with Christ through daily prayer and the living out of his commandment of love. [Pause] Lord, hear us.

For those for whom Christ is only a name: that they may get to know and encounter him in us his followers. [Pause] Lord, hear us.

For ourselves: that we may respect our bodies as temples of the Holy Spirit. [Pause] Lord, hear us.

For our own special needs: that God may grant our prayers. [Longer pause] Lord, hear us.

President: God of grace, grant that the Lord Jesus may not walk ahead of us, we may not follow; nor walk behind us, we may not lead; but may just walk beside us and be our friend. We make this and all our prayers through the same Christ our Lord.

REFLECTION   **God's call**

> God's call is mysterious;
> it comes in the darkness of faith.
> It is so fine, so subtle,
> that it is only with the deepest silence within us
> that we can hear it.
> And yet nothing is surer or stronger,
> nothing is so decisive and overpowering,
> as that call.
> This call is uninterrupted:
> God is always calling us.
>   *Carlo Carretto*

Third Sunday of the Year
REPENT AND BELIEVE THE GOOD NEWS

INTRODUCTION AND CONFITEOR

Jesus began his preaching with a call to repentance. We begin each Mass with a similar call: we are asked to call to mind our sins and to repent of them. Let us do that now. [Pause]

Jesus also announced the good news of God's forgiveness.

Lord Jesus, you came to heal the contrite. Lord, have mercy.

You came to call sinners to repentance. Christ, have mercy.

You plead for us at the right hand of the Father. Lord, have mercy.

HEADINGS FOR READINGS

First Reading (Jon 3:1-5.10). The preaching of Jonah met with an immediate response in the pagan city of Nineveh.

Second Reading (1 Cor 7:29-31). Believing that the return of the Lord was imminent, Paul counsels an attitude of detachment from the things of this world.

Gospel (Mk 1:14-20). Jesus begins to preach and calls his first disciples.

SCRIPTURE NOTE

The first half of Mark's Gospel (1:1–8:26) describes Jesus' ministry of healing and preaching in Galilee.

Jesus begins his preaching by calling on people to repent and embrace the Good News. For Mark, 'believe in the Gospel' meant 'believe in the good news of salvation through Jesus Christ.'

Repentance is one of the main themes of the readings. The First Reading relates how the preaching of Jonah met with an immediate response in the pagan city of Nineveh. The story shows the possibility of a heathen city repenting and turning to God. It also shows the mercy and forgiveness of God.

If the Ninevites responded so fully to the preaching of Jonah, how much more fully should we respond to the preaching of Jesus. The Gospel shows the prompt response of the first disciples to his call to follow him.

Even though we can't share Paul's belief that the Second Coming of Christ is imminent, he still has an important message for us, namely, that this world is not the be-all and the end-all. We are destined for the next world. This should profoundly affect the way we live in this world.

HOMILY 1   **The meaning of repentance**

Jesus began his public mission with the call: 'Repent, and believe the Good News.' Who was this call to repentance directed to? While it was directed to sinners in the first place, it was in fact directed at everyone, even the good.

Jesus had more trouble with good people than with sinners. Why? The hardest people of all to convert are the good, because they don't see any need of conversion. It's hard enough to get those who are ill to go to the doctor, but try getting those who are convinced they are well to go! Sinners who openly admitted they were sinners didn't cause Jesus the same trouble.

To answer the call to repentance one must feel a dissatisfaction with oneself, and have a longing for something better. There must be a sense that something is wrong, or at least that something is missing. The conversion experience begins with the realisation that we are not what we could and should be. This realisation is the first stage of a process, the first step of a journey.

To take on board the call to repentance demands openness, honesty, humility, and above all courage – the courage to put an end to self-deception, and confront a painful reality. The courage to admit one's guilt, ask for forgiveness, and resolve to change. People can become so set in their ways, so sunk in ruts, that it's almost impossible to move them.

Some people can see a better future, and still won't move. They realise that this future can't be achieved in the twinkling of an eye or by means of a magic wand. They realise that the road forward will be long, and the progress slow and painful. The present self can't dwell in the house of the future; only a transformed self can. This is why some people opt to stay as they are.

Repentance is often presented as a harsh, negative and sad thing, as if it merely consisted in feeling guilty about one's sins and doing penance for them. Repentance is a very positive thing. True, to repent is to admit that all is not well with oneself. But it is also to discover something wonderful about oneself, namely, that one has potentialities which one didn't know one had. It means acquiring a new vision, taking a new direction, setting oneself more worthwhile goals, living by better values. In a word, it opens the way to a new life. Understood like this, repentance is exciting, and always leads to joy.

To repent means to be converted. Conversion is the starting point of every spiritual journey, and is a prerequisite for entry into the kingdom of God. The Christian life is a continuous process of conversion.

HOMILY 2   **The call to repentance**

The theme of repentance is one of the main themes of today's readings. We see how the prophet Jonah preached repentance to the pagan city of Nineveh, and met with an immediate and whole-hearted response. And Jesus began his public mission with the call: 'Repent and believe the God News.' Unfortunately, he didn't meet with the same kind of response.

Many find the idea of repentance a disturbing one. To repent means to change one's outlook on life, and to adjust one's actions accordingly. It means a change of heart and a change of life, perhaps even a complete reversal of life. As such it is bound to be painful. That is why people are slow to embrace it, and just want to be left alone.

There is a story from the days when Christianity had just arrived in Rome. The story concerns a young Roman soldier by the name of Livinius who fell in love with a girl who was a Christian. However, she would have nothing to do with him because he was not a Christian. One night he followed her to a secret meeting of the little group of Christians, where, unknown to anyone, he listened to the service.

As he listened to the preaching of St Peter, something happened to him. A new and blessed vision of what life could be like opened up before him. But he knew straight away that if he wished to follow that teaching, he would have to make a bonfire of his old thoughts, habits, goals and character. Then he would have to open himself to a life that was altogether different. We don't know if he loved the girl enough to make such a sea change in his life.

That is an example of conversion – turning away from things that are manifestly evil, such as drunkenness, dishonesty, adultery. But it is only one kind of conversion. There is also a conversion to goodness. Here the change is not necessarily that drastic, or that radical. The change may be from a life that is completely selfish to a more loving and caring life. This kind of change also hurts. Who wants to be shaken out of a life of sensuality, comfort-seeking and self-indulgence?

Repentance is something essentially positive. True, to repent is to admit that all is not well with oneself. But it is also to discover something wonderful about oneself, namely, that one has potentialities which one didn't know one had. It means acquiring a new vision, taking a new direction, setting oneself more worthwhile goals, living by better values. In a word, it means a new life.

The new life cannot be achieved quickly and painlessly, otherwise everybody would opt for it. Rather, it involves a journey and a struggle in which the victory is not achieved completely.

Unlike regret, repentance opens the way to rebirth. Understood like this, repentance is exciting, and always leads to joy. It means that we have heard the Good News and embraced it.

HOMILY 3   **The call to discipleship**

St Mark gives the impression that the call of the first disciples was a very formal event, and one that came out of the blue without any previous knowledge of, or relationship with, Jesus. But St John shows that this was not the case. John makes it clear that their relationship with Jesus passed through a stage of growth and development. People don't just up and follow a complete stranger. If they do they are fools.

It's clear that the four (Simon and Andrew, James and John) had previous contact with Jesus. They probably began by standing in the crowd, listening to him. That would have resulted in admiration, which made them want to get to know him personally. Once they met him, and felt the magnetism of his personality, they were attracted to him. This is what made possible their decision to follow him.

This explains why, when the call finally came, their response was so immediate and complete. They left everything – livelihood, possessions, security, family ties – and devoted themselves exclusively to the following of Jesus. Down the ages many believers have made the same total commitment to Christ. Even though his call 'Follow me' sounds like a command, it was of course not a command but an invitation.

Who were these men? They were fishermen. Fishing was an important occupation. But Jesus called them to an even more important occupation. He offered them not just a new work but a cause to which to dedicate their lives. They knew he wasn't calling them to a life of ease. Quite the contrary. But as fishermen they would have been well acquainted with hardship already.

They understood also that Jesus' call was a call to service of others: 'I will make you fishers of people.' When the leaders of cults call people to follow them, they turn them into their personal slaves. Jesus called the apostles, not to service of himself, but to service of others.

His call meant sacrificing their own plans, ambitions, securities, and so on. It was a dangerous adventure, because they were moving from the known to the unknown. But they also knew that his call offered an opportunity to live a fuller and more worthwhile life. Up to this they had a career. Now they would have a vocation.

A career and a vocation are different though not mutually exclusive. We might express a vocation through a specific career … teacher, nurse, doctor … But a vocation can never be reduced to these activities. It is something deeper. It involves vision, motivation, dedication. A career usually means furthering oneself. But a vocation means serving others.

The fact that they accepted this challenge so whole-heartedly tells us a lot about the kind of men they were. Yet they weren't supermen. They were just ordinary people. No one ever believed in the ordinary people as much as Jesus did. One doesn't have to be an exceptional person to be a disciple of Jesus.

The Lord still calls people today, and the need is just as great today. And there still are those who respond. Some people (like the four apostles) are called to dedicate themselves totally and in a 'professional' way to the following of Christ. But not all Christians are called to follow Christ in this way.

The idea of a call runs counter to the prevailing culture. The thinking today is that we can live an uncalled life – one not referred to any purpose beyond oneself. It's not easy to allow oneself to be chosen. Left to ourselves we tend to follow the line of least resistance. Hence, we need someone to challenge us, who has our best interests at heart, and who will not let us settle for anything less than the best that we are capable of.

What does the following of Christ mean for the ordinary person? It means to be a Christian where you are and in your chosen profession. There are more ways than one of serving Christ and his Gospel. The call in the first instance is not to an *apostolate* but to *discipleship*.

ANOTHER APPROACH   **Who are you working for?**

Peter, Andrew, James and John were ordinary workers (fishermen). Yet they left everything and followed Jesus. It wasn't that they were fed up with fishing – fishing is an important occupation. It was that they knew Jesus was calling them to do something more worthwhile with their lives.

The Lord still calls people today. And there still are those who respond. Some people (like the four apostles) are called to dedicate themselves totally to the following of Christ. But not all Christians are called to follow Christ in this way. What does the following of Christ mean for the ordinary person? It means to be a Christian where you are and in your chosen occupation or profession.

Not many people today do the kind of work they like to do. Instead of choosing their jobs freely, they are forced by economic necessity to work at tasks that fail to satisfy them. 'I do it only because I get paid for it,' is what many say. Such an attitude tends to result in badly done work. On the other hand, those who choose their work because it fulfils a purpose they approve of, and they grow in stature through that work.

A sense of vocation is sadly lacking today. But every work, viewed in its proper perspective, can ennoble us. Every task has two aspects. First, there is our purpose in doing it. And second, there is the work itself. Today the first aspect of working has become paramount, and we tend to ignore the second, so that many workers lead half-lives in their labouring hours.

Work begins when you don't like what you're doing.

But when you take pride in your work it relieves it of much of its drudgery. Some craftsmen get a thrill out of any job they do. They know the satisfaction and feeling of self-respect that comes from a job well done. Work can afford a genuine sense of well-being and increases one's indifference to pleasures that are pleasures in name only.

The thing is to try to link these two things: the joy of doing a good work with the purpose of doing it at all (to earn a living). We play golf to get exercise; but we play the game as well as possible, just for the joy of doing it well.

There is a story about a holy rabbi. In the town where he lived, the houses of the rich stood in an isolated area so that they had to hire men to watch over their property at night. Late one evening as the rabbi was coming home he met a watchman walking up and down.

'For whom are you working?' the rabbi asked.

The man told him and then inquired in his turn, 'And for whom are you working for, Rabbi?'

The words struck the rabbi like a shaft. 'I am not working for anyone just now,' he barely managed to say. Then he walked up and down beside the man for a long time. 'Will you be my servant?' he finally asked. 'I should like to,' the man replied, 'but what would be my duties?' 'To ask me that question every now and then,' said the Rabbi.

It's a question each of us might ask ourselves every now and then: Who or what am I working for?

PRAYER OF THE FAITHFUL

President: Let us pray that God may make his ways known to us and teach us to follow his path.

Response: Lord, hear our prayer.

Reader(s): For all the baptised: that they may live up to their calling to be disciples of Christ in the world. [Pause] Let us pray to the Lord.

For the leaders of governments: that God may give them strength and wisdom so that the nations may live in peace. [Pause] Let us pray to the Lord.

For those who have consecrated their lives to the service of Christ in the priesthood and/or religious life. [Pause] Let us pray to the Lord.

For those in pain: that they may know that God cares for them. [Pause] Let us pray to the Lord.

For each of us here: that, whatever our task in life, we may listen to Christ's call to a deeper and a more authentic life. [Pause] Let us pray to the Lord.

For our own special needs. [Longer pause] Let us pray to the Lord.

President: Lord, in your gentle mercy, guide our wayward hearts, for we know that left to ourselves we cannot do your will. We make our prayers through Christ our Lord.

REFLECTION   **Good news for sinners**

Today we are in danger of being drowned in bad news.
Jesus began his ministry by announcing good news.
What was this good news?
That the kingdom of heaven had come.
The kingdom stands for the fulfilment of the promises,
the fullness of God's blessings,
in short, the new order of things.
Forgiveness is available. Recovery is possible.
God's love is unconditional
and is available to us in Christ.
All we have to do is recognise our need,
and seek his help with humility and sincerity.
Unless we repent we can't hear the good news.

Fourth Sunday of the Year
TEACHING WITH AUTHORITY.

INTRODUCTION AND CONFITEOR

Jesus' words carried great authority with the ordinary people. Why? Because his words had the ring of truth, and people knew he meant them. Jesus' words can change our lives if we act on them. But sometimes we are content merely to listen to them. [Pause]

Lord Jesus, your words guide us when we are in error. Lord, have mercy.

Your words comfort us when we are sad. Christ, have mercy.

Your words inspire us to live good and holy lives. Lord, have mercy.

HEADINGS FOR READINGS

First Reading (Deut 18:15-20). Moses foretells the coming of a prophet who will speak God's word to the people.

Second Reading (1 Cor 7:32-35). Paul urges everyone, but especially those who are celibate, to give their undivided attention to the Lord.

Gospel (Mk 1:21-28). The prophecy of Moses is fulfilled in Jesus.

SCRIPTURE NOTE

Here Mark begins to tell us the kind of things Jesus did in proclaiming the kingdom.

Deuteronomy presents Moses as the ideal prophet (First Reading). The prophet can never speak on his own authority, but speaks on behalf of God. The Jews believed that God would raise up in the last days a prophet like Moses. The early Christians regarded Jesus as the awaited prophet. His teaching was given with authority and confirmed by miracles, the sign that God was with him. In today's Gospel we see how Jesus spoke with authority, and how the ordinary people recognised this.

HOMILY 1   **He taught with authority**

Ralph Waldo Emerson stands as one of the great literary figures of nineteenth century America. A hugely influential lecturer, essayist and poet, he became one of his country's most vital voices. He was a fierce foe of slavery and political corruption. In one of his essays he said something that has great relevance in the light of today's Gospel:

Only so much do I know as I have lived. Instantly we know whose words are loaded with life. I learn immediately from any speaker how much he has lived. One person speaks *from within*, or from experience, as a possessor of the fact; another speaks *from without*, as a spectator, or as acquainted with the facts on the evidence of a third person. It is no use to preach to me from without. I can do that myself.

In today's Gospel we read that Jesus' teaching 'made a deep impression on the people because, unlike the Scribes [the official teachers], he taught them with authority.' Why did Jesus make such an impact on his listeners? Because, in the words of Emerson, 'Jesus spoke always from within, and in a degree that transcended all others. But this is the way it should always be. All people stand continually in the expectation of the appearance of such a teacher.'

In the spiritual life the second-hand is of little worth. Here the only person who speaks with authority is the one who has experienced what is being talked about. There is no authority like the authority of the one who has lived what he is saying.

As soon as Jesus began to teach, the people recognised at once that there was a freshness and a transparency about his teaching. Yet he didn't have the same kind of background as the rabbis of his day. But in a way this was an advantage. Van Gogh said, 'In a way I'm glad I have not learned painting.' There are more ways of learning than from books. There is the great school of life.

What most impressed Jesus' listeners was the authority with which he taught. Yet he held no official position. But one doesn't have to hold an office in order to be able to speak with authority. In fact, sometimes the opposite is nearer the truth. The person in the official position is seen as not being his/her own person. He is forced to toe the party line. Whereas the person who has no such position has the freedom to say it as it is.

At the time of Jesus no Scribe ever expressed an opinion of his own. He would always begin by quoting his authority. He would buttress his statement with quotations from the great legal masters of the past. The last thing he would do was give an independent judgement.

Jesus spoke with his own voice, with his own authority. He didn't justify everything he said by quoting the Bible or some other master. That would only have shown lack of authority.

We must distinguish between authority and influence on the one hand, and power and control on the other. Some of the people with greatest moral authority are quite powerless, and the most influential have no need to control those they influence. One can have all the authority in the world, and still fail as a teacher.

There are certain human beings who possess an unaccountable spiritual superiority. This gives them enormous moral authority. They have this authority, not by virtue of an office they hold, but by virtue of the kind of persons they are. This is the greatest and highest authority of all. It has its roots in the authority of God himself. Without it the holder of an office is a mere functionary, a mere mouthpiece.

Jesus possessed this kind of authority to a degree unequalled by anyone else. Every Christian, irrespective of whether or not he/she holds an office, can and should have some of this kind of authority – the kind that comes from being a person of transparent integrity.

HOMILY 2   **Speaking with authority**

Today we have a glut of words from public figures. But there is a depressing predictability about what they have to say. How few speak with real authority. There is a terrible scepticism at present about the words of people in authority. Their statements of policy may be obeyed, but nobody seriously regards them as having authority.

If many public figures lack credibility, what is it that damages credibility? When the speaker himself doesn't believe what he is saying. That which I do not believe I cannot adequately say, no matter how often I repeat the words.

Then the character of the speaker is very important. If a person's character is flawed, his credibility is seriously undermined. You would find it hard to drink wine out of a rusty or dirty tin.

And when the speaker doesn't live according to his own words. This is perhaps the most damaging thing of all. Emerson put it like this: 'Do not say things. What you are stands over you and thunders so loudly that I cannot hear what you say to the contrary.'

A large portion of the ministry of Jesus was given over to teaching. And his teaching was refreshingly different from that of the official teachers of the day, the Scribes. No Scribe ever expressed an opinion of his own. He would always begin by quoting his authority.

Jesus, on the other hand, spoke with his own voice, and needed no other. He cited no authorities and quoted no experts, yet he spoke with great authority. Nor had he any official position. From where, then, did his authority come? It came from the fact that he spoke the truth. 'One word of truth outweighs the whole world' (Russian proverb).

Besides, his teaching was fresh, direct, and had a transparency about it. Some examples: 'No one can serve two masters ... A city on a hill cannot be hidden ... A camel cannot pass through the eye of a needle ... You can't pluck figs from thistles.'

The teaching of the Scribes failed to nourish the people. The teaching of Jesus nourished the heart and the spirit. Some teachers just provide facts. Others provide vision, inspiration, and meaning.

And of course his authority came from his character, which was such that it compelled people to listen. Then there was the fact that he backed up his words with deeds. Even though St Mark says that 'his teaching made a deep impression on the people,' he doesn't tell us what Jesus said. This seems to suggest that Jesus himself was the sermon.

A man was out walking in the early morning. The sky was clear all over. At a certain point he heard the noise of a jet plane. He stopped to see if he could locate it. In his search he was guided by the sound, which seemed to be coming from directly overhead. That was his mistake. He searched there, but no plane.

Then he saw a trail of vapour in the sky. By following this trail to its origin he found the plane – a tiny silver triangle which was barely visible against the canopy of blue. The plane was away out there in front, whereas the sound was still only overhead. But that sound was loud enough to awaken the dead.

In a manner of speaking, the plane acted first, and spoke later. Ideally this is how it always should be – deeds should precede words. When people who have done something, or are doing something, begin to speak, people listen. Their words carry enormous weight. They have real authority. People may doubt what you say, but they will believe what you do. The weakness of a lot of words arises from the fact that they are not preceded, or accompanied, or even followed by words.

There is nourishment for our lives in the words of Jesus. But it's not enough to listen to them; we have to do them. If we are living by anything other than the truth we are undernourished.

HOMILY 3   **Leave us alone**

As Jesus was preaching in the synagogue at Capernaum, a poor demented man created a scene. He cried out, 'What do want with us, Jesus of Nazareth? Have you come to destroy us?' In effect what the man was saying was, 'Leave me alone! I'm no good. I'm evil. I'm not worthy of love or care.'

It's a cry we hear more than once in the Gospel from people who believed they were possessed by devils. 'Don't meddle with us. Leave us alone. Don't try to change us.' They recognised that change is painful. Whether they were actually possessed by devils we do not know. But what we do know is that they were sick, broken, isolated, unloved people, who had no dignity and whose self-worth was nil.

There are many such people in our world today – in our prisons, in our psychiatric hospitals, and so on. Any of us can be caught in some desperate situation. At least the man in the synagogue didn't try to hide how he was. He came to Jesus. Jesus wasn't put off by his desperate cry. In the cry, 'Leave me alone!' Jesus heard a cry for help. And he cured him.

People find it hard to admit that they can't manage their problems. Pride tells them: I should be able to handle my own problems. Recognition that there is a problem is the first step towards rehabilitation. The acknowledgement of our weakness and need would open the way to recovery. It's the courageous ones that go for counselling.

Psychologists tell us that sometimes people don't really want to be cured. Why is this? Because a cure can be painful – it involves a process which requires a lot of change, and all change is painful. The idea of recovery can even be terrifying.

Often we are afraid to talk about something that is hurting us. We keep it locked up inside us where it festers. We may not say, 'Leave me alone,' but that is what it amounts to: 'You wouldn't know, you couldn't possibly understand.' Unvoiced suffering is more harrowing than suffering that cries aloud.

Shortly after the birth of her son a young mother discovered that he was blind. She called her family together and said, 'I don't want my child to know that he is blind.' She insisted that from that point on everyone should avoid using words such as 'light', 'colour', and 'sight'. The child grew up believing that he was like everyone else until one day a strange girl jumped over the garden wall and used all the forbidden words.

The story symbolises much of our behaviour. We all seek to hide what is strange and painful, and to act as if things are normal. We act as if we had no problems, no abnormalities, no pains, no wounds, no failures. This urge to hide is very powerful, and can be more harmful than what it tries to conceal.

When we have the courage to face our problems, new creative energies became available to us. Fear, shame, and guilt often make us stay in isolation. It is by showing our wounds, by allowing ourselves to touch and be touched that we are healed. It is in our brokenness, our woundedness, that God heals us – if we give him a chance.

ANOTHER STORY

Once a number of orthodox rabbis gathered for a festivity, and each began to boast of his eminent rabbinical ancestors. However, there was one exception – a man by the name of Abram. The son of a simple baker, Abram possessed some of the forthright qualities of a man of the people.

At a certain point each rabbi was asked to hold forth on a text culled from the sayings of one of his distinguished ancestors. One rabbi after another delivered their learned dissertations. At last it came time for Abram to say something. He arose and said, 'My father was a baker. He taught me that only fresh bread was appetising, and that I must avoid stale bread at all costs. This can also apply to teaching.' And with that he sat down.

It certainly applied to the teaching of Jesus. As soon as he began to teach, the people recognised at once that there was a freshness and a transparency about his teaching. Yet he didn't have the same kind of background as the rabbis of his day. But in a way that was an advantage.

PRAYER OF THE FAITHFUL

President: Let us with confidence bring our needs before the Lord, knowing that he will listen to our cries as Jesus listened to the cry of the sick man in the synagogue.

Response: Lord, hear our prayer.

Reader(s): For the Pope and the bishops: that they may preach the Gospel with authority. [Pause] We pray to the Lord.

For all who hold public office: that their deeds may match their words. [Pause] We pray to the Lord.

For the victims of broken promises. [Pause] We pray to the Lord.

For those who are suffering from mental illness, and for those who care for them [Pause] We pray to the Lord.

For all gathered here: that our lives may bear witness to the faith we profess with our lips. [Pause] We pray to the Lord.

For our own special needs. [Longer pause] We pray to the Lord.

President: Lord, grant that what we have said with our lips, we may believe in our hearts, and practise in our lives. We ask this through Christ our Lord.

REFLECTION   **Speaking with authority**

Ideally words should always be preceded by deeds.
When people who have done something
begin to speak, people listen.
Their words carry enormous weight.
They have real authority.
The weakness of a lot of words arises from the fact
that they are not preceded, or accompanied,
or even followed by words.
At the root of innumerable wrongs in our world
is the discrepancy between word and deed.
It is the weakness of Churches, parties, and individuals.
It gives people and institutions split personalities.
Lord, grant that what we have said with our lips,
we may believe with our hearts,
and practise with our lives.

Fifth Sunday of the Year
JESUS' RESPONSE TO SUFFERING

INTRODUCTION AND CONFITEOR

Most of us live very busy lives. As a result we may be spiritually impoverished. Today's Gospel shows us how in the midst of all his work Jesus took time out to pray. The Eucharistic Celebration provides us with a great opportunity to take time out to be with the Lord. [Pause]

Let us now bring before the Lord our concerns, problems, and sins, so that we may receive his forgiveness and help.

Lord, we have sinned against you. *Lord, have mercy.*

Lord, show us your mercy and love. *And grant us your salvation.*

HEADINGS FOR READINGS

First Reading (Job 7:1-4.6-7). Wrestling with the problem of why the innocent should suffer, Job takes a rather pessimistic view of life.

Second Reading (1 Cor 9:16-19.22-23). St Paul tells how he has made himself all things to all people in order to bring them the Good News of salvation.

Gospel (Mk 1:29-39). In the midst of his work of teaching and healing, Jesus finds it necessary to escape to a lonely place to pray.

SCRIPTURE NOTE

The Book of Job confronts the problem of suffering. The common explanation was that suffering was a punishment for sin. But, though Job is a good man, he suffers greatly. His suffering causes him to take a gloomy view of life (First Reading).

This sets the scene for the Gospel. However, what we see in the Gospel is not Jesus' answer to the question 'why suffering?', but his response to actual suffering. He heals the sick and proclaims the good news of salvation. The Gospel also shows the urgency with which he dedicated himself to preaching the Gospel, something we see exemplified also in Paul (Second Reading).

In the midst of his activity Jesus found time to pray in quiet places. It was during these hours of solitude that he maintained and fostered the most important thing in his life – his relationship with the Father. Here lay the secret of his successful ministry.

HOMILY 1   **Response to suffering**

The question of human suffering, especially that of the just, was a big problem in biblical times. This was the problem Job was wrestling with.

Job was a good man yet he suffered terrible tragedies. This resulted in his gloomy view of life.

Suffering is still a big problem. There are lots of people today who could identify with Job. Think of all who suffer from poverty, hunger, sickness, injustice, oppression, tragedy ... In Old Testament times suffering was seen as a punishment from God for sin.

What was Jesus' answer to the problem of suffering? He did not accept the view that suffering was a punishment from God. God does not do evil. God does good. What we see in the Gospel is not so much an answer to the question 'why suffering?', as Jesus' response to actual suffering.

That response was a very practical one – as we see from today's Gospel. Here we see Jesus surrounded by throngs of physically and mentally sick people. And he gives himself to each of them, healing them one by one. He didn't insulate himself against human pain. He made himself totally vulnerable before the wounded and the sick.

Suffering is a lonely condition. Jesus wasn't sentimental about suffering. Nor did he preach resignation as we often do. He did not like to see people suffer. Suffering was one of the evils he came to fight. He had compassion on sufferers and made them well. He cast out the devils of guilt, fear, shame, despair ... that held people bound.

The problem of suffering became an opportunity for Jesus – an opportunity to show what God is like. By the way he gave himself to the sick, he reveals to us the compassion of God in the face of human suffering.

The suffering of others is an opportunity for us too. We may not be able to cure, but it is always within our power to care. And to care is a very healing thing. Just to be with the sufferer, is in itself a very worthwhile thing. But it's no easy thing, because it means that instead of relieving someone's pain, we have to be prepared to share it.

We come to sufferers with empty hands. What can we do for them? We can use those empty hands for comforting. All they ask is that we do not desert them. That we stand our ground at the foot of the cross as Mary did on Calvary. Simply to be there – that in some ways is the hardest thing of all. The one thing the sufferer longs for is in our power to give – human warmth. A person can be healed without being cured.

As regards our own suffering. Suffering is an unavoidable element of the human condition. Nevertheless, the road of suffering is a narrow and dark one. It's a great comfort to us to know that Jesus went down this road, and went down it to the end. It is not the same since he travelled it. A bright light illuminates it. He shows us that though it leads to Calvary, it doesn't end there. It ends at Easter. Thus for Christians suffering becomes an opportunity to share in Christ's Passion in the hope of sharing in his Easter victory.

HOMILY 2   **Taking time out**

Once a man was riding a galloping horse. As the horse and rider thundered past, an old farmer standing by a gate called out,

'Where are you going?'

'Don't ask me, ask the horse,' the man yelled as he flashed by.

The man on horseback stands for the person whose life consists of non-stop activity. Such a person is not free; he is a slave to his work. But his problem goes deeper. He is not in control of his life. It's as if some power has got into him that is driving him along. This is not a good way to live.

People can get so caught up in work that they haven't a minute for themselves. Activity can become a disease. This is a dangerous situation. People can suffer burn-out or breakdown. Generous people are more at risk than selfish people. We need to take care of ourselves. It can't be all out-put and no in-put. Only by paying careful attention to our own physical, emotional, mental and spiritual needs can we remain joyful givers.

Even Jesus needed to take time out for himself, as we see from today's Gospel passage. He was surrounded by the physically and mentally sick. Everybody was clamouring for him. He was in danger of being consumed. Yet in the middle of this hectic scene, we read, 'Early in the morning, he got up and left the house, and went off to a lonely place to pray.' Jesus prayed not only out of a sense of duty but also out of a sense of need.

What did the lonely place do for him? It enabled him to recover lost energy. It helped him to keep focused. But above all, it was during these hours of solitude that he maintained and fostered the most important thing in his life – his relationship with the Father. Here lies the secret of his successful ministry.

The most beneficial prayer of all is just to be in the presence of God, without saying or doing anything. Just to sit in his presence, as one might sit by a fire. This may sound easy, but in practice it's very difficult. Because as soon as we stop, we feel empty, perhaps even useless. Most people get their sense of self-worth from doing. Their value as persons depends on their usefulness. They don't know how to cope with idleness and stillness. The result is that their lives can be shallow and superficial. On the other hand, when we immerse ourselves in the quiet and stillness of God's presence, our projects lose their power over us, and we experience our true worth, which consists not in doing but in being.

The most important way to love God is simply to be in his presence, just taking care of God himself. A lot of people tend to equate love of God with social action. Of course prayer can become a selfish thing. It can be a cop-out and an escape. But so too can work. Work can be a cop-out from prayer, from seeking God. And without prayer it can easily become totally self-directed, self-propelled, rather than inspired by God.

We can lose ourselves in work. But we can also find ourselves in work.

This is why we need a lonely place in our lives. We need to learn from the example of Jesus how to combine action and contemplation. Going away is not escaping, but leads to re-engagement. There is a time to give and a time to receive. For a healthy life we need to take care of both.

HOMILY 3   **A lonely place**

There was a man who was in the habit of going off by himself into a remote wood. One day a friend, curious to know what he was up to, followed him into the wood. When he caught up with him, he found him sitting quietly on a log.

'What are you doing?' he asked the man.

'I'm praying,' came the reply.

'But why come to this remote spot to pray?'

'Because I feel close to God here.'

'But isn't God to be found everywhere, and isn't God the same everywhere?'

'God is, but I am not.'

While it's true that we can find God and pray to God anywhere and everywhere – in the kitchen, in the street, in the car, in the farmyard, in the workshop – still, it's a good idea to have a special place to which we can withdraw from time to time – the shore, the park, the mountains, the church, or wherever.

In such places God somehow seems to be nearer and more friendly. The whole atmosphere seems to be pervaded with the divine presence. God speaks to us in the wind, in the sound of a stream, in the song of a bird, in the beauty of a wild flower, in the very silence.

And in such places we are different too. We are calmer, quieter, more relaxed, and are thus more open to what God is offering us at all times and in all places.

It is very good to have a special spot, a little tabernacle, our own sacred space, from which we exclude everything else. Such a spot is especially helpful for quiet meditation and for talking to God from the heart, person-to-person. Even just to sit in such a special room is a good thing. In your sacred space you not only find God but find yourself. We lose touch with ourselves when we are too busy. It's impossible to see one's face in troubled waters.

Everybody, whether they realise it or not, is in need of such a space. It is absolutely necessary if we want to have an inner life. The further we get into it, the more we will be at peace with whatever happens. Best of all, it helps us to find, or to create, a sacred space within ourselves. We can live from that centre even while we remain in relation to the world.

To be relaxed we need space – our own private space, the place of solitude, where we can really be in touch with our deepest being. If we do not have this, if our space is taken away or violated, if we are under too much pressure, or overwhelmed with things to do, then we risk falling into confusion. This is what Jesus was doing when he rose early and went off to a lonely place to pray.

PRAYER OF THE FAITHFUL

President: God hears the prayers of the humble. Let us now bring our petitions before him in humility and confidence.

Response: Lord, hear us in your love.

Reader(s): For all followers of Christ: that they may realise that, without time for prayer and reflection, their lives are in danger. [Pause] We pray in faith.

For those in authority: that they may promote peace and goodwill among people. [Pause] We pray in faith.

For doctors and nurses and all who work for the sick. [Pause] We pray in faith.

For all in this congregation: that through our own sufferings we may learn to feel the sufferings of others and show them compassion. [Pause] We pray in faith.

For grace to bring our own special needs before God. [Longer pause] We pray in faith.

President: Merciful God, help us to learn from your Son, who shows us your compassion in the face of human suffering, and how to combine action and contemplation. We ask this through the same Christ our Lord.

REFLECTION   **A lonely place**

Jesus often went off to a lonely place to pray.
Yet the same Jesus who prayed in lonely places said,
'When you pray, go into your room,
and pray to your Father in secret.'
This means that the lonely place
is not necessarily a place far away,
or that by 'room' he means four walls
that separate us physically from others.
The room is the room of our innermost heart.
This room is with us at all times.
We should make it a place to which we can go
to find rest and spiritual recovery
when the world is too much with us.
Then we will discovery that the inner room
is not empty after all, but is occupied
by the God of love who dwells in us all.

Sixth Sunday of the Year
CURE OF THE LEPER

INTRODUCTION AND CONFITEOR

In biblical times people did not touch lepers for fear of contagion. Yet Jesus reached out and touched lepers. He still reaches out to us. Let us approach the Lord now, realising that we need his healing touch. [Pause]

Lord, you raise the dead to life in the spirit. Lord, have mercy.

You bring pardon and peace to sinners. Christ, have mercy.

You bring light to those who live in darkness. Lord, have mercy.

HEADINGS FOR READINGS

First Reading (Lev 13:1-2.45-46). Lepers were considered ritually unclean and were compelled to live apart from the community.

Second Reading (1 Cor 10:31-11:1). St Paul urges us never to do anything offensive to anyone but to do everything for the glory of God.

Gospel (Mk 1:40-45). This tells of the cure of a leper by Jesus.

SCRIPTURAL NOTE

Leprosy is the clear theme of the First Reading and the Gospel. In biblical times lepers were treated as pariahs. Leprosy was the ultimate uncleanness. It made the victim an outcast not only socially, but also in the religious sphere.

Jesus broke through all the religious and social taboos and reached out a loving and healing hand to the leper. In this way we see how a Christian community should deal with sinners and people society rejects. Besides, a Christian is one who has been 'cleansed' by Christ in baptism, and who ought to spread the 'good news'.

In the Gospel we have an early instance of what scholars call Mark's 'Messianic Secret,' whereby Jesus seems to hide his identity as the Messiah and Son of God until it is made apparent after his death and resurrection.

HOMILY 1   **The kindness of Jesus**

In biblical times leprosy was believed to be highly contagious. For this reason lepers were forced to live outside the community. They were known as the *untouchables*.

Theirs was a cold, lonely existence. They had said good-bye to home, family, and friends. Once they were somebody in life; now they were nobody. Their life was a living death. People believed they were cursed by God. They considered them to be not only sick but also unclean.

This was the kind of man who approached Jesus. He shouldn't have appeared in public without ringing a bell, or shouting a warning. He ran the risk of being chased away with stones. But he was determined to meet the one man he believed would not reject him.

Jesus saw the leper approaching, and allowed him to come right up to him. Would he or wouldn't he touch the leper? If he did touch him, what would he be saying? If he didn't touch him, what would he be saying? Well, seeing the pitiful state he was in, Jesus took pity on him, and reached out and touched him. It was a symbolic act which no doubt shocked the onlookers. (We've seen the trouble even a simple handshake could cause in Northern Ireland.) By touching the leper Jesus became ritually unclean himself.

Most of us are afraid of the sick and the very poor. We may give a few pennies to a beggar, but we make sure there is no contact between us. Yet we love to be touched ourselves. We feel honoured when someone important shakes hands with us or gives us a pat on the back.

Physical contact is precisely what gives people, especially sick and wounded people, a sense of warmth and joy. By the very act of touching another person we accept that person exactly as he or she is. Jesus touched lepers, sinners, sick people, and the dead.

Imagine how good the leper felt when Jesus touched him. He felt he was a human being after all. His body was horribly wounded by leprosy. But his spirit was even more deeply wounded – by the sense of having been rejected and abandoned by everyone, including God. By touching him Jesus healed his wounded spirit.

Then the leper said, 'Sir, I believe you can cure me if you really want to.'

'Of course I want to,' Jesus replied. And he cured him. Now he was cured in body too, wholly cured.

Kindness is almost as important to a sick person as medicine. When people come out of hospital after an operation or a bout of illness, one of the things they always comment on is how they were treated by the doctors and nurses.

Jesus asked the leper to keep quiet about his cure. But the man broadcast everywhere what Jesus had done for him. And it wasn't just the fact that Jesus had cured him that he spoke about, but the astonishing kindness and respect with which he had treated him.

Jesus reached out a loving and healing hand towards a pariah. He challenges us his followers to reach out to those society rejects today: prisoners, drug addicts, the Travellers, AIDS victims ...

It's amazing what people can do for others. People can rekindle hope, bring back the zest for living, inspire plans for the future, restore self-respect and pride. They can even mirror dimly the infinite charity of God.

HOMILY 2   **Acceptance and rejection**

Leprosy is without doubt a terrible disease to have, but not as terrible as feeling unloved, unwanted, or abandoned. One of the worst things that can happen to a human being is to be rejected. Rejection hurts beyond any other state or emotion. It damages one's self-worth. It makes a person feel worthless. It makes one want to shrivel up or openly rebel. There's an African tribe in which capital punishment consists in being ostracised.

Rejection is devastating for children, the elderly, the handicapped … To a child, abandonment by its parents is equivalent to death. The elderly fear rejection more than all their infirmities together. The deepest wounds of the handicapped are caused, not by their physical or mental limitations, but by the rejection they have known. Those who create (writers, artists, and so on) are painfully vulnerable, no matter what success they've had. Each of us to some extent has felt the pain of rejection.

There are ways of insulating oneself from rejection – risking little, wanting (needing) nothing, avoiding relationships. It seems better to build walls and avoid relationships than to risk suffering rejection. But this is like cutting off our feet so as not to need shoes.

The man who approached Jesus was a reject. As a leper he was forced to live outside the community. People wouldn't even touch him. At that time illness was seen as a punishment for sin. Hence, the leper was considered to have been rejected by God too. The leper's worst suffering was not the leprosy itself, but the pain of being rejected by everyone.

When we reject people we are in effect treating them as 'lepers', even though we may not be conscious of this. We can reject a person in small but subtle ways – by the tone of our voice or even by a look. But pinpricks of rejection can accumulate with serious long-term effects.

The interesting thing is not that Christ cured the leper, but the manner in which he cured him. Excluded and rejected by everybody, lepers were forced to ring a bell to warn people of their approach; nobody would come near them for fear of contamination and of being branded unclean.

But Jesus cut through all of this. He was moved with compassion on seeing the plight of the leper. He allowed the leper to approach him. Then he did the unthinkable. He reached out and touched him. In this way he gave him a sign of welcome, and repaired his sense of being dirty and unworthy, of being nothing but human scrap. Before healing his broken body, he healed his broken self-image.

Jesus accepted the leper just as he was. Acceptance is the answer to rejection. It is one of the loveliest things that can happen to us. When people accept us they give us a feeling that we are worthwhile.

Each of us longs to be accepted for what we are. It is the love and acceptance of others that makes us the unique persons that we are. When we are accepted only for work we do, then we are not unique, for others can do the same work perhaps even better than we can. But when we are accepted for who we are, then we become unique and irreplaceable, and are able to realise our full potential.

This is how Christ accepted the leper, and how he accepts us. And how in our turn we may learn to accept others, and to reach out to those who are suffering the pain of rejection. In our turn we could rekindle hope, bring back the zest for living, in someone else, and thus mirror dimly the infinite compassion of God.

HOMILY 3   **Importance of the small gesture**

Little gestures can give us greater insight into a person's character than the big gestures. The big things show us a person's power. The little ones show us a person's humanity. We have a very good example of this in today's Gospel. It concerns Jesus' gesture of touching the leper before he cured him. Though it was a small thing in itself, in the context it was a very big thing. It is small gestures like that which affirm the dignity and value of people.

Today leprosy is not feared as much as it once was. If those who are infected are treated in time, they can be completely cured, and nobody will know that they have had the disease. In biblical times leprosy was one of the most feared diseases. It was to the people of that time what AIDS is to us today.

Lepers were forbidden to live in the community. This was to protect the community against infection. Lepers were also excluded from religious services because they were considered ritually unclean, as was anybody who came in contact with them. Thus they were social and religious outcasts. They were rejected and despised by people, and believed themselves rejected and despised by God too. If pronounced cured they had to undergo a purification rite before being re-admitted to the community.

Jesus knew all of this. Nevertheless, he cut through the religious and social taboos. He allowed the leper to approach him. Then he did the unthinkable. He reached out and touched him before he cured him. Why did he do what the Law forbade? That touch shows Jesus' great compassion for the outcast, the sinner, and the sufferer.

He touched the leper that he might show that all things are clean to the one who is clean himself. To show that external uncleanness does not defile the clean of heart. He touched him to teach us to despise no one, or regard them as pitiable because of some bodily affliction. He touched the infirmities of people, not so that those infirmities might adhere to him, but that he might drive them from those who were afflicted.

That simple gesture would have meant the world to the leper. The leper's worst suffering was not the leprosy itself, but the pain of being rejected by everyone. In touching him Jesus gave him a sign of welcome, and repaired his sense of being dirty and unworthy, of being nothing but human scrap.

Jesus had this great understanding of, and feeling for, people who were suffering. Oscar Wilde put it like this:

> Jesus understood the leprosy of the leper, the darkness of the blind, the fierce misery of those who live for pleasure, the strange poverty of the rich, the thirst that can lead people to drink from muddy waters.

Jesus stretches our capacity for compassion. He challenges our idea of love. Each of us has a great capacity for love. The pity is that it often goes unused. We have it in our power to reach out to those who are suffering the pain of rejection. We could rekindle hope, bring back the zest for living, in someone else, and thus mirror dimly the infinite compassion of God.

By looking at Jesus we see how a Christian community should deal with sinners and people society rejects. Who are the 'lepers' (the outcasts) of our day? We know how Jesus would have treated them. How do we treat them? And on a personal level, each of us has been 'cleansed' by Christ in baptism, and ought to spread the 'good news'.

PRAYER OF THE FAITHFUL

President: Let us now bring our needs before the Lord who in his great compassion reached out to the leper and healed him.

Response: Lord, graciously hear us.

Reader(s): For the Christian community: that it may be warm and caring towards those whom society rejects. [Pause] Lord, hear us.

For the human family: that God may bind its members in ties of friendship and mutual acceptance. [Pause] Lord, hear us.

For prisoners, drug addicts, and all those who feel the pain of rejection. [Pause] Lord. hear us.

For all gathered here: that the Lord may open our hearts and our eyes to those who suffer so that they need not carry their cross alone. [Pause] Lord. hear us.

For our own special needs. [Longer pause] Lord, hear us.

President: God of love and mercy, you know our weakness. May we reach out with joy to grasp the hand you stretch out to us in Christ, and so walk more readily in your ways. We make this prayer through the same Christ our Lord.

REFLECTION   **Touching**

Many of us are afraid to touch other people.
We give a few pennies to a beggar,

but make sure there is no contact between us,
not even eye-contact.
Jesus didn't stand off or keep his distance.
He wasn't afraid to touch others.
He touched lepers, sinners, sick people,
and even the dead.
Physical contact is precisely what gives people,
especially sick and wounded people,
a sense of warmth and joy.
By the very act of touching another person,
we accept that person exactly as he or she is.
Lord, give us a warm heart and kind hands.

Seventh Sunday of the Year
FORGIVENESS OF SIN

INTRODUCTION AND CONFITEOR

In today's liturgy one message comes through loud and clear, and it's a message we can never hear too often. The message is that God forgives the sins of his people. Each of us need God's forgiveness. Let us now pause to call to mind our sins. [Pause]

Loed Jesus, you pay heed when of the depths we cry to you. Lord, have mercy.

You heal us of all our sins Christ, have mercy.

With you there is mercy and fullness of redemption. Lord, have mercy.

HEADINGS FOR READINGS

First Reading (Is 43:18-19.21-22.24-25). Isaiah tells the people that God will give them a fresh demonstration of his love, and blot out all their sins.

Second Reading (2 Cor 1:18-22). Conscious that he represents Christ, who is fidelity itself, Paul declares that he is a man of his word.

Gospel (Mk 2:1-12). Jesus declares that he has authority to forgive sins, and proves it by curing a paralysed man.

SCRIPTURE NOTE

In 2:1–3:6 Mark tells of five objections raised by the Scribes and Pharisees to what Jesus does and says. We have the first of these today – his claim to have authority to forgive sins.

The main theme of the First Reading and the Gospel is that of forgiveness of sins. Isaiah tells the people that God will give them a fresh demonstration of his love, and blot out all their sins. This wonderful promise is fulfilled in Jesus, who demonstrates that he has authority on earth to forgive sins.

HOMILY 1   **Curing the whole person**

In the olden days in rural Ireland when a person got sick, the priest was the first one sent for. Then maybe the doctor. Nowadays the opposite is more likely. But for Christians, both the doctor and the priest have a role to play in the care of the sick. This is not to imply that the body is the doctor's province, the soul the priest's. To say this would be to condemn both doctor and priest to see but one half of reality.

When the paralysed man arrived in front of him, Jesus saw at once that the man was in need of physical healing. But he saw something else. He saw that he was in need of spiritual healing too. And he decided to begin with that.

He began the cure of the paralytic with the forgiveness of his sins. Why? He wasn't implying that the sins of the paralytic were the cause of his illness. Nor was he suggesting that the man was a greater sinner than any of the others in the room. He was simply stating that like everyone else he too was a sinner. By beginning there, he was saying that sin too is an illness, an illness of the soul. Jesus didn't distinguish rigidly between sickness of the body and sickness of the soul, but took them both as different expressions of the one supreme ailment of humanity.

Many therapists today would agree with the approach of Jesus. Many bodily ills are related to and spring from ills of the soul. Today they talk about 'holistic health'. This means that we have to take into consideration not just the physical side of a person, but also the psychological and the spiritual sides. It was Christ's intention that the whole person should be cared for.

It has been claimed that counselling comes to nothing when people refuse to see their pain as other than a purely physical problem. In therapy the problem is always the whole person, never the symptom alone. Pain affects not just the body, but also the mind, the feelings, and the spirit. What appears, namely, the physical, may only be an outer manifestation of an inner malaise.

As we have seen, Jesus began with the spiritual, saying to the man, 'Your sins are forgiven.' This scandalised the Scribes. But Jesus went on to prove that he had indeed the power to forgive sins by curing the man's physical illness too.

Jesus came to save the whole person, soul and body. So now he said to the paralytic: 'Take up your bed and walk.' And the man left the room on his own feet. He didn't need to be carried any more. Besides, his soul was

[194]

clean and bright and at peace.

Here was a new and mighty deed. The people realised this at once. They were astounded and praised God saying, 'We have never seen anything like this.'

We may not need physical healing at this moment, but we certainly need spiritual healing. This is how the miracle applies to us. Sin can be regarded as a spiritual paralysis which affects us all. It affects our heart – it impairs our ability to love. It affects our will – we are unable to reject evil decisively and commit ourselves once-and-for-all to the good. It affects our spirit – we are unable to live in freedom, hope and joy.

We need the Lord's forgiveness and healing. We need to bring our sins and ills to him in humility and trust. Then he will say to us, 'Your sins are forgiven. Now go and live freely and joyfully as a child of God.' And hearing those words we too will praise God, and walk in the freedom of the children of God.

HOMILY 2   **The forgiveness of sins**

We live in an age of confessions. People are telling their stories, baring their fragile souls, not just privately to psychotherapists, but publicly in books and on radio and television. However, while there are lots of confessions, there are no absolutions – at least none in the name of Christ.

Going to a therapist doesn't relieve people of guilty feelings. Sometimes therapists are too ready to say, 'That's okay, you meant no harm, lots of people do that, you were under pressure, and so on.' People feel sustained by therapists but they do not feel forgiven.

Human forgiveness often comes too cheaply and too easily. God, on the other hand, takes our sins seriously but loves us enough to forgive them. It's as if he says to us, 'What you did matters, and matters very much, but I forgive you for it.'

What people need is a sense of radical forgiveness that simultaneously recognises the sinfulness of what they did and affirms them as people worth caring about. Human beings can't grant that kind of forgiveness; only God can.

Forgiveness is a wonderful thing. While it doesn't condone or excuse, it allows for a clean slate, a fresh start. The forgiven are no longer paralysed by feelings of guilt. They are set free to walk in friendship with God and with the persons they have offended.

Forgiveness was at the heart of Jesus' ministry. And he passed this power on to his apostles when he said to them, 'Whose sins you shall forgive, they are forgiven; whose sins you shall retain, they are retained.' The power to forgive sins in his name is one of the greatest gifts Jesus left to his Church, and is exercised mainly through the Sacrament of Reconciliation (Confession).

Many of us approach Confession with a prepared list of sins. The same sins appear on the list time after time – usually trivial matters for which we have neither sorrow nor purpose of amendment. In Confession we run through the list, hardly hearing what the priest says to us, and find ourselves living no differently afterwards. No attempt is made to get down to the roots of our relationship with God and other people.

We have to distinguish between sin as an event, an act, and sin as a condition. The second is more serious. You may do something very wrong, but that doesn't make you a chronic wrong-doer. There is a big difference between the person who does wrong once or twice, and the person for whom wrong-doing is a way of life. A person may steal once, under pressure of temptation or economic hardship. Or a person may steal regularly, so that it becomes a way of life.

Our sinfulness is not the same as our sins. The first is the disease, the second the symptoms. We are a sinful, fallen people – that is the reality. Hence, we have to go beyond lists of sins. The Sacrament of Reconciliation demands that we search our hearts. Our sins may be an outer manifestation of an inner malaise.

Sin is not something we can throw off once and for all like an old garment. Rather, it is a condition in which we live. We are sinful people, always in need of redemption. What is important is not so much our failures, as our struggle for goodness. The purpose of a good life is not to win the battle, but to wage it unceasingly.

The Sacrament of Reconciliation is not an impersonal laundering service. It is an encounter with Christ who draws us forward to walk in the freedom of the children of God.

The paralytic got up, took up his mat, and walked away. When we are forgiven, we are set free from our past, and are able to move forward again, shouldering our own burdens and responsibilities.

HOMILY 3   **Why confess to a priest?**

God's forgiveness is available through the ministry of any priest, a man who himself bears the scars of sin and needs forgiveness. By sharing in the power of Christ every priest becomes a wounded healer. However, it is not the priest who forgives, but Christ acting through him.

For many the problem arises: Why confess to a priest and not directly to God? From God's point of view the answer is simple: there is no reason. We have to look to ourselves to find the reasons. There's more to it that simple forgiveness.

Confession is good for the soul. The unspoken evil a person has done is a worm eating his heart away. We have a need to talk about what is worrying us. In Confession we can say absolutely everything about ourselves and know it will never be betrayed. Thus it fulfils a deep human need to open ourselves. We also may need guidance. Confession meets that need too.

To go a little deeper. We have a need to externalise – with words, signs, and gestures – what is in our minds and heart. We need a tangible expression of God's forgiveness. We need to see, hear, and feel forgiveness – not just think about it. We need other human beings to help us externalise what is within, and open our hearts before God. They help us to experience and proclaim the mercy of God in our lives.

We don't go directly to God about the ills of the body. So why go directly to him about the ills of the soul? It's so easy not to go to Confession at all. It's easy to deceive ourselves, to let ourselves off the hook, to keep putting off the day of reckoning, the day when we draw the line and add up the bill. Confession means facing the reality about ourselves.

But the mere fact of going to Confession isn't enough. Grown people can make the same Confession they made at the age of ten or twelve. People often refuse to see beyond the individual fault. After all, the transgression itself is only the eruption, the symptom. We have to consider the whole of ourselves. We have to look at our deeds, sufferings, temptations, our struggle for goodness, and our failures in that struggle.

Confession involves a painful scrutiny of self. We have to come to terms with the dark side of ourselves. But we must remember that Christ did not come to judge us, but to save us. We are invited to judge ourselves, to look at ourselves, to examine ourselves. It's not easy to admit our poverty, our weakness, our sins. But we must make a clean sweep if we are to find cleanness, wholeness and peace.

Some people keep bringing up their past sins, as if they didn't really believe that God has forgiven them. Perhaps the real problem is that they haven't forgiven themselves. Such people could learn from St Peter. I'm sure that Peter never forgot the fact that he denied Jesus. Yet I doubt if it haunted him the way some people are haunted by their sins.

Peter learned a lot from his fall. He found out a very painful truth about himself. He wasn't as strong, or as brave, or as generous as he thought he was. And he also learned a wonderful truth about Jesus. He learned that in spite of his denials, Jesus still loved him. It was Jesus' love that enabled him to turn an hour of pain and shame into an hour of grace and salvation.

We too can learn from our sins. We learn about our own weakness. And we learn about the goodness of God, because it is in our sins that we experience God's love and mercy. When we learn from a fall, the recalling of it is more likely to evoke gratitude than self-recrimination.

PRAYER OF THE FAITHFUL

President: The Lord healed the paralytic and forgave him his sins. Let us pray that he may pardon our guilt and heal the wounds of our sins.

Response: Lord, hear our prayer.

Reader(s): For the Church: that through its ministry, sinners may experience the loving forgiveness of God. [Pause] Let us pray to the Lord.

For world leaders: that God may bless them with wisdom and integrity. [Pause] Let us pray to the Lord.

For the handicapped: that they may have a life of dignity. [Pause] Let us pray to the Lord.

For those who are fearful or anxious about past or present sins: that they may open their hearts to God's merciful forgiveness. [Pause)] Let us pray to the Lord.

For this community: that the Lord may help us to walk freely and joyfully in the path of his commandments. [Pause] Let us pray to the Lord.

For our own special needs. [Longer pause] Let us pray to the Lord.

President: All-powerful God, you know our weakness. May we reach out with joy to grasp your hand, and walk more readily in your ways. We ask this through Christ our Lord.

REFLECTION   **Forgiveness**

> Forgiveness is like the child's dream of a miracle.
> Through forgiveness what is broken is made whole again,
> what is soiled is made clean,
> and what is lost is found.
> Nothing greater can happen to a human being
> than that he or she is forgiven.
> Those who are forgiven are no longer trapped in their past.
> They are set free – free to move forward again.
> The Lord not only forgives our sins,
> but helps us to learn from them.
> We learn about our own weakness.
> We learn about the goodness of God.
> And we learn to be compassionate towards others who sin.

Eighth Sunday of the Year
THE NEW WINE

INTRODUCTION AND CONFITEOR

The teaching of Jesus was new and exciting. He compared it to new wine which cannot be contained in old wineskins. The Gospel should be new for us every time we hear it. It would be a tragedy if it become old and stale. [Pause] Jesus has shown us that God is forgiving and merciful. Let us turn to God now, and ask pardon for our sins.

Lord, you are slow to anger and rich in mercy. Lord, have mercy.

As far as the east is from the west, so far do you remove our sins from us. Christ, have mercy.

As a father has compassion on his children, so you have pity on those who revere you. Lord, have mercy.

HEADINGS FOR READINGS

First Reading (Hos 2:16-17.21-22). Hosea uses the image of marriage to describe the relationship between God and his people. Here God calls his bride (his people) back to her first fervour.

Second Reading (2 Cor 3:1-6). Paul is confident of the success of his work, because it is God's work.

Gospel (Mk 2:18-22). In Jesus the prophecy of Hosea reaches fulfilment. Jesus established a new marriage covenant between God and his people.

SCRIPTURE NOTE

We hear today the second of five objections raised by the Scribes and Pharisees to what Jesus does and says – the failure of his disciples to fast.

In the Old Testament, marriage is often used to describe the relationship between God and his people. Hosea was the first to so describe it (First Reading). But the people have proved unfaithful. Nevertheless, God hasn't discarded them. Instead he wants to win back his 'spouse', and restore the intimacy they enjoyed in earlier times and especially during the Exodus.

What Hosea foretold is fulfilled in Jesus. A new 'wedding' takes place. Jesus, the Bridegroom, restores the broken relationship between God and his people. What he inaugurates goes way beyond anything that went before it. It is radically new and different. This should be a cause not for fasting but for rejoicing. Jesus' disciples are like guests at a wedding, and so cannot be expected to fast. They will fast when the bridegroom (Jesus) is taken away from them – a reference to his impending death.

HOMILY 1   **Christian joy**

We don't appreciate something until we lose it, or it is taken away from us. It's the same story with people. There are lots of tears when people die, yet during life these same people may have been taken for granted, and their presence gone uncelebrated.

If we try to appreciate people more, if we celebrate more with them, if we open our hearts more to them, then we will find that we are also closer to God.

Jesus spoke of his presence as being like the presence of the bridegroom among his guests at a wedding feast. It was no time for fasting. Rather, it was a time for joy and celebration. But he said that the time for sorrow and fasting would come – when the bridegroom would be taken away. This was a thinly-veiled hint at his passion and death.

Jesus was not against fasting as such. What he was saying was that there was a time for it. A wedding feast was not an appropriate time for fasting.

There was only one day in which fasting was compulsory for all Jews – the Day of Atonement. Nevertheless, it was a regular practice among stricter Jews. The Pharisees fasted twice a week. But it seems that they weren't doing it for the honour and glory of God, or the benefit of others. They were doing it for their own sakes – to win the admiration of people, and to put God in their debt.

There is a story about a rich man who was also a very pious man. One day he went to his rabbi to ask for his blessing.

'Tell me,' asked the rabbi, 'do you eat well?'

'Oh, I live very modestly,' the rich man answered, thinking that thereby he would win the admiration of the rabbi. 'My meals consist of a crust of dry bread and salt.'

The rabbi was not impressed. 'Why do you deny yourself food appropriate to a man of your wealth?'

'What should I eat?'

'You should eat meat and drink wine,' the rabbi said.

When the rabbi's disciples heard the advice he had given to the rich man they were filled with amazement. Turing to the rabbi they asked, 'What's the meaning of this? What difference does it make whether this man eats bread and salt or meat and wine?'

'Oh, it matters a great deal,' said the rabbi. 'If he lives well and eats well, as he can afford, then at least it will be possible for him to grasp the fact that the poor can dine only on a dry crust and salt. But if he denies himself all the pleasures of life, even if out of piety, then he will soon begin to think that the poor ought to eat stones.'

This probably explains why the Pharisees were so hard on others. But it need not be like this. Fasting, even for a brief period, can serve as a reminder to us of what is almost a permanent condition for many people in the world today.

There are some who think that joy and celebration are not part of Christianity. And what's worse, they would have others share their lonely, bleak landscape. The characteristic attitude of a Christian life ought to be one of joy and celebration.

One thing we are guaranteed is that suffering and sorrow will come. But sorrow and joy are closely related. There is much painful joy in life, and much sweet pain. It takes both rain and sunshine to make a rainbow. It takes cloud and clear sky to make a brilliant sunset. The quality of joy we feel depends on the sorrow we've known. If you've experienced a lot of pain and darkness, when you get a chance to clasp light and life, you grab them with all your might.

If we have the cause, we shouldn't be afraid to celebrate and to taste joy. This is not the same as the pagan attitude: 'Eat, drink and be merry for tomorrow we die.'

The capacity for celebration is very important. We cannot live without joy, without celebration. Religion should be a cause of joy and celebration, because it enables us to delight in God's greatest gift to us – the gift of existence. Such delight is a source of immense energy.

Jesus restores the broken relationship between God and his people. We are not just members of God's people. We are members of God's family. This should be a cause not for fasting but for rejoicing. Genuine, unforced joy is a great way of witnessing to the truth of the Gospel.

HOMILY 2 **Open to the new**

In today's Gospel we hear Jesus talking about the newness he wanted to bring. He uses two images to describe this newness: a new garment and new wine.

There's little point in putting a new patch on an old garment. All it will do is make matters worse. You have to get a whole new garment. But of course some might settle for patching the old one.

You can't put new wine into an old wineskin. New wine is still fermenting. As it ferments, it gives off gases. If the skin isn't able to expand, it will burst. This is why old skins won't do. They have become hard and unyielding. New skins, on the other hand, have a certain elasticity in them, and thus are able to expand.

Jesus was talking about a new teaching, a new movement, a new spirit. The new cannot be confined within the limits of the old. The new spirit is not a piece added to the old, or a new element poured into the old container.

Jesus was demanding an openness of mind. It is fatally easy to become set in our ways. It can happen unconsciously that as we grow old our minds become closed. We develop a dislike for what is new and unfamiliar. We become unwilling to make any adjustments in our habits and ways of living, so that we are unable to accept new truth or to try new ways.

Worse still, we might even become bitter, unforgiving and cynical. This would be understandable if we had some bad experiences. Even so, it would be a tragedy. It would cut us off from new life, new possibilities, and above all from joy. In fact, it would be to die before our time. It would be to turn into a fossil.

Pity those who have attained old age with little obvious joy or sense of gratitude, and who have to live with themselves in such hardness and bitterness of heart. Who would want to end up like that?

Jesus even went so far as to say, 'Unless you become like little children you will not enter the kingdom of heaven.' We need the child to help us to stay young at heart, because nothing is easier as life goes on than to grow old in heart, dry and disillusioned, cynical and selfish. Nothing is easier than to lose the fire and energy, the ardour and selflessness, the idealism and enthusiasm of youth.

The Gospel continually challenges us to discard old habits, to cast aside prejudice, and to see with fresh, clear eyes. This gets harder as we go on. Our eyes grow tired. Even our devotion to religion can easily harden with time into rigidities and exclusions.

We must try to remain open to the wonderful mystery of life, open to see more, to understand more, to enjoy more, so that we may live more fully and richly, and thus prepare ourselves for the mystery of eternal life.

HOMILY 3   **The newness of the Gospel**

There are two ideas in today's Gospel: joy and newness. Though they are obviously connected, I want to concentrate on the second. The newness is conveyed in two similes: the garment and the wine.

Jesus was suggesting that the old garment (the old teaching) was no longer adequate. Nor was it any good putting on a few new patches. A completely new garment was called for. He also said that the old wineskins were no longer any use, for he had new wine to offer. New wine demands new wineskins.

The newness Christ spoke about obviously went beyond mere teaching, but perhaps in a short homily we might do well to concentrate on that aspect only. Let us look at some examples of how Christ's teaching was new to the ears of his listeners.

[In what follows two voices could be used.]

For whom should you love and show concern?

Your friends of course, say the Pharisees. Those who are good to you. Those who are deserving of your love.

No, says Jesus. When you give a party don't invite your friends who will invite you in return. Invite those from whom you can expect nothing in return. Then you will have a reward in heaven.

If you are offering a gift to God and suddenly you remember that you have offended someone, what should you do?

Go ahead and offer the gift of course, say the Pharisees. The worship of God comes before all else.

No, says Jesus. Leave your gift there. Go and be reconciled with the person you have offended. Then come back and offer your gift to God and it will be acceptable to him.

If someone treats you badly, how should you react?

Give him back the same kind of medicine, say the Pharisees. Teach him a lesson he'll never forget. Otherwise he'll just go on doing it and end up walking all over you.

No, says Jesus. Do not retaliate. Do not return evil for evil. Pray for those who persecute you and who make life difficult for you. Don't try to overcome evil by resorting to evil. Evil can be overcome only by good.

Who is the greatest, the person who sits in the place of honour at the top table, or the waiter?

The one at the top of the table of course, say the Pharisees.

No, says Jesus. The one who serves is the greatest. Those who put the needs of others before their own are the greatest in the kingdom of heaven.

Who puts in the most in the collection for the poor – the wealthy person who puts in £10, or the poor person who puts in 10p?

The one who puts in £10 of course, say the Pharisees.

No, says Jesus, but the poor person who puts in 10p. A sacrifice is judged, not by the amount given, but by the cost to the giver.

What is God like and how does he deal with us?

He's just and gives us what we deserve, say the Pharisees. If we keep his laws he will reward us. If we break them he will punish us.

No, says Jesus. God is loving and treats everybody with compassion. There is joy in heaven when even one sinner comes back to him.

Who is my neighbour?

Anyone who is from my religion, or my tribe, or my class, or my race, or my nation, say the Pharisees.

No, says Jesus. My neighbour is any one who needs my help, regardless of class, or creed, or race, or nation.

Who is the person blessed by God?

The one who has an abundance of the goods of this earth and who has made a success of his life, say the Pharisees.

No, says Jesus. The one who is truly blessed by God is the person who knows that no matter how much he owns he is always poor before God, and who therefore puts his trust in God rather than in money.

Who is the fortunate one?

The man who enjoys the honour and esteem of his contemporaries, say the Pharisees.

No, says Jesus, but the one who is honest, and truthful and just in all his dealings. If he makes enemies, and if people try to discredit him, let him rejoice. He is in good company. That is how all true prophets have been treated.

One could go on, but the point has been made. The teaching of Jesus was refreshingly new. Yet it was profoundly disturbing for those who clung to the old ways and the old values. The Gospel is the announcement of something absolutely new, everlastingly new, not a message that was once new but is now two thousand years old.

However, it is only when we live according to the teaching of the Gospel that the new wine begins to flow for us. And that new wine is still being offered to us – this very day we can taste it.

PRAYER OF THE FAITHFUL

President: With confidence in God's goodness let us now brings our needs before him.

Response: Lord, graciously hear us.

Reader(s): For the Church: that through its preaching people may hear the Gospel in all its freshness and purity. [Pause] Lord, hear us.

For government leaders: that they may find inspiration in the Gospel to work for justice and peace. [Pause] Lord, hear us.

For those who have heard the Gospel but whose lives remain untouched by it. [Pause] Lord, hear us.

For those who are sick: that in their pain they may know God's comforting. [Pause] Lord, hear us.

For all gathered here: that we may realise that we will never understand the words of Christ until we act on them. [Pause] Lord, hear us.

For grace to bring our own special needs before God. [Longer pause] Lord, hear us.

President: Heavenly Father, open our ears so that we can hear the Gospel of your Son; guide our minds so that we may understand it; and strengthen our wills so that we may live it. We ask this through the same Christ our Lord.

REFLECTION   **Newness**

Jesus spoke about new times.
Those who want to belong to these times
must put aside the old garment and put on a new one;
they must cast aside the old wineskin and get a new one.
Yet he was not really talking about new clothes,
but about new attitudes;
for he condemned the Scribes and the Pharisees
who went around in fine robes,
but whose hearts were full of mould and decay.
Lord, touch our minds with your grace,
so that they will always be open to the truth.
And touch our hearts with your love,
so that they will always be open to others.

Ninth Sunday of the Year
THE SABBATH

INTRODUCTION AND CONFITEOR

Sunday takes its name from the sun. The early Christians decided to keep the same name but gave it a new meaning. It reminded them of another sun – the Son of God, the light of the world. People like to sit in the sun. In a sense that is what we are doing each Sunday when we come to church: we are turning our face towards the sun. We are enlightened and warmed by the light of Christ. [Pause]

On this day we bring our fragmented lives to God and ask him to mend them.

Lord, you were sent to heal the contrite. Lord, have mercy.

You came to call sinners to repentance. Christ, have mercy.

You plead for us at the right hand of the Father. Lord, have mercy.

HEADINGS FOR READINGS

First Reading (Deut 5:12-15). The Sabbath is a day of rest, and a re-minder to the people of their deliverance from slavery in Egypt.

Second Reading (2 Cor 4:6-11). Though the ministers of the Gospel may be heavily burdened with tribulations, nevertheless the life of Jesus flows from them to others.

Gospel (Mk 2:23-3:6). Jesus states that the Sabbath was made for people, not people for the Sabbath.

SCRIPTURE NOTE

Today's Gospel contains the last two of the five conflict stories referred to above (see Seventh Sunday). We have two further objections to Jesus. He and his disciples are accused of doing what was not lawful on the Sabbath.

Two reasons are given in the Bible for the Sabbath law. According to Exodus it imitates God who rested on the seventh day after his work of creation. According to Deuteronomy it serves to remind the people of their deliverance from slavery in Egypt (First Reading). Later the Sabbath observance was seen as one of the great signs of the covenant, and grew in importance. However, through hair-splitting over what was per-mitted and what was not, the spirit was lost, and it became an end in itself. People had become slaves to Sabbath observance.

It was against this attitude and casuistry that Jesus spoke and acted, restoring the spirit and true meaning of the Sabbath. Early on, Christians came to observe not the Jewish Sabbath, but the day of the resurrection, which became known as 'the Lord's Day'.

HOMILY 1   **The Sabbath: a gift from God**

In the charming little book, *The Little Prince*, the Prince travels to earth from a small planet. Along the way he meets different people at various stopping-off points. In one tiny planet he meets a very conscientious lamplighter. Even though he is the only person on the planet, he lights the lamp each evening and extinguishes it each morning.

'I follow a terrible profession,' he moans. 'In the old days things were reasonable. I lit the lamp in the evening and had the rest of the night for sleep. I put it out in the morning and had the rest of the day for relaxation. In those days the planet turned slowly, now it turns faster and faster.'

'And the orders haven't changed?' asked the little Prince.

'That is the tragedy,' replied the lamplighter. 'Even though from year to year the planet has turned more rapidly, the orders have remained the same. It's got so bad that now the planet makes a complete revolution every half-hour so that I get no rest night or day.'

The Little Prince felt sorry for the lamplighter – always on the go, but with no time for himself. His once lovely job had become a monotonous chore. The lamplighter had become old and anguished and disillusioned.

Our world too has changed. It has become very impersonal. People who work for big companies are not appreciated at a personal level. Their work is often dull and repetitive. And the pace of life is getting faster and faster. People cannot find time to relax, or to reflect on their lives.

We need to stand back and look at where we're going. Above all, we need a chance to take care of the 'spirit'. This is where the Sabbath comes in. And this is the revolutionary aspect of today's Gospel. Jesus says that the Sabbath was made for us, not us for the Sabbath.

Some find Sunday a depressing day. They find it hard to stop and be still. When deprived of their work, they experience feelings of loneliness and emptiness. Unable to face this, they rush out to do other things, and so the merry-go-round continues. When given the gift of some free time they immediately throw it away. Sailors who are undismayed in a storm often can't stand a calm. 'There are people who pray for eternal life who don't know what to do with themselves on a rainy Sunday' (Chesterton).

Sunday was once a day for putting down one's burdens. However, in recent times there has been a gradual erosion of Sunday. Sunday is rapidly becoming just another weekday. This is a pity. The Sabbath is a gift from God. It is meant to be a day of joy and freedom. On this day we are free to care for the seeds of eternity planted in our souls.

The Sabbath offers us time to relax, time to recollect ourselves. And it has a social function too. It redeems us from our isolation. It takes us out of ourselves and puts us in touch with the community. It gives us time for the various expressions of love and unity that we are often too busy to show each other.

We are a community of Christ's disciples. Our destinies are inseparably linked. Sunday is our great gathering day. We gather to celebrate the Eucharist. The community which during the week has been scattered, on Sunday is gathered together as grains of wheat are gathered to form one loaf.

It's very difficult to remain a Christian in today's secular world in isolation from others. This is where the community comes in. Through the community we support one another.

On this day we celebrate the Lord's resurrection from the dead, and are reminded that life is a pilgrimage to God's eternal kingdom. We listen to the Word of God, which is 'a lamp for our steps and a light for our path'. And we receive the Eucharist, which is the food of our journey.

We don't keep the Sabbath; the Sabbath keeps us. No matter if a certain melancholy is mixed with it, or assails us during it.

HOMILY 2   **The sacredness of everyday life**

The Sabbath Day is the one day out of the week that we owe to God. That's why we refer to the Sabbath as the Lord's Day. Correct? No. It's true that the Sabbath is in a special sense the Lord's Day. As such, it reminds us that God has the first place in our lives. But what about the other days of the week? Do they not belong to the Lord too? And are we not to think of him and serve him on those days as well?

Keeping the Sabbath Day has become almost synonymous with church-going. However, there are two ways of looking at church-going.

According to the first way, we go to church in order to be in the presence of the holy, and to have our everyday lives influenced by that presence. This is a rather narrow and impoverished view.

According to the second way, we go to church in order to be able to see the sacred dimension of everyday life. This is a broader and richer view.

For some, religion is merely a Sunday affair. They think of divine things as a round of duties separated from life. They regard the Sabbath day as holy and the other days of the week as secular. When we leave religion to church at the weekend, it remains on the periphery of life, even if that periphery is an exalted one. Without an effort to incorporate the sacred into life, religion can become so far removed from the human situation as to be irrelevant. People can be extremely religious in a formal way and on formal occasions, and yet profess values in everyday life that are thoroughly secular.

For others, religion is a week-long observance that is inspired and sustained by the Sabbath. For them the function of the Sabbath Day is to help us recognise the holiness, not just of the first day of the week, but of all the days in the week. It serves to sensitise us to the sacred dimension of everyday life. They make no distinction between religious activity and the acts of every day.

This second kind of spirituality is especially nourishing for the soul. It has the effect of drawing together the secular and the sacred, and thus making the holy close to life. Making it precious and too removed from life can actually hinder a genuine sensitivity to what is sacred.

For Jews the Sabbath was very important. It was a day reserved for the essentials: for prayer, reflection and relaxing with the family beneath the gaze of God. It was not an escape from the work of the other six days, but a time to re-find the energy to return to that reality with renewed strength.

For the Jews the Sabbath was a day when they celebrated their deliverance from the slavery of Egypt. For the early Christians it was a day when they celebrated Jesus' resurrection from the grave. For us it is a sign that we are no longer slaves but God's children, and helps us to live in joy and freedom.

Religion is not about how we pray on Sunday but about how we live every day.

HOMILY 3   **Earthenware vessels**

St Paul says, 'We are only the earthenware jars that hold the treasure' (Second Reading). The treasure he is talking about is the divine glory of Christ, a glory which he has shared with us. The image of a priceless treasure being carried in a cheap container is a very beautiful one.

An earthenware jar is one of the most ordinary, commonplace things you could think of. It's not made of precious material but of the stuff of this earth – clay. It has no beauty or radiance of any kind. It is so brittle that it has to be handled with great care. In itself it has little or no value. Even if you possessed a thousand such jars you wouldn't think of yourself as rich.

A beautiful image indeed, but doesn't it sound incredible. A priceless treasure contained in a worthless jar. Yet this is precisely how a Christian sees the human condition.

In his love for us God has given each of us a treasure – the treasure of our divine dignity. But we carry this priceless treasure in a vessel made of clay, namely, the body. Since the vessel is fragile we have to treat it with care and respect. Thus God has given us the dignity of being responsible for his gift.

But we see only the container, the body, a body made of perishable material – clay, earth, dust. The treasure itself is hidden from our eyes. Therefore, we have to take its existence on faith. But those who believe in it have a sure anchor in life. They know that even though at death the vessel is broken and turns into dust, the treasure is not lost. God gathers it up and brings it to himself.

Therefore, we no longer need to fear death, because even though the vessel of clay is broken, the treasure is not lost. Furthermore, we believe that through the power of God, the vessel will be restored on the last day and become like Jesus' risen body.

We are a polarity between a divine image and worthless dust. It is because of our being dust that our sins can be forgiven, and it is because of our being an image of God that righteousness is expected of us.

Today we are celebrating the Sabbath Day, a day which Jesus said was made for us. On this the first day of the week we celebrate the Lord's resurrection from the dead. When the Son of God came on earth, he hid the treasure of his divinity inside a vessel of clay similar to ours. He clothed himself in the cloak of our weak, fragile, mortal humanity. In that humanity he lived, suffered, and died. But by rising from the dead, he clothed our mortal humanity with immortality.

The Sabbath is a wonderful opportunity to remind ourselves of just how great is the treasure that we carry, and to make sure that we take good care of this treasure.

OTHER STORIES

1. There was a man who lived on the Great Blasket island (off the coast of Kerry), who worked from dawn to dusk every day of the week. He owned a small flock of sheep. His family being young, he was short of help, and had no time to go and check on his sheep except on Sundays. So, instead of going across to the mainland to attend Mass with the other islanders, he would take his stick and his dog, and go up to hill to check on his sheep. It wasn't that he had no faith. His faith was as strong as that of his neighbours. It was just that he was a stubborn man who always did what suited himself.

His wife often tried to get him to change his ways. She told him that he was not setting a good example for his children. Why couldn't he check on his sheep after returning from Mass, as his neighbours did? But he ignored her.

One Sunday, when all the islanders had gone to Dunquin to Mass, he went up the hill as usual. Since the wind was from the south, he went to the northside of the island, expecting to find the sheep there. But there wasn't a sheep to be found there. Puzzled, he then went to the southside, and to his surprise found the sheep there. He was amazed to see them gathered into one spot with this marvellous beam of light shining down on them through a break in the clouds.

This simple scene made a deep impression on him. The result was that next Sunday he was the first to arrive on the pier to get the boat to Dunquin for Mass. And he never again missed going to Mass on a Sunday.

It seems that it suddenly dawned on him what he was missing by separating himself from the community on Sundays. While all of the community was gathered into God's house, with God's light shining down on them, he was left outside.

It is a beautiful image of what Sunday is about. In a sense, each Sunday when we go to church: we are turning our face towards the sun. We are enlightened and warmed by the light of Christ.

2. There is a story of a rabbi who once asked his son, 'Where does God live?' The child couldn't understand the question. To him the question should have been: 'Where does God not live?' So he answered, 'The Lord fills the heavens and the earth.' 'No,' said the rabbi. 'God lives wherever we let him in.'

Perhaps that is the meaning of the Sabbath. It is the day when we abandon our own devices and desires and let God in.

PRAYER OF THE FAITHFUL

President: Gathered together on this, the Lord's Day, let us bring our many needs before him.

Response: Lord, hear our prayer.

Reader(s): For Christians: that they may have a richer understanding of the Sabbath, the Lord's day and ours too. [Pause] We pray to the Lord.

For all those in charge of civil affairs: that they may fulfil their responsibilities worthily and well. [Pause] We pray to the Lord.

For those for whom this day has no meaning. [Pause] We pray to the Lord.

For all gathered here: that we may see the Sabbath as an opportunity to give more attention to God, and to share more of ourselves with those we love. [Pause] We pray to the Lord.

For our own special needs. [Longer pause] We pray to the Lord.

President: God of love and mercy, we thank you for the gift of the Sabbath. May our celebration of it be a sign that we are no longer slaves but your children. We ask this through Christ our Lord.

REFLECTION   **The Sabbath**

Six days a week we work under strain,
    beset with worries, and slaves to material things.
But on the Sabbath we turn our attention
    to the things of the spirit.
Here we are given time to be thankful,
    to be joyful, to be free;
time to look at where we are going in life,
    and, if needs be, to correct our compass;

time to be with the Lord and with one another.
The Sabbath provides us with a window into eternity,
and a halting place on the road to the kingdom of God.
We don't keep the Sabbath;
the Sabbath keeps us – if we observe it.
Thank you, Lord, for the gift of the Sabbath.

Tenth Sunday of the Year
THE DIVIDED KINGDOM

INTRODUCTION AND CONFITEOR

One of the things that brings good projects to a bad end is when divisions occur. As today's Gospel puts it: 'Any kingdom that is divided against itself cannot stand.' Our world is full of division. Each one of us is full of division – we are pulled towards good and evil at the same time. Let us turn to the Lord and ask him to heal our divisions. [Pause]

Lord Jesus, you came to reconcile us to one another and to the Father. Lord, have mercy.

Lord Jesus, you heal the wounds of sin and division. Christ have mercy.

Lord Jesus, you intercede for us with the Father. Lord, have mercy.

HEADINGS FOR READINGS

First Reading (Gen 3:9-15). We are shown the consequences of the fall of Adam and Eve, and also God's promise of salvation.

Second Reading (2 Cor 4:13-5:1). Paul is sustained in his trials by the firm hope that God has a permanent dwelling prepared for us in heaven.

Gospel (Mk 3:20-35). God's promise of salvation is fulfilled in Jesus, who overthrows Satan and establishes the Kingdom of God.

SCRIPTURE NOTE

In the First Reading we see the pathetic efforts of Adam and Eve to shift the blame for their sin from themselves on to the serpent, and even onto God himself. We also see the consequences of sin: loss of intimacy to God, and a breakdown between man and woman – the man betrays the woman. It is not God who has changed but the man and the woman. However, the sad scene ends with a promise of salvation.

The Gospel shows the promise of salvation as being fulfilled in Jesus. He overthrows Satan and establishes the Kingdom of God. For those who believe in him, and who do the will of God, a new kinship is formed.

Mark highlights the frustrations Jesus had to contend with. His relatives, worried about the direction his life had taken, wanted to bring him back home. Then there is the argument with the Scribes concerning the source of Jesus' healing power. While the ordinary people recognized the God-given nature of Jesus' power, the Scribes put a horrible spin on Jesus' healing miracles, perversely claiming that it was through the power of the devil that he did these deeds. This shows the sheer hardness of heart of the Scribes.

At first Jesus tries to reason with them, but with little success. Such people are not open to the truth. Then he warns them against committing the gravest sin of all, blasphemy against the Holy Spirit – the sin of deliberately twisting the good so that it is made to look bad.

HOMILY 1   **Adam, where are you?**

When God gave Adam and Eve the gift of free will, he gave them the capacity to be moral, that is, to choose to do what is right. But they chose evil. To choose evil is to abuse freedom. And like children who have done wrong, they tried to hide rather than face the consequences. But God came looking for them and called out to Adam, 'Where are you?'

But there seems to be a problem here. If God knows all things, why did he have to ask Adam, 'Where are you?' Are we to conclude that God didn't know where Adam was. Oh, God knew all right. It was Adam who didn't know. In asking the question God does not expect to learn something he doesn't know. What he wants is to produce an effect on the person which can only be produced by just such a question.

The question 'Where are you?' is a profoundly disturbing question. And it a question which is addressed not just to Adam but to every person. In every era, God calls to every person in sin, and says: 'Where are you … in your relationship to me, to others, and to yourself?'

Adam hid to avoid rendering an account, and to escape responsibility for what he had done. We hide for the same reason, when we find ourselves in Adam's situation. When we do wrong, we become afraid, and try to hide from the consequences. In trying to hide from God (which is impossible), we are hiding from ourselves, we are running from ourselves.

But there is Something who seeks us out. We hear the voice of God in our heart asking: 'Where are you?' God is not indifferent. God pursues us when we would rather not deal with him. He does so, not to punish us, but to get us to face up to what we have done. He loves us enough to forgive our sins, but he wants us to take responsibility for them and to try to atone for them. Confrontation is a sign of love.

Adam and Eve trembled on hearing the voice of God. They were ashamed of what they had done, and ashamed of themselves. Everyone's heart (like that of Adam) trembles on hearing the question 'Where are you?' That question is not meant as a threat but as a help. It is the voice of

Someone who cares about us.

Adam and Eve felt guilty. Today guilt has almost become a dirty word. But guilt can be constructive. It is a sign of a healthy conscience. If people do wrong they ought to feel guilty. It is a sign of being truly human. Only a psychopath feels no guilt: what one encounters is a scary moral numbness. We don't consider such a person normal or fully human.

Just as pain is a warning that all is not right with us physically, so guilt is a sign that all is not well with us morally. In some people the throbbing pain of guilt calls them to change, to seek the truth, to repair past faults, and to ask for forgiveness – all of this is positive. However, taken too far, guilt can become a spiritual sickness. Here we are talking about someone who is 'guilt ridden', or crippled by guilt. It has been said that the purpose of guilt is to make us feel bad for the right reasons so that we can feel good for the right reasons.

When Adam and Eve sinned there were consequences. Before they sinned they enjoyed a delightful familiarity with God. They are portrayed as walking with God in the cool of the evening. After their fall they are afraid of God and try to hide from him. And there is a breakdown between themselves: Adam betrays Eve. Where once unity and harmony existed, now there is division, fuelled by mistrust, mutual-recrimination, and fear. It wasn't God who brought this punishment on them. They brought it on themselves. We are not punished so much for our sins as by our sins.

The sad scene ends with a promise of salvation. God takes pity on Adam and Eve and promises to send them a saviour. The Gospel shows the promise fulfilled in Jesus. Jesus overthrows Satan and establishes the Kingdom of God. For those who believe in him, and who do God's will, a new kinship is formed and a new intimacy with God becomes possible. As a result of what he did, we are not just God's creatures, but members of God's family. And a new bond is formed between us. Thus the old divisions are overcome.

HOMILY 2   **The divided kingdom**

Jesus said that a kingdom which is divided cannot stand. It doesn't require much reflection to see the truth of this. We see countries where there is internal conflict torn asunder. (Give a current example.) We see the breakup families in which there is conflict.

The problem affects us on a personal level too. Each of us is a divided kingdom. We are divided within ourselves; we are pulled in opposite directions. There is a war going on inside each of us, a war between light and darkness, good and evil.

Brian Keenan, who was held hostage in Lebanon in the 1980s, said: 'In captivity I was forced to confront the man I thought I was, and discovered that I was many people.' And Dostoevsky said: 'Human nature is a mass of contradictory urges, impulses, voices, all seen and heard together.'

Even the saints experienced this internal division. This is what St Paul was talking about when he said, 'The good which I want to do, I do not do; the evil which I want to avoid I find myself doing.'

We have to face this inner division, and come to terms with it. Within each of us there is division, fragility, darkness, and evil. What we need to do is engage in a process – a process of growth towards wholeness and unity. By the grace of God, the divided self can be made whole. Those who are unified have great strength. Those who have peace within themselves radiate it to others. Those who don't, project onto others the conflict going on within themselves.

Sin divides each of us in two: part of us is pulling with God, and part of us is pulling against God. Sin is not something we can throw off once and for all like an old garment. Rather, it is a condition in which we live. What is important is not so much our failures as our struggle for goodness. Once we are seriously struggling for goodness, we are facing in the right direction, and we are on the side of Christ.

Sin also divides us from one another, because essentially sin is a refusal to love. It means that we always put our own needs before those of our neighbour. By their disobedience Adam and Eve not only brought about a rift between God and them, but also between themselves. Christ restores us to God's friendship. And by the power of his Spirit we are able us to reach out to our neighbour in forgiveness and reconciliation. And so the divisions are overcome. And the Kingdom of God is seen to have come among us.

HOMILY 3   **Closeness to Christ**

The Gospel passage seems to imply that Jesus had brothers and sisters. However, according to the traditional teaching of the Church this was not so. The confusion results from the fact that in Aramaic they used the same word to denote brother, sister, and cousin. Even to this day Africans in a group are called by familial names such as uncle, brother, sister, mama, papa, even when not related by blood.

When Jesus left Nazareth to begin his public ministry he 'lost' his natural family. However, in the meantime he had gained another family – the family of his disciples. So when he was told that his mother and brothers and sisters were outside asking for him, he replied, 'Who are my mother and my brothers? Anyone who does the will of God, that person is my brother and sister and mother.' Those who hear and do the will of God are now Jesus' brothers and sisters and mother.

Relatives are not always the people to whom we are closest. In fact, our best friends are usually people with whom we have no blood relationship. Blood relationship is important but it is not everything. It doesn't automatically confer closeness. The natural family is only the beginning. Jesus was calling people to a new community, into a spiritual family.

Family or racial ties don't necessarily create community. Belief in Jesus and the practice of God's will are what create community. These expand the boundaries of our own communities and families. Witness the bonds we who are gathered in this church today have with one another because of our faith in Jesus.

The woman in the Gospel said that the mother of Jesus was a very privileged and fortunate person. But Jesus responded to this by saying that those who hear the word of God and keep it are even more fortunate.

In saying this he wasn't putting down his mother. He was making an important point. He was not only the son of Mary but also the Son of God. Mary had to learn that she could not keep the child for herself. All parents have to learn this painful lesson – to let go of their children.

No, Jesus wasn't putting his mother down. Quite the opposite. He was saying that she was doubly blessed. Mary was blessed because she was the physical mother of Jesus, and she was also blessed because she heard the word, and acted on it. If we want the intimacy Mary had with Jesus we can have it provided, like her, we hear the word of God and do it.

Once there was a rabbi who had a great reputation for sanctity. One day a stranger arrived from a faraway town to see him. On his arrival he was introduced to one of the rabbi's disciples.

'I have heard that your rabbi is a very holy man,' the stranger said.

'Is that so?' the disciple answered.

'Well, we have a rabbi in our town who is also very close to God.'

'How can you tell that?' asked the disciple.

'Because he works miracles,' came the reply.

'I see,' said the disciple.

'What miracles has your rabbi performed?' the stranger asked.

'There are miracles and miracles,' the disciple answered. 'It seems clear that the people of your town regard it as a miracle if God should do your rabbi's bidding. Well, we in this town regard it as a miracle that our rabbi does God's bidding.'

Magic tries to manipulate God. Religion tries to serve God.

PRAYER OF THE FAITHFUL

President: Let us now bring our needs before God, confident that he will listen to us because we pray in the name of his Son.

Response: Lord, graciously hear us.

Reader(s): For the Church: that it may be a sign of unity and an instrument of peace in a divided world. [Pause] Lord, hear us.

For unity among the nations of the world, and especially in countries where divisions exist. [Pause] Lord, hear us.

For unity in families. [Pause] Lord, hear us.

For all those who have lost their lives through warfare or violence. [Pause] Lord, hear us.

For each of us here: that we may strive to be a source of unity among our friends and neighbours. [Pause] Lord, hear us.

For grace to entrust our own special needs to the Lord. [Longer pause] Lord, hear us.

President: Lord, in your gentle mercy, guide our wayward hearts, for we know that by ourselves we cannot do your will. We make this prayer through Christ our Lord.

REFLECTION   **A divided kingdom**

A kingdom that is divided within itself cannot stand.
I myself am a divided kingdom;
I am divided within myself.
The good that I want to do, I do not do;
the evil that I want to avoid, I find myself doing.
I am like a field in which wheat and weeds
are struggling for supremacy.
Who will save me from myself?
Who will keep my kingdom from falling down?
You, Lord, who overpowered Satan,
will heal the division within me,
and help me to take complete possession of my house.
Then I shall be free, united, and at peace.

Eleventh Sunday of the Year
SMALL BEGINNINGS

INTRODUCTION AND CONFITEOR

Life calls for a lot of patience and trust. You can't plant an acorn today and expect to sit in the shade of an oak tree tomorrow. The same holds true for spiritual matters. We have to make the effort. But then we must be patient and trust that God's grace will take over. [Pause]

Lord, you make the just flourish like trees that are planted by a running stream. Lord, have mercy.

You plant them in the house of the Lord, to flourish in the courts of our God. Christ, have mercy.

You make them bear fruit even when they are old. Lord, have mercy.

HEADINGS FOR READINGS

First Reading (Ezek 17:22-24). The prophet foretells the fall of Jerusalem. At the same time he tells of the establishment of a universal kingdom (by the Messiah).

Second Reading (2 Cor 5:6-10). Since Paul's priority at all times is to please the Lord, he has no fears of appearing before him.

Gospel (Mk 4:26-34). Two parables about the steady growth of the Kingdom of God from insignificant beginnings, a growth brought about by God.

SCRIPTURE NOTE

In Mark 4:1-34 we have a collection of parables, most of which deal with the growth of seed. They serve as a commentary on what has been happening in Jesus' proclamation of the kingdom.

The prophet Ezekiel foretold that God would take a twig from the top of the cedar and plant it in Zion (First Reading). Under God's protective power that twig would grow into a great cedar. Thus Ezekiel dreamed that God would transplant the exiled people of Israel back to the land of their fathers. He glimpsed a future son of David whose kingdom would be universal.

The promise is fulfilled in Jesus who ushers in the kingdom of God. The parables of the seed that grows by itself and the mustard seed were meant to encourage the early Church which was worried about the slow growth of the kingdom. They were telling the disciples to be patient, to trust, and not to expect instant results. Through the power of God, from small and insignificant beginnings the kingdom will grow into something great.

HOMILY 1   **The seed growing of itself**

In Jesus' parable of the seed growing of itself what is stressed is the certainty of the harvest once the sower has done his job. It was meant to give encouragement to those early disciples who had become discouraged because little seemed to be happening. It was telling them to be patient, to trust, and not to expect instant results. It is a very encouraging little parable.

Like those early disciples we too want results and we want them fast. We live in the age of the instant product. We have instant soup, instant tea, instant photos ... pretty well instant anything. We know that the quality suffers, but we are willing to sacrifice that for quick results and time and effort saved.

We forget that certain things cannot be rushed. To grow to maturity as a human being is the job of a lifetime. To build a good relationship with someone takes time. To get to know and understand one's children takes time. To overcome one's sins and weaknesses takes time.

Our age could also be called the age of the push button. All we have to do is press a button or turn a switch and things happen.

Many of today's labour-saving devices are good. They take some of the monotony and drudgery out of life and work. But there is a danger in living in the world of the push button. The push button encourages the minimum effort, the least cost, the shortcut approach to everything. It may lure us into always seeking the easy option, even when there is no easy option – at least not if we want the genuine article. Why bother to visit that old or sick person if you can phone them?

Besides, the old problems remain in the age of the push button. There is the problem of bringing up one's children well. There is no magic switch for that. There is the problem of acquiring a skill. There is no button you can press that will make that happen painlessly. In other words, for some things there are no shortcuts.

In Jesus' story the farmer did his part – he sowed the seed. Things were now beyond his control. The one thing he wanted to see happen, namely, for the seed to grow, he couldn't do anything about. All he could do was wait in patience, humility and hope. These are not easy virtues.

Yet life calls for these virtues. Some people think they must always be up and doing – as if everything depended on them. They are unable to take time out, to let things be, to trust, to be patient, to be humble, to wait.

There is something we can do, and which God will not do for us. But that done, we have to acknowledge that we can't do everything. Spiritual development, and indeed human development, is a process. It will go on provided we do not resist it. In the great processes of growth, healing, recovery, and spiritual progress we are only facilitators. We can plant the seed, but we can't make it grow. God has to take over. It is God who gives the increase.

We should learn patience from watching nature. Things take time to grow. And they take time to ripen. Nature doesn't take shortcuts. All the seasons are needed.

We need all the seasons too. Nothing is wasted. Look at the example of Jesus. Before beginning his public ministry, he spent thirty years at Nazareth. To some it might seem a waste of valuable time. Nothing could be further from the truth. In his humanity he needed those years. During them he was growing quietly in the shadows.

The lovely little parable of the seed growing of itself shows us that there is an almighty power working for us. Our job is to sow the seed. Then God has to take over. And God does. Any farmer will tell you that. If we do the right thing, the harvest will come. But can we be patient, can we wait, can we trust?

HOMILY 2   **Small beginnings**

The parable of the mustard seed was a reply to the question: Could the kingdom really grow from such humble beginnings? Mark's reply was that the little cell of disciples could indeed become a kingdom. Like the first parable (the seed growing of itself) this also is a very encouraging little parable.

It seems that what life intends to be great it first makes small. Perhaps that is where we go wrong. We're too impressed by the large. We tend to despise the small. Yet look at the atom. It is the smallest unit of matter, yet what energy it contains.

Many great things and undertakings begin in small and often hidden ways. Examples: a building begins with one brick on another, a book begins with one word on a page, a journey with a single step, a forest fire from a single spark, a giant oak from an acorn, a huge river from a tiny spring, a lifelong friendship from a chance encounter. Things that have a certain integrity and truth always seem to start from humble beginnings.

Seeds need the darkness, isolation, and cover of the earth in order to germinate. Therefore, for something to begin small, hidden, anonymous, is in fact an advantage. It means it can develop away from publicity. There are no pressures. No burden of expectations. It can develop at its own pace. There is no hurry. Hurry ruins many things.

Hence the importance of beginnings, of taking care of things in their beginnings. If you wish the adult to turn out well, then take good care of the child. We ignore the small at our peril. It is not the mega-rows that lead to marriage break-up, but the mini-rows. The treacheries which are destined to reach furthest in their consequences do not begin in an obvious or dramatic way. They begin humbly and unostentatiously, to bear their bitter fruit in maturity. We ascend the heights or sink into the depths a step at a time.

The true savour of life is not to be gained from big things but from little ones. To sample a wine the taster needs only a sip. Bad habits and illnesses creep up on us slowly and in little steps. The first step was of no seeming consequence. The roof leaks for the want of a handful of thatch. Alcoholism takes hold of a person a glass at a time.

Just because we may not be able to go a mile today shouldn't stop us for going a yard. Great things are not done by impulse, but by a series of small steps taken over a period of time. Our lives are made up of little things – little deeds, little happenings, and so on. The person who prays for little things is innocent.

If there is something which we want to do, let us not hesitate and think too much. Let us make a start, however small. Let us take one step. Let us plant one seed. For, as Van Gogh says, 'The only thing that accumulates in the long run is the meagre work of every day.'

HOMILY 3   **Partners with God**

There is a version of the creation story that goes like this. When God was creating the world, he did it bit by bit. He made the trees, the grass, the animals, the birds, the fish, and so on. As he was making these things, the angels kept asking, 'Is the world finished yet?' To which God would reply with a simple 'No'.

Finally God made people, and said to them, 'I'm tired. I want you to finish the world. If you agree to do so, then I promise to be your partner.' They agreed. After this, whenever the angels enquired of God if the world was finished, the reply would come, 'I don't know. You'll have to ask my partners.'

There is something we can do, and which we have to do. God will not do it for us. Not that he couldn't do it. It's just that he wants us to be partners with him. We have to plant the seed. That's our part. But having done that, we have to acknowledge that we can't do everything. We can't make the seed grow. That's God's part. And God does his part. Any farmer or gardener will tell you that.

So, if there is something which we want to do, or goals we'd like to achieve, let us not sit around dreaming about them. Let us do something about them, even if it's something very small. Let us take that first step. Let us plant one seed. If we do that, then we can be sure that in good time God will see to it that we have a harvest to reap. Meanwhile, as Paul says, 'We have to go by faith and not by sight' (Second Reading).

Once the food buyer for a residential school in Boston went to the Farmers' Market. Passing a stand that was heaped with beautiful sweet corn, the buyer asked the farmer who was selling it, 'Did you grow this corn?' 'No,' came the reply. 'I planted the seed.'

After gathering in a bountiful harvest, a farmer took off his cap. Then standing in the middle of the empty cornfield, he looked up to heaven and said, 'Thank you, Lord, for the fine harvest.' And the Lord looked down and said, 'And thank you. We did a good job.'

We are the work of God's hands, but we are also God's hands at work.

ANOTHER STORY

Montgomery, Alabama, 1955. Although 70% of the passengers using the city bus lines were black, the first seats on all buses were kept for whites. And if those seats were taken and more whites got on the bus, black people seated in the rear were forced to get up and give them their seats.

On December 1, 1955, Mrs Parks, a 42-year-old black woman boarded a bus to go home after a long day working and shopping. She found a seat at the start of the black section. At the next stop some whites got on so the driver ordered her to get up and give her seat to a white man. She refused to get up. The driver called a policeman. Mrs Parks was arrested.

Word quickly spread. A meeting was called and Martin Luther King addressed it. They made one basic demand: that passengers be seated on a first-come first-served basis. To achieve this end they began a boycott of the buses. People walked to work.

It was an extraordinary scene. Everywhere the sidewalks were crammed with people walking to work, and the buses went by empty but for whites. The boycott dragged on all that winter, and through the spring and summer of 1956. Meanwhile the leaders of the movement were arrested. Martin Luther King's home was bombed. Finally the Supreme Court declared that Alabama's segregation laws were unconstitutional.

Victory was achieved and an unjust situation put right because one day one woman decided to act. The spark ignited by Mrs Parks started a fire.

PRAYER OF THE FAITHFUL

President: Let us pray for the growth of God's Kingdom on earth and in our lives.

Response: Lord, hear us in your love.

Reader(s): For the Church: that Christ may sustain it in its task of being a leaven in the world. [Pause] We pray in faith.

For government leaders that they may speak wisely and act justly, for God has made us responsible for the world. [Pause] We pray in faith.

For all those who are discouraged because of lack of results. [Pause] We pray in faith.

For those who work on the land: that their work may bear fruit. [Pause] We pray in faith.

For all here: that each of us may play our part, however small, in making the world a better place to live in. [Pause] We pray in faith.

For grace to bring our needs before God in silence and in trust. [Longer pause] We pray in faith.

President: Almighty and ever-loving God, help us to have confidence in your unchanging love for us, so that when things are difficult we may have the strength to persevere in goodness. We make our prayers through Christ our Lord.

REFLECTION   **The seed that grows by itself**

On many an idle day have I grieved over lost time.
But it is never lost, my Lord.
You have taken every moment of my life in your own hands.
Hidden in the heart of things
you are nourishing seeds into sprouts,

buds into blossoms, and ripening flowers into fruitfulness.
I was tired and sleeping on my idle bed
and imagining all work had ceased.
In the morning I woke up
and found my garden full with wonders of flowers.

Rabindranath Tagore

Twelfth Sunday of the Year
STORM ON THE LAKE

INTRODUCTION AND CONFITEOR

When the apostles got caught in a storm they turned to Jesus for help
and found it. From time to time we too get caught in storms. Our storms
usually take the form of trials of one kind or another. We must know
how to turn to the Lord, and trust that he will see us through the storm.
[Pause]

Lord Jesus, you bring us peace of mind by forgiving our sins. Lord,
have mercy.

You calm our fears by your presence with us. Christ, have mercy.

You uphold us with your grace in times of trial and difficulty. Lord,
have mercy.

HEADINGS FOR READINGS

First Reading (Job 38:1.8-11). God alone has mastery over the sea.

Second Reading (2 Cor 5:14-17). Christ showed his love for us by dying
for us. We are to imitate that love.

Gospel (Mk 4:35-41). By calming a storm Jesus shows his divine power
and his care for his disciples.

SCRIPTURE NOTE

In 4:35–5:43 Mark follows the section on the parables with four miraculous actions of Jesus. The first of these was the calming of the storm.

In the Bible the calming of a storm is a characteristic sign of divine
power, because the sea and the wind are seen as forces of evil and chaos
which only God can control (First Reading). But the storm can also stand
for the trials and tribulations which the righteous suffer, and from which
only the power of God can save them.

In the calming of the storm, the apostles witnessed a work that only
God can accomplish, which means that Jesus has divine power. At the
same time the miracle shows Jesus' care for his apostles. Mark is using

the story for catechetical purposes. The storm reflects the post-Easter experience of the early Church. The disciples have run into all sorts of difficulties, and feel that the Lord has abandoned them. But they are summoned to have faith in his presence with them and care for them.

HOMILY 1   **Out of control**

In the Bible the sea, the wind and the storm are seen as forces of evil and chaos which only God can control. But the storm can also stand for the trials and tribulations which the righteous suffer, and from which only the power of God can save them.

As Jesus and his apostles were crossing the lake a storm blew up. For a while the apostles were managing. They were in control – if only barely. It's a good feeling to be in control. We are running the show. Things are within our power. The outcome is in our own hands.

In such circumstances it's easy to convince ourselves that we have faith, even great faith. But we could be on an ego trip. The ego is happiest when in control of a familiar and predictable world. We are setting the agenda. We are creating our own goals. Sometimes it can mean controlling the lives of others too. We don't really need God, except maybe to give us a pat on the back at the end of it all.

But that evening, when the storm arose, and the boat seemed to be on the verge of sinking, the apostles suddenly discovered that things were out of their control. Things were beyond their powers. The outcome was out of their hands.

To be out of control is not a pleasant experience. We experience small samples of this when we get caught in a traffic jam. It can be annoying and frustrating. But we can experience more serious cases of it in times of grave illness and/or tragedy. At such times everything seems to be falling apart. We feel confused and powerless. The ego is profoundly threatened by the approach of danger, and especially death, which it sees as utter chaos and the ultimate unknown.

To find oneself in a such a situation is both humbling and terrifying. But it is precisely in times like this that we discover whether or not we have faith. Our first reaction is to think that God no longer cares about us, and has abandoned us.

When things got out of control for the apostles it seems they too felt like this. They looked towards Jesus only to discover that he was asleep. Incidentally, the ability to sleep peacefully in the midst of a storm was a sign of perfect trust in God. The faith of Jesus contrasts with the 'little faith' of the apostles. Jesus chided them for their lack of trust, and then calmed the storm.

For the early Christians this miracle was a very relevant one. The boat represented the Church, and the storm the persecutions unleashed on it by evil powers that wanted to wreck it. They were filled with fear. To them it must have seemed that Jesus was asleep. But then their faith rose to the challenge. It was enough for them to 'awaken' him with their prayers, and to have trust and faith in his presence, for the storm of their fear to be stilled.

Even though Jesus was with the apostles in that boat, the storm still struck. So, just because a storm strikes doesn't mean that God has abandoned us. If we have faith, we will not doubt that he is with us, and we will turn to him in prayer, and know his help.

The story challenges us to trust in God's power especially when storms assail us. When you have faith you give up the need to be in control.

HOMILY 2   **Faith in a time of crisis**

It's easy to delude ourselves into thinking we have a strong faith when everything in our world is calm and smooth. It's only when the storm strikes that we discover what kind of faith we have, or if we have any faith at all. Faith here means not so much belief in God as trust in God.

Some people think that if God was with them, and if he really cared about them, then no storm would ever hit them. Life would be all plain sailing. So, when a storm does come, they immediately think that God has abandoned them. But today's Gospel story shows that this is not so. The storm still hit the apostles even though Jesus was present with them in the boat.

What real faith does is assure us that God is with us in the midst of the storm. It is that conviction that we are not alone, which enables us to get through the storm.

When the storm suddenly hit the apostles, what happened? Their faith failed them and they were overcome with fear. We can deduce this from what Jesus said to them: 'Why are you so frightened? How is it that you have no faith?' However, in their fear they cried out, 'Master, do you not care? We are going down!'

The cry of the apostles, 'Master, do you not care? We are going down!' offers comfort to us. It is a cry made by many, and probably by ourselves, when danger strikes and God seems not to care or even to be found. At such times we discover how little our faith really is. But our faith doesn't have to be perfect. Even a little faith can get us through. Gandhi said, 'A person with a grain of faith in God never loses hope, because he ever believes in the ultimate triumph of truth.'

In their grave need, the apostles turned to Jesus for help. Pretty well everybody turns to God in times of extreme danger. But there are some who turn to God only then.

There is a story about a sea captain who in his retirement skippered a boat taking day trippers to the Shetland Islands. On one trip the boat was full of young people. These laughed at the old captain when they saw him saying a prayer before setting out, because the day was fine and the sea calm.

However, they weren't long out at sea when a storm suddenly blew up, and the boat began to pitch violently. The terrified passengers came to the captain and asked him to join them in prayer. But he replied, 'I say my prayers when it's calm. When it's rough, I attend to my ship.'

There is a lesson here for us. If we cannot or will not seek God in the quiet moments of our lives, we are not likely to find him when trouble strikes. We are more likely to panic. But if we have learnt to seek him and to trust him in the quiet moments, then most certainly we will find him when the going gets rough.

Life can be compared to a voyage. Though each of us has to pilot our own little craft, the life of a Christian is not meant to be a solo voyage. We journey with our fellow Christians, and thus are able to support one another in times of difficulty. One of the shortest prayers ever composed was written by a French sailor. It goes like this: 'Lord my boat is small and the ocean is great.' This little prayer expresses everything. 'Lord, my boat is small and the ocean is great.'

HOMILY 3   **Turning to God only in times of crisis**

One day while on a journey across country a man came to a river. While attempting to cross the river, the current swept him off his feet, and to his horror he found himself being carried down river. Unable to swim, all he could do was to cry out for help. Luckily an alert passer-by heard his cries and threw a lifebelt to him. He grabbed the lifebelt and held on for dear life with both hands until he was pulled ashore. There he quickly recovered from the shock. Then he put the lifebelt back in its place on the riverbank, and resumed his journey.

Pretty well everybody turns to God in times of extreme danger. We see an example of this in today's Gospel. The apostles were rowing along in the quiet of the evening, making steady progress, when a storm suddenly struck. One minute they were in control. Next minute everything was out of control. They did what they could but it was not enough. And their faith seemed to have evaporated. In their grave need they cried out to Jesus for help: 'Lord, save us. We are going down.'

Yes, in times of danger everybody turns to God. But there are some who turn to God only then. In a time of crisis they turn to God, begging him to rescue them. And they are prepared to pay a high price if only God will come to their rescue. For it they are willing to give up their worldly possessions, their treasures, their lusts, their greeds, vanities and hates. But once the crisis has passed, they quickly snatch their treasures back and proceed to live as before.

For such people God is like a lifebelt – useful in a crisis but otherwise irrelevant. In the dark God is their only guarantor, their only shield against death. But in the light they disown God. If our relationship with God is based on fear rather than on love, very likely that is what we will do.

But for other people faith, in the sense of reliance on God, is the air they breathe, the bread they eat, the path they walk.

There is a lesson here for all of us. When things are normal and we are in control, we may think we have a firm faith. It is only when things get out of control that we find out how much faith we really have. Then we must know how to turn to God, and trust that he will see us through it.

Danger can be a grace. Danger sweeps our lives clean of trivia, leaving only the essentials. In the hour of danger we discover a lot about ourselves, about others, and about God. We can do in difficult times what in easier times seems impossible. Why? Because in difficult times we are forced to call on more of our inner resources.

But in the end, only God can save us.

ANOTHER STORY

The sycamore tree came crashing down during a modest storm which struck on the first day of June. The fact that it fell at the start of summer surprised many people. After all, it had withstood the storms of winter which usually are far more severe.

But the reason for its sudden collapse was not too deeply hidden. In winter the tree was bare. The wind whistled through its empty branches, unable to get a proper hold on it. But in summer it was a different matter. Now the tree was clothed with an abundance of large leaves. Hence, the wind was able to get a firm grip on it, and wrestled it out of the ground.

Trees are more vulnerable before summer storms because they are loaded with leaves. People too have more to fear from 'summer' storms than from 'winter' storms. By summer storms I mean ones that come when things are good. And the rich have more to fear when the storm hits than the poor. The poor seem to have more resilience, and of course have less to lose. This may account for the fact that when apartheid was still the system of government in South Africa, suicides were three times higher among whites than among blacks.

PRAYER OF THE FAITHFUL

President: The apostles cried out to the Lord in their trouble and he rescued them. Let us now bring our needs before the Lord, confident that he will hear our prayers too.

Response: Lord, hear our prayer.

Reader(s): For the Church, the barque of Peter: that it may not lose heart when storms of dissension or persecution blow up. [Pause] Let us pray to the Lord.

For world leaders: that they may persevere in their efforts to bring peace to those parts of the world where conflict exists. [Pause] Let us pray to the Lord.

For homes where there are stormy relationships. [Pause] Let us pray to the Lord.

For the sick and the lonely: that through our love they may know that God cares about them. [Pause] Let us pray to the Lord.

For all gathered here: that we may nourish our faith through regular prayer. [Pause] Let us pray to the Lord.

For our own special needs. [Longer pause] Let us pray to the Lord.

President: All-powerful God, grant that in the midst of life's storms we may experience the calming presence of your Son, so that we may find peace and tranquillity in your service. We ask this through the same Christ our Lord.

PRAYER FOR PEACE

Lord Jesus Christ, when a storm blew up and threatened to sink the apostles' boat, you said: 'Why are you frightened, men of little faith?' Then you spoke to the wind and the sea, and there came a great calm. Calm the storms which anger causes to blow up among us, so that we may enjoy the peace and unity of your kingdom where you live for ever and ever.

REFLECTION   **Faith tested**

My faith is tested many times every day,
and more times than I'd like to confess,
I'm unable to keep the banner of faith aloft.
If a promise is not kept, or if a secret is betrayed,
or if I experience long-lasting pain,
I begin to doubt God and God's love.
I fall into the chasm of disbelief and I cry out in despair.
But then the Spirit lifts me up again,
and once more I am secured in faith.
I don't know how that happens,
save when I cry out earnestly I am answered immediately
and am returned to faithfulness.
I am once again filled with Spirit
and firmly planted on solid ground.

Maya Angelu
(Wouldn't Take Nothing for My Journey Now
1993, New York, Bantam Books)

Thirteenth Sunday of the Year
JESUS' POWER OVER SICKNESS AND DEATH

INTRODUCTION AND CONFITEOR

In the Gospel we see that Jesus healed sick people by touching them. He touched people in various ways: with his words, with his hands, with his love. The Eucharist brings us very close to Jesus. And we too need his healing touch in our lives. [Pause]

Lord Jesus, you bring pardon and peace to sinners. Lord, have mercy.
You give new hope to those in anguish and despair. Christ, have mercy.
You comfort the broken-hearted. Lord, have mercy.

HEADINGS FOR READINGS

First Reading (Wis 1:13-15; 2:23-24). God did not make us for death but for life, here and hereafter.

Second Reading (2 Cor 8:7.9.13-15). St Paul is appealing to the Corinthians to contribute to a collection for the poor in the Church at Jerusalem.

Gospel (Mk 5:21-43). Both of the miracles related here are signs of God's power, restoring life and health through Jesus.

SCRIPTURE NOTE

In today's Gospel we have two more of the miracles referred to in the Scripture Note for last Sunday.

These miracles show that Jesus' saving power can overcome sickness and even death. The reading from Wisdom serves as a backdrop to this message. God did not create human beings in order to destroy them, but that they should enjoy a blessed immortality.

Both the woman with the haemorrhage and the daughter of Jairus were beyond the help of any earthly power. The great faith of the woman and of Jairus is stressed. Both believed that Jesus possessed a supernatural power to heal. Both miracles are signs of God's power, restoring life and health through Jesus. The raising of the little girl is a foreshadowing of Jesus' gift of eternal life to all who believe in him.

HOMILY 1   **Looking for a quick fix**

The woman who came to Jesus was desperate. For twelve years had been suffering from an illness and had many painful and fruitless treatments at the hands of various doctors. It had also cost her every penny she had. She had exhausted all human possibilities of healing.

Then she heard about Jesus. She believed that if only she could touch the hem of his garment she would be well. (In those days it was believed that it was enough to touch the clothes of a holy person to get a cure.) She showed great determination in getting through the crowd. However, she wasn't seeking an encounter with Jesus. What she was looking for was a 'quick fix'.

Often we too opt for the 'quick-fix' even though we realise that it is unsatisfactory and that we are being short-changed. We opt for the quick Mass, and the quick Confession (Tell your sins, make an act of contrition, get absolution, and run!) The same with a visit to the doctor – get a prescription and go.

Yet we don't like to be treated in a hasty and impersonal manner. So why then do we opt for the 'quick fix'? Because there is a part of us that shies away from a personal encounter. Why is this? Because we know that it is more demanding. We want to get it over with as quickly and painlessly as possible.

The woman's faith was rewarded. She got her quick cure. However, just as she was about to slink off into the anonymity of the crowd, Jesus sought her out. He didn't go in for this kind of cure. Some healers reduce human contact to a minimum. Not so Jesus. He always dealt with people on a personal level. Besides, he knew that power had gone out from him, which shows that every cure took something out of him.

He insisted on having a face-to-face encounter with her. In this he wasn't thinking of himself but of her. He knew she would feel better afterwards. He knew she needed not just physical healing, but psychological and spiritual healing too. After all her years of sickness she was feeling bad about herself and alienated from God too.

So he met her. In the encounter we see the sensitivity and courtesy of Jesus. A woman with a haemorrhage would have been ritually unclean. She had no business in the crowd, and, by touching Jesus, she rendered him ritually unclean too, or so others would have reckoned. Jesus did not scold her for her 'reprehensible' conduct. Instead, he commended her faith. And spoke lovely words to her: 'My daughter, your faith has restored you to health; go in peace and be free of your complaint.'

It was not enough just to touch him. Others touched him. She touched him with faith. Faith enabled this poor, frightened, sick, untouchable woman to recognise Jesus' power, and she awakened that power with a touch.

Jesus let her know that he was happy for her. In saying to her, 'Your faith has made you well,' he was telling her that she had played a part in her own healing. He confirmed the fact that she was cured. This would have given her comfort and assurance.

How good all this must have made her feel. How much better this was than an impersonal, hasty, and secretive cure. Jesus made her feel as if she was the only person in the world.

In therapy and healing the problem is always the whole person, never the symptom alone. Questions have to be asked which challenge the whole personality. It's not just the leg, or arm, that is being treated, but a person. Jesus never cured just an illness; he cured a sick person. His words healed the spirit; his touch healed the body.

HOMILY 2   **The price of healing**

To achieve success at something we have to put something of ourselves, of our very life and of our very soul, into it, so much so that we feel drained afterwards. This is especially true of healing.

Healing can be exhausting and painful for the healer. The healing act itself is often an occasion of suffering. We can't take away suffering without somehow and to some degree entering into it, if only by just trying to understand the sufferer, and drawing close to him or her. The healer must in some way suffer.

Sometimes what leads people to become healers is an experience of having been sick themselves and having been healed. Healers need to be very conscious of their own vulnerability. They are themselves vulnerable, and that is part of the reason they heal. Jesus was totally vulnerable to people. He took their pain into himself; he suffered with each one.

Even when he was surrounded by people, if someone touched him and was healed, he knew it. Why was this? It was because each cure took something out of him. In the words of the Gospel: 'power went out of him'. And he felt it going out of him. It was this power and the faith of the sick person that produced the cure.

Every time Jesus healed someone it took something out of him. His greatness was that he was prepared to pay the price of helping others. We are following in his steps when we give of ourselves in helping others.

Each of us could do some healing if we allowed ourselves to become his instruments. We may not be able to cure, but it is within our power to care. And to care is a very healing thing. We dress the wound, but it's God who does the healing.

However, each act of caring would cost us something. Power would go out of us. But we need never become rundown. If we maintain contact with the Lord, power will be continually restored to us.

Some people possess a self-confidence and optimism which acts as a tonic for the sick. Energy goes out from them and enters others. Through their touch, their look, their mere presence, they give life to others. They are happy when helping others, and helping others is healing.

All of us to some degree are wounded. But we tend to hide our wounds. The woman who came to Jesus was a deeply wounded person. In her case the wound was visible. But people can be wounded without it appearing on the outside. They carry invisible wounds – feelings of rejection, failure, worthlessness, loneliness, bitterness, hostility ... So all of us need healing.

And all of us can be healers. Our lives are continually touching those of other people. With a little sympathy we could heal a wounded heart. With a little care we could ease a troubled mind. With a little of our time we could ease the pain of loneliness for someone. From time to time each of us should stop and ask ourselves: 'What goes out from me through my words, my deeds, my relationships – hurting or healing?'

Healing is not a task only for the individual. If we can create communities where people can get together, work together, and support each other, then healing becomes a part of everyday life.

HOMILY 3   **Power even over death**

Jairus, the leader of the synagogue, came to Jesus begging for a cure for his twelve-year-old daughter. Even though she was still alive, like the woman with the haemorrhage, she was clearly beyond the help of any earthly power. The man's request showed that he believed that Jesus possessed a supernatural power, the power to heal.

Jesus immediately set out for the house of Jairus. But while they were on their way the news came that the girl had died. The messengers suggested that there was no point in troubling Jesus further. In effect they were saying was that even the power of Jesus could not prevail over death. We see the same attitude of hopelessness expressed in the weeping of the mourners.

But Jesus ignored the words of the messengers. And he rebuked and finally expelled the mourners. His serene hope contrasted sharply with the despair of those around him. He urged Jairus to have faith, faith that even in death his little child was not out of reach of his power. 'Don't be afraid; only believe.'

Jesus went into the child's room with her parents and the three disciples. Then taking her by the hand he said, 'Little girl, I say to you arise.' And immediately the little girl got up and began to walk about. Jesus told them to give her something to eat. There is such gentleness and tenderness in the scene. Jesus showed such love for the little girl and for her parents.

What are we to make of this story? We have to ask what the early Christians made of it. They too suffered illnesses, and members of their community were dying off.

For Mark and his readers the story was a manifestation of the power of the risen Lord to dominate death itself. Jesus raises the dead girl because he is 'the resurrection and the life'. Faith in Jesus can transform life, and is victory over death. That's what this story would have meant for the early Christians.

For those who believe in Jesus, death is only a sleep from which he can and will awaken them. In the case of most Christians, this awakening will not happen in this life, but in the world to come. Thus the early Christians described the dead as 'sleeping' because they believed that they will one day be awakened, just as people who are asleep are awakened. The word the early Christians used for a burial place means 'a sleeping place' – *koimeterion*, from which the word 'cemetery' comes.

Both stories show that, even when, humanly speaking, there is no hope, the power of God can prevail over sickness and even death itself. Mark is telling us that this power is present in Jesus.

ANOTHER APPROACH   **The difference faith makes**

The woman in the Gospel had been sick for twelve years. That's a long time, a huge chunk of life. But she was a woman of faith.

Patients who have no faith are at a disadvantage. They endure a threefold suffering: they suffer their disease; they suffer on account of its meaninglessness (for them it is nothing but a vexation, the result of blind chance); and they suffer because it suspends their life. They see their illness as something to be endured rather than lived. Their lives are on hold as they wait passively for things to get back to normal so that they can begin to live again. They are living in the future rather than the present.

On the other hand, patients with faith are in a much better position. Though faith may not deliver them from their disease, or diminish the suffering it causes them, believers continue to live as intensely as before, and even more so. They can seek God in sickness as well as in health, and their sickness can turn out to be such a fruitful experience that they will bless that sickness.

Nevertheless, it's not easy to deal positively with illness. But unless people do, the time of illness becomes a complete waste, just so much junk. They throw away the vital raw material instead of trying to transform it.

The sick must be helped to see their illness in the larger context of their life. To see it, not as some unfortunate episode in their life, but as an intrinsic part of it. This is not the junk of life. This is as true as any other part of life, and has the potential to enrich them.

Patients must be helped to tap into their spiritual resources in times of crisis. Spirituality can thrive in a hospital environment. Here the human spirit, stripped of power and status, is at its most vulnerable. It is then especially that spiritual resources can become available to us. It is then that we are forced to draw on them. So an enrichment, a deepening of the person can result.

God's love can be experienced even in suffering. God's presence does not necessarily take away suffering, but gives us the power to transform it. We need God to help us so that our souls are not reduced to pure passivity, to being mere objects, acted upon but never acting.

We are not caring for the soul when we protect ourselves from the impact of illnesses, visits to the doctor and/or hospital. The soul is nurtured by want as well as by plenty.

From our illnesses we can derive a new understanding of our vulnerability as human beings. 'Illnesses exist to remind us that we are not made of wood' (Van Gogh). A painful experience causes us to reflect on our lives, and teaches us to be compassionate towards other sufferers. Compassion is not learned without suffering.

PRAYER OF THE FAITHFUL

President: The Lord rescues us from all that depresses us, and even from death itself. Let us pray to him with great faith.

Response: Lord, hear our prayer.

Reader(s): For the Church: that through its ministry people may experience the healing power of Christ. [Pause] Let us pray to the Lord.

For our political and civil leaders: that God may enable them to carry out their responsibilities with wisdom and compassion. [Pause] Let us pray to the Lord.

For doctors, nurses, and all those who care for the sick. [Pause] Let us pray to the Lord.

For those who have no one to care for them, no one to touch their wounds. [Pause] Let us pray to the Lord.

For all gathered here: that we may be aware of the power we have to heal: a kind word can heal a wounded spirit; a kind deed can heal a wounded heart. [Pause] Let us pray to the Lord.

For our own individual needs. [Longer pause] Let us pray to the Lord.

President: Heavenly Father, you sent your Son into the world to heal our wounds of body, mind, and spirit. Help us to have complete faith in his healing power and in your love for us. We ask this through the same Christ our Lord.

REFLECTION   **The power to heal**

Each of us is capable of doing some healing,
because we have eyes that can see,
ears that can hear,
tongues that can speak,
hands that can touch,
and above all a heart that can love.
Lord, make us instruments of your healing power.
Where there is hatred, let us sow love.

Where there is injury, pardon;
where there is doubt, faith;
where there is despair, hope;
where there is darkness, light;
And where there is sadness, joy. Amen.

Fourteenth Sunday of the Year
REJECTING THE MESSENGER

INTRODUCTION AND CONFITEOR

When Jesus returned to Nazareth it was a sad occasion for him, because the people rejected him. But they themselves were the real losers, because he was unable to do anything for them. Jesus comes to us during this Eucharist. We have a chance to listen to him with faith and to receive him with love. [Pause]

Lord Jesus, you come to reconcile us with one another and with the Father. Lord, have mercy.

Lord Jesus, you heal our wounds of sin and division. Christ, have mercy.

Lord Jesus, you intercede for us now at the right hand of the Father. Lord, have mercy.

HEADINGS AND READINGS

First Reading (Ezek 2:2-5). God sends a prophet to his people to ensure that they do not remain in ignorance of their disobedience.

Second Reading (2 Cor 12:7-10). In his weakness Paul experiences the power of God's grace.

Gospel (Mk 6:1-6). True to the proverb that no prophet is honoured by his own people, Jesus is rejected by the people of Nazareth.

SCRIPTURE NOTE

A biblical prophet is someone who has received a divine call to speak God's word to his people (First Reading). Even though the Word of God could be a hard word, it was a word of love because it meant that God had not abandoned his people. God's spokesman had to be prepared for opposition and rejection. It was so for the Old Testament prophets, and for Jesus himself.

At the close of his Galilean ministry Jesus is rejected by the people of his home town, who can't bring themselves to believe in the greatness of someone who is one of themselves. Consequently, his power is ineffective there. Their rejection of him is an anticipation of his rejection by the

Jewish nation as a whole.

Christians today should not grow discouraged by lack of belief. Paul's experience of weakness ('a thorn in the flesh') taught him humility, and allowed him to experience God's power in a way that might not otherwise have been possible. The words 'My grace is sufficient for you', are spoken to us too, and should be a great consolation to us in our struggles.

HOMILY 1   **Rejected by his own**

Jesus went back to his native place, and to the people among whom he had grown up. It soon became clear to them that he had changed. Away from Nazareth he had found his true vocation (work), and his gifts (of teaching and healing) had blossomed. He now had a reputation as a teacher and a worker of miracles.

Often people have to go away from home and their native place in order to blossom. At home they may feel cramped, or stifled through lack of opportunity, challenge, and recognition.

When they come back home, people are not ready for this. They want to see the one who went away come back as he left them. Then they will feel comfortable with him and accept him. He will be no challenge to them.

Better again if he should come back down in his luck. Then they would all feel sorry for him. But let him come back a changed person, and they are likely to resent and reject him. They themselves may be stuck in a rut. Hence, they resent the one who went away and made something of himself. They try to cut him down to size – their own size.

Anyway, Jesus was back, and dearly wanted to share his gifts with his own people. But instead of being welcomed, he found people watching him, studying him, and scrutinising him.

As soon as he began to speak in the synagogue they could see that he had a special gift – the gift of wisdom. Initially they were impressed, even to the point of being amazed. Yet, instead of rejoicing at this, and opening themselves to what he had to offer, they ask, 'Where did he get all this?' They figured that someone must have given it to him. But the simple answer was: it was in him all the time.

'Where did he (she) get all this?' is a question many parents have asked on hearing a child of theirs come out with something that has made them wonder. Here we are dealing with the mystery of a person's development. Who are we to set limits and boundaries to what another person is capable of?

The people of Nazareth remembered Jesus' humble origins. After all, what was he but an ordinary artisan, whose family was well known to them. In effect they were saying: 'Who does he think he is?' They felt they had him summed up. They had set boundaries to his capabilities. An attitude like that doesn't allow for growth and development.

They refused to believe in him. They refused to take him seriously. Because of their attitude they made it impossible for him to do anything for them, and so did not benefit from his visit.

It's a sad but familiar story – the prophet not accepted by his own people. Often we fail to acknowledge the gifts and talents of those who are close to us, in our own house or in our neighbourhood. We don't appreciate or recognise them, and so limit their effectiveness. We don't give them a chance. Worse, we put them down. We do them a great injustice. And we too suffer because we do not benefit from their goodness and gifts.

It's hurtful to be rejected by anyone. But it's particularly hurtful to be rejected by one's own people. Jesus was amazed at their lack of faith. He greatly desired to help them but found himself unable to do so. You can't help people against their will. He was saddened but not angered. Rejection can easily turn into anger.

We've all experienced a little of this. We have wanted to help someone but our help was refused. We feel frustrated and helpless. When we meet with rejection, we may be tempted to say, 'That's it! I'm finished.' We decide not to help or care anymore. It's too painful.

Jesus didn't react like this. He didn't become embittered. He did what little he could in Nazareth – he cured a few sick people. Then he decided to take his light and his gifts elsewhere.

HOMILY 2   **Thorn in the flesh**

In a moment of great frankness, Paul tells us that he was granted all kind of visions by God which made him feel that he had one foot in heaven already. But he tells us that he was also given a 'thorn in the flesh' to remind him of his human weakness and to keep him humble.

A thorn in the flesh – it's a striking and powerful image. We've all had experience of a thorn in a foot or in a finger. And we are familiar with the expression 'a thorn in the side'.

The image suggests something raw and painful – a constant nagging thing, which is impossible to ignore. It is something which shouldn't be there. It is extremely annoying and makes us angry. It may be quite a small thing. But small thorns can be extremely painful.

The 'thorn' is an image of a problem, and can take many forms – an illness, a worry, a burden, an addiction, a compulsion … It may be another person who is difficult to live with. Paul doesn't tell us what his 'thorn' consisted in. Most likely it was a recurring physical illness.

But he does tell us that he dearly wanted to be rid of it. Many times he begged God to remove this 'thorn', but God did not do so. This shows that we shouldn't just accept the thorn. We should try to get rid of it.

Eventually Paul had to accept the fact that the thorn was there to stay. But God assured him that he would give him the strength to cope with it: 'My grace is sufficient for you.' We too may have to accept that our 'thorn' is there to stay. But the words 'My grace is sufficient for you' are spoken to us too, and should be a great consolation to us. God works in spite of human weakness, indeed, even through human weakness.

Paul eventually came to value and even boast of his thorn. It kept him humble. It gave him an experience of weakness and powerlessness. It was then that he experienced the power of God's grace. It is in times of calm, when his boat is going nowhere, that a sailor appreciates the power of the wind.

So it can be with us. In our weakness, we experience the power of God. In our darkness, we experience his light. In our sins, we experience his mercy. If the 'thorn' makes us rely more on the power of God, and have more recourse to him, then it will become a source of growth and grace for us.

HOMILY 3   **Rejecting the messenger**

A travelling circus was staying on the outskirts of a village. One evening, shortly before show time, a fire broke out in one of the tents. The manager sent the clown, who was already dressed up for his act, into the nearby village for help. There was a danger that the fire would spread across the fields of dry stubble and burn the village itself.

The clown hurried into the village. He asked the people to come out as quickly as possible to help to quench the fire. But the people didn't take him seriously. They thought it was a brilliant piece of advertising on the part of the management. He tried his best to make them understand that there really was a fire. But the harder he tried the more they laughed at him. Finally the fire reached the village and burned it to the ground.

The main reason why the villagers didn't listen to the man was that they looked upon him as a clown. This made it virtually impossible for them to examine the truth of what he was saying to them.

Something similar happened to Jesus when he returned to his native village of Nazareth. The people refused to listen to him. They knew too much about him. The message never had a chance because they rejected the messenger. In fact, they tried to do away with him.

What truth did he tell his fellow villagers that they found so threatening that they wanted to kill him? He pointed out to them that they were God's chosen people. That one would, therefore, expect to find some faith among them. Yet he told them that he found more faith among the pagans (the Gentiles). He went on to suggest that the Gentiles would take their place in the Kingdom. For this they wanted to kill him.

One of the signs of God's care for his people was that he kept on sending them messengers (the prophets) to call them back to the right path. Even though the word of the prophets was often a critical one, it was a word spoken out of love.

God does the same for us. He does not leave us in the darkness of error or wrong-doing. He sends us messengers, mostly those near us. Who else could it be? But we too may reject the messengers, especially when the message may not be one that we want to hear. The truth can hurt.

'You are working too hard. You're out of the house far too much. You have no home life for yourselves or the children ... You're spoiling your children ... You're too materialistic ... You drink too much ... You're full of prejudice ... You always put yourself first ... Your worship of God is mere lip-service.'

If someone were to say one or more of these things to us, how would we react? Might we not want to attack the messenger? The fact is, none of us have any particular appetite for the truth. We ought to pray for the courage to listen to the truth even though it may be painful and come as a blow to our pride. The truth, as Jesus says, will set us free.

The person who out of love for us tells us the truth, knowing that it is going to hurt, and at the risk of losing our friendship, is a true friend.

We should also pray for the courage to be able to speak the truth to others. To set a person on the right road is a great thing. But there is a way of doing this. It has to be done with love and concern for the person. The secret is to be totally honest and totally kind at the same time.

ANOTHER STORY

Two paupers wandered from town to town, begging for alms. One was a giant who had never been sick in his life; the other was a cripple who had never known anything but sickness. The giant used to laugh at the cripple. The cripple took his mockery very much to heart, and in his resentment prayed that God would punish his cruel companion.

At last the two paupers reached the capital city. They arrived just at the time when a great misfortune had happened to the king. Two of his most trusted servants had died suddenly. One was his personal body-guard, the strongest man in the land; the other was his personal physician, the most skilful physician in the entire realm. So the king sent couriers into all the towns and villages of his kingdom to gather into the capital all the strong men and doctors who wished to apply for the vacant posts.

The king finally chose one strong man and one doctor from among all the applicants. He then asked them to furnish proof of their fitness for the posts they were to fill.

'Your Majesty,' said the strong man, 'Bring to me the strongest and biggest man in this city and I will kill him with one blow of my fist.'

And the doctor said, 'Your Majesty, bring me the most helpless cripple you can find and I will make him well in one week.'

So the king sent messengers throughout the city looking for the strongest man and the most helpless cripple. Luck was with them, for they soon came upon the two paupers. So they brought them before the king.

With one blow of his fist the strong man killed the giant. Then the doctor examined the cripple, and after a week's treatment he made him well.

The strength of the strong often proves to be their downfall, while the weakness of the weak often saves them. People don't fall because they are weak but because they think they are strong. Paul was content with his weakness. He said, 'It is when I am weak that I am strong.' The recognition of his own weakness made him rely on Christ, whose power then became available to him.

May the Lord help us to be aware of our weakness, and strengthen us against it.

PRAYER OF THE FAITHFUL

President: God still speaks his word to us and to the world. Let us pray for the grace to be open to the truth.

Response: Lord, hear our prayer.

Reader(s): For Christians: that they may be able to speak Christ's truth to the world with courage and love. [Pause] Let us pray to the Lord.

For our political leaders: that they may listen to the voices of those prophetic people who speak the truth. [Pause] Let us pray to the Lord.

For all those who live in the darkness of error or prejudice. [Pause] Let us pray to the Lord.

For the grace to be able to cope with whatever is proving to be 'a thorn in the flesh' for us right now. [Pause] Let us pray to the Lord.

For grace to recognise the good in the people with whom we share our lives. [Pause] Let us pray to the Lord.

For our own special needs. [Longer pause] Let us pray to the Lord.

President: Merciful God, deliver us from the cowardice that shrinks from new truth; from the laziness that is content with only half of the truth; and from the arrogance that thinks it knows it all. We ask this through the same Christ our Lord.

REFLECTION   **Disturb us, O Lord**

Disturb us, O Lord,
  when we are too well pleased with ourselves;
  when our dreams have come true because we dreamed too little;
  when we have arrived safely

because we sailed too close to the shore.
Stir us, O Lord, to dare more boldly,
to venture more seas, where storms shall show your mastery,
where losing sight of land we shall find the stars.
In the name of him who pushed back the horizons of our hopes
and invited the brave to follow him. Amen.

Author unknown

Fifteenth Sunday of the Year
WORKING FOR CHRIST

INTRODUCTION AND CONFITEOR

We come to the Lord at his invitation, to receive from him. And at the end
of Mass we are sent out to share with others the gifts we have received
from the Lord. Here the Lord forgives our sins, speaks his word to us,
and nourishes us with the food of the Eucharist. By bringing us together
he makes it possible for us to support one another. [Pause]

Let us ask the Lord's forgiveness for the wrong we have done and the
good we have failed to do.

HEADINGS AND READINGS

First Reading (Amos 7:12-15). The prophet Amos is faithful to the task
God gave him, even though he is rejected by those to whom he is sent.

Second Reading (Eph 1:3-14). This is a hymn of thanksgiving to God for
the great spiritual gifts he had given us in Christ.

Gospel (Mk 6:7-13). Jesus sends out the twelve apostles in twos as his
representatives.

SCRIPTURE NOTE

Amos is sent to prophesy to the people of Israel (First Reading). In the
Gospel we have the sending out of the Twelve.

Amos was a prophet by divine call. In his case the call had come to a
poor, unsophisticated shepherd and 'dresser of sycamore trees', a total
outsider to the ranks of professional prophets. Much the same could be
said about the men Jesus chose 'to be with him'. Jesus having instructed
them, the time had come for them to take an active part in his ministry.
Their mission was an extension of his own mission, and he gave them the
power to accomplish this.

In understanding his instructions as to what they were to take with
them, we must remember that this was only a temporary mission, of short

duration and limited to the surrounding Jewish towns and villages. The final commissioning, in which they were sent to the whole world, was still in the future.

HOMILY 1   **He sent them out**

Jesus sent the apostles out. Christianity is always like that. It is never something to be kept to oneself. It always involves an outreach to others. Without that element it would not be Christianity. And it has been proved over and over again that every person is capable of sacrifice.

Up to now the apostles had been with Jesus. During that time he had instructed them. But he chose them for a mission – to help spread the news of the kingdom of God. The time had come for them to get involved in that work. He sent them out in twos so that they could support one another and learn to work with others. He empowered them to speak and act in his name.

Keep in mind that this was only a temporary mission, of short duration and limited to the surrounding Jewish towns and villages. The final commissioning, in which they were sent to the whole world, was still in the future.

Their mission in the first place was a spiritual one – to preach repentance and the imminent coming of the kingdom of God. But it was also concerned with physical and mental healing. This shows that Christianity is concerned with people's spiritual well-being and with their physical well-being. In other words, with the whole person.

They were to bring no material things with them to give to the people. In any case, they probably didn't have them. There is always the danger that if missionaries come loaded down with material gifts the message may be accepted for the wrong reasons. Their message must sell itself on its own merits, and has to be accepted principally for spiritual reasons.

As for personal possessions, they are to bring only the bare essentials – sandals and a staff. For food and lodgings they are to rely on the hospitality of the people to whom they are being sent. In effect, this means relying on divine providence. But in that way the people will feel that they are giving something also. There will be a sharing. This is good for the missionaries: they need the people to whom they are sent. And it is good for the people to whom they are sent: it is good for their dignity, and also encourages generosity among them.

The missionaries are to witness to poverty by their detachment from material things. And they are to show solidarity with the poor, by joining them in their struggles and sharing their poverty. Their main task is to preach the message. But they won't be able to control the response of the people, nor should they try to do so. They have to respect their freedom. And they have to expect that some will refuse it.

If their preaching is rejected they are to react only with a symbolic gesture – shaking the dust from their feet. This was a highly symbolic act for the Jews of that time. The people would have known exactly what it meant. It meant that the apostles were dissociating themselves completely from them and henceforth would regard them as heathens. However, it was meant as a gesture of concern. Its purpose was to make them think again about what was being offered them and the consequences of their refusal. It showed the fate of those who refuse the gifts of God.

This Gospel passage has great relevance for us. The Gospel still needs to be preached, and it needs those who accept it. Jesus' instructions are still relevant for missionaries of today. Though conditions have changed, the basic principles remain the same. They challenge those whose task it is to preach the Gospel, and those to whom it is preached – it shows the importance of being open to the word of God.

It's a great challenge to us all to be active, not passive followers; to be not only receivers but also givers. Not barren or dead branches of the Vine, but living and fruitful ones.

We saw how Amos was called away from his ordinary work to preach the message (First Reading). So too were the twelve apostles. We are not. Only a few are called to actually preach the Gospel. But all of us are called to witness to it. We do this principally by living it – by being disciples of Christ in fact as well as in name.

HOMILY 2   **God has made us responsible**

In a sense, belief in God is very uncomfortable because it increases our responsibility. If there was no God, then there would be no point in being responsible – it's just chaos and eternal night.

If someone comes to us and asks our help, we should not turn him away with pious words, saying, 'Have faith; take your troubles to God and he will help you.' In such cases we should act as if there was no God, as if there was only one person in all the world who could help this person, namely, myself.

Reliance on the providence of God is an essential part of Christianity. But it must not be used as an excuse for doing nothing. We mustn't stand back and wait for God to do it all. God is not going to come down and do it himself. God works through us.

One winter's day a man came upon a small boy sitting begging on a wind-swept city bridge. The boy was shivering from the cold and obviously in need of a good meal. On seeing him the man got very angry and said to God:

'Lord, why don't you do something about this boy?'

And God replied, 'I have already done something about him.'

This surprised the man so he said, 'I hope you don't mind me saying this: but whatever you did, it doesn't seem to be working.'

'I agree with you there,' God relied.

'By the way, what did you do?' the man asked.

'I made you,' came the reply.

There's nothing wrong in asking God to right wrongs and comfort the suffering. But what we must remember is that he has entrusted these tasks to us.

We are God's instruments. That is our dignity, and also our responsibility. We must become convinced that without our love others will not achieve the things God has willed for them. We see this so clearly from today's Gospel. There we see how Jesus shared his work of spreading the kingdom of God with the apostles.

Of course, we may ask ourselves: what can we do? We have to answer that question for ourselves. But the following example points us in the right direction.

An unemployed couple lived in Dallas, Texas. They were very poor and used to go around the city collecting aluminium beer tins which they sold for recycling. In their work they looked into many a refuse bin.

One morning they made a very sad discovery in one particular bin. In it they found the body of a new-born baby. They reported it to the police, who carried out an investigation but failed to trace the parents. So there was no one to bury the baby.

The couple then knew what they had to do. They themselves would see to it that the unknown baby got a decent funeral. But this would cost money, something they had very little of. The wife pawned her only valuable possession, a diamond engagement ring, to help pay the funeral expenses.

Thanks to their efforts, the baby went to its final resting place in a white coffin covered with flowers. The tears the couple shed were as pure as those shed by Jesus at the grave of his friend, Lazarus.

To be a source of light in the world one doesn't need to be either rich or famous. All one needs is a warm heart.

HOMILY 3   **Christ needs us**

The Korean war was raging. A little village came under heavy artillery fire. In the village stood a Catholic church. Outside the church, mounted on a pedestal, was a fine statue of Christ. However, when the smoke of battle cleared away, the statue had disappeared. It had been blown off its pedestal and lay in fragments on the ground.

A group of American soldiers helped the priest to collect up the fragments. Carefully they put the statue together again. They found all the pieces except the hands. They offered to fly the back to America and have hands made for it. But the priest refused.

'I have a better idea', he said. 'Let's leave it without hands. And we'll write on the pedestal the words: FRIEND, LEND ME YOUR HANDS. In that way passers-by will come to see that Christ now has no hands but ours with which to raise up the fallen; no feet but ours to seek out the lost; no ears but ours to listen to the lonely; no tongue but ours to speak words of comfort to the lonely.'

This little incident brings out very well the message of today's Gospel. Jesus involved the apostles in his work. He shared his divine mission with them. He gave them his own authority and power. No doubt they made mistakes, which is not surprising considering they were ordinary men.

Amos was a simple shepherd (First Reading). Yet God sent him to preach a message of repentance to his people. Most of the apostles were fishermen. Yet Jesus didn't hesitate to share his work with them. Even more surprising – the day came when he entrusted his entire work to them.

Many in authority have a fear of involving people in a work, especially so-called ordinary people. Hence, people are left with the feeling that they have nothing to contribute. It is good for people to be involved. It makes them responsible. It gives them an opportunity to use their talents. It builds up a community spirit.

But sometimes people don't want to be involved. It's easier to leave it to the experts. The practice of leaving it to the professionals is very common today. Thus, all healing is left to doctors and nurses. All teaching is left to teachers. All the work for the poor is left to the Government or the Vincent de Paul Society.

Of course experts are needed for specialised jobs. But the non-specialist too has a lot to contribute and often has a warmer heart. The sick have as much need of companionship as of medicine. The old need someone to spend time with them. The young need someone to show an interest in them. This is work we all can do. It does not call for any expertise – only a caring heart.

The Bible starts with the story of how God made human beings partners in the work of creation. And Christ made his disciples partners in the work of salvation. A great responsibility has been laid upon us. A great honour has been conferred on us. We are responsible for God's world and for one another. We are stewards of creation. We are co-workers with Christ.

OTHER STORIES

1. The mayor of a certain town decided to hold a harvest festival. All, without exception, were invited. The mayor himself offered to provide the food. To ensure that there would be adequate wine, each guest was asked to bring along a bottle of white wine. The wine would be poured into a huge cask from which all could drink.

The day of the festival arrived. Every man, woman and child in town showed up. Thanks to the generosity of the mayor, there was an abundance of food. Each guest duly arrived with a bottle of wine and poured it into the cask. When all was ready the mayor went to the cask. An aide tapped it and filled the mayor's glass. Holding up the glass, the mayor said, 'I declare the festival open.'

Then he took a drink out of the glass only to discover that it was not wine but water. It seems that each guest had argued like this: 'My contribution won't be missed.' So instead of bringing a bottle of wine they had brought a bottle of water. The festival was ruined

It's a great challenge to us all to be active, not passive followers of Christ; to be not only receivers but also givers. Something is asked of every person. And everybody's contribution, no matter how small, is important. For the forest to be green, the individual trees must be green.

2. Once a knight set out on a long journey. He tried to foresee all the possible problems and dangers he was likely to encounter, and to take precautions against them.

He took a sword and a suit of armour in case he met an enemy. He took a jar of ointment to guard against sunburn. He took an axe to chop wood for a fire at night. He took a tent and several blankets. He took pots and pans for cooking. And of course he took a sackful of oats for his horse. Thus, heavily laden, he set forth.

However, he hadn't gone very far when he came to a rickety old bridge which straddled a deep gorge. He was only halfway across when the bridge collapsed under him, and he fell into the gorge and got killed.

When Jesus sent out the apostles he urged them to place complete trust in God. They were to travel light, taking with them only the essentials. God would take care of his workers.

If we wish to travel speedily and safely, even taking normal precautions, then travel light. But to travel light requires a lot of faith.

PRAYER OF THE FAITHFUL

President: Let us now bring our needs before God, whose help is near to those who turn to him in humility and trust.

Response: Lord, graciously hear us.

Reader(s): For all Christians: that they may realise that Christ has made them his co-workers in building the Kingdom of God on earth. [Pause] Lord, hear us.

For all those in positions of leadership: that they may learn the art of involving others. [Pause] Lord, hear us.

For missionaries and all those who preach the Gospel today: that God may sustain their efforts and their hope. [Pause] Lord, hear us.

For the members of the voluntary organisations in the parish: that God may bless and reward their generosity. [Pause] Lord, hear us.

For ourselves: that we may show forth in our lives the faith we profess with our lips. [Pause] Lord, hear us.

For our own special needs. [Longer pause] Lord, hear us.

President: Lord, may everything we do begin with your inspiration, continue with your help, and reach perfection under your guidance. We ask this through Christ our Lord.

REFLECTION   **Working for Christ**

To do the work of Christ is really quite simple.
It means to be faithful in little things,
for to be faithful in little things is a big thing.
It means to do one's task, no matter how humble,
not only thoroughly but joyfully.
It means to make oneself available,
yet never to seek the limelight.
It means to make oneself useful,
without seeking to push oneself.
It means to carry one's own burden, without,
as far as possible, becoming a burden on others.
In a word, it means to be at one's post,
helpful and faithful, loyal and constant.
Lord, make me an instrument
for the building of your kingdom.

DISMISSAL

At the end of Mass we are not simply dismissed.
We are sent out in the Lord's name and with the Lord's power
to build up of his kingdom in the world ...

Sixteenth Sunday of the Year
SHEEP WITHOUT A SHEPHERD

INTRODUCTION AND CONFITEOR

Every page of the Gospel shows that Jesus cared about people. He cares about us too. He makes us into one people, the people of God, the community of his disciples. Therefore, let us approach him in a spirit of trust and love. [Pause]

Lord, you are our shepherd, granting us all we need. Lord, have mercy.

You are with us even if we walk through the valley of darkness. Christ, have mercy.

You call us to dwell in your own house for ever and ever. Lord, have mercy.

HEADINGS FOR READINGS

First Reading (Jer 23:1-6). The leaders of Israel are indicted for their neglect of the people, but better leaders are promised.

Second Reading (Eph 2:13-18). By his death Christ broke down the wall between Jews and Gentiles, and united all peoples as children of the one Father.

Gospel (Mk 6:30-34). We see the care of Christ for his apostles as well as his compassion for the ordinary people.

SCRIPTURE NOTE

Jeremiah indicts the official leaders for neglecting their duties towards the people (First Reading). They must shoulder the blame for the misfortune that has befallen the people. But God will not let his people languish. He himself will assume the mantle of leadership, and entrust the flock to good and faithful shepherds.

This ties in neatly with the Gospel. Jeremiah's promise is fulfilled in Jesus. We see Jesus, the Good Shepherd, in action. Firstly, we see his care for the Twelve, who have just returned from their missionary work and need a break. Secondly, we see his care for the ordinary people, whom he teaches at length. What a contrast there is between him and the official leaders of his time. Little wonder that the people flocked to him. In Jesus we see the divine compassion in action.

HOMILY 1   **A costly caring**

Once a man went to see a friend of his who was a professor at a great university. However, as they sat chatting in the professor's office, they were continually interrupted by students who came knocking at the door, seeking the professor's advice about something or other. Each time the professor rose from his chair, went to the door, and dealt with the student's request. Eventually the visitor asked the professor, 'How do you manage to get any work done with so many interruptions?'

'At first I used to resent the interruptions to my work. But one day it suddenly dawned on me that the interruptions were my work,' the professor replied.

That professor could have locked himself away and devoted his time to his own private work. In that way he would no doubt have had a quieter life. But being the generous and unselfish person that he was, he couldn't do that. Instead he made his work consist in being available to his students. It was no surprise that he was greatly loved by the students. And it was no coincidence that he was one of the happiest and most fulfilled professors on the campus.

Unselfishness is never easy. Yet at certain times it's easier than at others. It's easier when we are able to plan our good deeds – when the deed is of our own choosing, and we happen to be in the mood, and it causes us the minimum inconvenience and disruption. At other times unselfishness is particularly difficult: when the deed is not of our own choosing, when we don't feel in the mood, and when it is sprung on us at an awkward moment. In such cases we have to forget ourselves, and set aside our feelings and our plans. A real sacrifice is involved.

An act of kindness is judged, not so much by its importance, but by the disruption it causes in the life of the one who does it. It's a great test of people when, at the drop of a hat, they put aside their own plans to help another person.

It's a consolation for us to know that Jesus too had to cope with interruptions. He too had his plans upset. Today's Gospel tells us that he was in such demand that he and his apostles scarcely had time to eat. However, at some point he decided that enough was enough, and took the apostles off to a quiet place for a break.

This time he wasn't thinking of himself but of his apostles. They had just come back from the mission on which he had sent them. He saw that they needed a rest. So he decided to take them off to a quiet place. The carers too need to be cared for.

However, things didn't work out as planned. The people followed them. How did Jesus react? Far from getting annoyed, he received the people. This tells us a lot about the kind of person he was. He was moved with pity for them. He saw that they were leaderless. The official teachers had no time for the ordinary people. But Jesus had time for them. This is why they flocked to him.

Caring is never easy. Some people are willing to care a little, provided they are in the mood, and it's not too inconvenient, and doesn't upset their own plans. But to care as Jesus did, when it does upset one's plans – that's the real test. Parents do it all the time. How many times they have to get out of bed at night to see to a child?

All of us are capable of caring. The need for caring people is great. Neglect is widespread in our society. There are many people in our world who are like sheep without a shepherd. (Give some examples.) When we care, we are living the Gospel.

Good can come out of interruptions. They prevent us from becoming totally preoccupied with ourselves. Selfishness is a kind of prison. Love, on the other hand, sets us free. Helder Camara says:

> Accept surprises that upset your plans, shatter your dreams, give a completely different turn to your day and – Who knows? – to your life. It's not chance. Leave God free to weave the pattern of your days.

HOMILY 2   **On becoming a shepherd**

Amos was the shepherd of a large flock. Tonight it was his turn to act as watchman. The night was bitterly cold. A slight mist had started to fall, so he drew his heavy coat more tightly around him. As he stood there shivering, his mind went back to when it all began.

Right from his youth he had dreamed about becoming a shepherd. He loved sheep and wanted to devote his life to them. But in those far-off days he was very naive. His youthful mind was brimming with romantic ideas. To him a shepherd was someone who loved sheep, and who devoted himself totally to them. What could be simpler? But now his eyes were being opened. The task of shepherding was turning out to be a far more complicated and demanding thing than he had imagined.

How many jobs this one job embraced! At times he was more like a builder than a shepherd, so much time did he spend building and repairing walls and fences. At other times the job required of him the ability of a weather-forecaster. Again at other times it demanded the expertise of a veterinary surgeon, and the skill of a professional tracker. And tonight he was a watchman, no different from countless other watchmen, lost in the silence of the night.

'How different the reality is from the dream,' he said to himself. But then another voice said, 'You are now being given the chance to become in earnest what you naively dreamed about when you started out. There is no such thing as a born shepherd. One becomes a shepherd.'

A shepherd is used in the Bible as an image of a caring person. Thus God is described as the shepherd of his people. And God appointed leaders who were to be shepherds to his people. It's clear from today's First Reading that these failed in their duty.

God indicted the leaders of Israel because they neglected the people. Neglect is a sad thing. Yet it's a cry often heard today: 'You don't care about me.' Or it may be said about our leaders, 'They only care about themselves.' Sometimes it's unfair; but other times, alas, it is justified.

Mother Teresa tells how one day she visited an old people's home in Sweden. It was efficiently run. The food was good. The staff was trained, and treated the old people well. It seemed an ideal place in which to end one's days.

There were about forty elderly people in the home. They seemed to have everything they wanted. Yet as she went around she noticed that none of them smiled. She also noticed something else. They kept looking towards the door. She asked one of the nurses why this was so.

'They are longing for someone to come to visit them,' the nurse replied. 'They are always looking, and thinking, "Maybe my son, maybe my daughter, maybe somebody will come and visit me today." But no one comes. It's the same every day.'

'No one comes!' The phrase haunted Mother Teresa. These elderly people had been put away in this home by their families and then abandoned. That sense of having been abandoned was by far their greatest suffering.

Sometimes a person may have no choice but to put an elderly parent in a home. However, it's the spirit in which this is done that matters. Having put an elderly parent in a home, one person may abandon that parent, whereas another visits that parent regularly.

A Christian who doesn't care is like a lamp that doesn't give light. But caring is never easy. Yet all of us are capable of caring. All that is required is an open heart. When we care, we are living the Gospel.

HOMILY 3   **He had compassion on them**

Counsellors and therapists are told that in dealing with their clients they must at all times control their emotions. They must maintain a certain distance and detachment. This advice makes sense. Otherwise they would not be able to maintain the necessary perspective. They would leave themselves open to manipulation and possible take-over by their clients. They would also be in danger of burn-out. Hence, at all times they must maintain their professional cool.

Yet this coolness, this detachment, can be carried too far. The quality of the relationship between therapist and client is far more important than procedures and techniques. A cold, detached, unsympathetic attitude on the part of the therapist is not conducive to healing. The patient must experience warmth, sympathy and care if healing, change and growth are to take place.

The most successful psychotherapists are those who are able to show warmth and empathy. Therapy works best when the therapist is affected by the plight of the patient, and is not afraid to let the patient see this. The famous psychologist, Carl Jung, said, 'I have learned that only the physician who feels himself deeply affected by his patients could heal.' And Scott Peck, author of *The Road Less Travelled*, goes so far as to say that it is essential for the therapist to love a patient for the therapy to be successful.

When as a patient you meet someone who seems to understand what it is like to be you, without wanting to analyse you or judge you, then you find it easier to open up. When you discover that your pain is felt by the person in whom you have confided, it makes you want to get well.

Yet professionals often come across as cold – cold to people who are extremely vulnerable. Many people are unable to deal with pain. You hear some people say, 'I could never be a doctor or a nurse – I can't bear to see people suffer.' The best doctors and nurses are precisely those who can't bear to see people suffering, and therefore try their best to relieve that suffering. But this doesn't mean that there aren't limits.

While professionals tend to keep their distance amateurs tend to get more involved with patients. The former often look down on the latter, yet the latter sometimes achieve more. This is not surprising when you realise that the word 'amateur' comes from the Latin word *amare* , which means 'to love'. In the long run, love is the thing that heals.

Jesus was no detached healer. He showed care and compassion for those who suffered. And he wasn't afraid to let the sufferers know that he cared about them. There is a fine example of this in today's Gospel. On stepping ashore, he was met by a large crowd. But he didn't see them as a crowd, but as a collection of individuals, each with problems and worries. He had compassion on them, precisely because they were wounded and in need.

Caring is essentially a matter of the heart. One actually is less exhausted by a total involvement of self than by an attempt to barricade oneself behind defences, provided one knows how to replenish one's reserves. Those who give themselves, somehow recharge themselves at the same time.

PRAYER OF THE FAITHFUL

President: Let us pray to the Father who cared about us so much that he sent his Son to be our Shepherd and Friend.

Response: Lord, hear us in your love.

Reader(s): For the Christian community: that it may strive to make the love of Christ visible in the world. [Pause] We pray in faith.

For all the followers of Christ: that as he broke down the barrier between Jew and Gentile, they may strive to overcome all forms of tribalism. [Pause] We pray in faith.

For the leaders of our country: that they may carry out their office in a caring way. [Pause] We pray in faith.

For all who are lost, and who feel that nobody cares about them. [Pause] We pray in faith.

For all gathered here: that through our own suffering we may learn to feel the suffering of others and show them compassion. [Pause] We pray in faith.

For our particular needs. [Longer pause] We pray in faith.

President: God of power and love, may we who have experienced the love of Christ,the Good Shepherd, show that same love to others. We ask this through the same Christ our Lord.

PRAYER/REFLECTION   **Sheep without a shepherd**

> Lord, look upon us and take pity on us,
> for at times we too are like sheep.
> Save us from a blind following of the herd.
> Help us to listen to your voice,
> to trust you and to follow you,
> even if it means leaving the crowd
> and walking a lonely path.
> Lead us from fear to trust, from error to truth,
> from hate to love, from war to peace,
> from despair to hope, and from death to life. Amen.

Seventeenth Sunday of the Year
FOOD FOR THE HUNGRY

INTRODUCTION AND CONFITEOR

Christ fed the hungry, and did so with great generosity. Here he feeds us with the food of the Eucharist. We receive this precious food, not because we are worthy of it, but because we need it and he invites us to receive it. [Pause]

Lord, you give food in due time to all those who look to you. Lord, have mercy.

Lord, you are just in all your ways and loving in all your deeds. Christ, have mercy.

Lord, you are close to all who call on you, who call on you from their hearts. Lord, have mercy.

HEADINGS FOR READINGS

First Reading (2 Kgs 4:42-44). The miraculous food which the prophet Elisha gave to hungry people was a sign of God's concern for his people.

Second Reading (Eph 4:1-6). St Paul pleads with the Ephesians to live a life in keeping with the Gospel, placing special emphasis on the need for unity and harmony.

Gospel (Jn 6:1-15). Like Elisha, Jesus feeds the people miraculously, but does so even more astonishingly.

SCRIPTURE NOTE

For this and the next four Sundays the Gospel readings come from Chapter Six of St John's Gospel. John has no account of the institution of the Eucharist. But this chapter more than compensates for that.

The miracle described in the First Reading shows God's concern for his people during a time of famine. The bread in question was the bread of the first-fruits, which was meant to be offered to God. But instead of offering it to God, Elisha, the prophet of the old covenant, gave it to the people. The left-overs stress God's generosity.

Like Elisha, Jesus, the prophet of the new covenant, feeds hungry people, and does so even more astonishingly. There are clear eucharistic overtones in the way the miracle is related. Jesus '*took* the loaves, *gave thanks*, and *distributed* them to the people.' Such language is meant to remind us of what he did at the Last Supper, and of what happens every time we celebrate the Eucharist.

Even though both feedings are miraculous there is an essential human element in each, without which no miracle is possible.

HOMILY 1   **Food for the hungry**

In the readings we see God's concern for the hungry. In the First Reading we see how Elisha cut through the red tape and insisted that the bread be given to the people, even though the bread was that of the first fruits which was marked out for offering to God, And in the Gospel we see Jesus providing bread for the people who had followed him into the wilderness.

Food is the first necessity of life. Without food no life is possible, much less a higher form of life. Feeding the hungry is the first of the great corporal works of mercy. At the last judgement Jesus will say, 'I was hungry and you gave me food,' or 'I was hungry and you did not give me food.'

When Jesus met hungry people he gave them the only thing that mattered to them at that moment. He gave them food, and did so with great generosity – all ate as much as they wanted, and there still were twelve baskets left over.

Jesus took the five loaves and gave thanks. So should we when we eat. In a world in which millions are hungry, we shouldn't take food for granted.

Every loaf [maybe use a real one as a visual] is as much a miracle as those Jesus gave to the people. Every loaf is touched by many human hands and by the hand of God. This is expressed beautifully in the prayer which the priest says over the bread at the Offertory of the Mass: 'Blessed are you, Lord, God of all creation. Through your goodness we have this bread to offer, which earth has given and human hands have made. It will become for us the bread of life.'

God does the same miracle through the seasons and the harvest. In the corn fields he multiplies not loaves but grains, so that if we do our part there is enough for everyone. A single grain of wheat can produce as many as seventy grains.

Today there is a preoccupation with food, but it varies greatly from one part of the world to another. In the developed world, we have too much food. The main preoccupation of many people has become how to cut down on food with a view to reducing weight. But this leaves people preoccupied with themselves, which is the death of love. In the Third World, however, the problem is how to get anything to eat at all.

The miracle of Jesus should make us thankful to God for the food we have, and careful not to waste it. It should also made us actively concerned about those who have none. It is said that there are over 700 million people in the world today who do not have enough to eat. One third of all African children are undernourished.

The problem of what to do with our surplus food is a profoundly disturbing one for Christians. One answer is to stockpile it. But surely the stockpiling of surplus food is as great a scandal as the stockpiling of nuclear weapons. Another answer is to reduce the amount that is produced. But this leads to the scandal of farmers being paid to leave good land idle. Most farmers are unhappy with this arrangement.

The miracle of the multiplication of the loaves is a miracle of generosity. We experience that generosity every time we sit down to eat and especially when we receive the Eucharist. The experience of generosity should result in an enlarging of our hearts, and a desire to be generous towards those who are not as fortunate as ourselves.

HOMILY 2   **A miracle of generosity**

A priest celebrating Mass in a Dublin parish and preaching on today's Gospel referred to the miracle of the loaves and fishes as a miracle of generosity. And it's easy to see why.

First of all there is the marvellous generosity of the boy, who, with his gift of five loaves and two fish, made the miracle possible. It was a small thing in itself, but for the little boy it was a big thing because it was all he had. There are many who are willing to make a contribution out of the relative plenty that they have, but very few who are willing to give when it means going without themselves.

Then there is the astonishing generosity of Jesus. Not only did he feed all the people, but he saw to it that each got as much as he wanted, and even so there were twelve full baskets of left-overs.

The priest left the altar at the end of Mass happy in the belief that he had preached a nice little sermon. As he was unvesting in the sacristy an elderly woman came to enquire if anyone had left in a shopping bag. She said she had brought it into the church with her, but now couldn't find it. The sacristan gave her the bad news: no one had left in a bag.

The priest was expecting her to say: 'What kind of person would steal from another person in the house of God?' or some such thing. But she said no such thing. Without a trace of anger or bitterness, she said simply, 'Maybe the person who took it needs it more than I do.'

'What was in the bag?' the priest asked.

'Two loaves of bread,' the woman replied.

Her answer delighted the priest. But it also humbled him, because he knew that in her position he would not have been so generous in his response to the theft of his property. He was also humbled for another reason. He was preaching generosity; this woman was practising it. Hers was generosity of heart.

The Lord nourishes us here in the Eucharistic banquet as surely and as generously as he fed the people in the desert. He nourishes us so that we in our turn may be able to nourish others.

Generosity should have a central place in the life of every Christian, and we get many opportunities in our everyday dealings with one another to practise it. It's not only about giving things, but also and more especially about giving of ourselves – of our time, our energy, and our love.

Joy is one of the lovely fruits of generosity. You rarely meet a generous person who is sad. And you will never meet a happy miser.

HOMILY 3   **Understanding God's goodness**

The practice of saying grace before meals is an excellent one. In describing the miracle of the multiplication of the loaves and fishes, the evangelists tell us that 'Jesus took the loaves and gave thanks.' We too should give thanks when we eat. In a world in which millions are hungry, we shouldn't take food for granted.

One evening a man sat down with his family to a full table, and he and his wife bowed their heads as their little girl said the grace: 'Thank you, God, for your goodness to us. Thank you especially for giving us such a lot of food. Amen.'

Normally this little ritual brought great joy to the father. But that evening for some strange reason he felt uneasy. He was conscious that we in the developed world have too much food, while those in the Third World have too little. He had read recently how some forty million people die annually from hunger and related diseases, and that one third of all African children are undernourished. And he asked himself, 'Why are we the ones to receive such gifts from God? Is it that we deserve them more than the many people who will go hungry tonight, and who instead of thanking God will go to bed in bitterness?'

He had raised a profound and disturbing question which didn't do his appetite any good at all. Does the fact that we have food to eat mean that we have won a special position of favour in God's sight? Does it mean that he feeds his favourite children and lets the unworthy go hungry? May God protect us from adopting such an attitude. Rather, may he lead us to a true understanding of his goodness.

God's goodness becomes a curse if it causes such thoughts to arise within us, and if we thank God for his goodness to us without becoming conscious of the responsibility which that goodness lays upon us.

In order to understand God's goodness in his gifts, we must think of them as held in trust for our brothers and sisters. Therefore, let no one say, 'Thank you, God, for having blessed me with money and possessions,' and then proceed to live as if he were alone in the world. For the time will come when he will realise that he has been worshipping the idols of his good fortune and his selfishness. Possessions are indeed signs of God's blessing and goodness, but they are also opportunities of service which he entrusts to us.

We can't multiply the food as Jesus could. But we do not have to. All we have to do is share it, or the money to buy it. Jesus continues to ask us the question he asked Philip: 'Where can we buy bread for these people to eat?'

In the light of all this what would be a more appropriate grace before meals? How about the following: 'Thank you, Lord, for your goodness to us, and especially for this plentiful food. May we use your gifts in such a way that others too will know your goodness, and give you thanks as we do.'

ANOTHER STORY

In the days of King Solomon there lived in Jerusalem a rich miser by the name of Simeon. Simeon treated his servants very badly. He worked them hard but didn't give them enough food, so that they and their children were constantly hungry.

It happened that once there came a great famine in the land. All the wealthy citizens opened their granaries and gave food to the poor. But not Simeon. He put on additional locks on the doors of his granaries.

The stories of Simeon's meanness reached the ears of King Solomon. Solomon devised a stratagem. He sent a messenger to invite him to dine at the royal palace on the following evening. Simeon felt highly honoured. In order to enjoy the king's meal to the full, he fasted all day and arrived at the palace ravenously hungry.

A servant showed him into a waiting room and said, 'The king will eat with you alone tonight. Now there are some rules of conduct which you must observe. Firstly, you must never ask anything either from the king or the servants. Secondly, you must ask no questions and make no complaints. Thirdly, if the king should ask you how you are enjoying the meal, you must say that you are enjoying it enormously. Are you willing to obey these rules?'

'I am,' Simeon answered.

'Well then, wait here and I'll call you when supper time comes.'

As he waited, the most delicious aromas came to him from the kitchen. He was so hungry that the smells almost drove him mad. Finally supper time arrived. 'Do sit down, my friend,' Solomon said. 'I want you to eat to your heart's content.'

Simeon sat down. A servant placed a baked fish on a golden platter before the king. The king started to eat, and as he ate he said, 'The fish is delicious.' When he finished, the servant placed a plate of fish before Simeon. However, just as he was about to delve into it, the servant took it away again and carried it back to the kitchen. Simeon was about to protest, but remembering his instructions, kept quiet.

The servant then placed a fine broth in a golden bowl before the king, who drank it with relish. When he had finished it, the servant placed a bowl of broth in front of Simeon, but took it away immediately again. The same happened with the main course and the dessert. By this time Simeon was beside himself with anger and hunger. He cast a look of hatred at the servant, while trying to show a smiling face to the king. At the end of the meal the king said to Simeon, 'I do hope you enjoyed your meal.'

'Oh, everything was delicious,' Simeon replied.

'I'm glad to hear that,' said the king.

Faint with hunger, Simeon rose to make his departure. But the king said, 'Don't go, my friend. The night is still young. I want my musicians to entertain you.'

The musicians entered and entertained him with beautiful music for a couple of hours. When they had finished, once again Simeon rose to go. But the king said, 'Don't go, my friend. It's late. Stay the night.'

Simeon had no option but to stay. However, because of the pangs of hunger, he didn't sleep a wink. Lying awake in bed he began to reflect on the possible meaning of the king's conduct. 'Why did he invite me here and then not allow me to eat?' he asked himself.

Suddenly the answer dawned on him. The king wanted to teach him a lesson about hunger. And what a sharp lesson he had taught him. Well, the lesson was learned. Simeon resolved that never again would any of his servants go hungry.

PRAYER OF THE FAITHFUL

President: Let us now bring our needs to the Lord, who is just in all his ways and loving in all his deeds.

Response: Lord, hear our prayer.

Reader(s): For Christians: that they may be generous in sharing what they have with those who are less fortunate than themselves. [Pause] We pray to the Lord.

For public authorities: hat the vast amounts of money being spent on armaments is used instead to feed the hungry. [Pause] We pray to the Lord.

For the hungry of the world: that their hunger may be satisfied. [Pause] We pray to the Lord.

For ourselves: that the Lord may open our hearts to those who suffer, so that they won't have to carry their cross alone. [Pause] We pray to the Lord.

For our special needs. [Longer pause] We pray to the Lord.

President: All-powerful God, grant that all who participate in the Eucharist, may experience you goodness, and so grow in love. We ask this through the same Christ our Lord.

REFLECTION   **Discovering one's own riches**

I lived on the shady side of the road
and watched my neighbours' gardens across the way
revelling in the sunshine.
I felt I was poor
and from door to door went in my hunger.
The more they gave me from their careless abundance
the more I became aware of my beggar's bowl.
Till one morning I awoke from my sleep
at the sudden opening of my door
and you came and asked for alms.
In despair I broke open the lid of my chest
and was startled into finding my own wealth.

Rabindranath Tagore

Eighteenth Sunday of the Year
THE FURTHER HUNGER

INTRODUCTION AND CONFITEOR

Last Sunday we saw how Jesus gave bread to the people in the wilderness. But when they came back the next day for more he said to them, 'Do not work for perishable food, but for the food that endures to eternal life.'

We are here because we know that we need another kind of food, the food that only God can give us. [Pause]

Lord, you nourish our minds with the bread of faith. Lord, have mercy.

You nourish our spirits with the bread of hope. Christ, have mercy.

You nourish our hearts with the bread of love. Lord, have mercy.

HEADINGS FOR READINGS

First Reading (Ex 16:2-4.12-15). God feeds his people in the desert.

Second Reading (Eph 4:17. 20-24). Paul urges the Ephesians to live lives that are in keeping with their baptismal calling.

Gospel (Jn 6:24-35). Jesus declares that he himself is the true bread from heaven of which the manna provided by Moses was but a foreshadowing.

SCRIPTURAL NOTE

The First Reading tells how God fed his people in the desert with manna. This is regarded as the classic example of God's care for his people.

Jesus too fed people who were hungry. But the Gospel makes it clear that the Son of Man did not come down from above merely to satisfy physical hunger. He came to give a heavenly bread that people will eat and never become hungry. The manna was but a foreshadowing of the spiritual food which was now being offered by Jesus to his followers. The manna nourished people physically and sustained life temporarily. The new bread will nourish people spiritually and sustain life eternally.

The 'bread' in question is primarily the teaching given by Jesus. Only at a secondary level does it refer to the Eucharist.

HOMILY 1 — Our many hungers

In 1885 Vincent van Gogh visited a museum in Amsterdam in order to see Rembrandt's famous painting, 'The Jewish Bride'. Having seen it he said, 'I would give ten years of my life if I could sit before this picture for a fortnight, with nothing but a crust of dry bread for food. My first hunger is not for food, though I have fasted ever so long. The desire for painting is so much stronger, that when I receive some money I start at once hunting for models until all the money is gone.'

It's not only the body that gets hungry; the heart and the spirit get hungry too. The bread of material things can never satisfy the heart of a human being. To nourish a human being is not the same as to fatten cattle. We are creatures not with one hunger but with a hundred hungers. We hunger for lots of things besides bread.

Not all of our hungers should be satisfied. Some of them are appetites which could destroy us if we feed them. The more they are fed, the hungrier and more demanding they become. We should be aware that such appetites exist within us. But let us stay with the hungers that should be satisfied if we are to be properly nourished as human beings and children of God.

We hunger for a feeling of importance. Nobody wants to be a nobody. We all want to matter, if only to one person.

We hunger for acceptance. If we are not accepted it becomes almost impossible for us to realise ourselves.

We hunger for relationships. Without them we are at the mercy of cold winds of anguish and loneliness. We are like a lone tree on a hilltop.

We hunger for motivation. Without it we are like a sail boat without the wind.

We hunger for faith – for a set of positive beliefs to guide us. Otherwise we are like a ship without chart or compass or port of destination.

We hunger for hope. To give up hope is akin to going on a spiritual hunger strike.

We hunger for love. If this was fully satisfied then most of our other hungers would disappear.

However, there is one further hunger, a deeper one, and one that underlies all our other hungers, including that of love. It is the hunger for eternal life. In other words, the hunger for God. To experience this hunger is not a misfortune but a blessing. It saves us from stagnation and keeps the stream of our lives moving forward towards the sea.

Every day we see people emerging from supermarkets with trolleys loaded down with food and drink. But we won't find this other bread in supermarkets. If we could, we would be well nourished. Only God can give us this food. Only God can satisfy our deepest hungers.

The manna sustained life temporarily. The food Jesus gives sustains life permanently. To us, pilgrims on the streets of time but driven by an irrepressible desire for immortality, Jesus comes with the promise: 'He who eats the bread that I give will live forever.' Who would not want to eat of this bread?

HOMILY 2   **Trusting in God**

The feeding of the people in the desert with manna is regarded as the classic example of God's care for his people. Yet the manna probably was a natural phenomenon. But this doesn't mean it wasn't a gift from God. It may have been a sweet resinous food which drips from a certain desert tree during the night and hardens in the cool of the night. It has to be collected in the early morning before it melts in the heat of the day. As for the quails: they migrate from northern Europe to Africa, and are forced down to rest in the desert, where they are easily caught.

God said to Moses, 'I will rain down bread for you from the heavens.

Each day the people are to go out and gather the day's portion; I propose to test them this way to see whether they will follow my law or not.' How are we to interpret these words?

If you ask the ordinary believer if he believes that God is the only God in the world, he will answer without hesitation, 'Of course.' But if you ask him if he trusts that God will see to it that he has all that he needs, he will be taken aback and is likely to say, 'Well, I haven't reached that stage yet.'

We must distinguish between faith and trust. Though they are closely linked they are not the same thing. The person who firmly believes, trusts completely. But if someone has not perfect trust in God, his belief will be faint as well.

The desert experience was an opportunity for the Israelites to get close to God. It was meant to teach them to rely on God, to trust in Providence on a daily basis. Hence, they are told not to store up the manna so as to ensure that they will have some for tomorrow. No, they must collect only what they need for today. God will provide for them tomorrow.

Jesus taught the same truth. He said we should pray, 'Give us this day our daily bread.' This teaching will sound strange, and even foolish, to those who put all their trust in savings accounts, insurance policies, and warranties. We don't leave much room for God. This is the opposite to living by faith.

When all is said and done, it wasn't the manna that sustained the Israelites during their time in the desert. What sustained them was their faith and trust in God. The same 'food' is available to us. Faith and trust in God will nourish us at all times but especially during times of trial. It's not we who keep the faith; it's the faith that keeps us.

No matter how difficult life may be, for those who trust in God, and live a day at a time, the manna falls every day.

HOMILY 3   **The price of freedom**

After every great moment there comes a moment of reaction – and it is in the reaction that the danger lies. It seems to be a law of life that just after our resistance power has been at its highest it nose-dives to its lowest.

Writing about his Auschwitz experience, the Italian writer, Primo Levi, said:

> In the majority of cases, the hour of liberation was neither joyful nor light-hearted. Many suicides occurred immediately after the liberation. By contrast, suicides were rare during imprisonment. In my own case release was a critical moment which coincided with a flood of rethinking and depression.

And Elie Wiesel, another Auschwitz survivor, said:

During the ordeal, I lived in expectation ... of a miracle, or of death. It was only later, after the nightmare was over, that I underwent a crisis, painful and anguished, questioning all my beliefs.

In theory, having been released, they should have lived happily ever after. Yet it frequently happened that those who came back died fairly soon after their 'return to life'. How does one account for this? While they were in limbo it was the dream of being released that gave them the strength to survive. But freedom didn't always live up to expectations. Some of them had nothing to go back to. 'The cruelty of prison starts when you come out' (Oscar Wilde).

The Israelites had a similar experience. They left the slavery of Egypt in joy, and set off into what they believed would be a bright future. Yet a short time later they wanted to go back to Egypt. They were willing to be slaves again. What happened?

In a sense, their real troubles began after their release. Freedom didn't turn out to be what they thought it would be. They found themselves in the desert, and short of food. They discovered that freedom involved a journey to a promised land that was remote and hazy. All they could see immediately ahead of them were hardships, trials and dangers.

In truth, the Israelites of Moses' day were not ready for liberty, and the Bible faithfully records their quarrels and troubles. It took a new generation to be ready to cross the Jordan and enter the promised land. It has been said: 'It took one day to get the Israelites out of Egypt, but it took forty years to get Egypt out of the Israelites.'

Freedom presents its own challenges. It means taking responsibility for one's life. This is no easy thing especially for those who have got used to others making all the decisions for them. Freedom calls for self-discipline. It's easier to be disciplined by others than to discipline oneself. It's easier to turn a man into a slave than a slave into a man.

The Israelites looked backwards and thought, 'Maybe we were better off in Egypt; at least we had enough to eat there.' And so they start to complain against Moses. If only they had brought with them the qualities that had enabled them to endure enslavement. But they didn't put the same work into freedom as into enslavement .

We can feel sympathy for them. They could not have foreseen that their dream of freedom, once realised, would entail new challenges and fresh perils. Still, their attitude is sad. To think that they were ready to give up their freedom for a bellyful of the old food they ate in Egypt. Nevertheless, God took pity on them and gave them manna to sustain them in their journey through the desert.

This has great relevance for us. We are the new People of God, journeying in faith towards the promised land of eternal life. By our baptism we have been called out of slavery – slavery to sin, slavery to material comforts and securities, and so on (see Second Reading). We are led, not by Moses, but by Jesus. We have to live by faith and not by sight.

And we are bound to experience the desert of trial and difficulty. At times we may feel that God has abandoned us. And so we hunger for the fleshpots of this world. We are tempted to fall back into the slavery of sin rather than live in the freedom of the children of God.

But just as God sustained the Israelites, so he sustains us through faith in Jesus, and the special bread Jesus gives us, especially in the Eucharist. It is not we who keep the faith; it is the faith that keeps us. No matter how difficult life may be, for those who trust in God, and live a day at a time, the manna falls every day.

ANOTHER APPROACH   **The bread that endures**

In the miracle of the loaves and fishes, Jesus had fed the people with ordinary food, and did so with great generosity. Afterwards he and his disciples crossed the lake. But the people followed them. Jesus knew that they followed him in the hope of receiving more of the same kind of food.

But this time Jesus refused to give it to them. He wouldn't do what business people do – give people what they want. It's called catering to consumers' tastes and pleasures. Producers simply provide what there is a demand for. Their sole aim is to try to meet the needs of the market or the potential buyer's taste.

For a spiritual teacher to do this would be a disaster. The spiritual teacher must challenge people to go beyond their tastes.

It was the first temptation all over again: turn these stones into bread. The temptation to use his special powers to give the people all the material things they could possibly want. But Jesus knew that material things by themselves will never satisfy people. These needs can never be satisfied, and increase when yielded to. Food is only the beginning. We eat in order to live; we don't live just to eat.

It was the temptation to give people what they want rather than what they need. The temptation to please the crowd by giving them what will satisfy their immediate wants, when they don't know what they really need.

Jesus made it clear that the Son of Man had not come down from above merely to satisfy people's physical hunger. He came to give them heavenly bread that people will eat and never again become hungry. He challenged them to go deeper. He said: 'Do not work for food that perishes, but for the food that endures for eternal life, food that the Son of Man will give you.'

If Jesus had given the people more loaves and fishes he would have made himself very popular – in the short term. After the miracle of the loaves they called him a prophet and wanted to make him their king. But in the long term such a move would have betrayed them. To give priority to physical needs would be to diminish humanity, to treat them as no higher than beasts.

Jesus challenged them to face the deeper hunger, the spiritual hunger. He urged them to seek food for that, food that he could give them. But when he taught them about spiritual food, and about eternal life, they began to murmur and turned their backs on him.

We too are tempted to live for material things alone. It's not that we deny the spiritual, but that we neglect it.

Physical food sustains life temporarily. But the food Jesus gives sustains life permanently. Who would not want to eat of this food?

PRAYER OF THE FAITHFUL

President: God is close to all who call on him from their hearts. Let us call on him now in our many needs.

Response: Lord, graciously hear us.

Reader(s): For all Christians: that they may hunger for the bread that only God can give. [Pause] Lord, hear us.

For the human family: that all of God's children may be nourished with the bread of faith, hope, and love. [Pause] Lord, hear us.

For those who are going through a desert of hardship or pain; that God may give them the bread of endurance. [Pause] Lord, hear us.

For all gathered here: that we may be able to live in the freedom of the children of God. [Pause] Lord, hear us.

For grace to bring our own special needs to the Lord. [Longer pause] Lord, hear us.

President: God of mercy, you heard the prayers of your people in the desert. Hear our prayers now as we journey towards the eternal life promised us by your Son. We ask this through the same Christ our Lord.

REFLECTION   **A day at a time**

God provided a mysterious food called *manna*
for the Israelites during their time in the desert.
However, they were told not to stockpile the manna,
but to gather only what they needed for one day.
Jesus told his disciples not to worry about tomorrow.
He said, When you pray to your heavenly Father,
you are to say, 'Give us this day our daily bread.'
No matter how difficult life may be,
for those who trust in God
and who live a day at a time,
the manna falls every day.

Nineteenth Sunday of the Year
FOOD FOR THE JOURNEY

INTRODUCTION AND CONFITEOR

We are God's people, journeying in faith towards the promised land of eternal life. We are bound to encounter doubts and difficulties along the way. The Lord in whose name we gather, is not only the goal of our journey, but our companion on the way. [Pause]

Lord, you strengthen us when we are weak. Lord, have mercy.

You raise us up when we fall. Christ, have mercy.

You renew our hope when we grow discouraged. Lord, have mercy.

HEADINGS FOR READINGS

First Reading (1 Kgs 19:4-8). Fed by an angel, a broken and dispirited Elijah is able to walk all the way to the mountain of God.

Second Reading (Eph 4:30–5:2). St Paul urges the Ephesians to walk in the way of love and thus live up to their calling.

Gospel (Jn 6:41-51). Jesus is the new manna from heaven. Those who eat this food will live forever.

SCRIPTURE NOTE

The First Reading gives us a glimpse into the heart of a prophet, and we see how very human he is. Elijah, the great champion of Yahweh, flees into the desert, a broken and dispirited man. But like the Israelites of old, he is fed with 'bread from heaven'. Strengthened by this food he continues his journey to Horeb, the mountain of God.

In the Gospel Jesus declares that he is 'the bread that has come down from heaven.' The bread in question is primarily the revelation given to people by Jesus. Only at a secondary level does it envisage the Eucharist. The fundamental reaction called for is one of 'coming to him', which is a synonym of belief. Even though faith is a gift from God it does demand openness on our part.

HOMILY 1   **Food for the journey**

Elijah was the greatest of the Old Testament prophets. So much so that it was thought he would come back to usher in the Messianic era. Yet in the First Reading we see him weak, exhausted, terror-stricken. He is sick and tired of being God's prophet. He is on the run for his life. He wants to throw the towel in. He begins to doubt himself: 'I am no better than my fathers.'

What was it that brought him so low? He had pursued a fierce war on the idolatry which was rampant at the time. This brought him into conflict with the wicked queen, Jezebel, who wanted him killed. So he fled into the desert where he lay down and prayed that God might take his life away. Then all his troubles would be ended.

He had lost his spirit. When we lose our spirit we lose our greatest source of strength. Our spirit is to us what wings are to a bird or roots are to a tree.

Even the great know periods of weakness, weariness, and despair. They feel life is so difficult that they can't cope any more. They are no less great because of that. It shows that they are human after all, and therefore limited. Jesus himself knew such an hour in the garden of Gethsemane.

Many people are reluctant to admit their human limitations. They want to appear strong all the time. They think they will lose face before others if they show weakness and fear. But, in fact, the opposite is the case. People are touched and moved to help us when they see that we are human like them. In the words of Picasso: 'You are overcome with compassion when you find in each person the source of tears.'

Still, some may feel that such feelings aren't worthy of someone who has faith in God. But weakness is not incompatible with faith. Besides, how can we get help if we won't even admit our need? Recognition is the first step on the road to rehabilitation.

God sent an angel with food and drink for Elijah. Most likely the 'angel' was none other than his servant who had accompanied him to the edge of the desert. On the strength of this food Elijah walked all the way to Horeb, the mountain of God. Just as his previous condition was not produced by lack of food (though there was a famine at the time), so his new strength didn't come from the food alone. It came from the assurance that God was with him. It was this assurance that breathed new life into him and gave him the heart to go on.

We too are journeying towards the mountain of God – eternal life. We too will experience moments of weakness on that journey. We need help – human help in the first place. Ideally this should be available through the Christian community. And of course we need the help that comes from God. What is especially sustaining is a sense of God's presence with us and love for us. And we need bread for our journey. However, ordinary bread will not suffice. We need the bread that Jesus gives – the bread of the Eucharist.

The Eucharist has been called *Viaticum*, that is, bread *for a journey*, somwhat like a soldier's rations. However, over the years *Viaticum* came to be applied in a very narrow sense. It came to mean Communion given to someone who was dying. Thus it was seen as the bread for the last stage of the Christian's earthly journey. But the Eucharist is meant to sustain us all through our journey.

On the strength of the food which Jesus gives us in the Eucharist, we will walk all the way to God's eternal Kingdom. And along the way we may have the privilege of being God's angel to another human being who is experiencing a low moment. It's only the kind of love and support that you expect from people who eat at the same table.

HOMILY 2   **How God's help comes**

Elijah was the greatest prophet of the Old Testament. He opposed and defeated the prophets of Baal at Mount Carmel. This earned him the hatred of the idolatrous queen, Jezebel, who wanted him killed. So he fled into the desert, where he lay down and asked God to take his life away. Then all his troubles would be over.

God heard the prayer of Elijah and answered it, but not in the way Elijah had wanted. God sent an angel to him with food and water. And strengthened by this food 'from heaven' he was able to make his way to Horeb, the mountain of God.

There may not have not been anything supernatural about the incident. It can be explained in a perfectly natural way. The 'angel' who fed Elijah was probably the prophet's own servant whom he had left a short distance away. But it still could be an expression of God's care for his prophet. The normal way in which God works is through human agencies.

There is a little story which illustrates this. There was a bad flood and the cellar of Thomas' house filled up with water. A man came by in a canoe and said, 'Do you want a lift to safety?' 'No,' said Thomas. 'I have faith in God. He will save me.'

The water rose and flooded the ground floor. Thomas was forced to go upstairs. A man in a motor boat came by and offered to take him to safety, but Thomas said, 'I have faith in God. He will save me.'

The water rose higher still and Thomas had to take to the roof. A helicopter came by and the pilot offered to take him to safety. But once again Thomas declined, saying, 'I have faith in God. He will save me.' And he sat there waiting for God.

But the water continued to rise and he drowned. On arriving in heaven he said angrily to God, 'I had faith in you, and still you let me drown.' To which God replied, 'Not once, but three times, I sent you help, and each time you refused it.'

We don't always recognise God's help when it comes. Prayer is answered not in God doing things for us, but in God helping us to do things for ourselves and for one another. We will wait in vain for a heavenly angel. But God sends us human angels. All of us have experienced the ministry of such angels.

And we also get opportunities to be such an angel to someone in distress. Sometimes it may mean doing something, providing some basic service such as a hot meal. Other times it may mean saying a word of encouragement. Still other times it may mean just being there beside someone, providing a comforting presence, so that the person doesn't have to suffer alone.

Many people go through a bad period. It is only the care of some human angel that helps them get through it. Ultimately the 'angel' God sent to us is his Son, Jesus. Jesus stays by our side, and gives us, not ordinary bread, but the 'bread of life'. In the strength of this bread he will walk all the way to the mountain of God, namely, eternal life.

HOMILY 3   **Religion is not escapism**

Elijah spent a lifetime battling against the idolatry which was rampant in his time. This brought him into conflict with Queen Jezebel, who wanted to kill him. So he fled into the desert to escape. But there things caught up with him. Having given his all, he felt drained. So he lay down and asked God to take his life away. Then all his troubles would be over.

Elijah was perhaps the greatest of the Old Testament prophets. Yet here we see him weak, exhausted, terror-stricken, and just wanting to die. Far from being shocked at this we should take heart from it. Elijah was a great man. Greatness can't be conferred on people; they have to achieve it. And they do so, not by avoiding difficulties, but by confronting them and overcoming them. But even the great know moments of weakness, doubt and fear like the rest of us.

Elijah was running away from something that was going to follow him. Instead of granting his wish, God sent an angel to him with food and drink. There may not have not been anything supernatural about the incident. The 'angel' was probably the prophet's own servant whom he had left a short distance away. Still, it was an expression of God's care for his prophet. In any case, strengthened by this food 'from heaven' Elijah was able to make his way to Horeb, the mountain of God.

At Horeb he had an experience of God. The purpose of this experience was not to encourage escape on his part. It was meant to comfort and strengthen him so that he could go back and face the mess and danger he left behind. And that is exactly what he did.

Prayer and religion are not meant to be an escape from life but are to help us to face it. From our own daily journey in search of God, and in our effort to live the life of a Christian, we return again and again to prayer and the sacraments. Not, however, for refuge and escape, but for rebirth and renewal of courage and energy, so that we may commit ourselves again to the journey.

Religion is meant to comfort us in times of trouble and to console us in times of sorrow. But if it did not do more than that then it would involve neither risk nor strain. It must give us something to work us up, a good cause to energise us. It should challenge and stretch us to our limit and beyond, so that thereafter we have new standards by which to judge ourselves.

There is a religion of devotion, and a religion of commitment. Faith can be a crutch or a pair of wings.

The Christian life is not about evasions, escapism, soft options, comfort. It is about the very opposite to these. The God who loves us, expects the best of us, nothing less.

God gives us a special food to nourish us. The food that Elijah received enabled him to walk to the mountain of God. The food that Jesus gives us in the Eucharist enables us to walk all the way to his eternal kingdom.

PRAYER OF THE FAITHFUL

President: Let us now bring our needs before God, trusting that he will listen to our prayers as he listened to the prayer of his servant Elijah.

Response: Lord, hear us in your love.

Reader(s): For all the followers of Jesus: that their lives may bear witness to the hope they carry in their hearts. [Pause] We pray in faith.

For our political and civil leaders: that they may work to create the kind of society in which people can live in freedom and dignity. [Pause] We pray in faith.

For those who are going through a difficult period: that they may find comfort and support. [Pause] We pray in faith.

For this community: that we may be friends with one another, forgiving one another as readily as God has forgiven us in Christ. [Pause] We pray in faith.

For our own particular needs. [Longer pause] We pray in faith.

President: Almighty and ever-loving God, may the bread which only you can give sustain us as we journey in hope towards the promised land of eternal life. We ask this through the same Christ our Lord.

PRAYER/REFLECTION   **Trust in God**

Lord, I've no idea where I'm going.
I do not see the road ahead of me.
I cannot know for certain where it will end.
Nor do I really know myself.
And the fact that I think I'm doing your will,
doesn't mean that I'm actually doing it.
But I believe that the desire to please you
does in fact please you, and I hope that I have this desire.
Though I may seem to be lost and in the shadow of death,

I will not fear, for you are with me,
and you will never leave me face my perils alone.   *Thomas Merton*

Twentieth Sunday of the Year
THE BANQUET OF THE EUCHARIST

INTRODUCTION AND CONFITEOR

We hunger for many things. However, only God can satisfy our deepest hungers. We are gathered in God's house to celebrate the Eucharist, the banquet God has provided for us, his pilgrim people. Let us prepare ourselves to receive the nourishment God wants to give us in this banquet. [Pause]

Lord, you nourish us with the bread of your word. Lord, have mercy.

You nourish us with the bread of the Eucharist. Christ, have mercy.

You bind us together as members of your family, pilgrims to your kingdom. Lord, have mercy.

HEADINGS FOR READINGS

First Reading (Prov 9:1-6). Wisdom is described in terms of a banquet. Christians will see this as a foreshadowing of the Eucharistic banquet.

Second Reading (Eph 5:15-20). The wise Christian will make the most of the present time, being alert to the will of God, and shaping conduct accordingly.

Gospel (Jn 6:51-58). This contains Christ's great promise of eternal life to those who eat his body and drink his blood (in the Eucharist).

SCRIPTURE NOTE

The First Reading talks about the sumptuous banquet that Wisdom offers its devotees. It suggests the great blessings that would coincide with the coming of the Messiah. But Christians will see it as a foreshadowing of the Eucharist, and of the heavenly banquet which the Eucharist anticipates. Thus it prepares us to hear the Gospel.

In the Gospel the theme is exclusively eucharistic. The language shifts to eating and drinking, to flesh and blood. 'Flesh and blood' is a Hebrew idiom for the whole person.

In a poetic way John has laid out the basic elements that makes the Christian Eucharistic Celebration nourishing. In the Service of the Word we are fed with divine revelation; in the Service of the Sacrament we are fed with the flesh and blood of Christ.

HOMILY 1   **In communion with the Lord**

Physical presence is a great thing. We don't always realise this until a loved one is absent. And it is brought home to us more forcefully still when a loved one dies, leaving a great emptiness.

Physical presence is a great thing. But it is not everything. Physical presence doesn't always produce the intimacy we long for. In fact, people can be sitting side by side without being really present to one another. There may be no communication, much less communion, between them. Indeed, for all that passes between them, they might as well be miles apart. But then the opposite can happen. People can be separated by a great distance and yet be very much present to one another.

We believe that Jesus is present in the Eucharist. But he is not physically present. Nevertheless, he is really and truly present. The mode of his presence is beyond our understanding. We call it 'the real presence' because it is presence in the fullest sense. To receive the gift of the Eucharist is to receive the Lord himself.

Of course, an act of faith is required. But for those who believe that God is present in all things and in all places, his unique and special presence in the Eucharist ought not to be a big problem. Besides, we have the word of Jesus: 'This is my body ... this is my blood.' St Cyril says: 'Do not doubt whether this is true, but rather receive the words of the Saviour in faith, for he cannot lie.'

The expressions 'to eat his flesh' and 'to drink his blood' must not be taken with a crude literalism. 'Body and blood' stand for the whole person. When we eat the bread and drink the wine of the Eucharist we are not receiving a body and blood. We are receiving a person, a living person.

In the Eucharist Jesus comes to us, not under the form of something like a radio, or a coat, or even medicine. He comes under the form of something more basic still, something which is essential for life – food. More specifically he comes under the form of bread. Bread nourishes us and gives us life. But it is also something which we can take into ourselves, and make part of ourselves. Through the food of the Eucharist Jesus nourishes in us the undying life of God which we received in baptism. This is why he says, 'Anyone who eats this bread will live forever.'

When we receive the Eucharist, Jesus comes to each of us personally, as though each of us was the only person in the world at that moment. We are able to enter into a deeper intimacy with him than if he were physically present. We are not merely in communication with him, but in communion with him, a holy communion. Through the Eucharist a spiritual bond is forged between us and Jesus. The Eucharist enables us to grow in intimacy and friendship with the Lord.

And through our shared intimacy with Jesus in communion, we are united also with one another, something which we must try to live out in our ordinary lives through mutual love, forgiveness and concern.

HOMILY 2   **From Eucharist to life**

The theme of today's Gospel is exclusively eucharistic. Absolutely central to what we believe about the Eucharist is that Christ is really and truly present there. Not physically present, but nevertheless really present. For those who believe that God is present in all things and in all places, his special presence in the Eucharist ought not to be such a big problem. Besides, we have the word of Jesus: 'This is my body ... this is my blood.' And the Lord cannot lie.

When we receive communion, Jesus comes to each of us personally, as though each of us was the only person in the world at that moment. A spiritual bond is forged between us and him, with the result that we are able to enter into a deeper intimacy with him than if he were physically present. We should avail of this wonderful time to grow in intimacy and friendship with the Lord.

However, we must never forget that the Jesus we receive in the Eucharist is the same Jesus who gave his life for us. The words of the consecration remind us of this: 'This is my body given for you ... This is my blood shed for you.' Hence, communion should evoke a spirit of sacrifice in us. To receive this food is to be reminded that, like Christ, we too must be willing to give ourselves in the service of others.

Mother Teresa of Calcutta had a rule that when a newcomer arrived to join her Order, the Missionaries of Charity, the very next day the newcomer had to go to the Home of the Dying. One day a girl came from outside India to join, so Mother Teresa said to her: 'You saw with what love and care the priest touched Jesus in the Host during Mass. Now go to the Home for the Dying and do the same, because it is the same Jesus you will find there in the broken bodies of our poor.'

Three hours later the newcomer came back and, with a big smile, said to her, 'Mother, I have been touching the body of Christ for three hours.'

'How? What did you do?' Mother Teresa asked her.

'When I arrived there,' she replied, 'they brought in a man who had fallen into a drain, and been there for some time. He was covered with dirt and had several wounds. I washed him and cleaned his wounds. As I did so I knew I was touching the body of Christ.'

To be able to make this kind of connection we need the help of the Lord himself. It is above all in the Eucharist that he gives us this help. Mother Teresa put it like this:

In the Eucharist I receive the spiritual food which sustains me in all my labours. Without it I could not get through one single day or hour of my life.

HOMILY 3   **Places at table**

Once there was a wealthy merchant who had his newly married son and his wife living in his household. The son had a kind heart, and devoted himself to charitable works, helping every poor person who asked for his assistance.

In time the young wife gave birth to a son. In honour of the occasion, the happy grandfather arranged a great feast. Shortly before the festivities were about to begin, the son asked,

'Tell me, father, what arrangements have you made for the seating of the guests? If you do the conventional thing and seat the rich at the head table and the poor near the door, it will distress me. You know very well how I love the poor. As this is my celebration, let me honour those who get no honour. Promise me, then, to seat the poor at the head table and the rich at the door.'

His father listened attentively and replied, 'My son, it is difficult to change the world. Look at it this way: Why do poor people come to a feast? Because they are hungry and would like to eat a good meal. And why do rich people come to a feast? To get honour. They don't come to eat, because they have enough at home.

'Now just imagine what would happen if you seated the poor at the head table. They would sit there, very self-consciously, feeling everybody's eyes on them, and so would be ashamed to eat their fill. And what they'd eat they wouldn't enjoy. Don't you think it would be better for their sake that they sat unnoticed at the door, where they could eat to their hearts content without being ashamed?

'Then again, suppose I were to do what you're asking and seat the rich at the door. Don't you think they'd feel insulted. They don't come for the sake of the food, but for the honour. And if you don't give them that what will they get?'

The Eucharist is the banquet Jesus provides for his followers. All of us come to this banquet hungry; all of us need the bread that only Jesus can give – the bread of eternal life. And all of us come here poor before God. Here all of us are nourished. And here all of us are honoured, because here every place is a place of honour.

Furthermore, through the Eucharist a spiritual bond is forged between us. Through our shared intimacy with Jesus, we are united also with one another, something which we must try to live out in our ordinary lives through mutual love, forgiveness and concern.

PRAYER OF THE FAITHFUL

President: Those who seek the Lord lack no blessing. Let us now bring our needs to the Lord and seek his help and his blessing.

Response: Lord, hear our prayer.

Reader(s): For the Church: that the Eucharistic Banquet may be a sign and a source of unity for its members. [Pause] We pray to the Lord.

For all temporal rulers: that they may promote justice and unity in the world. [Pause] We pray to the Lord.

For the lapsed: that they may hear the gentle voice of Christ, the Good Shepherd, calling them back to be part of the flock he nourishes. [Pause] We pray to the Lord.

For all gathered here: that we may receive Jesus in communion with faith and humility, and so deepen our love for him and for one another. [Pause] We pray to the Lord.

For our own special needs. [Longer pause] We pray to the Lord.

President: Father, your Son Jesus gave us the gift of the Eucharist. May all who come here experience the joy of his friendship, and grow in his love. We ask this through the same Christ our Lord.

BEFORE COMMUNION

When the host is held up before us we ought to look at it. And when the Eucharistic minister says, 'The Body of Christ,' we should respond with 'Amen.' In this way we are making an act of faith in the presence of Christ in the Eucharistic bread. Having received the host with reverence, we return to our places to spend some time in communion with the Lord.

PRAYER/REFLECTION   **The presence of Christ**

Christ be near at either hand,
Christ behind, before me stand.
Christ with me where e'er I go,
Christ around, above, below.

Christ be in my heart and mind,
Christ within my soul enshrined.
Christ control my wayward heart,
Christ abide and ne'er depart.

Christ my life and only way,
Christ my lantern night and day.
Christ be my unchanging friend,
Guide and Shepherd to the end.

Twenty-first Sunday of the Year
WILL YOU ALSO LEAVE ME?

INTRODUCTION AND CONFITEOR

In the Gospel we read how many people left Jesus, and walked no more with him. Many still leave him. But by the grace of God we are here. Each Sunday gives us an opportunity to confirm our faith in him who alone has the words of eternal life. [Pause]

Lord Jesus, you confirm our faith in you. Lord, have mercy.

You confirm our hope in what you promise. Christ, have mercy.

You confirm our love for you and for one another. Lord, have mercy.

HEADINGS FOR READINGS

First Reading (Josh 24:1-2.15-18). Joshua confronts the people with a vital decision – to serve the one true God or to serve false gods.

Second Reading (Eph 5:21-32). St Paul uses the image of a marriage relationship to express the bond that exists between Christ and the Church.

Gospel (Jn 6:60-69). The disciples of Jesus are faced with a vital decision – to stay with Jesus or to leave him.

SCRIPTURE NOTE

The First Reading deals with a covenant-renewal ceremony that took place at Shechem shortly after the people had entered the promised land. Joshua called upon them to make a choice: to serve the God of their fathers or to serve other gods. All the tribes of Israel declared, 'We will serve the Lord.'

In a similar way Jesus called upon the people who had listened to his discourse on the Bread of Life to make up their minds whether or not they were going to believe in him and follow him. Sadly, apart from the Twelve, many deserted him. Even among the Twelve a traitor lurked.

Even though Jesus was sad to see those people leaving him, he let them go. It wasn't great crowds that excited him. What mattered to him (and what should matter to the Church) was the authenticity and sincerity of those who stayed.

Just as Mark's account of the ministry in Galilee ends on a note of disbelief (Fourteenth Sunday), so it is here. And in Peter's reaction we have John's parallel to the synoptic scene at Caesarea Philippi (Twenty-fourth Sunday).

HOMILY 1   **Coming to a personal acceptance of the faith**

People's beliefs and convictions are almost always got second-hand, and without examination, from some authority. This is especially true of religious beliefs. It is hard to find a person who has acquired his beliefs by personal proof. This is especially true of us who, for the most part, are cradle Catholics.

A so-called 'born Catholic' woke up one day and got a shock. It suddenly dawned on him that he was not a volunteer but a conscript. I don't know what triggered off this line of thought in him. But for the first time in his life he realised that everything relating to the faith had been given to him. It was all second-hand, like clothes handed down to him from an older brother.

He had been baptised as a baby, and naturally had no memory of it. All the way through his growing years, religion had been imposed on him by his parents and by Church and school authorities. Not that he had resisted this or even resented it to any degree.

But now that he was a young adult it suddenly hit him. He had accepted it all unthinkingly. He had never made the faith his own. But what bothered him most was the fact that he had never been consulted about it. He had never been offered the opportunity to made a personal choice about his faith.

It was not a happy moment for him. In fact, it was a very disturbing moment. Of course, he soon realised that the faith was not the only thing he had inherited. Most of what he was, of what constituted his identity, was not his either – his name, his family, his nationality, and so on.

But the faith was the thing that worried him most. He had not owned the faith. He began to wonder if he had any convictions at all about it. What, if anything, did it mean to him? Would his life be any the poorer without it? These were questions he had never asked himself before.

It was a worrying moment for him, and a dangerous one too (the danger of throwing out the baby with the bath water). But it also carried great possibilities. He was being given a chance to make a personal choice regarding the faith. It was not unlike the choice which Joshua put to the Israelites on taking possession of the promised land (First Reading). He told them that the faith of their forefathers would not do them. They would have to make their own commitment to God there and then. Jesus put a similar choice before his apostles.

It is no longer enough to be born into the faith. A second-hand faith is an impoverished faith. It will not do us, especially in hard times. 'A knowledge of religion, as distinguished from experience, seems but chaff in moments of trial' (Gandhi).

As we go through life, things happen to us which cause us either to make this faith our own and to try to live it with some conviction, or to drift away from it. For some, the transformative experiences may be quiet and undramatic. Others have their beliefs transformed by painful experiences such as addiction, or war experiences, or the loss of a loved one ...

We need to make the faith our own. We have to find meaning in it through personal experience if it is to come alive for us. But we have to be clear what that word 'faith' involves. It is not in the first place the acceptance of a set of beliefs, but a belief in, and commitment to, the person of Jesus.

When Jesus saw that many of his disciples were leaving him, he turned to the apostles and said, 'Will you also leave me?' These words are addressed to us too. It's not the Lord who leaves us, but we who may leave him. But why would we want to leave the Lord, who alone has the words of eternal life?

We need to make our own Peter's profession of faith. I think this is happening in the Church. For more and more people, faith is no longer something inherited and taken for granted, but the fruit of a personal decision. They live as members of a community of believers whose common faith strengthens the faith of each individual.

The Lord himself is the one who strengthens our faith. But we also need to confirm one another. Our presence at the Sunday Eucharist can make both of these things happen.

HOMILY 2   **Words of eternal life**

'Lord, to whom shall we go? You have the words of eternal life. We have come to believe and know that you are the Holy One of God.' This is one of the clearest and greatest professions of faith in the Gospel. It went to the heart of who Jesus was and what he was about. He was not just a teacher or healer or prophet. He was the Holy One of God. Later the first Christians came to believe that he was, in fact, the Son of God.

As for what he was about. Though he healed and fed the bodies of people, his main concern was to nourish their minds and hearts with what Peter so aptly called 'the words of eternal life.' His words truly brought life to people. Here are some examples of the kind of words he spoke to people.

'Go in peace, your sins are forgiven.' With these words he set sinners free.

'Fear not, it is I.' With these words he calmed the fears of his apostles when they thought they were going to drown.

To the woman at the well he said, 'Anyone who drinks the water I can give will never get thirsty again.' There is a thirst in every human heart that only God can quench.

To the people he said, 'I am the bread of life. Anyone who eats this bread will live for ever.' Who would not want to eat of this bread?

Again he said, 'I am the light of the world. Anyone who follows me will never walk in darkness, but will always have the light of life.' The light of Jesus was such that no darkness, not even that of death, could overpower it.

To the Jewish leaders he said, 'I am the good shepherd. I know my sheep and they follow me. I give them eternal life.'

To the grief-stricken Martha and Mary he said, 'I am the resurrection and the life. Anyone who believes in me will never die [eternally].'

To the apostles, who were distraught on hearing him say that he was leaving them, he said, 'Let not our hearts be troubled or afraid. I am going to prepare a place for you.'

'This day you will be with me in Paradise.' With these words he brought hope to a condemned man.

On one occasion the religious leaders sent the temple guards to arrest him. But they never laid a hand on him. Instead, they were spell-bound by his teaching. Even they recognised that Jesus' words were special, and went back to their masters and declared, 'No one ever spoke like this man speaks.'

Jesus truly has the words of eternal life. And those words of Jesus have been preserved for us in the Gospels. Each Sunday we are invited to listen to them.

'Will you also leave me?' These words are now addressed to us. It's not the Lord who leaves us, but we who may leave him. Many still do so.

We need to make our own Peter's profession of faith: 'Lord, to whom shall we go? You have the words of eternal life.' We have done so. Our presence here is a sign of that. But we need to reaffirm our commitment, just as the Israelites did on taking possession of the promised land. Every Sunday we get a chance to do this. We need the Lord to strengthen our faith. We also need to confirm one another.

Eternal life is not something that lies in the future. It has already begun in Baptism. Its full flowering is still to come. It's something we accept on the word of Jesus.

HOMILY 3   **Freedom to choose**

In recent years we have seen the appearance of a large number of cults. One of the most disturbing things about them is the hold they get on those who join them. The leaders are invariably people who have a lust to control other people. And the members are often insecure and fragile people, easy prey for such leaders.

There is a big difference between Christ's approach and that of the false messiahs. In the cults we have the personal glorification of the leader. Christ never sought glory for himself. He referred everything to his heavenly Father, whose will he came to do. He made himself the servant of all. The false messiahs usually promise their followers an earthly paradise in some shape or form. It becomes a form of inducement. Christ made no such promise to his followers. In fact, quite the contrary. He told them that they would suffer persecution if they followed him. True, he did promise eternal life – but only to those prepared to do, not his will, but the will of the Father.

When the cult leaders see that the ship is sinking, they usually try to ensure that the crew goes down with it. Christ, the Good Shepherd, laid down his life to save the lives of his sheep.

Through a combination of inducements and indoctrination, recruits to the cults become little better than flies caught in a spider's web. Their freedom is almost completely taken away. But freedom is the greatest thing we have. The only thing that has moral value and that helps us to grow is what is done freely. Jesus forced no one to follow him. We have a splendid example of this in today's Gospel.

The cross was already beginning to cast its shadow over him. His disciples were faced with a decision – to stay with him or to leave him. Some stayed with him as long as his career was on the way up, but at the first shadow of the cross they abandoned him. Others had come to him to get something from him; when it came to suffering for him, and giving to others, they quit. Incredibly, even one of his twelve had already opted out, having made up his mind to betray him.

But a remnant stayed with Jesus. Peter spoke up for these. His decision to stay was based first of all on a personal loyalty to Jesus. Then to his teaching. Even though there are many things he didn't understand, he knew that Jesus had the words of eternal life.

If we follow Christ we will always be free. We are free, not when we do whatever we please, but when we do what is right. When we do what is right we are like an instrument that is being played as it was meant to be played.

ANOTHER APPROACH   **Freedom of choice**

There are decisive moments when one has to come out of the shadows and declare where one's loyalties lie, or to take a definite stand, or to make a definite commitment one way or another. The First Reading provides us with a splendid example

It deals with a covenant-renewal ceremony that took place at Shechem shortly after the people had entered the promised land. Joshua called upon them to make a choice: to serve the God of their fathers, or to serve other gods. He issued a solemn warning: if they chose to follow others gods, they would be cursed; but if they chose to follow the true God, they would be blessed. It was a stern, stark choice, which represented a rather forbidding morality. Jesus gave a different perspective – to obey not under threat of punishment but out of love. Anyway, all the tribes of Israel declared, 'We will serve the Lord.'

One of the greatest gifts God has given us is freedom of choice. No doubt we would have an easier life if God pulled all the strings. If we were God's puppets, then we would make only good choices. But that would be to make automatons out of us. It would make sin impossible, but at the same stroke it would make virtue impossible.

The fact that God respects our freedom is a sign of his love for us. Possessive love tries to control the loved one. God doesn't control us. He has given us the freedom to choose between good and evil. We have to choose one or the other. Even to make no choice is a choice.

Even when we disobey his commandments, God doesn't stop loving us. But this doesn't mean that God is permissive, that it doesn't matter what we do. It matters an awful lot. God sees every human act. He does not condone sin or wrong-doing.

Since we are free, we are responsible for our choices, and for the consequences of our choices. Sin brings its own punishment. We are punished, not *for* our sins, but *by* our sins. There is no true wisdom, no life as God would have us live it, without obedience to God's commandments.

In the New Testament we see that God has not left us to ourselves. He has given us his grace to help us make the right choices.

We are never more free that when we choose to walk in God's ways. Are homing birds free? In one sense they are not free. But in another sense they are completely free. They are free to go home. That is where they long to go. Happy those who experience a kind of homing instinct for God. We can be free even on a hard road provided it is freely chosen.

PRAYER OF THE FAITHFUL

President: The Lord hears the cries of his people and rescues them from all their distress. Let us pray to him now with confidence.

Response: Lord, hear our prayer.

Reader(s): For all the followers of Jesus: that they may realise that they are truly free only when they do the will of God. [Pause] We pray to the Lord.

For government leaders: that they may respect the rights and freedoms of their people. [Pause] We pray to the Lord.

For the sick: that God may lighten their burden and comfort them with his presence. [Pause] We pray to the Lord.

For all those who have become slaves to wrong-doing, or who are in the grip of some compulsion or addiction. [Pause] We pray to the Lord.

For all gathered here: that our lives may bear witness to the faith we profess with our lips. [Pause] We pray to the Lord.

For grace to place our own particular needs before God. [Longer pause] We pray to the Lord.

President: Heavenly Father, help us to follow Christ your Son, who by doing your will at all times showed us how to live in freedom and dignity on this earth. We make our prayers through the same Christ our Lord.

REFLECTION   **Will you also leave me?**

When many of his disciples were leaving him,
Jesus turned to the apostles and said, 'Will you also leave me?'
These words are addressed to us too.
It's not the Lord who leaves us, but we who may leave him.
But why would we want to leave the Lord,
who alone has the words of eternal life?
We need to make our own Peter's profession of faith.
Every Sunday we get a chance to do so.
We need the Lord to strengthen our faith.
We also need to confirm one another.
Lord, confirm our decision to stay with you.
Draw us closer to you in bonds of trust,
so that we may follow you in love and freedom.

Twenty-second Sunday of the Year

INTRODUCTION AND CONFITEOR

The primary reason why we are here is to worship God. Jesus said of the Pharisees: 'This people honours me with their lips, but their hearts are far from me.' Hence, their worship was hollow and empty. It's a danger that faces us all. We need God's help in order to give him the kind of worship that will honour him and transform our lives. Let us turn to God now with sincere and humble hearts. [Pause]

Lord, you help us to worship you with a sincere heart. Lord, have mercy.

Lord, you help us to worship you with a humble heart. Christ, have mercy.

Lord, you help us to worship you with a loving heart. Lord, have mercy.

HEADINGS FOR READINGS

First Reading (Deut 4:1-2.6-8) Moses urges the people to be faithful to God's law, which is not a burden to be endured, but a source of life and wisdom.

Second Reading (Jam 1:17-18.21-22.27). It is not enough to listen to the word of God; we must put it into practice.

Gospel (Mk 7:1-8.14-15.21-23). Jesus tells the Pharisees that they have substituted their own laws for the Law of God, and are more concerned about outer cleanness than cleanness of heart.

SCRIPTURE NOTE

Today, as we resume the reading of Mark's Gospel, we meet a controversy over ritual cleanness.

All three readings tie in with one another. In the First Reading Moses urges the people to be faithful to God's Law, without adding to it or subtracting from it. It is not a burden to be endured, but a source of life and wisdom. The Gospel shows what happened in practice. To the Law of God (given through Moses) they added their own traditions, which came to be regarded as equally authoritative and binding. Worse, they got in the way of God's Law.

Mark is making clear to Gentile Christians that being followers of Christ does not involve them in the observance of Jewish practices.

The Second Reading (the first of five from the Letter of St James) shows the essential link between faith and love. Nothing could be more practical than this. Nowhere is the way to sanctity so clearly indicated.

HOMILY 1 **The primacy of the heart**

In education we attach more importance to the head than to the heart. Indeed, the heart hardly gets a look in. We make more of a clever child than of a good child. The world of business and politics rewards cleverness rather than goodness. And yet in our everyday language we acknowledge the primacy of the heart. Here are a few examples.

We judge a person by the heart. One of the most damning things we can say about anyone is that 'he has no heart', or that 'he has a cold heart', or 'a hard heart'. But then one of the best things we can say about anyone is that 'he has a heart', or 'he is warm-hearted', or 'soft-hearted'.

We judge the degree of a person's commitment to something in terms of the heart. Of one we say, 'his heart is not in it', or 'he is only half-hearted'. As a result, he will probably quit. Even if he stays, he will not put his best into it. Of another we say, 'his heart is in it', or 'he is whole-hearted'. Then in all probability he will not only persevere but put his best into it.

We describe sorrow and joy in terms of the heart. We say, 'her heart was broken', or 'she went with a heavy heart'. Or we say, 'her heart overflowed with joy', or 'she went with a light heart'.

We describe burdens and wounds in terms of the heart. A 'heavy heart' is the most wearisome burden of all. A 'broken heart' is the most painful wound of all.

There are many more examples that could be given. However, let us end by looking at two telling examples from today's Gospel.

The first concerns worship. The most damning thing that can be said about someone's worship is that the person's heart is not in it. In which case it is mere lip-service, like that of the Pharisees. And one of the best things than can be said about someone's worship is that the person's heart is in it. That it comes from the heart.

The second concerns badness and goodness. A corrupt heart is the worst form of badness. It means to be bad at the core. A pure heart is the best kind of goodness. It means to be good at the core.

The Gospel places great emphasis on the heart, and we can see why. The heart is the source from which all our thoughts, words and deeds flow. If the heart is clean, then all that flows from it will be clean, like water flowing from a pure spring. The Pharisees paid more attention to the outside than the inside. They were more preoccupied with having clean hands than having clean hearts.

It's the heart that matters. But only God can see what is in the heart. And only he can make it into what it should be.

HOMILY 2   **The evil within**

Only a fool would wash the outside of a cup and ignore the inside. We make sure to wash at least the inside, whatever about the outside. Jesus said we should do the same with ourselves. We should get the inside clean, whatever about the outside. In fact, if the inside (the heart) is clean, the outside (our behaviour) will also be clean. But if the inside is unclean, then the outside will be unclean too. The outside will reflect the state of the inside.

The Pharisees saw evil as something outside themselves – in things and especially in other people. They prided themselves on being virtuous and despised everyone else. If evil was outside themselves, then they could protect themselves from it by avoiding contact with people, or where this was not possible then by ritual washings.

The Pharisees were sincere people. It's just that their efforts were directed at the wrong target. For them the exterior was everything. Hence, their concern about outer cleanness, and neglect of what was more important – inner cleanness, or cleanness of heart.

Jesus said that the source of evil is within us. It has its roots in the heart. We can't guard ourselves from it by separation from others. All those horrible things he lists, and which we read about in the newspapers – fornication, theft, murder, adultery, greed, malice, deceit, indecency, envy, slander, pride – all these things start inside a person. Their seeds are within us all. These are the things which make a person unclean in the eyes of God.

This is a very disturbing truth, and one we ignore at our own peril. A great problem of our time is our failure to know ourselves, to recognise evil and deal with it within ourselves. Yet there is a kind of comfort and freedom in knowing and accepting this humbling truth.

Today there is a huge preoccupation with cleanness of body. Hence, all the ads about soaps and perfumes. And there is great preoccupation with the environment – with the quality of the water we drink, the food we eat, and the air we breathe. It's not that these are unimportant. It's just that there is another environment which is even more important – the moral environment. Evil is the worst kind of pollution of all.

But if the source of evil is within us, so too is the source of good. All our thoughts, words, and deeds flow from the heart like water from a hidden spring. If the spring is clean, then all that flows from it will be clean. We must purify the source.

There is a story about a master who one day put the following question to some of his disciples: 'What is the thing that one should avoid most in life?'

'An evil eye,' said the first.

'A treacherous friend,' said the second.

'A bad neighbour,' said the third.

'A bad heart,' said the fourth.

The Master liked the last answer best, because it included all the others. Then he said, 'And what is the most desirable thing to strive for in life?'

'A good eye,' said the first.

'A good friend,' said the second.

'A good neighbour,' said the third.

'A good heart,' said the fourth.

The Master liked the last answer best, because it included all the others.

We must strive for cleanness of heart. Total purity of heart is unattainable here on earth. It is a struggle that will always go on. A pure heart is not the same as an empty heart. A heart that is full of love is a pure and healthy heart.

HOMILY 3   **Lip-service versus service of the heart**

An answering machine is a good thing in itself. But when we make a phone-call, we prefer to be greeted by a human being rather than by a machine. Yet, thanks to the marvels of modern technology, a person's voice can be there while the person is absent.

Long before such gadgets as answering machines were invented people were able to do that – to be present in voice only. Nowhere is this seen so clearly as in the case of worship. Jesus said of the Pharisees, 'These people honour God with their lips, but their hearts are far from him.'

People can be present in church in voice only, and so their worship becomes mere lip-service. And to make matters worse, that voice may not be their ordinary voice. It may be a solemn and serious one, put on specially for Sundays. Such people are no better than answering machines. The most important element is missing, namely, the heart.

The same applies to any meeting or gathering of people. It is most likely to manifest itself at public functions and on formal occasions. People are there, yet it is not their true self that is there. It is an artificial self, a dressed-up likeness. To meet such people is to meet a shadow. You are left with an empty feeling.

How different real presence is! The heart is in it, and the words that are spoken flow from there. For our words to ring true, they must be spoken from the heart. If they come only from the lips, they will have a hollow sound. And while they may be clever, they will not convince or inspire.

Take the word of forgiveness for instance. If it does not come from the heart, of what use is it? It will not set the offender free. Nor will it result in a true reconciliation between the parties.

And the word of peace. If it is not spoken from the heart, can it bring peace? Of course not. And the word of welcome. I may open the door of my house to a person with kind words, but unless I make room for him in my heart, he will still be a stranger to me.

It is only with the heart that we can speak rightly. And a presence without the heart is like a fireplace without a fire.

What is the quality of my presence here on a Sunday? I can tell by whether or not my heart is in it. What does it mean to put one's heart into one's worship? It implies sincerity, depth of commitment, and above all, love.

ANOTHER APPROACH   **Looking into the perfect mirror**

It has been said that we need mirrors to see what without them we would hardly see at all. St James likens God's word to a mirror (Second Reading). He says, 'To listen to the word of God … is like looking at our own features in a mirror.' (Note: this verse is omitted in our reading). He says that to examine ourselves against the word of God, is to look into 'the perfect mirror.'

The word of God holds a rare and revealing mirror to our lives. We learn much by looking into it. This mirror will search out our impurities. It will make us aware of all that is hollow in ourselves – our greed, our pride, our selfishness. Some do not look into the mirror because they fear they might not like what they see. They try to avoid the self-questioning the mirror demands by staying away from it.

However, we shouldn't be afraid to look into this mirror, and to draw our own conclusions from what we see. Putting off the encounter with the mirror only makes it harder. What have we to fear? Only the truth –

and the truth will set us free.

When we look into an ordinary mirror we see ourselves as we are, physically only, of course. But when we look into the mirror of God's word we see ourselves as we are, not physically, but spiritually. But we see more than that. We see ourselves as we could be. It shows us what we are capable of becoming. We see our possibilities, and what we are called to be. God's word challenges us to a bolder, truer and deeper living.

It is into this 'perfect mirror' that we must gaze. If this doesn't accuse us, then we have nothing to fear. But it's unlikely that we shall not find something amiss, something wanting.

Of course, as St James says, it's possible to look into the mirror and then go away and forget what one saw. Needless to say, no good will come from that. It's deeds that count.

And if we look into the mirror James holds up before us in today's reading what will we see? This lovely reading shows the essential link between faith and love. There he says, 'Pure, unspoilt religion, in the eyes of God is this: coming to the help of orphans and widows [the most vulnerable members of the community] when they need it, and keeping oneself uncontaminated by the world.' Nothing could be more practical than this. Nowhere is the way to sanctity so clearly pointed out.

PRAYERS OF THE FAITHFUL

President: Standing before the Lord with open and humble hearts, let us bring before him our own needs, those of the Church and of the world.

Response: Lord, hear our prayer.

Reader(s): For Christians: that they may honour and worship God not only with their lips, but also with their hearts and their lives. [Pause] Let us pray to the Lord.

For all those who work to improve our environment. [Pause] Let us pray to the Lord.

For people who work in the media. [Pause] Let us pray to the Lord.

For artists, craftspeople, and musicians: that their work may bring joy and inspiration into the lives of people. [Pause] Let us pray to the Lord.

That we may be aware of the evil within us, and strive to overcome it. [Pause] Let us pray to the Lord.

For our special needs. [Longer pause] Let us pray to the Lord.

President: All-loving God, give us pure hearts that we may see you, humble hearts that we may hear you, loving hearts that we may serve you, and trusting hearts that we may abide in you. We ask this through Christ our Lord.

REFLECTION   **Cleanness of heart**

Today pollution has become a big issue,
and rightly so.
People want clean water, clean air, and clean food.
But we should be even more concerned
about the most dangerous pollution of all, namely, evil.
Pride, anger, hate, lust, greed, envy ...
all these are dangerous pollutants.
So what must we do?
We must purify the source; the heart is the source.
It is the well-spring from which
all our thoughts, words, and deeds flow.
If the heart is clean, all that flows from it will be clean.
Blessed are the clean of heart: they shall see God.

Twenty-third Sunday of the Year
THE DEAF HEAR AND THE DUMB SPEAK

INTRODUCTION AND CONFITEOR

Jesus made the deaf hear and the dumb speak. We need God to touch our ears in order to be able to hear his word, and we need him to touch our tongues in order to be able to profess our faith. [Pause]

Lord Jesus, you open our ears so that we can hear your word. Lord, have mercy.

You touch our tongues so that we can profess our faith. Christ, have mercy.

You touch our hearts we that we can love you and love one another. Lord, have mercy.

HEADINGS FOR READINGS

First Reading (Is 35:4-7). The prophet urges the people to take courage, because God is coming to save his people.

Second Reading (Jam 2:1-5). Class distinction should have no place among Christians.

Gospel (Mk 7:31-37). Jesus cures a Gentile man who is deaf and has a speech impediment.

SCRIPTURE NOTE

Jesus performed this miracle in Gentile territory. The faith-response of the Gentiles contrasts sharply with that of many of his own people. In

Mark's mind Jesus was fulfilling the prophecy of Isaiah, 'The ears of the deaf will be unsealed, and the tongues of the dumb sing for joy' (First Reading). In other words, Jesus is the one who brings salvation to Israel.

This miracle is the only cure in the Gospels that is described as taking place gradually. Mark saw it as an illustration of growth in faith. It is what happens to every Christian at Baptism. Christ touches our ears so that we can hear his word, and touches our tongues so that we can profess our faith. Hence, we too can say, 'He has done all things well; he makes the deaf hear and the dumb speak.'

HOMILY 1   **The gifts of hearing and speech**

The ability to hear and to speak are two great gifts. Like all gifts they can be taken for granted or even misused. They are connected. We see this especially in the case of the elderly. When their hearing goes they retreat into silence. The man who came to Jesus was deaf and also had an impediment in his speech. The latter may have been due in part to the former.

People with diminished hearing are often seen as doddering or buffoonish. Diminished hearing leads to embarrassed silences and misunderstandings. Today hearing aids have lessened their pain but not removed it entirely.

The gift of speech is our chief means of communicating with other people. People with speech impediments are often subjects of fun and amusement to others.

We see the trouble Jesus went to on behalf of this poor man, and the care with which he dealt with him. He took him away from the crowd so that he could deal with him in private and give him his undivided attention. Rather than speak to him, he touched his ears and tongue. Thus he made him feel what he could not hear.

The miracle has great relevance for us, not because we are deaf or dumb (which happily most of us are not), but precisely because we have the gifts of hearing and speech. The fact that we have these gifts doesn't mean we use them well. Many people are very poor listeners. And many people have difficulty in expressing themselves.

A fate even worse than being born deaf is to have ears and yet fail to hear. Worse again is to have ears and refuse to hear, or to have a tongue and refuse to speak. So we need the Lord's healing touch if we are to use these two precious gifts well.

Our senses are precious and vital. We have to experience God with our senses too – with our eyes, our ears, our tongues, and especially our hearts.

The miracle is not so much about the physical healing of a man who was deaf and dumb. Rather, it's about the opening of a person's ears so that he may be able to hear the word of God; and the loosening of his tongue so that he may be able to profess faith in Jesus. A person could have perfect hearing, and yet not hear the word of God. And a person could have perfect speech, and be unable to make an act of faith.

Hence, it comes as no surprise that the ceremony of touching the ears and the tongue made its way into the rite of Baptism from early times, and is still there to this day. The minister touches the ears and mouth of the person being baptised and says, 'The Lord Jesus made the deaf hear and the dumb speak. May he soon touch your ears to receive his word, and your mouth to proclaim his faith, to the praise and glory of God the Father.'

We need to be able to hear the word of God. Then we need to be able to profess that word with our lips. Finally, we need to put it into practice in our lives. The word of God, when heard and acted on, is like seed falling on good soil; it makes our lives fruitful.

HOMILY 2   **Re-telling the story**

My name is James. Being completely deaf, I was deprived of so much that others take for granted. I couldn't hear the shouts of children at play, the singing of the birds, the sound of the wind in the trees ... I couldn't hear words of comfort, encouragement, or advice. Few people bother to try to communicate with the deaf. They find it too tedious. I felt terribly isolated.

The fact that I was practically dumb as well added to my sense of deprivation and isolation. I couldn't explain myself. I couldn't express my feelings Insensitive people laughed at my stammerings.

I had no opportunity to contribute anything to the community. Consequently, I felt useless and in the way. People even hesitated to touch me. To be handicapped is to be different. And when you are different, people are afraid of you. Furthermore, I was led to believe that my handicaps were a punishment from God.

I was full of self-pity. I craved for compassion. I was convinced that there wasn't a single person who understood or pitied me. That was until the day I learned about Jesus. Even though he was a Jew and I was a Gentile, that didn't deter me from seeking his help.

What an experience! The first thing he did was take me aside from the crowd, and gave me his undivided attention. This made me feel that I was important to him. At the same time it saved me from the curiosity of gawkers.

He did not speak to me as it would have been a waste of words. Instead he touched me. He made me feel what I couldn't hear. There was nothing rough or hurried about his touch. It was tender, patient and loving.

He put his fingers into my ears. Then he put his finger into his mouth, took some healing spittle from it, and put it on my tongue. Next he raised his eyes to heaven to show me that it was from God that help was to come. Then with a great sigh he said, 'Be opened!' And suddenly my ears were opened and my speech became normal. I was cured!

He told me not to broadcast what he had done for me. But I was unable to keep quiet. There was so much bottled up inside me that at first I talked incessantly. I couldn't pass anyone in the street without saying 'hello'. I couldn't remain silent in the presence of someone in pain if I felt a word would help. I couldn't bear to see an injustice done without denouncing it.

But soon I realised that I was over-talking. I wasn't listening. In that way I was hurting people. So I made a special point of trying to really listen to people, which meant that I had to stop talking. I listened too to the sounds of nature, to music, to laughter and crying ...

I discovered some interesting things during those early months after my cure. I discovered that everybody has certain impediments that prevent them from making full use of the gift of speech – shyness, insensitivity, apathy ... And they have impediments that prevent them from hearing well ... prejudice, inattention, refusal to listen ...

Why am I telling you all this? It is to save you from the fate of those who have ears but cannot hear, and tongues but cannot speak. What I discovered from my experience is this: the greatest tragedy is not to be born deaf or dumb, but to have ears and yet fail to hear; and to have tongues and yet fail to speak.

Hearing and speech are great gifts. But without a heart that is able to feel compassion, we will never be able to use them well. It is only with the heart that we can listen rightly, and it is only with the heart that we can speak rightly.

The man who touched my ears and my tongue also touched my heart. It was that above all that made me new. That was the real miracle.

HOMILY 3   **Class distinction**

Once a wealthy man invited all his fellow townspeople to a banquet. A man showed up at the banquet in a tattered suit, which was the only one he had, and was turned away at the door. Undaunted, he went home and borrowed an expensive suit of clothes from a wealthy neighbour. Then he returned to his host's house looking like a man of substance. This time the doorman welcomed him respectfully and showed him to a seat at the top table. During the meal as he reached for a piece of roast meat, his sleeve accidentally slipped into the dish.

'Pull up your sleeve,' the man next to him whispered.

'No, I won't,' said he. Then addressing his sleeve he said, 'Eat, my sleeve, eat and take your fill. You have more right to the feast than I, since they respect you above me in this house.'

The apostle James says: 'Do not try to combine faith in Jesus Christ with the making of distinctions between classes of people.' If this passage from James makes some of us uncomfortable, well then, so be it! Our society is riddled with class distinction. We see it in the cars people drive in, in the planes they fly in, in the areas they live in, in the clubs they frequent, and so on. There is a place for the rich and a place for the poor. Our society values people according to the amount of money they have. If you are wealthy, you are somebody. If you are poor, you are nobody.

It's not so much the fact that there are distinctions, but what results from these distinctions that concerns us. Class distinction leads to partiality; to the favouring of the rich and the slighting of the poor. It is used to keep people in their place, and give people an inferiority complex. It keeps people apart. Sometimes the poor are not allowed in the same building as the rich. But the rich too suffer, because it gives them a false sense of importance.

Class distinction leads to double standards and should have no place among Christians. Christians need to challenge these false standards, and not allow themselves to be lured into conforming to them.

There are times when the barriers of class fall down. In times of collective danger, or collective sadness, or collective joy, these distinctions are swept aside, and shown up for the silly things they really are. On such occasions people reach out to one another, and a great mutual enrichment occurs. Such occasions make one realise how much is lost through these artificial divisions.

If God shows any partiality at all it is towards the poor and the oppressed. God's concern for the poor doesn't mean that God loves them simply because they are poor, as if poverty were a virtue. God takes the side of the poor and oppressed because they are unjustly treated. The Bible sees the rich as oppressing the poor. And God is determined to vindicate the oppressed. Christians must try to make their standards conform to the standards of God.

Greatness cannot be defined by class, nor can goodness or evil. No class has a monopoly on good or evil, suffering or joy. But when it comes to faith, St James says that it is those who are poor according to this world who are rich in faith. The rich tend to rely on their riches, whereas the poor turn to God instinctively. This is why Jesus says, 'Blessed are the poor, the Kingdom of Heaven is theirs.'

Here in the house of God all barriers of class fall down. They look silly. Because here our true dignity becomes apparent. It is not based on the things which normally divide people, and which are held in such esteem by society. It is based on something much deeper – what people are. We are God's sons and daughters, and brothers and sisters of the Lord. Any other distinctions are trivial and insignificant. When we arrive here, these others distinctions vanish like early morning mist before the sun.

ANOTHER APPROACH   **The handicaps of the normal**

The Gospel concerns the cure of a handicapped man. For that reason we might dismiss it as having no relevance for us. But, in truth, all of us have got our handicaps. The fact that ours are not as visible as those of the man in the Gospel doesn't make them less real.

In one way or another all of us are wounded. We see evidence of this in husbands who take refuge in work because they are no longer attracted to their wives, or wives who are wounded by lack of attention and love from their husbands, or parents in conflict with their children, or children who don't receive the love they need or who are stifled by parents who are too possessive.

Some people carry deep wounds from bad childhood experiences. Others are wounded by sickness, or by the death of a loved one, or by the non-acceptance of themselves. More are wounded by failures in work and in relationships. People are wounded by the inability to forgive, and by the experience of rejection which makes them in turn reject.

Inside each of us there lies a hidden world of suffering. But some are more wounded than others. The deepest wounds are those that are not visible to the eye. What we see as the obvious sufferings of others are almost certainly not their deepest suffering.

In some people the inner wounds have led to drink and/or depression. In others the same inner wounds have bred a compelling need to prove themselves, to be successful, to win, to dominate, to be well known, even to save others.

The first step in the road to healing is to recognise our wounds. Then counselling may be called for. Psychology may help unravel the origins of some of these wounds.

Here is a paradox: people who are limited physically and intellectually due to mental handicaps, are often more gifted than others when it comes to the things of the heart and to relationships. A handicapped person observed: 'Living as a cripple in a wheelchair allows you to see more clearly the crippled hearts of some people whose bodies are whole and sound.'

It is above all the heart that has to be healed. If only the heart was right we could give so much more. But, alas, the heart is often empty, often cold and unwelcoming, often hard and unyielding, often weighed down with worry, often lonely, often wounded, and sometimes broken. We shouldn't be surprised that this is so. All it means is that we have a heart of flesh, and not one of stone. But we have to heal the wounds of the heart in order to be able to bear the fruits of love, joy and peace.

In touching the ears and tongue of that handicapped man, Jesus also touched his wounded heart. It was that above all that made the man new. That was the real miracle.

PRAYER OF THE FAITHFUL

President: All of us are poor in the things that matter in the sight of God. With faith in God's goodness, let us now turn to him in our many needs.

Response: Lord, hear our prayer.

Reader(s): For Christians: that they may strive to break down divisions between people, and so help to build a just and peaceful society. [Pause] We pray to the Lord.

For people of different ethnic, or social, or religious backgrounds: that they may listen with good will, and speak words of peace to one another. [Pause] We pray to the Lord.

For those who are hard of hearing, and those who find it hard to express themselves. [Pause] We pray to the Lord.

For this gathering: that we may listen patiently, speak kindly, see truly, and act rightly. [Pause] We pray to the Lord.

For grace to bring our own particular needs before God. [Longer pause] We pray to the Lord.

President: Lord Jesus, you made the deaf hear, and the dumb speak. Touch our ears to receive your word, and touch our mouths to proclaim our faith, to the praise and glory of God the Father.

REFLECTION   **Precious gifts**

The gift of hearing is a precious gift.
But it is only with the heart that we can hear rightly.
The cry of a needy person may reach our ears,
but unless it reaches our heart
we will not feel the person's pain,
and it is unlikely that we will respond.
And the gift of speech is a precious gift.
But again it is only with the heart that we can speak rightly.
For our words to ring true, they must come from the heart.
If they come only from the lips,
they will have a hollow sound and will have little effect.
They will be like a wind that ruffles the surface of the water
but leaves the depths untouched.
But words that come from the heart, enter the heart.

Twenty-fourth Sunday of the Year
PETER'S PROFESSION OF FAITH

INTRODUCTION AND CONFITEOR

In the Gospel we see that some people had no faith in Jesus. Others had a mistaken faith. But Peter showed true faith in Jesus when he declared, 'You are the Christ, the Son of the living God.' If the faith is to be alive and influential in our lives, we have to make the faith our own. [Pause].

Lord Jesus, you are mighty God and prince of peace. Lord, have mercy.

Lord Jesus, you are Son of God and Son of Mary. Christ, have mercy.

Lord Jesus, you are the Word made flesh and Splendour of the Father. Lord, have mercy.

HEADINGS FOR READINGS

First Reading (Is 50:5-9). The just person is sustained in all his trials by the firm belief that God is with him.

Second Reading (Jam 2:14-18). Faith without good works is dead.

Gospel (Mk 8:27-35). Even though Peter declares his belief in Jesus as the Messiah, he has no idea what that implies.

SCRIPTURE NOTE

We have now entered Part Two of Mark's Gospel (8:27–16:8). After having been consistently rejected and misunderstood despite all he has said and done, Jesus starts to proclaim the necessity of the suffering, death, and resurrection of the Son of Man in God's plan.

The First Reading talks about the Servant of the Lord who suffers, not in spite of his innocence, but because of it. But he is sustained in all his trials by the firm belief that God is with him. The Suffering Servant represents the many suffering just people. The New Testament sees Jesus as the Suffering Servant *par excellence.*

In the Gospel we have Peter's profession of faith. In response to that confession, Jesus makes a threefold disclosure: that the Messiah must suffer, that his disciples must be prepared to share his suffering, and that his and their suffering will lead to ultimate glory.

HOMILY 1   **Two kinds of faith**

There are two kinds of faith. The first is the faith of those who believe because they follow the traditions of their ancestors, strongly maintaining their tradition of faith. This could be called an inherited faith. The second is the faith of those who have gained it through reason and philosophical thinking. The second could be called a personal faith. There is an important difference between the two.

The possessors of an inherited faith have the advantage that they are not easily tempted. Even when confronted with philosophical arguments that might contradict their faith, that faith remains strong because of the traditions they have inherited from their ancestors. Besides this, they have never depended on philosophical speculation. But they also have a disadvantage. Their faith is usually not well reasoned or thought out, and frequently is a faith of habit and routine.

The possessors of a personal faith also have an advantage. They have discovered God with their reasoning, and for that reason are very strong in their faith. But they too have a disadvantage. They can be persuaded by logic, and if confronted with strong contrary arguments, they can be tempted to abandon their faith. In order to be able to withstand challenges, faith must be grounded in something that goes beyond one's own personal experience.

The people who gain their faith in both of these ways have every advantage. They depend strongly on the traditions of their ancestors, while at the same time taking advantage of their ability to think things out for themselves. They thus have the best and most perfect faith.

No longer is it enough to be born into the faith. An inherited faith is a second-hand faith and can be very empty. It's not enough to say, 'My parents were believers.' Every generation has to be converted anew. It has been said that many church-goers are little better than baptised pagans. That seems unduly harsh. Nevertheless, we see many sad and tired faces in church, the faces of people who come late and leave early.

The question Jesus asked the apostles is the most important question in the Gospel. It concerns the identity of Jesus. He asked the question not for his own sake but for their sake. A question forces people to think about their beliefs.

First he asked: 'Who do other people say I am?' They told him. The answers were way off the mark. Then he turned to them and said, 'And *you*, who do *you* say I am?' And Peter replied, 'You are the Christ.' 'The Christ' means the Messiah. St Matthew puts Peter's answer like this: 'You are the Christ, the Son of the living God.' This is the core faith on which the Church was founded.

It is important for us to come up with our own answers; to be able to state our own values and beliefs as Christians. It is no longer sufficient merely to repeat the official answers. We have to make the faith our own for it to be alive and influential in our lives. Our parents' faith is not ours until we walk the journey ourselves.

We need to grow in our understanding of the faith. We must believe out of personal conviction. The more of such people we have in the Church, the more it is founded on rock.

It's clear that Peter didn't fully understand what he had said. When he recognised Jesus as the Messiah, he didn't know that Jesus would be a suffering Messiah. That was something he had to learn, and learn the hard way.

Peter made a perfect profession of faith. He got it absolutely right – with his words. But when it came to acting on that faith, he failed. His lowest point was when he denied he ever knew Jesus. This shows us that we need God's grace, not only to profess our faith, but also to live it.

HOMILY 2   **Faith without good works**

Mrs O'Reilly received the news that one of her neighbours was seriously ill. She said to the person who gave her the news, 'Tell her that I'll remember her in my prayers, and that I hope she'll soon be feeling better.'

And she was as good as her word. That same night as she said her customary night prayers she prayed very sincerely and fervently for her neighbour. She said to God, 'Lord, I want to commend my neighbour to you. She's very seriously ill. She needs a lot of help, a lot of support.'

When she finished her prayers, she felt better. And yet, something was bothering her. She sat down to think about it. Then she fell into a dream-like state in which she heard God saying to her, 'I can see that you're very concerned about your neighbour.'

'Yes, Lord, I really am,' she replied with no little pride.

'And I understand that your neighbour is in great need of help,' said God.

'So I've been told,' said Mrs O'Reilly.

'You know, what she most needs is someone to spend a little time with her,' said the Lord.

'You're absolutely right Lord. I was thinking the same myself,' Mrs O'Reilly answered.

'Now when you asked me to help her, you weren't expecting me to come down from heaven to visit her, were you?'

'No, Lord, I wouldn't expect you to do that. Nor would my neighbour expect it either. In fact, I think the shock of it might kill her.'

'But she does need someone to call on her?'

'She does, Lord.'

'Who can I send?'

After a long pause, Mrs O'Reilly said, 'Send me, Lord.'

When she woke up from her dream, she knew exactly what she had to do.

St James says, 'If someone comes to you who is lacking food or clothing, it's not enough just to say to him, "I wish you well," and leave it at that.'

It's not enough to say to a needy person, 'I'll pray for you.' We must not think that we have done our bit once we have referred the matter to God. That sounds very like passing the buck. When we pray for another person we are in effect saying to God, 'Here I am, Lord. Send me.'

Our prayer should commit us to some positive action, no matter how small. But even a small act, such as a visit, could prove to be a costly gesture, because it means putting ourselves alongside a suffering person. And to do that is to lay ourselves open to that person's pain. We will inevitably absorb some of that pain.

To pray for people, or to wish them well, is a good thing. It gives them the comfort of knowing that they are not alone. But it is not enough. That is a dead faith. If our faith is alive we will express our concern in action also.

Peter got the identity of Jesus absolutely right. His faith was perfect as far as words went. But when the time came for action, he was woefully lacking. When Jesus asked him to watch with him during his agony in the garden, he fell asleep. And later that night he denied that he had ever known Jesus.

There is a faith that consists only in words. And there is a faith that flows into deeds. We need God's grace, not only to profess our faith, but also to live it.

HOMILY 3   **Being true to oneself**

G. K. Chesterton has a story about a popular philanthropist. The main reason for his popularity was his unfailing good humour. No one bothered to ask how he managed to be always happy. They assumed he was born an optimist.

But then one day he was found dead in mysterious circumstances. Foul play was immediately suspected. However, the case completely baffled the police. Eventually it was Chesterton's unlikely detective, Fr Browne, who solved the case. His verdict – the man committed suicide.

At first the people refused to accept Fr Browne's verdict. They couldn't imagine how such a happy man could commit suicide. But then it emerged that there was a serious side to the funny man. The man who made others laugh was in fact a deeply depressed man. But he could never tell anyone how he really felt.

The man had two lives. One open, seen and known by all. The other secret, and known only to himself. In public he was the man who smiled at everyone. But in private he was wounded and desperate.

He felt he had to live up to people's expectations in return for their attention and esteem. He was never able to be himself. Finally, he realised that his whole life was based on a lie. The strain of trying to maintain the public image became so great that he could no longer cope with it. So he committed suicide.

Everybody likes to be well-thought of. Hence, people try to carve out for themselves a favourable image in the eyes of others. They will do anything to maintain that image.

In today's Gospel we see how little attention Jesus paid to what other people thought of him, even though their image of him was a favourable one. The people regarded him as a great prophet. Peter went further. He declared him to be the Christ (that is, the Messiah).

It would be impossible to exaggerate what the Messiah meant to the Jews. Many thought that he would be a great military leader – another King David who would restore Israel to its former military greatness. Obviously this is what Peter thought.

But this wasn't Jesus' idea of the Messiah. He told the apostles that the Messiah would suffer as Isaiah had foretold (see First Reading). He didn't want them to have false hopes only to be disappointed later, and feel that he had deceived them.

But Peter couldn't countenance the idea that Jesus would suffer. He was determined to save him from such a fate. We can sympathise with him. We want to save those we love from suffering. But much as we might love someone, we have no right to stand in the way of his/her destiny.

Jesus reprimanded Peter. He had no intention of living up to the popular expectations. He was not swayed by what people thought, or wanted, or expected of him. He was true to himself and to what God wanted of him.

Whatever our path in life, what really matters is that we should be ourselves, our unique selves, but the best that we can be – the kind of people God intended us to be. The only thing that matters is to be true to ourselves. Any other path is a false trail and will not result in growth, or happiness, or fulfilment, or holiness.

PRAYER OF THE FAITHFUL

President: God is gracious, just and compassionate. Let us now bring our needs and concerns before him.

Response: Lord, graciously hear us.

Reader(s): For all Christians: that their deeds may bear witness to the faith they profess with their words. [Pause] Lord, hear us.

For government leaders: that they may strive to create a society in which all of God's children can live in freedom and dignity. [Pause] Lord, hear us.

For those who have a heavy cross to carry: that God may lighten their burden and comfort them with his presence. [Pause] Lord, hear us.

For this congregation: that each of us may strive to be the unique people that God made us to be. [Pause] Lord, hear us.

For all gathered here: that the prayers we say for others may never take the place of the things we should do for them. [Pause] Lord, hear us.

For our own special needs. [Longer pause] Lord, hear us.

President: God of compassion, you know our weakness. May we reach out with joy to grasp your hand, and so walk more readily in your ways. We ask this through Christ our Lord.

REFLECTION   **Faith without works**

A watch may have a gold chain,
but if it doesn't tell the time it is useless.
A fruit tree may be teeming with blossoms,
but if it doesn't produce fruit it is useless.
A lamp may be studded with diamonds,
but if it doesn't give light it is worthless.
And a faith that doesn't result in good works is dead.
The fruit of prayer is faith.
The fruit of faith is love.
The fruit of love is service.
And the fruit of service is peace.

Twenty-fifth Sunday of the Year

INTRODUCTION AND CONFITEOR

As Christians we are called to live in peace and harmony with one another. One of the things that is very damaging to unity is false ambition. This causes us to put ourselves and our own interests first. [Pause]

Let us ask the Lord to pardon our sins and to help us live by his values.

Lord, you said, 'Blessed are the gentle; they will inherit the earth.' Lord, have mercy.

You said, 'Blessed are those who serve; they will be greatest in the kingdom of heaven.' Christ, have mercy.

You said, 'Blessed are the peacemakers; they will be called the children of God.' Lord, have mercy.

HEADINGS FOR READINGS

First Reading (Wis 2:12.17-20). The godless plot to do away with the just one, because his blameless life is a reproach to them.

Second Reading (Jam 3:16-4:3). Jealousy, ambition, and self-seeking lead to disharmony and fighting. Gentleness. reasonableness, and mercy lead to peace.

Gospel (Mk 9:30-37). Jesus tells his apostles that he will suffer bitter humiliation and death, and says that true greatness shows itself in service towards the weaker members of the community.

SCRIPTURE NOTE

The First Reading talks about the just one who serves the cause of righteousness, and suffers for it at the hands of the wicked. The 'righteous' are those who hold on to their faith in God and obey his commandments. This passage has been seen in Christian tradition as anticipating the hostility suffered by Jesus, the suffering just one *par excellence*. Our reading forms a unified theme with the Gospel and with the reading from James.

In the Gospel we have the second prediction of the Passion: once again the disciples do not understand. Instead, motivated by selfish ambition, they get involved in an argument as to which of them is the greatest. This kind of ambition is condemned by Jesus and by James (Second Reading).

It is not ambition itself that is condemned, but false ambition. False ambition involves a desire to rule others. It creates conflict and division, and is very damaging to the unity of the community. True ambition, on the other hand, is the desire to serve others. The best and purest kind of service is that which is rendered to the little ones, that is, to the most insignificant persons in the community.

HOMILY 1   **True and false ambition**

There's nothing wrong with being ambitious. Indeed, it is good to be ambitious, to have goals, to want to be good at what one does and to succeed in it. But ambition can get out of hand. It can cause us to forget everything else in the pursuit of success in business or in a career.

Hence, we must be careful what we are sacrificing in the pursuit of our goals. We may be sacrificing family life, justice, kindness, even life itself. Drive and ambition can cause one to treat others in a cruel or unjust way. What good will it do us if we gain the whole world but lose ourselves?

In the Gospel we see the apostles fighting over who would be first in Jesus' kingdom. The scene is not an edifying one. That they are driven by selfishness and false ambition shows how little they had learned from Jesus. It shows how poor was their understanding of his mission. Jesus called them together and gave them a lecture on the meaning of true greatness.

Jesus did not abolish ambition. Rather, he redefined it. For the ambition to rule others he substituted the ambition to serve others. For the ambition to have others do things for us he substituted the ambition to do things for others. So, it is not ambition itself that is being condemned, but false ambition.

False ambition is very damaging to the unity of the community. It springs from jealousy and selfishness. And it can result in all kinds of ugly behaviour. So much of the violence and evil in our society results from greed and selfishness. Self-interest creates conflict and often results in painful divisions.

There is a good form of ambition which Christians should not shy away from. Jesus did not tell the apostles that they should not seek greatness in his kingdom. He just showed them where true greatness was to be found. It is not to be found in being the masters of others, but rather in being the servants of others, especially the weaker members of the community.

It's easier to serve the great, because we feel honoured through our association with them, and there is a better chance of rewards. But the real test is serving the least, from whom we cannot expect any rewards. Jesus says, 'Whoever welcomes one such child, welcomes me.' 'Welcome' means loving service. And 'child' stands for the weakest members of the community, who are the most needy. Service rendered to the least is best of all. We hear the same words in the last judgement scene: 'As long as you did it to one of these, the least of my brethren, you did it to me.'

Jesus set the example himself. Though he had authority from God, he never used that authority to dominate others. Instead, he used it to serve others. And that service was directed towards the poor, the sick, the maimed, the outcasts ...

The really great people, those who are fondly remembered, are not those who sought to further themselves and their own interests, but rather those who devoted themselves to furthering the interests of the community.

Service implies that you're not there for yourself. You are there for others. In order to serve, one has to be very self-effacing. A servant has to get used to being taken for granted.

HOMILY 2   ### The kind of person one is

When Nelson Mandela was a student lawyer in Johannesburg he had a friend whose name was Paul Mahabane. Mahabane was a member of the African National Congress (ANC), and had the reputation of being a radical. One day the two of them were standing outside a post office when the local magistrate, a white man in his sixties, approached Mahabane and asked him to go inside to buy him some stamps. It was quite common in those days for a white person to call on a black person to perform a chore. Paul refused. The magistrate was offended.

'Do you know who I am?' he said, his face turning red with anger.

'It is not necessary to know who you are,' Mahabane replied. 'I know *what* you are.'

The magistrate boiled over and exclaimed, 'You'll pay dearly for this,' and then walked away.

That white man was convinced that he was superior to Mahabane simple because he was a magistrate. And it's clear that it had become second nature to him to expect others, especially if they were black, to serve him.

We tend to define and evaluate people in terms of the job they do. Hence, if we learn that a person is a doctor, our estimation of the person soars. But if we learn that a person is an ordinary worker, our estimation stays earthbound. This is unfair and rather silly. There is something more important than the job, namely, the kind of human being behind the job.

The mistake the apostles made was to put the job, or the position, first. In their eyes, the greatest among them was the one who had the highest position. They obviously thought that Jesus would set up an earthly kingdom, and so each wanted to get a top position in his kingdom.

But Jesus told them that his kingdom was not about seeking honour and glory for oneself, but about serving others. If they were prepared to serve others, then by all means they could have a top place in his kingdom. But they would not be sitting on high chairs or soft seats. They were more likely to be down on their knees with a basin of water in one hand and a towel in the other, washing the feet of 'the little ones' (the weakest members of the community).

It's not what I do but what I am that is important. One's self-worth should not depend on the work one does. It's possible to possess an attitude of self-worth and accomplishment, regardless of what one does for a living.

There's a lot of talk nowadays about self-esteem. And rightly so, because it is pretty basic thing. But if we want to feel proud of ourselves, we've got to do things we can be proud of. Feelings follow actions. What might those kind of things be? Jesus tells us what they are. They are deeds of love and service. He set the example himself. He gave his life in the service of others. No one can go higher than that. He is the greatest in the kingdom.

HOMILY 3   **Persecution of the just**

Good people have always suffered at the hands of the wicked. They suffer because their blameless lives are a reproach to the wicked. They make evildoers uncomfortable by what they say in confronting injustice and evil, and sometimes just by the goodness and uprightness of their lives. It is precisely because they are good that they suffer.

Elie Wiesel (Jewish writer and Nobel Peace Prize winner) tells a very disturbing story in one of his books. Once after delivering a lecture in New York he met a man who looked vaguely familiar. He began to wonder who he was and where they had met before. Then he remembered. He had known him in Auschwitz. Suddenly an incident involving this man came back to him.

As soon as children arrived by train at Auschwitz, together with the elderly and the sick, they were immediately selected for the gas chamber. On one occasion a group of children were left to wait by themselves for the next day. This man asked the guards if he could stay with the children during their last night on earth. Surprisingly his request was granted.

How did they spend that last night? He started off by telling the children stories in an effort to cheer them up. However, instead of cheering them up, he succeeded only in making them cry. So what did they do? They cried together until daybreak. Then he accompanied the little ones to the gas chamber. Afterwards he returned to the prison yard to report for work. When the guards saw him, they burst out laughing.

This story has most of the ingredients of our readings. In it we see the brazenness of evil-doers, the persecution of the innocent, and the apparent triumph of evil, which is the subject of the First Reading. It also has a marvellous example of service done to the little ones, something that Jesus valued so highly, and which is highlighted in the Gospel.

The man's heroic act of service towards the little ones shines out all the brighter because of the darkness of the background. In Auschwitz all that was good and decent was trampled into the ground. There, self-interest was the name of the game. Compassion was as rare as a flower in winter.

Yet this man rose above all that. He risked his life to befriend the little ones. He had no answers to give them, no salvation to offer them. All he could do was accompany them during their last hours so that they would not suffer alone.

He is a Christlike figure. He would not participate in evil. Neither would he stand idly by and watch others suffer without trying to alleviate their sufferings.

Even though he was just an ordinary prisoner, with no rank or status of any kind, he was undoubtedly the greatest person in that sad place on that sad occasion. What made him great was his goodness.

Christ was the supremely just one. Yet he too suffered. Throughout his public ministry he was hounded by his enemies. This was so because he was too good, too just for them to contemplate. But it was especially on the cross that he suffered the taunts of his enemies and of the godless.

Christ was victorious, not by avoiding evil, but by confronting it and overcoming it. He gives courage and hope to all who sacrifice themselves for others in the cause of right.

Persecution has always been the lot of the righteous. However, it gives them an opportunity to show their true mettle. Besides, the just know that God is on their side. The *Credo* of the righteous is their unswerving belief in God's love for them. God never abandons the upright, but their reward is in the life-to-come.

'On the third day he will rise.' The resurrection assures the ultimate triumph of good over evil, of life over death.

STORIES   **Welcoming the little ones**

1. Dostoyevsky has a marvellous story about a Russian prince who came to a little village in the Swiss Alps in order to be treated for TB. While there he befriended the children of the village. At first the children made fun of him because he was clumsy and strange. But gradually he won them over by listening to them and telling them stories.

Now in the village there was a young woman called Marie. She lived in a ramshackle house with her mother who was an invalid. Marie also was suffering from TB which she had contracted as a child. Even though she was twenty years old, she was very weak. Yet she was forced to go from house to house scrubbing floors and washing dishes.

Then one day a commercial traveller, who was passing through took her away, seduced her, and then abandoned her. She returned home in disgrace. The villagers looked on her with contempt. The children threw mud and stones at her.

In order to escape from it all, Marie hired herself out as a cowherd and stayed away from the village as much as possible, eating only a little bread and cheese. Then her mother died. Now she was all alone.

However, the prince befriended her. As a result he lost the children for a while. But slowly, by reasoning and example, he won them back, and they too began to befriend Marie. They visited her, bringing her food, clothes, shoes, and other things. The prince was now accused of corrupting the children, who were forbidden to visit Marie.

However, they continued to do so secretly. For the first time in her life Marie began to smile and feel happy. But it was clear that her health was declining. The time came when she wasn't able to go out herding, and had to remain at home alone in her cottage.

The children nursed her with touching care and tenderness. The villagers no longer had the heart to forbid them. They stayed with her until she breathed her last, and saw to it that she had a beautiful funeral. They packed the tiny church. Then they vied with one another to carry her coffin. Afterwards they planted roses all around her grave.

When finally the time came for the prince to go back to Russia, the children went to the railway station to see him off. They did their best not to cry, but were not very successful. They stayed on the platform waving until the train was out of sight.

Here we see a good person, a true servant, in action. The prince was a good friend to those children. Good people do not think of themselves, nor are they influenced by the neglect and prejudice of others. They are interested only in doing good. No difficulty or danger is too great to be faced and overcome.

Such a caring attitude, however, goes against the prevailing attitudes of the day. The Christian vocation is a call to service. Christians seek to extend to others the love of Christ, which they themselves have experienced.

2. There is a woman in Dublin who in 1988 started short-term fostering – she works for a Catholic Adoption Agency. She receives the baby when he/she is two or three days old, and usually has the baby for three months. Then the baby is either taken back by the natural mother, or adopted, or goes into long-term fostering. This dear woman, by no means well-off, has to date fostered over forty babies. She says, 'It can be hard work at times, but I enjoy it.' She enjoys it because she does it with love. 'Anyone who welcomes one of these little children, welcomes me', would be a fitting epitaph for her life.

PRAYER OF THE FAITHFUL

President: Those who serve are the greatest in the kingdom of heaven. Let us pray to God for our own needs and those of the Church and the world.

Response: Lord, hear our prayer.

Reader(s): For the Pope and the bishops: that they may give an example of humble and loving service to their brothers and sisters in the Church. [Pause] Let us pray to the Lord.

For those in positions of authority in society: that they may put the service of others before personal ambition. [Pause] Let us pray to the Lord.

For those who are suffering in the cause of right. [Pause] Let us pray to the Lord.

For those who do menial jobs: that they may receive a just reward for their labours. [Pause] Let us pray to the Lord.

For all in this congregation: that as followers of Christ we may as willing to give as to receive. [Pause] Let us pray to the Lord.

For our own particular needs. [Longer pause] Let us pray to the Lord.

President: Lord, grant that what we have said with out lips, we may believe with our hearts, and practise with our lives. We make all our prayers through Christ our Lord.

REFLECTION   **The rewards of the just**

God's inspiration is at work in everyone.
However, there are people in whom divine inspiration
seems to have no effect;
people who commit crimes cold-bloodedly,
and who never rejoice at the sight of the true and the beautiful.
Even though they may seem to prosper,

their punishment is assured even in this world.
The anxieties and fears that assail them
make their prosperity a bitterness to them.
As for the just, even though their passage through life
is often dogged by misfortune,
the inward satisfaction of obeying divine inspiration
gives them great strength,
and is sufficient reward for them.

Twenty-sixth Sunday of the Year

INTRODUCTION AND CONFITEOR

Modern life has brought us closer to one another than ever before. We influence one another in all sorts of ways. God wants us to be stepping stones for one another. Unfortunately sometimes we are stumbling blocks to one another. [Pause]

Let us ask pardon for the harm we do and the good we fail to do to our brothers and sisters.

HEADINGS FOR READINGS

First Reading (Num 11:25-29). Joshua resents the fact that the gift of prophecy is now given to many others besides Moses, but Moses himself welcomes it.

Second Reading (Jam 5:1-6). We hear a strong condemnation of wealth, especially when it is obtained through exploitation of the weak.

Gospel (Mk 9:38-43.47-48). This contains a lesson in tolerance and in the avoidance of scandal and occasions of sin.

SCRIPTURE NOTE

The First Reading tells of the institution of seventy elders who were to assist Moses in ruling the people of Israel. They were endowed with the spirit of leadership and prophecy which was given to Moses. The main point of the reading is that God's choice is not a personal privilege to be guarded jealously, but a call to serve his people.

This leads into the Gospel because the apostles had to be reminded of this very truth. Jesus utters a grim warning against anyone who would hurt the 'little ones' who have faith in him. He talks about hell and compares it to Gehenna, a ravine near Jerusalem, which was a dump where offal and refuse was burned. Only a crass literalism could have led to the later notion of hell as a place of fiery torment.

Even though the practical points contained in the Gospel were originally addressed to the leaders in the community, they have relevance for all disciples of Jesus. Jesus' command to receive the little ones (the insignificant members of the community) underlines the inclusiveness of the kingdom. The warning about the danger of giving scandal would be heard by Mark's readers as applying to them also. The directions for dealing with temptation are not meant to be taken literally. They forcefully make the point that sin is to be avoided at all costs.

HOMILY 1   **Practical advice for disciples**

The Gospel makes a number of important and very practical points. Though these were addressed originally to the leaders in the community, they have relevance for all disciples of Jesus.

1. The apostles came upon a man, not of their company, who was healing people in the name of Jesus. They tried to stop him. Why? Because they were jealous of their special relationship with Jesus. (There is a similar example in the First Reading.) We remember the narrow attitudes we had towards Christians of other denominations prior to Vatican II.

But Jesus said, 'Do not stop him.' The fact that he was acting in his name meant that he was not against them. Thus Jesus gave them a lesson in openness and tolerance. All our official prayers are said, and all the sacraments are administered in the name, that is, in the power of Jesus. But Catholics have no monopoly on Jesus.

Some people are threatened by the gifts or achievements of others. If only they had a more open attitude they would find themselves enriched rather than diminished by those gifts. The person who is different from me does not diminish me but enriches me. God bestows his gifts freely. Our responsibility is to welcome those gifts wherever they appear.

2. Jesus said that anyone who gave the little ones even a cup of cold water would be rewarded. The 'cup of cold water' is a symbol of the small kind deed. Few of us are given the chance to perform great deeds. But the chance to give a cup of water can come our way several times in the course of a day. A small act of kindness can turn winter into summer at least briefly for another person.

Deeds don't have to be big in order to be of help and comfort to the person for whom they are done. They just have to have a certain quality. That quality is warmth. All deeds which come from the heart have this warmth.

3. Then Jesus deals with the sin of scandal – causing others to sin. He issues a grim warning against those who would lead astray any of the little ones who believe in him. When we think of the crimes committed against children today, whether through neglect or abuse, the words of

Jesus are a warning that we should take very seriously.

4. Then Jesus goes on to talk about the causes of sin in ourselves. A person's enemy may be within himself. Occasions of sin are to be ruthlessly cut off. Jesus urges people to make the costliest sacrifices in order to avoid sin, even to the extent of cutting off a hand or foot, or plucking out an eye.

These words must not be taken with a crude literalism. The point Jesus is making is that serious sin is to avoided at any cost. We ought to be prepared to go to any lengths in order to eliminate evil from our lives. His aim was to impress indelibly on us that the kingdom of God is worth any sacrifice.

5. Jesus talked about hell and compared it to Gehenna. Gehenna was a ravine south of Jerusalem, where at one time infants were sacrificed to Moloch. Josiah put an end to its use for worship, and later it was used as a dump for offal and refuse. As a site of ill-omen it came to symbolise the place of future punishment.

As always, the words of Jesus give us much food for thought. We would do well to heed them.

HOMILY 2   **A stumbling block or a stepping stone**

Today people live closer to one another than ever before. Therefore the influence they have on each other is greater. Whether we are aware of it or not, we are stumbling blocks in the path of others, or stepping stones for them on the road to salvation. Here are some of examples of the way we can be a *scandal*, that is, a *stumbling block*, to another person.

You are a scandal to me when you are unkind or unjust in the way you treat me. You make me feel small. You damage my self-confidence.

You are a scandal to me when you fail to understand my weakness, mistakes, and sins, and write me off as a result of them. When you condemn me you make me feel that I am evil.

You are a scandal to me when you humiliate me because I do not live up to your expectations. You hurt my pride and damage my self-image.

You are a scandal to me when you keep me down, or hold me back. When you grab the limelight I am forced to retreat to the shadows and made to feel inferior.

You are a scandal to me when you exclude me or ignore me. You make me feel a stranger and an outsider.

You are a scandal to me when you heap unjust criticism on me, and sour me with your own cynicism. You tear down my ideals, and destroy my dreams.

You are a scandal to me when you pay me poor wages (see Second Reading). You turn me into a slave so that you can live like a lord. You impoverish me so as to enrich yourself.

If you do any of these things to me you are a darkness to me. You are an obstacle in my path. You are a scandal, a stumbling block, to me in the road to self-development, and you make it difficult for me to reach the kingdom of heaven.

But you can also be a stepping stone to me.

You are a stepping stone to me when you support me in moments of weakness and doubt.

You are a stepping stone to me when you give me a belief in myself, when you boost my self-confidence.

You are a stepping stone to me when I'm feeling inadequate, and you help me to discover the special talents God has given me.

You are a stepping stone to me when you make demands on me, are challenging to me, not to hurt me, but to help me to grow and to develop my potential.

You are a stepping stone to me when you accept me, though others reject me.

You are a stepping stone to me when you refuse to join the mob and throw the stone of accusation and judgement at me when I sin.

You are a stepping stone to me when you forgive me. You liberate me from my past, and I am free to move forward again.

You are a stepping stone to me when you understand me and listen to me.

You are a stepping stone to me when you employ me and pay me a just wage.

If you have done any of these things for me, you are a light to me in my darkness. You are a signpost to me in my moments of doubt. You are a bridge over troubled waters. You make it easier for me to enter the kingdom of heaven.

Jesus said if you gave me as much as a cup of cold water, you would be rewarded for it. But you have done much more than that. You have led me to your own well and shared it with me.

HOMILY 3   **Condemnation of riches**

Very many people admire and envy the rich. Yet St James makes a scathing attack on them (Second Reading). However, it is not riches in themselves that are being condemned. Basically he makes two points.

The first is the ultimate worthlessness of wealth. Whatever comfort and luxury wealth affords is transitory; in the end it is vanity. Wealth does not lead to happiness. Therefore, placing one's hope in material wealth is foolish.

This is something we all need to be reminded of from time to time, because we live in a culture that tells us the opposite. In so many ways it tells us that possessions do lead to happiness. This is a seductive message which ruins many lives.

The second point St James makes concerns the manner in which wealth is acquired. More often than not acquiring and keeping wealth involves acting unjustly and exploiting the weak. Here we are not talking about foolishness. We are talking about something that is both evil and sinful.

Two further points should be made.

There is the affect of wealth on the one who possesses it. Preoccupation with material things concentrates a person's thoughts and interests on this world to the exclusion of the other world. Furthermore, possessions can make a person arrogant, proud, and self-satisfied. Wealth fosters selfishness, thus hardening the heart of the possessor. No one saw the danger of material things more clearly than Jesus.

Finally, all of this has to be seen against a background in which millions of people are living in poverty and hunger. For every person who has too much, there are at least ten who have too little. Some have a surfeit while others are in dire need. In some parts of the world babies are dying before their mothers' eyes.

According to an article in *The Tablet* (December 1996) the wealth of 358 richest billionaires is the same as the wealth of 2.3 billion poor people, who make up 45% of the world's population. These are grotesque inequalities. The gap between rich and poor countries is an ever widening one.

This inequality is a great evil. It explains the uneasiness felt by contemporary people, an unease felt not only by the poor but also by the rich. It demands decisive solutions. But where to begin and what to do? The first step is to become conscious of it.

Wealth is a responsibility. People will be judged by two criteria: how they got their wealth, and how they used it.

ANOTHER APPROACH   **A cup of cold water**

For months the chapel was decorated with artificial flowers. While they looked pretty they lacked one vital thing – they emitted no scent. Then one day someone brought in a small bunch of fresh bluebells and placed them on the altar. As soon as you walked into the chapel you noticed the difference. The fragrance given off by the little bluebells filled the entire chapel.

How the genuine article shines out, how it quietly makes its presence felt. It doesn't have to be big. Even the dew lessens the heat.

Jesus said that anyone who gave one of his disciples even a cup of cold water would be rewarded. The 'cup of cold water' is a symbol of the small kind deed.

Few of us are given the chance to perform great deeds. But the chance to give a cup of water can come our way several times in the course of a day. A small act of kindness can turn winter into summer at least briefly for another person. It becomes a small but significant stepping stone for that person.

Deeds don't have to be big in order to be of help and comfort to the person for whom they are done. They just have to have a certain quality. That quality is warmth. All deeds which come from the heart have this warmth.

PRAYER OF THE FAITHFUL

President: Let us bring our needs before God who wants us to be, not stumbling blocks, but stepping stones for one another on the road to his Kingdom.

Response: Lord, graciously hear us.

Reader(s): For Christians: that they may be a light to others and never a source of darkness, a stepping stone and never a stumbling block. [Pause] Lord, hear us.

For our political and civil leaders: that God may give them strength and wisdom. [Pause] Lord, hear us.

For all employers: that they may treat their employees in such a way as to further their dignity and self-respect. [Pause] Lord, hear us.

For all those who have been victims of exploitation or abuse: that they may be able to recover from the sins committed against them. [Pause] Lord, hear us.

For all gathered here: that we may be conscious of the evil that is within us, and strive to overcome it. [Pause] Lord, hear us.

For our own private needs remembered in silence. [Longer pause] Lord, hear us.

President: God of love and mercy, we are weak and each of us is poisoned by sin. We ask the grace that we may never drag our brothers or sisters down; rather, let our hands be the hands by which you lead them along the path of eternal life. We ask this through Christ our Lord.

REFLECTION   **Children**

Jesus warned those who would lead the little ones astray,
but he blessed those who care for them.
One of the most touching things about children
is their openness.
But this same openness
leaves them extremely vulnerable.
They may not say much but they feel everything.
They are like crocuses
which appear in the open in February –

[311]

frail, delicate, beautiful creatures –
innocents abroad in an unpredictable climate.
If they are embraced by the sun,
they will bloom to their full potential.
But if they are assailed by hail,
they will die a premature death.
Love is to a child what sunshine is to a flower.

Twenty-seventh Sunday of the Year

INTRODUCTION AND CONFITEOR

It's not easy to be a Christian in today's world. And it's almost impossible on one's own. But we are not alone. Christ has called us into a community. Let us reflect for a moment on the fact that we don't always speak and act in a way that builds up community. [Pause]

Lord, you are the vine, we are the branches. Lord, have mercy.

You unite us with you so that we may bear fruit. Christ, have mercy.

You unite us with one another as your brothers and sisters. Lord, have mercy.

HEADINGS FOR READINGS

First Reading (Gen 2:18-24). God made man and woman for each other. The bond of marriage means they are no longer two but one.

Second Reading (Heb 2:9-11). By entering fully into human life, and by experiencing the bitterness of death, Christ became a brother and a saviour to all people.

Gospel (Mk 10:2-16). Christ teaches that the marriage bond comes from God and is therefore indissoluble.

SCRIPTURE NOTE

Genesis has two accounts of the institution of marriage. The first (1:26-28) sees marriage as a means of procreation. The second (2:18-24) – our First Reading – sees marriage as meeting the human need for companionship and equality.

On the basis of Deuteronomy 24:1-4, the Pharisees allowed a husband to divorce his wife because of 'an indecency in her'. Appealing to Genesis 1:27; 2:24, Jesus stressed the unity created by marriage, which would forbid breaking the marriage bond, so that remarriage after a divorce would constitute adultery. Jesus leaves no doubt as to what the ideal marriage ought to be. But this doesn't mean he wasn't aware of, and sympathetic towards, the problems that can arise in living out that ideal.

The Gospel also shows Jesus' love for the little ones, and tells us that we must receive the kingdom the way children receive a gift.

From today until the Thirty-Third Sunday inclusive, the Second Reading is taken from the Letter to the Hebrews. Hebrews presents Christ as the Perfect Priest.

HOMILY 1   **Not good to be alone**

In the beginning of life, when we were infants, we needed others if we were to survive. And at the end of life, we will again need others so that we can survive. Now here's a secret: in between, we need others as well.

The Bible says, 'It's not good for a human being to be alone.' Sometimes it is a good and necessary thing for us to be alone – but not as a permanent condition. Human beings are social animals. Of ourselves we are incomplete. Humanity can never be acquired in solitude. We need others. To feel this need is not a sign of sickness but of health. Insanity has been defined as a condition in which people are no longer able to connect with other people.

The most dangerous lion is not the gregarious one, or the one that roars the loudest, but the silent one that walks alone. Serial killers nearly always turn out to be lonely, angry individuals. People who commit suicide are often people who have slipped into total isolation.

Isolation is the most painful condition of all. It causes people to turn in on themselves, and can lead to violence and/or alcoholism. Fear, shame, and guilt make people want to stay in their isolation.

God first gave Adam the animals. But Adam was unable to find a suitable partner among them. A survey was carried out among elderly people in America. When asked who was closest to them? Two out of three said it was their pet dog or cat. This is sad.

Then God gave Adam a woman, Eve. And as soon as Adam saw Eve he recognised in her a fitting companion and partner. She was made of the same material as himself, possessed the same dignity as himself, and therefore was his equal. True community can be created only among equals.

In marriage God answered the human need for friendship, companionship, closeness and warmth – all those things we pine for but find so difficult. These needs can also be met by belonging to a community. And those who have a close relationship with God are never alone.

When people get married they bring to it, not only their strengths, but also their weaknesses. All of us are wounded by sin and selfishness. To enter marriage is to enter a school of love, a school in which all are slow learners. The bond which two people seal on their wedding day is not made of unbreakable material, but of human, and therefore breakable material. The only bond that is unbreakable is the bond which God formed with us in Christ.

What are the things which weaken the marriage bond? Lack of respect, poor communication, selfishness, and above all infidelity. Respect, good communication, unselfishness, and fidelity strengthen the bond.

Relationships have to be worked on. They suffer from neglect just as surely as a garden does. People should not be afraid to seek help if they experience difficulties in their marriage. Relationships which have weathered some storms are the deepest. Couples must be determined to put their marriage and their children above economic success.

Indissoluble monogamy is not just a clerical hobby-horse. It finds a powerful justification in the special needs of children to be nurtured and cared for over a much longer period of time than almost any member of the animal species.

HOMILY 2   **The marriage commitment**

Harold Kushner, an American rabbi, tells how a young couple came to see him one evening. Their wedding was coming up and he was to officiate at it. At one point the young man said to him, 'Rabbi, would you object if we made one small change in the wedding ceremony? Instead of pronouncing us husband and wife 'till death do us part', could you pronounce us husband and wife 'for as long as love lasts'? We've talked about this and we both feel that, should the day come when we no longer love each other, it wouldn't be morally right for us to be stuck with each other.'

But the rabbi replied, 'I do object, and I won't make the change. You and I know that there is such a thing as divorce, and we know that a lot of marriages these days don't last until one of the partners dies. But let me tell you something. If you go into marriage with an attitude of "If it doesn't work out, we can always split", then I can almost guarantee you that things won't work out for you.

'I appreciate your honesty. But you must understand that a marriage commitment is not just a mutual willingness to live together, but a commitment to accept the frustrations and disappointments that are an inevitable part of two imperfect human beings relating to each other. It's hard enough to make a go of marriage even when you give it everything you've got. But if only a part of you is involved in the relationship, then you have virtually no chance.'

The result would inevitably be a fragile, tentative relationship that was sure to fail. Some enter into marriage expecting it to make their lives pleasurable all the time, and when at times it offers pain and conflict they want out of it.

When two people get married, their lives are linked together. From that point on they have a common destiny. They are committed to one another, and are responsible to and for one another. God then seals and blesses this bond. However, the bond is not made of unbreakable material. It is made of human, and therefore, imperfect material.

God made us for love – to receive it and to give it. However, the ability to love is not something that is given to the couple on their wedding day with all the other gifts. Love is something that has to be learned. The real journey married couples have to make, and not just them but single people too, is the journey from selfishness to love.

Nothing is a greater challenge to love, nothing provides a greater opportunity for growth in it, than marriage. It calls for a lot of maturity. Gold fish in a bowl get along easily. But bring two human beings together and you soon have problems. When two people get married they bring to it their strengths and weaknesses, loves and hates, hurts and wounds, hopes and fears.

However, the difficulties they encounter can become opportunities for growth. There is more depth to a relationship that has weathered some storms.

HOMILY 3   **The kingdom of childhood**

Jesus says to us, 'Unless you become like little children you will not enter the kingdom of heaven.' We tend to regard childhood as something that we must grow out of, leave completely behind, as if there was nothing in it that was worth keeping.

We have to distinguish between being *childlike* and being *childish*. To be childish implies immaturity, throwing tantrums, being silly, being irresponsible ... children are not angels. These are things we should grow out of. But there are lovely childlike qualities which we should try to hold onto – openness, receptivity, sense of wonder, ability to live in the present ...

Unfortunately what tends to happen is we lose some of the good qualities of the child and keep some of the worst. We cease to be childlike but continue to be childish. What have we lost with the loss of our youth?

Imagination is infinitely stronger in childhood. Every child is blessed with a sense of wonder. Their vision is so fresh and clear. Wordsworth put it beautifully: 'Heaven lies about us in our infancy.' Children are seeing everything as for the first time. Picasso's ambition was to paint like a child. He said that art should startle us into seeing the world anew like a child does.

Children teach us how to live. They have not yet got into grooves, or become prisoners of routine, habit, and prejudice. They are always themselves. This is what makes them so charming and unique.

Happiness is the natural state of little children. They have the capacity to wring enjoyment out of simple things. The shabbiest doll will delight a child's heart for half a year, but adults need so much more. Why? Because they have lost the soul of a child. It's one of the tasks of the Church to keep alive that soul.

Nothing is easier as life goes on than to grow old in heart, dry and disillusioned, cynical and selfish. Children put us in touch with the gentler and more innocent part of themselves that we may have discarded in the struggle or battle of life. They revive in us too a sense of wonder, and it is the sense of wonder above all that keeps us young.

When Jesus says to us, 'Unless you become like little children you will not enter the kingdom of heaven,' he is recalling us to our lost childhood, so that though old and frail in body, we might be reborn in innocence of character.

Jesus says we can't enter the Kingdom unless we receive it like a child. The kingdom is a gift. Children are more suited for the kingdom because they know how to receive a gift. No one can enter the kingdom who is not open to receive it as a gift.

ANOTHER APPROACH   **The boy I was**

A priest who was chaplain to a school tells the following story. Late one night one of his past pupils came to see him. In the intervening years the young man had got involved in crime. But now he wanted to get out of it. He knew that he had tarnished himself, and that he had been a bad influence on others. Now he felt a longing for the unstained innocence of his boyhood. He was so full of promise then, but now he was full of shame. He was full of brightness then, now he was full of darkness.

Anyway, he told his story very frankly to the priest. Then he made his request: 'Make me the boy I was when I was sixteen.' The boy's earnest request moved the priest deeply. He knew what the boy meant. He was saying, 'I want to find my way back to a path I once knew.' But was it something the priest could grant him? Was it even possible?

Just as Adam and Eve lost their original innocence, so we lose our childhood innocence. However, we can regain it. But this recovered innocence is different from the first. The first innocence was immature, not responsible, unacquainted with sorrow and evil; the second innocence is transfigured through responsibility and acquaintance with sorrow and evil. The first does not know how to sin; the second rises above sin. The first is harmless through weakness; the second is innocent through virtue. The first is incapable of committing sin; the second is unwilling to commit sin.

There is in every human heart a longing for the lost Eden. When the Lord says to us, 'Unless you become like little children you will not enter the kingdom of heaven,' he is recalling us to our lost childhood. No matter how old we may be, he makes it possible for us to be reborn in innocence of character.

PRAYER OF THE FAITHFUL

President: God made us not for isolation but for community. Let us now bring our common needs before him.

Response: Lord, hear us in your love.

Reader(s): For the Christian community: that it may be a sign and a source of unity for a fragmented world. [Pause] We pray in faith.

For political leaders: that through their work for justice and reconciliation the nations may live in peace. [Pause] We pray in faith.

For husbands and wives: that God may give them comfort in time of sorrow, strength in time of trial, and an enduring love for one another. [Pause] We pray in faith.

For marriages that have broken down: that Christ may heal the wounds that result. [Pause] We pray in faith.

For single people: that they may find love and support within the Christian community. [Pause] We pray in faith.

For our own special needs. [Longer pause] We pray in faith.

President: O God, strengthen the bonds that exist between us. We do not ask that these bonds never be tested. All we ask is for the grace to be faithful to you and to one another. We make our prayers through Christ our Lord.

REFLECTIOn 1   **Youth and age**

Youth is not a time of life, it is a state of mind.
Nobody grows old merely by living a number of years;
people grow old only by deserting their ideals.
Worry, doubt, self-distrust, fear and despair,
these are the long, long years that bow the head
and turn the growing spirit back to dust.
You are as young as your faith, as old as your doubt;
as young as your hope, as old as your despair.
So long as your heart receives messages of beauty,
cheer, courage, grandeur and power
from the earth, from man, from the infinite,
so long are you young.
When the heart is covered with the snow of pessimism
and the ice of cynicism,
then I am grown old indeed,
and may you, Lord, have mercy on my soul.

General Douglas MacArthur

REFLECTION 2   **To all children**

I tell you little children, not to hurry across the years:
All that age has for you is a field of worry, a sea of tears;
A mountain hard to climb where many fall,
and why should you not wander, pure and small?
Romance around our early morning lingers, but not for long,
And beauty moves no more her magic fingers o'er cords of song.
Sweetness will pine amid the sunless glades,
And innocence be gathered to the shades.
I tell you, little children, not to squander sunny hours
Too soon will come the storms of life, the thunder and leaden showers:
O children, you are growing up too soon,
And you will weep the morning when 'tis noon.

Patrick Kavanagh

FINAL BLESSING

May God, the almighty Father, bless you with his joy.
May the only Son of God have mercy on you, and help you in good times and in bad.
May the Holy Spirit of God always fill your hearts with his love.

From the marriage ceremony

Twenty-eighth Sunday of the Year
THE RICH YOUNG MAN

INTRODUCTION AND CONFITEOR

In the Gospel we read how riches kept a young man from becoming a disciple of Jesus. We are gathered here because we are disciples of Jesus. But we don't always follow him as closely as we should – something prevents us. That something is probably different for each one of us. Let us reflect for a moment on what that might thing might be. [Pause]

Let us ask pardon for our lack of courage and generosity.
Lord, we have sinned against you.
Lord, show us your mercy and your love.

HEADINGS AND READINGS

First Reading (Wis 7:7-11). This is a passage in praise of wisdom. It is presented as a speech of Solomon.
Second Reading (Heb 4:12-13). God's word is effective and is a source of true wisdom for us.

Gospel (Mk 10:17-30). The case of a good young man who refuses to follow Christ because he is unwilling to part with his wealth.

SCRIPTURE NOTE

Wisdom teaches us how to live rightly, and enables us to use the things of this world in a way that will help us achieve the end for which God put us on earth. Wisdom, therefore, should be prized even more than gold (First Reading).

The Gospel is a discipleship story. The Jews believed that the prosperity of the rich was a sign of God's blessing. But Jesus presents wealth as a stumbling block to the kingdom. Love of material possessions and comforts is one of the chief obstacles in the way of discipleship. Those who trust in themselves and their possessions can never be saved. Salvation is always God's achievement.

When Jesus says, 'Sell what you have … ' he doesn't mean that a disciple must be destitute. The life of the poor, with its hardship and suffering, is not set forth in Mark's Gospel as an ideal for the Christian disciple. But neither is the desire for possessions and the accumulation of wealth.

HOMILY 1   **True goodness**

Why did the young man come to Jesus? Many a young person in his position would have been more than happy with his lot. Was it that he was still questioning? Was it that his heart hadn't yet been hardened by riches? We don't know. But we do know that people can become so self-satisfied that they no longer hear the call of a better life.

He asked, 'What must I do to gain eternal life?' As a young person, he longed for action. He realised that it's deeds that count. This would have endeared him to Jesus. As we grew older, we tend to settle for words.

And he had firm ground under his feet. He could say, 'I have kept all the commandments: I haven't killed anyone. I haven't stolen from anyone, or cheated anyone. I haven't committed adultery. I haven't dishonoured my father or my mother … '

Here undoubtedly was a good-living, respectable young man – the kind of son any parent could be proud of. A model? Yes – up to a point. When we examine his claims to greatness they are less than convincing. So he hasn't killed anyone, or robbed anyone, or committed adultery, or … In a nutshell, what he was saying was, 'I haven't done anyone any harm' – which is a negative criterion. It's surprising how many people think this is the highest criterion of virtue.

We certainly are dealing with a good young man, one who has no blot on his copybook. But an outstanding young man? A young man who has been through the mill and proved himself? No. He simply has not been tested. But he is about to be tested.

Jesus looked at him with love and admiration. He saw great potential in him. Then he offered him a new vision of goodness – a positive one. This consisted, not merely in avoiding evil, but in doing good. He said, 'If you want to be perfect, sell what you have. Give it to the poor. Then come back and follow me, and you will have treasure in heaven.'

Jesus wanted to free the young man from his addiction to possessions, and to show him the path of sharing and compassion. But the young man wasn't up to it. So he went away sad.

Why was he sad? Because the challenge Jesus issued to him caused a vision of true greatness to flare up in his generous young heart. However, the price was too high. So he returned to his old life, and to his old comforts and securities. No doubt he would continue to dream about doing something really worthwhile with his life. But in time, the dream would fade. It's interesting that Jesus let him go.

It's very hard for people to give away their wealth, because it means depriving themselves of the resources on which they have come to rely for status, security, and enjoyment of life. But that is precisely the reason why disciples of Jesus must give up wealth. The essence of Christian faith is to put one's trust in God, and to rely on God as the sole source of security and well-being.

When Jesus says, 'Sell what you have … ' he doesn't mean that a disciple must be destitute. The life of the poor, with its hardship and suffering, is not set forth as an ideal for the Christian disciple. But neither is the desire for possessions and the accumulation of wealth.

Like the young man we too sometimes dream of a more authentic Christian life. We dream – but are we prepared to act? We are no better for merely desiring things, without striving towards them. For those who do strive, the rewards are great even in this life, in terms of meaning, fulfilment, and joy – in spite of trials and difficulties.

Just as he did with the young man, Jesus will not allow us to settle for an answer which does not demand the best of us. A true friend is someone who holds us to the best dreams of our youth. The friend challenges and stretches us to the limit of our ability and beyond, so that thereafter we have new standards by which to judge ourselves.

HOMILY 2   **Asking the important questions**

The young man asked Jesus, 'Master, what have I to do to inherit eternal life?' It's obvious that he had already asked another question, if not of Jesus, then of someone else. That question was: What is the purpose of life? The answer to which is: to gain eternal life.

These are the two most important questions in life. Most of us asked the same sort of questions when we were young. Perhaps we don't ask them any longer? Here we are, on the train of life, being carried forward inexorably, and it seems at an ever increasing speed, but where the train is bound for is no longer a burning issue with us.

Why is this? Could it be that we are so preoccupied with the baggage, or with amusements and distractions, that we simply have no time for such matters? Or could it be that, like the young man who came to Jesus, we have found that it is dangerous to ask such questions?

The climate we live in doesn't encourage this kind of questioning and reflection. Spiritual questions are seldom a topic of conversation at dinner tables, or even in intimate talks among friends. People focus more on work, family problems, and the political and economic issues of the day. Discussions about moral values and spiritual beliefs seldom happen. In fact, they are more or less taboo.

We are practical people. We want answers, not problems. Moral and spiritual matters are difficult issues. An American psychiatrist has said:

To a large extent our lives are spent in avoiding a confrontation with ourselves. Most of our daily activities facilitate this. They distract us from ourselves, and from reflection. We are tranquillised by the trivial.

Jesus answered the young man's question thus: 'Keep the commandments.' And the young man said, 'I have kept the commandments.'

For Jesus, keeping the commandments was just the bare minimum. He saw that this young man was capable of more. In fact, he was capable of greatness. So he said to him, 'If you want to be perfect, sell what you have, give the money to the poor, and then come and follow me.'

The young man stood on the brink of a new and exciting world. However, he realised at once that he could not enter this new world without saying good-bye to his old world. He hesitated. He thought about it. He looked back at that old world, and began to weigh up the things he was leaving. Suddenly he realised he couldn't do it. There was too much in that old world which he loved and wanted. So he refused the invitation of Jesus.

Some people are unwilling to let go of a single one of their old values in order to acquire a new one. If we fear to lose the pleasures of the old world, we will never taste the joys of the new.

Jesus demands the best of us as he did of the young man. He will not allow us to settle for anything less. The challenge – 'if you wish to be perfect' – is issued to us too. However, the thing we might be called upon to sacrifice in order to take up that challenge could vary for each of us. We have to look into our own hearts to see what it is that we would have to give up in order to respond to it.

Our presence here every Sunday brings us face to face with these great questions. We are reminded that life is a pilgrimage to God's eternal kingdom. We listen to the Word of God, and receive the Eucharist. But we must remember that salvation is always God's achievement. Those who trust in themselves and their possessions can never be saved. Those who trust in the saving power and redeeming love of God can enter freely into salvation.

HOMILY 3   **Sacrifice**

One day a young boy went to his grand-dad and asked him to go fishing with him. The grand-dad, who was a blacksmith, said, 'Just as soon as I finish shoeing these couple of horses, I'll be with you.'

The kid began to wander around the forge. The grand-dad warned him not to touch the horseshoes because some of them were very hot. But when his back was turned the boy picked one up. Finding it burning hot, he dropped it immediately, emitting a cry as he did so. The grand-dad heard the boy's cry. 'Did you hurt yourself?' he asked.

'No,' the boy lied.

'Are you sure?'

'Yes.'

'But if you're hurting, I can help you.'

'No, I'm all right.'

'So you didn't burn your hand?'

'No.'

'Well then, if you didn't, how come you dropped the shoe so quickly?'

'It didn't take long to look at it,' came the reply.

It doesn't take long to look at something and then drop it – as Jesus's story shows us.

Obviously the young man who came to Jesus did so because he admired Jesus – he called him 'Good master'. It's easy to gain admirers, but difficult to find people willing to make sacrifices. When Jesus asked him to give up his wealth and become his disciple, it proved too big a sacrifice for him. He went away sad. Why sad? Because the challenge Jesus issued to him caused a vision of true greatness to flare up in his young mind. He found this vision exciting but too costly. He knew that in turning his back on Jesus, he was turning his back on this vision too. So he went away sad.

And Jesus let him go. He respected his freedom. There is no point in forcing people to make sacrifices. If you take things away from them, they are impoverished. But if you can get them to give them up freely, they are enriched. People are essentially good. But this goodness has to be awakened and called forth if they are to enter the kingdom of love.

It is not what we receive that makes us great but what we give away. It is by giving that we grow. There is a danger that religion can become too easy. All the great religions teach that there is no reward without renunciation, without paying the price.

A questionnaire was once sent around a New York high school which asked, 'What would you like to be?' Two thirds of the students replied, 'A celebrity.' They had no idea of having to give of themselves in order to achieve something.

Deep down we all have a longing for goodness. We have a dream of doing something really worthwhile with our lives. We know that to follow that dream would involve sacrifice but would bring great joy too. It was God who put this longing in our hearts.

Jesus promised an earthly reward too to those who follow him – the reward of friendships, and of a life of purpose and meaning. Paradoxically, it's not an easy life but rather a life of sacrifice, that leads to fulfilment and joy.

PRAYER OF THE FAITHFUL

President: Let us turn to God for the wisdom and grace we need to use the things of this world in a way that will help us to gain eternal life.

Response: Lord, hear our prayer.

Reader(s): For the disciples of Jesus: that the faith they profess with their words may be borne out in their lives. [Pause] Let us pray to the Lord.

For government leaders: that they may work to ensure that all of God's children can live in dignity. [Pause] Let us pray to the Lord.

For the conversion of the rich. [Pause] Let us pray to the Lord.

For all gathered here: that we may not allow the love of wealth and comfort to stifle the spiritual side of ourselves. [Pause] Let us pray to the Lord.

For each other: that we may make whatever sacrifice is necessary in order to become authentic Christians. [Pause] Let us pray to the Lord.

For our own special needs. [Longer pause] Let us pray to the Lord.

President: Lord, help us to see you more clearly, to follow you more nearly, and to love you more dearly, so that under your gentle urging we may make steady progress along the road that leads to your kingdom. We make this and all our prayers through Christ our Lord.

REFLECTION   **Entering the kingdom of love**

Jesus saw that the rich young man had great potential,
so he invited him to enter the world of sharing.
But he wasn't up to it – riches got in the way.
As he went away a sadness descended on him,
the sadness that descends on us
when we choose to live for ourselves.
Even though Jesus was sad to see him go,

nevertheless, he let him go.
There's no point in forcing people to make sacrifices.
If you take things from people, they are impoverished;
but if you can get them to give them up, they are enriched.
People are essentially good,
but this goodness has to be awakened and called forth,
if they are to enter the kingdom of love.

Twenty-ninth Sunday of the Year
AUTHORITY AS SERVICE

INTRODUCTION AND CONFITEOR

The Letter to the Hebrews (Second Reading) tells us that in Jesus we have a High Priest who was tempted in every way that we are, though he is without sin. He has been through the mill, so to speak. Therefore, he can understand our struggles and help us. Let us approach him with confidence. [Pause]

Lord, you give us strength when we are weak. Lord, have mercy.
You raise us up when we fall. Christ, have mercy.
You give us courage when we are down-hearted. Lord, have mercy.

HEADINGS AND READINGS

First Reading (Is 53:10-11). The servant of the Lord takes on himself the sins of his people, and thus becomes a source of blessings for many.

Second Reading (Heb 4:14-16). We can approach Jesus with confidence because he knows our weaknesses and was like us in all things except sin.

Gospel (Mk 10:35-45). Jesus is the Suffering Servant who gave his life in the humble service of his people.

SCRIPTURE NOTE

The First Reading is an excerpt from Isaiah's fourth Servant Song. The Servant offers his life in atonement for the sins of his people. His death will be the beginning of glorification for him and be a source of blessings for others. By reflecting on passages such as this, the early Christians came to an understanding of the saving sufferings and death of Jesus.

In the Gospel we see how far the apostles are from this spirit of self-sacrifice. James and John want the top places in Jesus' kingdom. Obviously they thought that his kingdom would be modelled on worldly kingdoms, where those in high places enjoy honour, power, and glory. But

Jesus tells them that his disciples are not to imitate the Gentiles, whose rulers lord it over people. In his kingdom, service is what makes one great. He would set the example himself. He came 'not to be served but to serve, and to give his life as a ransom for many' (a reference to his saving death). Authority in his Church must wear the unmistakable livery of service.

HOMILY 1   **Authority as service**

The Gospel deals with a very important subject – the exercise of authority. It touches us all. Many people have had bad experiences of authority.

People seek authority for different reasons. Some people like the power that goes with it; it makes them feel important. Others like the prestige it brings. Others like the higher salary. All these reasons have one thing in common – authority is seen as an opportunity to promote oneself.

Jean Vanier (founder of L'Arche) distinguishes two kinds of authority: an authority which imposes, dominates and controls; and an authority which accompanies, listens, liberates, empowers, gives people confidence in themselves, and calls them to be aware of their responsibilities.

There is even a third kind of authority, silent, loving and hidden – the authority of powerless love, which waits, builds trust, and sometimes watches night and day in anguish. Parents have sometimes to wait and watch their children who have gone astray, hoping that they will come back.

Some people have a lust for power, and use their authority to dominate others. This is an abuse of authority. The lust for power is rooted not in strength but in weakness. Only the weak measure their worth by whom they can dominate. Authority exercised like this isolates the possessor, and tends to bring out the worst in everyone.

When James and John asked Jesus if they could have the top places in his kingdom they were thinking only of themselves. They did not mind how much envy and resentment they aroused in their companions. They obviously thought that his kingdom was modelled on worldly kingdoms. Those in high places would enjoy honour, glory, and power. But Jesus told them that it wasn't like that at all. In his kingdom the greatest would be those who were willing to serve others rather than serve themselves.

Jesus first outlined the accepted standard of civil authority: domination, with rulers lording it over their subjects. But this is not how it must be in his community. He saw authority as an opportunity to serve. As always, he set the example himself. He did not lord it over people. He appealed, he invited, but left the response to them. He would lead, but he would not control. His authority mirrored that of God. God uses his power not to control but to enable.

This is how he wanted authority to be exercised in his community. Authority should not be given to those who seek it, but only to those who have proved that they are willing to serve. Those entrusted with power over their fellow human beings ought to be caring, just, merciful, wise, tolerant, and lenient.

In order to serve, one has to be ready to drink the cup that Jesus drank – the cup of sacrifice and suffering. One can serve in any position. However, those in positions of authority are the best placed of all. We are recovering this spirit in the Church, and it is a very good thing. Power used for Christian service can be a tremendous force for good.

HOMILY 2   **Role reversal**

During the Last Supper Jesus washed the feet of the apostles. He was hammering home a lesson he had taught them earlier (see Gospel), namely, that for them authority was to be a form of service. So that there would be no doubt in their minds as to what he meant he said, 'If I, the Master, have washed your feet, you must wash each other's feet. I have given you an example so that you may copy what I have done' (Jn 13:14-15).

Today there is often a gulf between those who rule and those who are ruled. A lot of hurt results especially for those below. Those in low positions feel they are not appreciated by those in high positions. They see the latter as remote and uncaring. It's easy for those who have worked their way up into high positions to forget what it is like to be 'in the trenches'. To remember is to understand. A good parent remembers what it was like to be a child.

Would that those above might follow the example Jesus gave at the Last Supper. Let the policeman be arrested; the priest sit in the pew; the teacher sit at the desk; the foreman get down into the trenches; the warder be locked up; the doctor get seriously ill; the judge be put in the dock; the general go to the front line; the man with the secure job join the dole queue ... Might we not have a more caring and sensitive exercise of authority?

Of course the opposite also happens – those above are not understood by those below, and harsh judgements are sometimes handed up.

One day a watch was crossing the town square just as the big clock on the church steeple was chiming twelve noon. The watch looked up at the big clock and said, 'You think you're better than the rest of us, don't you? You ought to take a look at yourself. Your face is so common, your hands so clumsy, and your voice so coarse!'

But the big clock calmly replied, 'Come up here, my little brother, and I'll show you something.'

The little watch climbed up the long stairs, and at last stood beside the big clock. What a view there was from here. But pretty soon it realised that it was dangerous up here, very exposed, and ever so lonely.

'Little brother, there is a man down there who wants to know the time.

[326]

Why don't you tell him?' said the big clock.

'Oh, I couldn't make him hear me from here or see me either,' the watch replied.

'So you can't tell him,' said the big clock. 'But I can tell him. We each have a job to do. I can do what you can't do. You can do what I can't do. Let us therefore not criticise one another. Instead, let each of us in our own way, and from our own place, tell people the time. In that way, we will not only be equal but brothers as well.'

Jesus abolished the distance between the master and the servant. In him the two became one.

HOMILY 3   **Drinking the cup**

One of the images the Bible uses for life is that of a cup. Just as a cup may be filled with a bitter-sweet drink, so the life of each of us could be said to be a mixture of the sweet and the bitter. It's a rich and powerful image.

As well as standing for life as a whole, it can stand for a particular segment of life. Thus, there may be times when the cup of life is full of bitterness. It may be so bitter that we don't want to drink it, or feel we are not able to drink it. But at other times the cup may be over-flowing with sweetness. At such times we can't get enough of it. And at still other times the cup may be flat and tasteless. Finally, there may be times when the cup of life is empty.

James and John came to Jesus with a very selfish request. They asked that one might be allowed to sit at his right hand and the other at his left hand in his kingdom. They obviously thought that Jesus' kingdom would be modelled on worldly kingdoms. Those in high places would enjoy honour, glory, and power.

Jesus answered by asking them a question: 'Can you drink the cup that I am to drink?' They immediately said they could, because they thought it would be a very sweet cup.

But what Jesus was really asking the two disciples was, 'Are you willing to go through the suffering that I am going to go through?'

This was no easy thing – to drink a cup of sacrifice and suffering. Indeed, when the time came for Jesus himself to drink it, he shrank from it. Three times he asked the Father to remove it from him: 'Father, if it is possible, let this cup pass from me' (Mt 26:39). But then he added, 'Yet not my will but thine be done.' And he did drink it.

The apostles didn't know at this time that the Lord's cup would be a very bitter one. Nor did they know their own weakness. So when the time came, far from drinking the cup with him, they left him to drink the bitter cup alone.

We don't know in advance what the cup of life holds for us. We find out as we go along. Jesus, the Innocent One, chose to drink a very bitter cup. But, as we have seen, he didn't find it easy. Yet he drank it to the dregs. And did so out of love for us. Love can make a bitter cup drinkable. (So can dire necessity – think of a medicine that must be drunk.)

Even though Jesus was without sin, he experienced weakness and temptation as we do. He understands our weakness. Hence, we should approach him with confidence, knowing that he can and will help us.

If we find the cup of life particularly bitter, there is no need for us to pretend that it is sweet, or to think that we can drink it by our own strength. Unlike the two apostles, let us not be afraid or ashamed to say, 'No, Lord, I can't drink it. I don't want to drink it. But if I have to, then with your help I will.'

To drink the cup of life, especially a cup made difficult by a life of sacrifice and service of others, is to follow Christ. But those who share the bitterness of his cross will also share the sweetness of his Easter victory.

PRAYER OF THE FAITHFUL

President: The Lord loves justice and right, and fills the earth with his love. Let us now with confidence bring our needs before him.

Response: Lord, graciously hear us.

Reader(s): For the Pope and the bishops: that they may be true servants of the servants of God. [Pause] Lord, hear us.

For the disciples of Jesus: that they may follow him along the road of sacrifice and service. [Pause] Lord, hear us.

For temporal rulers: that they may exercise their authority in a gentle and just manner. [Pause] Lord, hear us.

For peoples who are subjected to oppression: that they may achieve their freedom. [Pause] Lord, hear us.

For prisoners: that they may be treated in a just and humane way. [Pause] Lord, hear us.

For those who right now are drinking a bitter cup. [Pause] Lord, hear us.

For our own special needs. [Longer pause] Lord, hear us.

President: God of power and love, cleanse us of greed and envy, and clothe us in gentleness and humility, so that we may become more like your Son and so come to share his glory in heaven. We ask this through the same Christ our Lord.

REFLECTION   **The request that Jesus refused to grant**

James and John were two opportunists.
Their one aim was to rise in the ranks.
To achieve their end they did not hesitate to beg.
They did not mind how much envy and resentment

they aroused in their companions.
Their aim was to scramble up the career ladder.
But at what price to themselves?
If in the course of their rise to the top,
people lose themselves, their own souls,
whatever they do or achieve will be worthless.
Power hardens the human heart.
A hard-hearted person is incapable of love.
It is by giving that we receive,
and it is by serving that we grow in love.

Thirtieth Sunday of the Year
BARTIMAEUS

INTRODUCTION AND CONFITEOR

In today's Gospel we meet a blind man by the name of Bartimaeus. When he met Jesus his prayer was: 'Lord, that I may see.' It is a prayer which we can make our own because in many ways we too are blind. Jesus wants to open our eyes too. [Pause]

Lord Jesus, you opened the eyes of the blind. Lord, have mercy.
You free us from the darkness of sin. Christ, have mercy.
You help us to walk in the light of goodness. Lord, have mercy.

HEADINGS FOR READINGS

First Reading (Jer 31:7-9). The prophet foretells the return of God's people from exile in Babylon. Even the most helpless will share in the joy of this great event.

Second Reading (Heb 5:1-6). This reading sets out the things that are required of a priest, and shows how Christ met these perfectly.

Gospel (Mk 10:46-52). Jesus hears the cry of a blind man and gives him back his sight.

SCRIPTURE NOTE

The First Reading carries a message of joyful hope for the exiles in Babylon. The Lord will save what's left of his people and bring them back from exile. Even the most helpless will share in the joy of this great event.

In Mark's mind Jesus is the one who brings salvation to Israel. His healings are a sign of the coming of the kingdom (Gospel).

The story of Bartimaeus is as much a call story as a healing story. The expression 'followed him along the way' doesn't simply mean that he joined the crowd on the road to Jerusalem. There can be no doubt what Mark intends: Bartimaeus followed Jesus on the way of Christian discipleship. He is presented as a model of faith.

It seems that the story was used in the early Church as a model of encouragement to believers and would-be believers.

Bartimaeus serves as a model for those who are spiritually blind and whose lives lack direction. Through faith they can have purpose, energy and direction in their lives. An enthusiastic following of Jesus results in a happy and fulfilled life.

HOMILY 1   **Blindness**

A young man, blind from birth, fell in love with a girl. The more he got he know her, the deeper his love for her became. He found her full of charm and wit. A beautiful friendship developed between them. But then one day a friend told him that the girl wasn't very good-looking. From that moment on he began to lose interest in her. Too bad. He had been 'seeing' her very well. It was his friend who was blind. A blind person doesn't judge by appearances. We must remember that there is sight and insight.

In biblical times blindness was very common. Today we have eliminated many of the diseases that cause blindness. And we have invented all kinds of devices to improve our seeing. We have ordinary glasses, bifocals, magnifying glasses, field glasses, telescopes, microscopes ... We can see more and farther than ever before in our history. Indeed, the miracle Jesus performed for Bartimaeus happens regularly in our hospitals.

Because we are not blind we might think that the Gospel story has no relevance for us. It is precisely because we can see that it has relevance for us. The question is: how well do we see?

Bartimaeus was suffering from physical blindness. But there are other forms of blindness. We acknowledge this when we use expressions such as, 'I was completely in the dark,' or 'It suddenly dawned on me,' or 'It was right in front of me but I couldn't see it.'

Is it possible that a blind person could have more faith than a sighted person? Is it possible that a blind person could even 'see' more than a sighted person, in the sense of having more insight and more understanding?

St Mark seems to think so. In fact, this seems to be the whole point of his story. Bartimaeus, who was physically blind, had more faith in Jesus than many of his disciples who had perfect eyesight. Whereas he has no doubt, they are full of doubt and hesitation.

One of the saddest things Jesus said about his contemporaries was this: 'They have eyes but fail to see.' They witnessed the great things he did, yet had no faith in him. Lack of faith is a more serious kind of blindness than physical blindness.

There is a darkness worse than that of Bartimaeus – the darkness of unbelief. It cuts us off from more. Physical sight in a great thing, a gift which we should never take for granted. But spiritual sight is even greater.

The Gospel story is more a discipleship story, a call story, than a story of healing. When Bartimaeus was cured he could have gone off to live his own life, forgetting about Jesus. Instead he became an immediate and enthusiastic disciple of Jesus. He followed Jesus along the road. That is the climax of the story.

From being a mere believer, Bartimaeus became a disciple. There is a big difference. The latter implies living as a Christian. His willingness to follow Jesus contrasts with the disciples' misunderstandings and hesitations during the journey to Jerusalem.

Bartimaeus was in darkness until he met Jesus. We are in darkness when we doubt, when we hate, when we live in error and prejudice, when we choose evil. Hence, we can make our own the heart-felt prayer of Bartimaeus: 'Lord, that I may see.' That we may see what is truly important in life, and above all that we may see with the eyes of faith.

Here on earth, though we can have a sense of God, we do not see God himself. We have to be content to travel by the light of faith towards that land where we shall see as we are seen.

HOMILY 2   **Throwing away the cloak**

Bartimaeus was in a sad state. Blindness is terrible affliction. He was sitting by the side of the road, on the margins of life. He was forced to beg, and so was totally dependent on the charity of others. His situation was hopeless.

And yet it seems that he had one kind of riches. He had faith in Jesus. It may have been only the faith of the desperate, but faith is what matters. When he heard that Jesus was passing by, overcoming his pride and shame, he began to cry out, 'Jesus, Son of David, have pity on me.' He was not put off by the fact that Jesus didn't immediately grant his request, or by the fact that people tried to silence him. He went on crying out.

When he heard that Jesus was calling him, he jumped to his feet, threw aside his cloak, and made his way to Jesus. That cloak was the one thing of value that he had. It meant the world to him. It not only provided him with warmth, but also covered his wretchedness, thus giving him some measure of dignity and respectability. Yet he threw it aside and came to Jesus just as he was – in all his darkness, poverty, and wretchedness. And Jesus received him and gave him back his sight.

When we go to see a doctor we may be asked to take off some or all of our clothes. It's not something we find easy. To strip is to become very vulnerable. But how can we have our ills diagnosed and treated, if we won't even let the doctor see them in the first place?

We too are blind in many ways. We too are poor before God. Jesus calls us to come to him. He wants to make us well. However, we find it hard to throw the 'cloak' away, and come to him just as we are. Pride makes us try to put on an outward show.

We may believe that we have to be perfect, otherwise he won't love us. To admit our sins and weaknesses would cause him to reject us. But if we were perfect, if we were well, we wouldn't need him at all.

We have to make a radical act of faith and trust in Jesus. We must give up pretending, covering up, hiding behind various screens and masks, and be content to appear before him as we really are. We have nothing to fear but his kindness and healing. A patient does not feel accepted unless the worst in him/her is also accepted. So we will never feel accepted and loved by God unless we let him see our worst side.

Many people sit at the roadside of life begging, not for money, but for love, for attention, for a feeling that they are important and that life has a meaning. Many of them are too embarrassed to ask for help. They are afraid of being silenced by the indifference of others.

Bartimaeus serves as a model for others. Many people were blind and without direction, but have found purpose, energy and direction in their lives as a result of following Jesus. An enthusiastic following of Jesus results in a happy and fulfilled life, a life shared with others.

Lord, that we may see – see our needy brothers and sisters, that we may hear their silent cries, that we may not pass by. For we too were beggars, and you enriched me. We too was blind, and you enlightened us.

HOMILY 3   **Retelling the story**

My name is Bartimaeus. Let me try to tell you what it was like for me to be blind. To be blind is to be cut off from other people. It is to be in a world of one's own. At times loneliness enfolded me like a cold mist. I was cut off from all the things which make life worthwhile, things which sighted people take for granted.

I was forced to beg for a living, which meant I was totally dependent on the charity of others. I was sitting at the roadside of life. My future was a long road, but a road without a goal. Life would never be any different. I would always be in the dark. Always on the margins. Always lonely and cut off.

I longed for one thing – to be able to see. That longing would not leave me. If only it would go away then maybe I would have some peace inside myself.

Some kind people gave me a coin as they passed. But no one stopped to talk to me. No one entered my lonely world, not even for a minute. The indifference of others – that is what hurt me most. It's terrible to be treated as if you had no feelings – like a block of wood.

People speeded up as they approached me and slowed down once they were past. I could tell from the sound of their footsteps. I never could understand this. It made me feel that I was in some way contaminated.

The priest told me that my blindness was caused by sin. This meant that even God had no time for me, that he too had pushed me out.

That's how it was for me until one day I heard the sound of a large crowd. I enquired and was told that Jesus was passing by. Suddenly hope flared up inside me, and I began to cry out, 'Jesus, Son of David, have pity on me!'

The people tried to silence me. They said I was an embarrassment. But I refused to be silenced. I cried all the louder.

Then I was told that he had heard me and was calling me. Throwing aside my cloak, I groped my way to meet him. He asked me, 'What can I do for you?' I said: 'Please, let me to see'. He asked no further questions. He just said, 'Go on your way, it was your faith that saved you.'

How could I go my own way and forget all about him? I followed him along the road. I became a disciple of his. What a joy it was to be able to see! I wanted to reach out and touch everyone. I looked on them all as my friends. In my meeting with Jesus I had felt his love. He had not only brought me in from the margins, but had given me a place of honour at the banquet of life.

Jesus said that his mission was 'to open the eyes of the blind.' His mission was not so much a question of bringing physical sight to people, but of bringing them vision, of giving them another way of looking at life. It wasn't a question of opening people's eyes physically, but of opening their minds, their imaginations, and especially their hearts. The real voyage of discovery consists not in seeking new landscapes but in having new eyes.

Jesus opened the eyes of Zacchaeus to the danger of riches, and got him to share with the poor. He opened the eyes of the dying thief to God's mercy, and welcomed him into paradise.

We don't have to be physically blind to feel in the dark. At times any of us can feel lonely and cut off. We find ourselves on the margin of things. We are no longer useful or wanted. People ignore us. Without love the world is very dark. And people want us to keep quiet. And we ourselves may be too ashamed to cry out.

At those times we must have courage and the humility to cry out to the Lord, 'Lord, that I may see.' Jesus is the one who brings us in from the margins. He tells us that we are precious to the Father. He gives us a seat at the banquet of the Kingdom.

He wants us to do for others what he did for Bartimaeus. We must not pass the lonely person by or leave them on the margins. But by our love, our care, our time, we are to let a little light into a world of darkness.

ANOTHER APPROACH   **Vision**

To a person of average height standing on the seashore the horizon is a mere three miles away. If one were standing on a point a hundred feet higher, it recedes to about thirteen miles. And seen from about a thousand feet up the distance to the horizon becomes about forty miles.

Meteorologists speak in terms of 'visibility'. This has nothing to do with how far away the horizon is. Visibility is defined as 'the furthest horizontal distance at which a person can distinguish and identify an object, in normal conditions of daylight' – a concept that is not as simple as it seems.

The air is never completely clear. Even if it were, the maximum visibility would still be only about 130 miles. In practice, it is quite unusual to be able to see clearly a distance of more than forty miles. There is no such thing as unlimited visibility. The highest numerical value with which meteorologists concern themselves is something above fifty miles.

Some people have a very limited horizon. They can barely see beyond themselves. Their world is limited because of a preoccupation with themselves. And their vision is darkened by the gloomy view they take of things. But other people have a wider horizon due to the fact that they are able to see beyond themselves. And their world is brightened by the fact that they see things in a positive light.

Jesus belonged to the second category. There are many examples in the Gospel. He saw Nathanael as he sat under the fig tree. He spotted Zacchaeus up on the sycamore tree. He noticed the poor widow making her small but heroic offering. Though small in themselves, these examples provide us with a precious insight into his character. Besides, his stories show that he was a keen observer of life and of people. It wasn't that he didn't see the ugly things. He did. Yet for him the world was filled with signs of the kingdom of God.

We have to distinguish between sight and vision. Just because we have good eyesight doesn't mean we have great vision. It's not with the eyes only that we see. We also 'see' with the mind, the heart, and the imagination. A narrow mind, a small heart, and an impoverished imagination lead to loss of vision, and narrow our world. We should remember the lovely words of Saint-Exupery's Little Prince: 'It is only with the heart that we can see rightly.'

PRAYER OF THE FAITHFUL

President: Jesus heard the humble but persistent cry of Bartimaeus. The example of Bartimaeus encourages us as we turn to God in our need.

Response: Lord, that we may see.

Reader(s): For Christians: that they may see with the eyes and heart of Christ. [Pause] Let us pray to the Lord.

For those in positions of power: that they may be sensitive to the needs of those in their charge. [Pause] Let us pray to the Lord.

For the poor, the handicapped, the lonely, and all those who are on the edges of life: that Christians may show them respect and love. [Pause] Let us pray to the Lord.

For those who live in the darkness of unbelief: that they may be granted the light of faith. [Pause] Let us pray to the Lord.

For ourselves: that we may use well the wonderful gift of sight. [Pause] Let us pray to the Lord.

For our departed relatives and friends: that they may see the light of God's glory. [Pause] Let us pray to the Lord.

For our own special needs. [Longer pause] Let us pray to the Lord.

President: Lord God, let your light shine on us so that we may walk without stumbling along the road to your kingdom. We ask this through Christ our Lord.

REFLECTION   **The gift of sight**

Helen Keller, who went blind and deaf at nineteen months, said:

> 'One day I asked a friend of mine who had just returned from a long walk in the woods what she had seen. She replied, "Nothing in particular."
>
> 'How was this possible?' I asked myself, 'when I, who cannot hear or see, find hundreds of things to interest me through mere touch. I feel the delicate shape and design of a leaf. I pass my hands lovingly over the rough bark of a pine tree. Occasionally, I place my hand quietly on a small tree, and if I'm lucky, feel the happy quiver of a bird in full song.
>
> 'The greatest calamity that can befall people, is not that they should be born blind, but that they should have eyes, yet fail to see.'

Thirty-first Sunday of the Year
THE TWO GREAT COMMANDMENTS

INTRODUCTION AND CONFITEOR

Today's Scripture readings remind us of one of the greatest truths in the Bible, namely, that there are really only two commandments. The first is to love God, and the second is to love our neighbour. Let us call to mind

our failure to live the commandments of love. [Pause]
    Let us ask forgiveness from God and from one another.

HEADINGS FOR READINGS

First Reading (Deut 6:2-6). To love God means to keep his command-
ments, especially the great commandment of love.
    Second Reading (Heb 7:23-28). This reading shows the superiority of
Christ over the priests of the Old Testament.
    Gospel (Mk 12:28-34). Jesus tells us what the two most important of
God's commandments are.

SCRIPTURE NOTE

By rabbinical count, 'the Law' consisted of some 613 commandments.
The Scribe's question as to which commandment was the greatest was
one frequently discussed among the rabbis. Jesus was asked to name one,
but responded by naming two. Both are found in the Old Testament; the
first in Deuteronomy 6:4 (First Reading), the second in Leviticus 19:18.
What Jesus did was to put the two together, thus emphasising the essential relatedness of them. No rabbi had previously done this. The emphasis on love became for Christians the identifying characteristic of their
religion.
    The Scribe agreed fully with Jesus, and went on to declare that true
love of God and the loving service of others are more important than
elaborate cult. Nowhere else in the Gospels does a Scribe emerge in such
a favourable light.

HOMILY 1   **Not separating the two great commandments**

One of the most sacred things a Moslem can do is make the pilgrimage to
Mecca, birthplace of Mohammed. It is one of the five pillars of the Mos-
lem religion.
    Once upon a time the king of the cats made the pilgrimage to Mecca.
On his return the king of the mice felt obliged to go and congratulate
him. But when the other mice heard this they feared for their king's safety.
'The cat is our enemy, he can't be trusted,' they said.
    'Oh, now that he's been to Mecca, I expect to see a great change in him.
I'm told he prays five times a day,' the king replied.
    So the king mouse set out. On coming into the kingdom of the cats he
spotted his opposite number in the distance, and was very impressed by
what he saw. Still dressed in his pilgrim's robe, the king cat was deep in
prayer. However, no sooner had the king mouse come near him than he
jumped up and pounced. Fortunately the king mouse was a fast mover,
and succeeded in escaping down a hole. Later he rejoined the other mice.

'How did you get on?' they asked eagerly. 'Is it true that since he made the pilgrimage to Mecca he's a changed cat?'

'I'm afraid you were right,' came the reply. 'Though he prays like a pilgrim, he still pounces like a cat.'

How easy it is to separate the two great commandments; to think that we can have one without the other; that we can love God without loving our neighbour too.

The two commandments are essentially interrelated. True love of neighbour springs from the love of God; and on the other hand, there can be no true love of God which does not express itself in love of neighbour. This is better than all sacrifices. It's easy to let ritual take the place of love. Then we end up with a loveless religion.

Our greatest sin is not that we don't love our neighbours, but that we don't even know them. So how can we be neighbours to them in the Gospel sense? The worst thing of all is a cold indifference.

The Bible tells us to love our neighbours, and also to love our enemies. The reason for this, according to G.K. Chesterton, is probably because they are generally the same people. And there is a human reason for this. We think of a remote person in the right way; that is, we think of him as a person. But we do not think like that about our next-door neighbour. He is not a man; he is an environment. He is the barking of a dog, or the noise of a drill or a piano.

Many people are caused problems by a particular person, be it a neighbour or a family member. What can we do? We should avoid any kind of retaliation – this only makes things worse. We should try to keep communicating with the person, even if it's just a matter of saying 'good morning', or 'good evening'. Then we should pray for that person. If we can sincerely pray for a person, it will keep bitterness and hatred from accumulating in our hearts.

Where there is no love, let us sow love, and we will reap love.

Where there is no love, let us put love, and we will find love.

> I sought God and him I did not see.
> I sought my soul but it eluded me.
> I sought my neighbour
> and found all three.

HOMILY 2   **The greatest failure of Christians**

Failure to love is the great failure in a Christian. Often, alas, it is not even seen as a sin. Sin is recognised when it means doing harm to a neighbour, but not when it means failing to love, or withholding love.

A story is told about a man who sold an old 'banger' of a car to an unsuspecting stranger, and who later went to Confession. Afterwards he met one of his old pals in the local pub. When one of his pals heard he had been to Confession, he said, 'I hope you told the priest how you cheated that man over the car.'

'I did no such thing,' he replied. 'I tell the priest my sins. But he has no right to know my business.'

The great danger facing church-going people is that they don't see the connection between what they do in church on a Sunday and what they do in relation to their neighbour on a weekday.

People may examine their conscience but leave whole fields untouched: the conscientious carrying out of one's duty, honesty in business matters, justice, respect and co-operation among those who live under the same roof ... and so on. For such people religion is divorced from life. It is a private matter between them and God. According to the Bible, a religion like that is a distortion. Worse, it is an abomination.

It's very easy to separate the two great commandments. In a sense there is only one commandment – the commandment of love. It is like a coin, one entity with two sides. It is impossible to have one without the other. It's not that we hate our neighbours. No, we don't hate them. It's just that we refuse to take them into our heart. If the truth were told, we are indifferent to them.

All of us have a great capacity to love, but sadly we use it all too seldom. The actor, Christopher Reeve, was famous for his portrayal of Superman in the movies. However, as a result of a fall from a horse, he ended up in a wheelchair, paralysed from the neck down. He said he got 100,000 letters of sympathy and support from people. This led him to ask: 'Why does it take a tragedy before we show our appreciation for one another?'

We leave it too late and then are full of regrets. We wait until it is too late to tell or show others that we love them. We leave it too late to mend a quarrel, too late to enjoy health or the gift of our children or our parents.

Jesus said to the Scribe, 'You are not far from the kingdom of God.' Knowing which were the two most important commandments was the first step. Putting them into practice was the second step. We are not far from the Kingdom – just a step away. In order to take that step we need God to touch our hearts.

HOMILY 3   **The ladder of Charity**

We live in an age that encourages selfishness. In elections, candidates for public office often suggest that voters ask themselves, 'Am I better off today than I was four years ago?' This appeal to personal selfishness is far more successful than asking voters, 'Is society better off today than it was then?'

In the Bible we see that God is deeply concerned about the way we treat one another. Our vocation is to love. And, in spite of everything, we are moved by altruism. We are touched by the pain of other people. We feel enlarged by doing good, more so than by doing well materially or financially. Generosity brings its own rewards. Joy springs up within us when we do a good deed for another. But when we refuse to do a good deed for another, a strange sadness descends on us.

Maimonides was a famous Jewish teacher who lived in Spain in the twelfth century. He outlined eight degrees or steps in the what he called the ladder of charity.

1. The first and lowest degree is to give, but with reluctance or regret. This is the gift of the hand, but not of the heart.
2. The second is to give cheerfully, but not in proportion to the distress of the sufferer.
3. The third is to give cheerfully and in proportion to the need, but not until we are asked.
4. The fourth is to give cheerfully, proportionately, and even unasked, but to put it into the poor man's hand, thereby exciting in him the painful emotion of shame.
5. The fifth is to give in such a way that the needy may receive the alms and know their benefactor, without the benefactor knowing them.
6. The sixth is to know the recipients of our charity, while remaining unknown to them.
7. The seventh is to bestow charity in such a way that the benefactor does not know the recipient, or the recipient the benefactor.
8. Lastly, the eight and most meritorious way of all, is to anticipate charity by preventing poverty. This can be done by giving a gift or a loan of money to enable an indigent person to get back on his feet, or by teaching him a trade, or by putting him in the way of business, so that he may earn an honest livelihood, and not be forced to the dreadful alternative of holding out his hand for charity.

'One of the nicest things that can happen to a person is to do good by stealth and be found out by accident.' (Mark Twain).

OTHER STORIES

1. In the sixteenth century, the Jews were expelled from Spain and went all over Europe. Jacob, a kind and devout shoemaker, ended up in Israel. He went to the synagogue every Sabbath, and even though he didn't understand a word of Hebrew, he listened intently to what the rabbi was saying.

One Sabbath the rabbi gave a sermon. Jacob understood only two words

– the word 'God' and the word 'bread'. He got very excited, and when he got home he said to his wife, 'The rabbi told us that God eats bread. You must bake bread and I'll bring it to God next Sabbath.'

His wife baked some lovely loaves of bread, and the following Sabbath Jacob brought them to the synagogue and placed them in the holy ark. He said to God, 'I've got your bread. You'll love it. My wife is the best baker in the country.'

No sooner had he left than in came the synagogue's caretaker. 'Lord, you know I love to come to this holy place. But seven weeks now I've been working and haven't been paid. I need a miracle. Maybe I'll open the holy ark, and there will be something to eat.' The caretaker walked to the ark and opened it, and there indeed was a miracle – seven fresh loaves of bread, one for each day of the week.

The next day when Jacob opened the ark and saw that the bread had been taken, you should have seen the joy that came over his face. And thus it went on week after week, year after year. Then one day Jacob came to the synagogue with his loaves of bread and said, 'Lord, I know your bread has been lumpy of late. My wife has arthritis. Maybe you could do something for her? You'd eat better.' Jacob put the bread in the ark and started to leave when the rabbi grabbed him. 'What are you doing?' the rabbi demanded.

'I'm bringing God his bread,' Jacob replied.

'God doesn't eat bread!'

'Well, he's been eating my wife's bread for many years!'

The rabbi and Jacob hid to see if they could figure out what was going on. Soon the caretaker came in. He began to mutter, 'I hate to bring it up, Lord, but your bread's been lumpy of late. Maybe you could talk with an angel.' As he reached in to take the bread, the rabbi grabbed him.

The rabbi began to yell at the two men, telling them how sinful they were. He ranted on and on until all three men began to cry. Jacob was crying because he wanted only to do good. The rabbi was crying because all this was happening because of his sermon. And the caretaker was crying because he realised there wouldn't be any more bread.

Suddenly the three men heard laughter in the corner. They turned round to see the great mystic, Isaac Luria, standing there. He was shaking with laughter. He said, 'Rabbi, these men are not sinful. They are devout men. God has got great fun from watching what goes on in your synagogue on the Sabbath. I mean this man brings the bread, that man takes the bread, and God get all the credit.

'You must beg forgiveness of these men, rabbi.' Then turning to Jacob he said, 'Jacob, you have been doing a great thing. But now you must do something even greater. You must bring your bread directly to the caretaker. And you must believe with perfect faith that God will be just as pleased and have just as much fun.'

And so it was.

2. There is a story about a poor man who went from house to house begging for a little money or a crust of bread. But no one showed him any compassion. Many a door was slammed in his face, and he was turned away with insults. Little wonder that the poor man grew despondent.

One wintry day, as he was trudging through the slippery streets, he fell and broke his leg. A passer-by took him to the hospital. When the people of the town heard that a poor stranger had been taken to the hospital suffering from a broken leg, they felt very sorry for him. Some went to comfort him, others brought him good things to eat. When he left the hospital they furnished him with warm clothes and gave him a tidy sum of money.

Before the poor man left town he wrote to his wife, 'Praise God, dear wife. A miracle happened: I broke my leg!'

Most people would sooner help one who has fallen than keep him from falling.

PRAYER OF THE FAITHFUL

President: As we bring our needs before God, we are mindful of the two great commandments of love, and of how much we need God's grace to be faithful to them.

Response: Lord, hear us in your love.

Reader(s): For Church leaders: that in word and in deed they may uphold the primacy of love in Christian living. [Pause] We pray in faith.

For all the followers of Christ: that they may show their love for God by loving others. [Pause] We pray in faith.

For our civil leaders: that they may work unselfishly for all members of society, but particularly the weaker and more vulnerable members. [Pause] We pray in faith.

For those who have known little love in their lives and who practise even less. [Pause] We pray in faith.

For the sick and the needy: that through our love they may know that God cares about them. [Pause] We pray in faith.

For this community: that our celebration of the Eucharist may strengthen our unity and deepen our love. [Pause] We pray in faith.

For our own special needs. [Longer pause] We pray in faith.

President: All-loving God, help us to make love the foundation of our lives. May our love for you express itself in our eagerness to do good to others. We ask this through Christ our Lord.

PRAYER/REFLECTION   **Bearing the fruits of love**

If only the heart was right we could give so much more.
Lord, open our hearts when they are closed,
soften them when they are hard,
warm them when they are cold,
brighten them when they are dark,
fill them when they are empty,
calm them when they are troubled,
cleanse them when they are sullied,
heal them when they are wounded,
and mend them when they are broken,
so that we, your disciples, may bear the fruits of love. Amen.

Thirty-second of the Year
THE WIDOW'S MIGHTY MITE

INTRODUCTION AND CONFITEOR

Jesus praised a widow who made a very small offering. He praised her
because it was all she had. Jesus didn't judge an offering by its size, but
by what it cost the giver. We tend to judge our own contribution and that
of others by standards other than those of the Gospel. [Pause]

God is generous with his forgiveness. Let us ask pardon for all the
unfair and false judgements we make.

HEADINGS FOR READINGS

First Reading (1 Kgs 17:10-16). In the middle of a famine, a poor widow
shares the last of her food with the prophet Elijah, and far from losing by
so doing, she is enriched.

Second Reading (Heb 9:24-28). Through his death Christ has taken our
sins upon himself and has opened for us the door to salvation.

Gospel (Mk 12:38-44). In the eyes of others the offering of the widow
was the least, but in the eyes of Christ it was the greatest.

SCRIPTURE NOTE

In biblical times widows were among the poorest of the poor. The widow
in the First Reading was a non-Jew, and she had a son to support. She was
down to her last handful of meal and drop of olive oil. After that she and
her child must starve. Yet, by sharing it with the prophet, she has an never-
ending supply of flour and oil. She represents those people, who, despite
poverty and oppression, place all their trust in God.

In the Gospel, Jesus' denunciation of the public display of the Scribes provides a background for an example of genuine religious behaviour on the part of a widow. Her example of true piety contrasts sharply with the counterfeit piety of the Scribes. The widow let go of every shred of security, and committed herself wholly to God. The story is as much about trust in God as about generosity. The widow's generosity results from her trust in God.

HOMILY 1   **When giving becomes a sacrifice**

The test of a gift is not what it amounts to in itself, but what its loss means to the giver.

We have to give what will cost us something. This is not just giving what we can live without, but what we can't live without, or don't want to live without. This kind of giving hurts. But this is love in action. When the gift is as desperately needed by the giver as by the receiver- that is true giving. Then our gift becomes a sacrifice.

Mother Teresa told a story how one day she was walking down the street when a beggar came up to her and said, 'Mother Teresa, everybody is giving to you, I also want to give to you. Today, for the whole day, I got only thirty cents. I want to give it to you.'

Mother Teresa thought for a moment: 'If I take the thirty cents he will have nothing to eat tonight, and if I don't take it I will hurt his feelings. So I put out my hands and I took the money. I have never seen such joy on anybody's face as I saw on the face of that beggar man at the thought that he too could give to Mother Teresa.'

Mother Teresa went on: 'It was a big sacrifice for that poor man, who had sat in the sun all day long and received only thirty cents. It was beautiful. Thirty cents is such a small amount, and I can get nothing with it, but as he gave it up and I took it, it became like thousands because it was given with so much love. God looks, not at the greatness of the work, but at the love with which it is performed.'

The readings today tell similar stories of generosity. Both concern two very poor people – two widows. We wonder how someone who was as poor as the widow in the Gospel was able to perform an act of such spontaneous goodness. One needs to have been faithful over many years to the practice of generosity to have a heart like hers. It is not achieved by a few great deeds but by a lot of little ones.

If you occupy a high station in life, you have a name to keep up. You are conscious of being in the public eye. So when you do a good deed, you may do it to impress others, rather than out of the goodness of your heart. This introduces an element of performance – you are performing for an audience.

To occupy a lowly station in life (like the widow) can be an advantage.

It means you won't get much attention. In that way what you do and give has a better chance of being anonymous. Your deed is more likely to come from the heart.

Even though no one else noticed what the widow had done, Jesus noticed it and praised it. It's nice to know that even such a small deed of love does not escape his attention. How good are we at recognising what others do and affirming them? Sadly, the truth may be that we are so self-absorbed that we don't notice, and don't care.

The widow in the Gospel story gave her all. She let go of every shred of security and committed herself wholly to God. Hence, the story is as much about trust in God as about generosity.

HOMILY 2   **Giving without losing**

On one level the story in the First Reading makes no sense. Indeed, it seems ridiculous and impossible. That is, if we take it in a literal sense. We could, of course, take it in a literal sense – in the sense of a miracle. But it can be taken in another sense. Then it becomes very true, and opens up whole horizons of meaning and application.

The widow was down to the last of her food. All she had left was a handful of meal in a jar and a little oil in a jug. Yet, by sharing what she had with the prophet, it never ran out. The point being made here is: It's possible to give without losing. In fact, to give can be a way of gaining. Not to give can be a sure way of losing what we have.

Take the example of a grain of wheat. If it is left in the barn, it remains just a grain of wheat, which in time will become mouldy and decay, and then there is nothing left at all. But if it is taken out and planted, it will die, but in doing so it is multiplied many times over.

Another example. If you light a candle, you can light a hundred candles from that original candle without it being diminished. It is able to share its light without losing its own.

So there is a sense in which we can share what we have without being impoverished. In fact, we are more likely to be enriched in so doing. Of course, here we are not talking about material things. A teacher loses nothing of his knowledge by sharing it with his pupils. A mother loses nothing of her love by sharing it with her children.

We can share such things as knowledge, love and peace with others without our own supply of these being in any way diminished. Giving liberates the soul of the giver. The giver is as enriched as the recipient. We see this in the case of the widow in the First Reading. When we give cheerfully, and accept gratefully, everyone is blessed.

Brian Keenan, who was held hostage in Lebanon for several years, gives us a further example. He says that if one kept to oneself, one was totally rapt up in oneself, never thinking of one's fellow hostages, or caring about them, or sharing with them ... that was a recipe for disaster. It drove one into oneself, and one became gloomy and self-preoccupied. He says, 'It is through what we give that we survive.'

'Love is like a basket of loaves and fishes: you never have enough until you start to give it away.' (Anon.)

HOMILY 3   **Results aren't everything**

There was a vixen who had three cubs. On one occasion she fell sick, so she had to send the cubs out one night in search of food. She told them to split up and go in different directions. They were not to go southwards because the town lay in that direction.

The first cub was strong but very lazy. He chose the easiest route. He set off eastwards across flat land. He hadn't gone far when he found himself in a field that was stirring with rabbits. He killed one and ate it. Then he caught another and made off home with it.

He was home in half an hour, without as much as a scratch on him. 'Oh, back already?' said the mother. 'And what a fine rabbit you've brought back. Well done!' And she gave him a lick of her tongue on the side of his face.

The second cub was very clever. He headed westwards across rolling fields. Seeing the lights of a farmhouse ahead, he approached it cautiously. He found a hole in the fence which gave access to a house full of geese. There was no guard dog. The cub stole into the house, killed two young geese, and dragged them away. When he was at a safe distance, he ate half of one. The other half he buried, determined to come back next day to finish it.

He was back home in just over an hour with the other goose, having taken care to wash the blood off himself in a stream. 'Well done!' said the mother. 'What a splendid goose you've brought back.' And she gave him two licks of her tongue on the side of his face.

The third cub was weak and somewhat sickly. He had no choice but to go northwards into hilly country. Here farmhouses were few and far between. The ones he found were guarded by vicious dogs. One of the dogs tore his face through the wire. An angry farmer fired a shot at him, narrowly missing him.

The night went by quickly. There was nothing to do but head for home. On the way home he managed to catch a sparrow. Though he was ready to collapse from exhaustion and hunger, he decided to take it home to his mother. He got home at dawn, covered with mud, and cuts, and bruises. On seeing him the mother said, 'What kept you? And look at the state of you!'

'I ran into trouble,' he answered feebly.

'Didn't I warn you to be careful,' snapped the mother. 'And what have you brought back to me after your night of gallivanting?'

With that he produced the sparrow. The other two cubs burst out laughing.

'What's this? A sparrow? Is that all you've brought back? A sparrow!'

'It was the best I could do,' said the little cub.

'Take it away from here and get out of my sight. Obviously I've wasted my time feeding and caring for you.'

With that she chased him out of the den. Then she spread a banquet. The menu consisted of rabbit and goose. She seated the strong cub on her right-hand side, and the clever cub on her left-hand side. But there was no place at the banquet table for the little cub, because in the eyes of the mother results alone mattered.

In one sense the mother was right. Judged by results the little cub had come a long way behind the other two. But in another sense the mother couldn't have been more wrong. Judged by the effort made and the spirit shown, the little cub was way ahead of the other two.

The little cub reminds us of the widow in today's Gospel. We live in a world in which the result is the only thing that matters. Prizes and certificates are given for results, never for effort. But Jesus had a different yardstick, as we see from the story of the poor widow. For him it was not the size of the offering that counted, but the cost of it. In other words, it's not the result that counts, but the effort made and the spirit shown.

With this in mind we could end the story of the foxes thus: The little cub got home at dawn, covered with mud, and cuts, and bruises. Giving the sparrow to his mother he said, 'Sorry, mother, but this is the best I could do.' On seeing the sparrow his two brothers burst out laughing. But the mother wasn't looking at the sparrow but at the little fellow's wounds. 'Well done,' she cried. 'You're a great little cub. I'm proud of you.' Then she hugged him. And having cleaned his wounds with her tongue, she gave him the central place at the banquet.

ANOTHER STORY

In a certain art gallery a small picture was hanging in the hallway, close to the main door. Most visitors passed by with scarcely a glance in its direction, as they hurried on to the paintings which made the museum a mecca for art lovers. The curator of the museum was very disappointed. He thought very highly of the little painting. So he decided to carry out a small experiment.

One night he took the picture and hung it in a crooked manner. And what happened? Next day one out of two visitors stopped to look at it.

The following night the curator decided to take his experiment one step further. He removed the painting altogether, leaving only the empty frame hanging there. And what happened? Everybody without exception stopped before the empty frame. And several went to the curator and asked, 'What happened to the lovely little painting that used to hang there?'

Some people (children, for example) may have to do something desperate to be noticed and to get attention. Others may have to die before they are missed and their contribution is recognised. Everyone comes out of the woodwork to praise them when they are gone. We never appreciate the value of another person's service until we need it ourselves.

Even though no one else noticed what the widow had done, Jesus noticed it and praised it. It's nice to know that even such a small deed of love does not escape his attention. How good are we at recognising what others do and affirming them? Sadly, the truth may be that we are so self-absorbed that we don't notice, and don't care.

PRAYER OF THE FAITHFUL

President: Let us pray that God may help us to imitate the faith and generosity of the widow.

Response: Lord, graciously hear us.

For the leaders of the Church: that they may teach and practise the values of Christ. [Pause] Lord, hear us.

For all those who have charge over others: that they may reward people, not according to results, but according to the effort made. [Pause] Lord, hear us.

For those whose work is hard and unrewarding, and who seldom receive recognition. [Pause] Lord, hear us.

For all gathered here: that we may work to please the Lord rather than to win human rewards. [Pause] Lord, hear us.

For our own special needs. [Longer pause] Lord, hear us.

President: Lord, you have been generous with us. Everything we have is a gift from you. Help us to be generous with others. We ask this through Christ our Lord.

REFLECTION   **Giving**

You give but little when you give of your possessions.
It is when you give of yourself that you truly give.
There are those who give little of the much which they have,
and they give it for recognition,
and their hidden desire makes their gifts unwholesome.
And there are those who have little and give it all.
These are the believers in life and the bounty of life,
and their coffer is never empty.
Through the hands of such as these God speaks,
and from behind their eyes he smiles upon the earth.   *Kahlil Gibran*

Thirty-third Sunday of the Year
MY WORDS WILL REMAIN

INTRODUCTION AND CONFITEOR

Thanks to the writers of the Gospels, the words of the Lord remain with us to this very day. They are with us to teach us, to guide us, to inspire us, to comfort us, and to challenge us. How well do we listen to his words, and how hard do we try to practise them in our lives? [Pause]

Lord Jesus, your words are a lamp for our steps and a light for our path. Lord, have mercy.

You yourself are our portion and our prize. Christ, have mercy.

You alone have the words of eternal life. Lord, have mercy.

HEADINGS FOR READINGS

First Reading (Dan 12:1-3). This is part of a vision of the prophet Daniel about the end of time. It introduces the belief in a resurrection of the dead and in retribution after death.

Second Reading (Heb 10:11-14.18). This reading insists on the superiority of Christ's sacrifice over all the sacrifices of the Old Law.

Gospel (Mk 13:24-32). This talks about the second coming of Christ, the time of which is known only to God.

SCRIPTURE NOTE

The First Reading is part of a vision of the prophet Daniel concerning the end of time. It is remarkable because it contains the earliest statement of belief in the resurrection of the dead, and the first mention in the Bible of 'everlasting life'.

In the Gospel we have part of Mark's Eschatological Discourse (13:1-37). Mark's account is coloured by what has already happened, for example, the persecution of the disciples in synagogues and before governors and kings. He believed that the *parousia* was imminent – a belief common among the early Christians.

The precise time of the end is known only to God. Therefore, the disciples must not allow themselves to be misled by claims or speculations that the end is near but must maintain a constant watchfulness. The purpose of the Lord's glorious coming will not be to execute judgement but to gather his elect.

While we cannot share Mark's view that the end is near, we do share his faith in God's victory in Christ. And, for each of us, the *parousia* will be our meeting with the Son of Man when we pass out of this life into eternal life.

Words that remain

'Heaven and earth will pass away, but my words will never pass away.' Words of Jesus we hear in today's Gospel.

In the course of a lifetime we hear a lot of words, and also speak a lot of words. Though we may forget most of the words we hear, some do remain with us. In fact, certain words burn themselves into our memory, so much so that we will probably remember them to our dying day. Some of these are words that hurt us, and remain to haunt us. Others are words that comfort us, and remain to inspire us.

Words can be very hurtful, and inflict deep and lasting wounds. However, sometimes it's not the words themselves, but the way they are said that does the damage.

A woman recalls: 'When we were young, mother sometimes said very hurtful things to us, mean-spirited, critical, accusatory things. And she would never apologise for them. When we raised the matter years later she excused herself by saying, "But I never meant them." And we were left wondering, Well then, if you didn't mean them, why did you say them?'

But words can remain to inspire us. A nun who studied theology recalls:

'During the course of my theology lectures I heard a lot of things. Most of these I will forget in time. Indeed, I've already forgotten a lot of them. But there is one thing which one professor said that I will never forget. He said: "Love keeps a low profile." I know it sounds a simple thing, but somehow it went straight to my heart, and has stayed there ever since.' Love keeps a low profile.

Words are very important and very powerful. Once uttered, they take on a life of their own, for good or ill. They can bring a blessing or a curse, healing or wounding, life or death. Words can continue to harm us or help us for many years after they have been spoken. Hence, we should be careful how we use words.

When we are very angry, it is better to remain silent. Words spoken is anger can cause deep hurt and make reconciliation very difficult. Choosing life instead of death, a blessing instead of a curse, often starts by choosing to remain silent, or being careful to choose words that open the way to healing. As one person put it: 'Sometimes loving others means keeping quiet and letting them be.'

Jesus says, 'Heaven and earth will pass away, but my words will never pass away.' The words of Jesus remain with us to this very day, comforting us, guiding us, challenging us. They turn our values upside down. Once heard, they can never be forgotten.

But for all that, they will benefit us little unless we act on them. They are like precious seeds. If left in a jar, they remain just so many seeds. But if they are taken out and planted, they produce a rich harvest.

In comparison with faith, there is nothing sure or lasting in the world. Human opinions are rooted in appearances, and change from day to day, but the words of Jesus do not change or pass away. We would do well to build the house of our life on his words.

HOMILY 2   **Handbook for Christians**

Here each Sunday we hear the words of Jesus, words that were written down by the early Christians, and which have been preserved for us over the centuries by the Church. Thus Christ's promise has come true: 'Heaven and earth will pass away, but my words will not pass away.'

The Gospel consists of a series of stories, all of which coalesce to form one great story – the story of Jesus. While we all like to listen to a story, we grow tired if we are told the same story over and over again. When that happens we switch off. The same thing can happen with the Gospel story. It may come across as old, stale, and lifeless.

How can we combat that stale and weary sense of the familiar? We have to try to hear the story afresh, indeed, as for the very first time. The Gospel is the greatest story ever told. And we need to recapture the wonder of it. We need to release the energy contained in it, if we are to experience the power it has to charm, surprise, shock, challenge, and inspire.

We need to hear it in such a way that we are dawn into it, and hear our own stories as we listen to it. When that happens, our stories merge with that of the Gospel, and are illuminated by it.

Everything we need is contained in the Gospels. Here we have the words of Jesus himself. Those who make this book their teacher will never go astray.

It's not enough just to turn to the Gospel in times of misfortune. It's not enough to turn it into an object of veneration (like the Book of Kells). We have to examine our lives against the words of the book. Those words should kindle a fire in our hearts, and others should feel the warmth.

The Gospel contains only those things that are the best and the deepest in life. 'Others are bothered by the part of the Bible they can't understand. I'm bothered by the parts I can understand' (Mark Twain).

There was a saint who, whenever he was faced with a difficult decision would ask himself: What would the Book say? The answer would come back from deep inside him: you must do what is right and best. Thus the Book had an enormous influence on him. It strengthened him in moments of weakness. It inspired him in moments of generosity. It shamed him in moments of cowardice. But through it all he had grasped the essential thing: that the Gospel has to be lived.

The Gospel is the handbook of every Christian. The opinions of human beings are rooted in appearances and change from day to day, but the words of Jesus do not pass away. We would do well to build the house of our life on his words.

HOMILY 3   **The end of the world**

A woman was hurrying home from work. This was her bingo night. Suddenly she spotted this fellow standing on the edge of the pavement holding aloft a placard which read: THE END OF THE WORLD IS NEAR. She went up to him and said, 'You say the end of the world is near.'

'That's right, missus,' he replied.

'But are you sure?'

'Quite sure, missus.'

'And you say it's near.'

'Yes, missus.'

'How near?'

'Oh, very near.'

'Could you be more precise?'

'This very night, missus.'

She paused for a moment to reflect on this. Then in a voice full of anxiety, she asked, 'Tell me, son. Will it be before or after bingo?'

The world in which we live is a very uncertain one. It seems to lurch from one crisis to another. This uncertainty can cause great fear and anxiety. In the midst of this uncertain and changing world we need something solid to rely on. For a Christian that can mean only one thing: faith in God. The psalm of today's Mass puts it like this: 'I keep the Lord ever in my sight: since he is at my right hand, I shall stand firm.' And of course we have the words of Jesus: 'Heaven and earth will pass away, but my words will not pass away.'

This is all we have. But then this is all we need. The assurance that things are in God's hands. That his plan for us and the world will be fulfilled. Christ will reign. God will reign. We will reign with him in everlasting life.

Many people have claimed to know when the end of the world will come. (There is likely to be a rash of such claims as we come to the end of the old millennium and the new one begins.) Some claim a special revelation from God or Mary, and others claim to have calculated it from the Bible. All such claims should be ignored.

Today's Gospel gives us a timely message about the end of the world. Jesus tells us that no one knows when the end will come except the heavenly Father. And with regard to the end – we should be hopeful rather than fearful. God made us for salvation, not for damnation.

Faith gives us the conviction that the world is not heading towards final, irreversible catastrophe. Nor is it headed towards mere ending. It is headed towards fulfilment. By his Easter victory Jesus has triumphed over evil and death. We should worry more about the end of our own individual world at death, which is certain, than about the end of the whole world, which is out of our hands.

PRAYER OF THE FAITHFUL

President: Since the Lord is at our right hand, we shall stand firm. Let us pray for our needs, the needs of the Church and of all the world.

Response: Lord, hear our prayer.

Reader(s): For the Church: that all its members may bear witness with their lives to the truths of the Gospel. [Pause] Let us pray to the Lord.

For those in charge of civil affairs: that the Gospel may inspire them in their work to promote justice and harmony in society. [Pause] Let us pray to the Lord.

For those in pain or distress: that the words of Christ may give them strength and hope. [Pause] Let us pray to the Lord.

For all gathered here: hat in spite of all the ugly things which happen in the world, we may remain hopeful and continue to trust in the goodness of God. [Pause] Let us pray to the Lord.

For our own special needs. [Longer pause] Let us pray to the Lord.

President: Lord, grant that amidst the changes of this uncertain world our hearts may be set on the world where true joys are to be found. We ask this through Christ our Lord.

PRAYER/REFLECTION   **Prayer of trust**

Preserve me God, I take refuge in you.
My happiness lies in you alone.
You are my portion and my cup,
you yourself are my prize
I keep you ever in my sight,
even at night you direct my heart.
With you at my right hand, I shall stand firm.
And so my heart rejoices, my soul is glad.
For you will not leave my soul among the dead,
nor let your beloved know decay.
You will show me the path of life,
the fullness of joy in your presence,
at your right hand happiness for ever.

From Psalm 15

Thirty-fourth Sunday of the Year
CHRIST THE KING

INTRODUCTION AND CONFITEOR

On this great feast we rejoice in calling Christ our King. We owe him an allegiance we would not give to any other power on earth. Our lives are meant to bear witness to his kingdom. What kind of witnesses are we? [Pause]

Lord Jesus, yours is a kingdom of truth and life. Lord, have mercy.

Yours is a kingdom of holiness and grace. Christ, have mercy.

Yours is a kingdom of justice, love and peace. Lord, have mercy.

HEADINGS FOR READINGS

First Reading (Dan 7:13-14). The prophet Daniel foresees the coming of one who will have dominion over all peoples. Christians see this as a reference to Christ, the Universal King.

Second Reading (Rev 1:5-8). Christ will take full possession of his kingdom only at the end of time.

Gospel (Jn 18:33-37). Jesus declares before Pilate that he is indeed a King, but that his kingdom is not like the kingdoms of this world.

SCRIPTURE NOTE

On the last Sunday of the Church's liturgical year, we think of the end and of judgement. The apocalyptic vision from the Book of Daniel sets the tone (First Reading). It talks about the coming of 'a son of man', a title for the future redeemer. It is not clear that Jesus referred to himself as 'Son of Man' in this apocalyptic sense, but the early Christians certainly did.

Basing itself on this same text from Daniel, Revelation looks to Jesus' coming at the end of time, when he will take full possession of his kingdom (Second Reading).

The Gospel, where the Lectionary once again shifts to John, contains a section from the Passion narrative: Jesus is being interrogated by Pilate. The issue here is the nature of Jesus' kingship.

HOMILY 1   **Allegiance to Christ**

We might think that idolatry belongs to primitive peoples and to the past. This is not so. Modern people have their idols too. And how they worship those idols! Money is the most common idol today. But there are others – possessions, pleasure, success, fame, power ... Idolatry leads at best to a superficial life, and at worst to a debased life. But the greatest harm idolatry does is that it causes people to forget the true God.

People can also make idols of themselves. The communist leaders made idols of themselves. One of the features of communism was 'the cult of personalities'. The leaders put themselves on pedestals. Everywhere you turned you saw pictures and statues of them. (We see this in Iraq with Sadam Hussein.) When communism collapsed many of these statues were pulled down and smashed. These monstrosities, these idols, stood for oppression and terror.

At the time when the statues were being toppled, *Time* magazine published a small but touching picture. The picture was taken in the Ukraine. It showed a group of ordinary people gathered in prayer around a simple altar in a public place. Standing on the altar was a small bust of Christ. This little picture said it all. After the idols had been toppled, Christ had been put back in his rightful place. What a contrast between his rule and the rule of the idols. The idols command; Christ invites. The idols rule through fear; Christ rules through love. The idols bring oppression and death; Christ brings freedom and life. No wonder we give him an allegiance, a loyalty, which we would not give to any other person or institution on earth.

The Gospel shows Jesus standing alone and unarmed before Pilate. As governor of a Roman province, Pilate was a powerful man. He had thousands of soldiers to call on. And there was Jesus – not one soldier to call upon. Yet Jesus was incomparably the greater of the two. And, in spite of his vulnerability, he is the one who is in control.

Political power is the capacity to coerce others to do one's will. This capacity resides in a position, such as king or president. It does not reside in the person who occupies the position. Political power is unrelated to goodness or wisdom. Many stupid and evil people have exercised this power.

Spiritual power, on the other hand, resides entirely in the individual, and has nothing to do with the capacity to coerce others. People of great spiritual power may be wealthy and may sometimes occupy positions of leadership, but they are more likely to be poor and lacking in political authority.

We have to distinguish between authority and influence on the one hand, and power and control on the other. Some of the people with greatest moral authority are quite powerless, and the most influential have no need to control those they influence. So it was with Jesus. Pilate had power over people; Jesus had influence on them. Jesus made his presence felt simply by the kind of person he was. There was a quiet authority about everything he said and did.

Christ is the hope of the human race. He shows us who God is, and how we can keep God at the centre of our lives. God is not some remote and uncaring figure. God is our heavenly Father, who is close to us, and to whom we are important and precious.

Christ did not come to establish a political sovereignty, but to bear witness to the truth of God's eternal and universal sovereignty.

HOMILY 2   **Incongruous title?**

Of all the titles we could bestow on Jesus that of 'king' would seem to be one of the most inappropriate. It smacks of the kind of things he rejected. When we think of a king we think of a throne, a crown, a palace, great wealth, power, prestige, a retinue of servants, and of course an army.

When we look at Jesus what do we see? There is no throne, no crown, no palace, no army. We see him walking the dusty roads of Palestine with a little band of disciples. He is surrounded by the poor and the sick, by sinners and outcasts. In short, by the kind of people who in worldly kingdoms are looking in through the gates of the royal palace, if they get even that close.

And yet the title 'king' is appropriate, and stands for something true and real in Jesus. First of all, it stands for his divinity. God is the Lord of all, the King of the universe, the One to whom all owe allegiance, the Ruler and Judge of all.

But even on a human level the title makes sense. He was the greatest source of goodness, light, and hope in a dark world. Jesus had immense moral and spiritual authority by reason of the kind of person he was. His presence could change beyond recognition the lives of those around him. His attitude towards sinners was one of kindness and persuasion rather than condemnation. There is a great person who makes everybody feel small. But the really great person makes everybody feel great. In that sense, Jesus was indeed a King.

We have to distinguish between authority and influence on the one hand, and power and control on the other. Some of the people with greatest moral authority are quite powerless, and the most influential have no need to control those they influence. So it was with Jesus. Pilate had power over people; Jesus had influence on them. Jesus made his presence felt simply by the kind of person he was. There was a quiet authority about everything he said and did.

And he did speak of a kingdom – the Kingdom of Heaven. His Kingdom represents all those things which the world doesn't stand for but which deep down it longs for – all that is right and true, all that is beautiful, just and good. His Kingdom will have come when God's will for us and for creation will be done.

Even though Christ the King doesn't need or want soldiers and tanks, he does need warriors – people who are ready to 'fight' for justice, truth, and peace. There is a battle being waged between the kingdom of darkness and the kingdom of light, the kingdom of lies and the kingdom of truth, the kingdom of evil and the kingdom of good. On which side are we?

HOMILY 3   **When it is the judge who is on trial**

This being the last Sunday of the Church's year, we naturally think of judgement – the Last Judgement and our own individual judgement after death. Today's Gospel then comes as a great surprise, because there the one who is being judged is Jesus himself, the one we call our King.

Sometimes in a court case it can happen that it is not so much the accused who is on trial but the judge. Indeed, sometimes it is the very concept of justice itself that is on trial.

Take the case of Louise Woodward, the 19-year-old English au pair whom a jury in Massachusetts convicted in 1998 of killing an eight-month-old baby, Matthew Eappen, who died in her care. But many people who followed the trial were convinced that a miscarriage of justice had taken place. In view of conflicting medical evidence, it was hard to see how the jury could have found, beyond reasonable doubt, that she had killed the baby. Her defence team appealed against the verdict.

At the start of the case, Louise was the one who was on trial. But now the focus shifted onto the judge, Hiller Zobel, who was reviewing the verdict. As we waited for his ruling, questions were raised as to his character. It was said that he was a very independent-minded man. A man not swayed by popular opinion, or one who bowed to pressure. The verdict he reached would show if those claims were true. Now it was Judge Zobel who was on trial.

After careful deliberation Zobel changed the jury's verdict of second-degree murder to involuntary manslaughter. Yes, a child was dead, and Louise bore some blame for his death. But she was not a murderer. And since she had already served seventeen months in prison, he set her free. In the eyes of most neutral observers, his verdict was a fair one. Judge Zobel emerged from the trial with an enhanced reputation. He was shown to be a man who was passionately concerned about justice.

Picture the scene in today's Gospel. Alone and unarmed Jesus stands before Pilate on trial for his life. He has been accused by the Jews of stirring up trouble among the people, and of telling them that it was wrong to pay taxes to Caesar.

However, Pilate soon saw that Jesus was innocent of the charges. He even declared him innocent before the religious leaders. But the religious leaders began to exert political pressure on him. They threatened to report him to Rome for letting someone they claimed was an enemy of Caesar, go free.

Now the focus shifted from Jesus to Pilate. Pilate was now the one on trial. Would he see that justice was done? Jesus made it easy for him by assuring him that his kingdom was no threat to Caesar. Pilate did struggle with it. But then he began to compromise. He tried to appease Jesus' accusers – first by having Jesus scourged, and then by releasing Barabbas. When this didn't satisfy them, he bowed to pressure and handed Jesus over to them.

Pilate knew what he had done. He called for water and washed his hands in the vain hope of cleansing himself of the stain of innocent blood. In the end, he is the one who stands condemned. With a click of his fingers he could have set Jesus free. Yet out of fear for his own position, he allowed the most innocent person ever to walk this earth to go to his death. His cowardice contrasts with the quiet courage of Jesus.

Today political leaders are frequently subjected to similar pressures. Pressure groups get on to them, threatening to put them out of office unless they get their way. At one time or another, all of us come under pressure. All of us find ourselves on trial.

By the way we live, especially by our attitude to truth and justice, we declare whether we are on the side of Christ and his kingdom, or whether like Pilate we take the way of evasion and cowardice. It is not possible to remain neutral.

Who judged Pilate? He judged himself. We too judge ourselves. Don't wait for the Last Judgement. It is happening now. It takes place every day, in little ways. Long before the end, people will already have judged themselves. In a thousand ways they will have already chosen for or against themselves, for or against their brothers and sisters, for or against the truth. God's judgement will not accomplish something new. It will merely show up what already is.

Let us never forget, however, that the Father's love and mercy are at the heart of the Kingdom. Jesus didn't tell us to fear the last day, only to be ready for it.

What a joy it is to belong to Christ and his kingdom. To let our lives be ruled by his spirit, and in our own small way to work for the spread of his kingdom – a kingdom of truth and life, holiness and grace, justice, love and peace.

PRAYER OF THE FAITHFUL

President: God is king over all the earth. Let us pray for the coming of the kingdom as Jesus taught us.

Response: Thy kingdom come.

Reader(s): For all Christians: that they may grow in the knowledge and love of Christ the King. [Pause] Let us pray to the Lord.

For world leaders: that they may work for a more just and a more human world. [Pause] Let us pray to the Lord.

For those who worship idols: that they may come to know, love and serve the one true God. [Pause] Let us pray to the Lord.

For unbelievers: that the light of faith may shine on them. [Pause] Let us pray to the Lord.

For all those who are suffering persecution in the cause of justice, or because of their allegiance to Christ. [Pause] Let us pray to the Lord.

For all gathered here: that we may give Christ the central place in our hearts and in our lives. [Pause] Let us pray to the Lord.

For our own special needs. [Longer pause] Let us pray to the Lord.

President: God of power and love, help us to be loyal and true followers of Christ on earth, so that we may share his glory in the kingdom of heaven, where he lives and reigns with you and the Holy Spirit, one God. for ever and ever.

REFLECTION   **The kingdom of Jesus**

Jesus said, 'My kingdom is not of this world.'
Jesus does not rule as earthly kings rule.
He has no palace, no throne, no crown, no army.
Yet we give him an allegiance and a loyalty,
which we would not give to any other person
or institution on earth.
Alone and unarmed he stood before Pilate.
Pilate, had thousands of soldiers to call upon.
Jesus had no soldier to call upon.
Yet Jesus was incomparably the greater of the two.
Jesus is the hope of the human race.
He rules, not by force, but by love.
Lord Jesus, may your kingdom come,
and may you remember me on that day.

SOLEMNITIES

'Madonna of the Magnificat'

ALBERT CARPENTIER, O.P.

Saint Patrick's Day

17 MARCH

In celebrating the feast of St Patrick we think of the great gift he brought us – the gift of faith. We know we don't live the faith as generously as we should. In all his doubts and difficulties Patrick turned to God for help. Let us turn to God now, confident that St Patrick is interceding for us in heaven.

Lord, you make us strong in faith. Lord, have mercy.
You make us joyful in hope. Christ, have mercy.
You make us untiring in love. Lord, have mercy.

HEADINGS FOR READINGS

First Reading (Jer 1:4-9). This tells of the call of the prophet Jeremiah. Patrick had a lot in common with Jeremiah.

Second Reading (Acts 13:46-49). Paul decides to preach the Gospel to the Gentiles who receive it with enthusiasm. Patrick's preaching to the Irish met with a similar reception.

Gospel (Lk 10:1-12.17-20). The sending out of missionaries to preach the Gospel has its origin in Christ's sending out of his disciples to preach the Gospel to their contemporaries.

HOMILY   **Patrick: a model Christian**

There is something very moving about the story of Patrick. He was born into a comfortable Christian family in Britain. But just before his sixteenth birthday he was snatched from his comfortable home by Irish raiders, and ended up minding sheep in the west of Ireland. It was something that might have destroyed him. Instead, through the providence of God, great good came from it for Patrick himself and for many others.

Strange as it may seem, faith can thrive in adversity. It resembles certain wild flowers: put them in a garden and they go to seed; put them on a mountainside and they bloom. Suffering can bring us closer to God, because we may only have God to rely on. Strange things happen when you have nothing to rely on except God's help.

This was certainly true in Patrick's case. In his *Confession* he tells us that when he was a boy at home God had seemed very far away. He even goes so far as to say: 'I did not know the true God.' But now that he was away from home and feeling the pain of loneliness, God became a faithful friend to him. He discovered the joy of believing, the rapture of faith in God. Daily prayer became as important to him as daily bread.

After six years, he escaped from Ireland. And after many wanderings and adventures he finally returned home. His relatives gave him a warm welcome and begged him never to leave them again. The experience of slavery left no obvious scars on him. This school of hardship and suffering didn't embitter him. In fact, it completely changed his outlook on life. On looking back, he realised that he had gained far more than he had lost during his years of slavery. In this way God had been preparing him for his future mission to the Irish.

He might have settled down to a comfortable life once more and forgotten the people who had imprisoned him. Instead, he heard those same people calling him to come and walk among them again. And, as we know, he did go back, as a bishop. And he tells us that he went back 'to share with them the gift God gave me in the land of my captivity' – the gift of the Christian faith.

Patrick is a saint whose life story will always be relevant. He was a humble man, with a friendly personality and a great capacity to forgive. There was no selfishness in him. Instead, there was a great generosity. He showed great courage and strength in the face of all kinds of trials and hardships. He had no interest in money and material possessions, but had a great love for people. His faithfulness to his vocation is an inspiration.

Patrick was a model Christian. His lifestyle, as well as his personal integrity, lent credence to his words. He was a living example of the Gospel he preached. People came to admire his goodness. Little wonder that he made so many converts.

The faith as preached by Patrick was a positive, life-giving faith. It banished many fears. It brought something new and hopeful into people's lives. It gave people a vision. A life without vision is like a night without stars. But it wasn't an easy faith. It was a challenging faith that inspired sacrifice and service in those who embraced it.

Patrick was driven by a desire to share his faith with others. This obviously rubbed off on his converts, because a missionary outreach has been a characteristic of Irish Christianity ever since. Christianity is never something to be kept to oneself. It always involves an outreach to others. Without that dimension it would not be Christianity.

Now that Ireland is enjoying great material prosperity, we are in danger of abandoning the gift of faith Patrick brought to us at such great personal cost. We must pray and strive to ensure that this doesn't happen. Because without faith, there is no reason for anything and nothing is in its proper place.

PRAYER OF THE FAITHFUL

President: God showed his love for us by sending his servant Patrick to bring the faith to us. Let us pray that we may be worthy of the gift that he has given us.

Response: Lord, hear our prayer.

Reader(s): For our religious leaders: that God may grant them courage and compassion in carrying out their ministry. [Pause] Let us pray to the Lord.

For our political and civil leaders: that under God's guidance they may speak wisely and act justly. [Pause] Let us pray to the Lord.

For our exiles, scattered all over the world: that they may remain firm in the faith. [Pause] Let us pray to the Lord.

For our young people: that the faith may take root in their hearts and bear fruit in their lives. [Pause] Let us pray to the Lord.

For all of us: that our sufferings may teach us to show compassion to other sufferers. [Pause] Let us pray to the Lord.

For all our dead, and all those who have gone before us marked with the sign of faith. [Pause] Let us pray to the Lord.

For our own special needs. [Pause] Let us pray to the Lord.

President: Lord, through the instrumentality of St Patrick you planted the seed of faith in our hearts. Nurture this seed with your grace, so that we may produce the fruits of justice and peace in the world. We ask this through Christ our Lord.

PRAYER/REFLECTION   **A Celtic prayer**

God's strength to pilot me,
God's might to uphold me,
God's wisdom to teach me,
God's light to guide me,
God's eyes to look before me,
God's ear to hear me,
God's hand to guard me,
God's love to warm me,
God's way to lie before me,
God's shield to protect me,
God's host to save me –
from the snares of the devil,
from temptations,
from all who wish me ill.
Amen.

The Assumption of the Blessed Virgin Mary
15 AUGUST

INTRODUCTION AND CONFITEOR

Mary's Assumption into heaven means that she shares in her Son's victory over death, and enjoys the fullness of eternal glory. During her earthly life, Mary was a humble person, who sought to do the will of God at all times. In this way she shows us the way we must go in order to share her glory. [Pause]

We turn to God who, as Mary said, is rich in love and mercy.

Lord, your mercy reaches from age to age for those who revere you. Lord, have mercy.

You fill the hungry with good things. Christ, have mercy.

You raise up the powerless who trust in you. Lord, have mercy.

HEADINGS AND READINGS

Vigil Mass

First Reading (1 Chron 15:3-4.15-16; 16:1-2). This shows the reverence with which the Ark of the Old Testament was regarded. Mary is seen as the ark of the New Covenant.

Second Reading (1 Cor 15:54-57). This celebrates Christ's victory over death, a victory in which Mary shares fully.

Gospell(Lk 11:27-28). Mary is blessed not only because she is the mother of Jesus, but because she heard the word of God and obeyed it.

Day Mass

First Reading (Rev 11:19; 12:1-6.10). This describes the battle between God and evil, with the ultimate triumph of God.

Second Reading (1 Cor 15:20-26). Christ is the new Adam who undoes all the harm done by the old Adam. (The Church sees Mary as the new Eve who by her obedience to God undoes the harm done by the old Eve.)

Gospel (Lk 1:39-56). This tells of Mary's visitation to Elizabeth, and contains her hymn of praise to God for his goodness to her and to his chosen people.

SCRIPTURE NOTE

This note refers only to the difficult First Reading of the Day Mass.

The Book of Revelation describes the ultimate battle between God and evil, represented here by the dragon (the serpent of Genesis). The woman represents the Church, and the child represents Christ (the Messiah). Like the woman in the vision, the Church was undergoing suffering and persecution at the time of the writing of the vision.

The dragon confronts the woman to devour her child. But the child is taken up to God – a reference to the ascension of Jesus. Jesus defeated the dragon and was exalted to God's right hand. The woman (the Church) flees to the desert to escape the persecution. There she is nourished by God, just as were the Israelites of old. The final verse praises the triumph of God and Christ.

The reading was meant to encourage the early Christians by assuring them that God would finally triumph. It should do the same for us. Even though the figure of the woman in the first place represents the Church, it can also be seen as representing Mary. As the mother of Jesus, she was at the heart of the battle between God and the powers of evil. Therefore, it is entirely fitting that (through her Assumption) she should share in the spoils of victory.

HOMILY 1   **Redeemed body and soul**

Sometimes the body is referred to as a shell, which is cast off at death, having served its purpose. At death the soul is freed from the body and floats away to its natural home, so that death can be regarded as a natural good.

But this is not Christianity. Firstly, such thinking diminishes the importance and significance of the body. Indeed, it amounts to contempt for the body. And secondly, it downplays death. Death is an enormous reality. When a person dies, it seems that not only the body, but the whole person has perished.

For Christians, eternal life is not merely the survival of a disembodied spirit. It must include the salvation of a person, not a disembodied spirit. The body in some way that we do not understand will also participate in eternal life.

It is fundamental to the Christian tradition that the soul and body go together. God has made us body and soul, and the soul and body belong naturally together, and therefore death is a disaster for us. Our salvation lies in the resurrection of the whole person, body and soul.

For the Church the human person is a unity of body and soul. The Church understands the resurrection from the dead as referring to the whole person. It stresses the reality of a true and integrated human life beyond the grave, not merely a partial existence. But there is no attempt to describe the nature of the risen state. The resurrection-body is very different from the human body that we know. It belongs to a new order. All we can say is that our risen bodies will be like the risen body of Jesus.

The feast of Mary's Assumption says that there is one human being who already is fully and completely redeemed, saved body and soul. That person is Mary, the mother of Jesus. Since she gave birth to him, and was intimately involved in the work of salvation, it is only right that she should share the full fruits of his victory over death.

The Assumption means that after her physical death, Mary's body was not allowed to remain on earth to corrupt, but was caused by God to come into its transfigured and glorified state. Mary has passed beyond death, and the glory she now shares is the same glory we hope to enjoy also.

By declaring that Mary was assumed 'body and soul' into heaven, the Church is declaring that the whole person will be saved, and affirms the goodness of all material reality. The bodily glorification of Mary is the anticipation of the glorification that is the destiny of all. We can look at her now in glory and say, 'That is how we will be one day.'

HOMILY 2   **Sharing his glory**

When things go wrong there is a tendency to blame one's parents. Psychologists trace everything back to childhood. Therefore, when things go right, we should give credit to our parents.

There was a poor boy who grew up in Los Angeles. As a teenager he became interested in boxing, and soon showed that he had exceptional talent. Were it not for this he probably would have drifted into crime like so many of his companions. The most significant person in his life was his mother. She encouraged him and went to all his fights.

He was selected to box for America in the Barcelona Olympics of 1992. He was thrilled but unfortunately his mother wasn't there to see him represent his country. She died a short time before the Games began. This greatly saddened him, but at the same time made him all the more determined to win the gold medal for her sake.

He did. And in his moment of triumph he didn't forget his mother. The very first thing he did, after the verdict was announced, was to get down on his knees right there in the ring, before the television cameras of the world, and say a prayer. Looking up to heaven he said, 'Ma, this is for you. I owe it to you.' As she had been at the centre of his struggle from the beginning, he now wanted her to share in his glory.

Mary was with Jesus from the very beginning, and stayed with him right to the end. She was beside him in all the joyful and sorrowful moments of his life. She brought him into the world in a stable. When he was but a new-born baby she took him into Egypt to save him from Herod's killers. She brought him back to Nazareth and took care of him as he grew up. She sought him in sorrow when he was lost in the temple. During his public ministry she sometimes feared for his safety and sanity. And she accompanied him all the way to Calvary, staying with him until he died.

Therefore, it is right and fitting that she should share his risen glory.

That is what we are celebrating on this feast – a mother sharing in the triumph of her son.

And it gives us great encouragement. After all, Mary was just a human being. What she has attained, all of us are meant to attain. We can look at her now in glory and say, 'That is how we will be one day.' As our spiritual mother, she wants nothing less for us. Just because she is in heaven doesn't mean that she can't help us. It is precisely because of where she is now, with God, that she can best help us.

HOMILY 3   **Mary's journey of faith**

This is a story about a drop of water called Daisy. Daisy started life as a snowflake on top of a high mountain. She lay there, pure and white, in the freezing cold until the sun came along and melted her. Then she began to move down the mountain. She joined up with a host of other drops to form a small but fast-flowing stream.

Like all the other drops, Daisy was weak and insignificant. Yet she was different. She had a greater consciousness of her dependence on the mysterious 'outside power' that was pulling them all to the ocean, and was more prompt in responding to it than any of the others. One day part of her broke off and formed a new droplet. Thus it was that her son was born. She called him Lux, because there was a brightness about him.

At first life was exciting for her and her son because it was full of movement. But at times it was frightening, like when they were bounced off rocks along the route. Finally they reached the bottom of the mountain, and the now greatly swollen stream slowed down. Life became so peaceful that at times they seemed to be going nowhere. Still, it was nice to lie in shallow pools and bask in the sunshine.

The stream merged with other streams and became a river. It was at this stage that Lux left her. He told her that he had work to do, and went on ahead of her. She was sorry to see him go but knew that this was the way things were meant to be. The pools got larger and deeper. She knew moments of anxiety and depression as she lay for days at the bottom of deep and dark pools, where only a glimmer of light filtered through.

But everywhere she went she discovered that Lux had been there before her. It was also becoming clear to her that through him a new element had been introduced into the river. He had given new direction, meaning, and hope to all seekers of the ocean. He had blazed a trail for them to follow.

In her heart she heard his gentle voice calling her to trust, to hope, and to follow. The worst danger she encountered came from the various pollutants that were dumped into the river. But once again she drew strength from knowing that Lux had also encountered these dangers, and had successfully negotiated them.

At last a vast expanse of water opened up ahead of her. The pull was now irresistible. At the sight of the broad ocean a new sense of excitement gripped her. It was marvellous to be part of something so great. Thus it was that she reached the ocean. But this is not the end of her story.

One day as she lay on the surface of the ocean under a bright sun she began to vaporise, and was slowly lifted up into the air, above the tops of the highest mountains, right up into the clouds in fact. It was an incredible feeling. As she looked down from her lofty perch on the meandering and often rocky course she had travelled, a glow of satisfaction came over her. Then out of the cloud she heard a familiar voice calling to her, saying: 'Welcome home, mother!' It was her son Lux. Now her joy was complete.

Daisy stands for Mary, and Lux for Jesus. During her life on earth there were times when Mary's life went along joyfully and peacefully. Yet she was spared none of the trials of life. At all times she sought to do the will of God. It was through her obedience that Jesus our Saviour came into the world.

On this day the Church celebrates the fact that the humble Mary was assumed into heaven to share in the victory her Son won over sin and death.

Each one of us has to make the same journey from mountain top to ocean and, we hope, beyond. We are straining towards the glorious state Mary has arrived at. Mary will watch over us at every turn in our journey.

PRAYER OF THE FAITHFUL

President: Let us pray to God who comes to the help of his people, and who never forgets his promises.

Response: Lord, hear our prayer.

Reader(s): For all Christians: that they may hear the gentle voice of Jesus calling them to trust, to hope, and to follow him. [Pause] Let us pray to the Lord.

For the world: that all peoples may see heaven as their final goal, and come to share in God's glory. [Pause] Let us pray to the Lord.

For those who can't find any meaning in life. [Pause] Let us pray to the Lord.

For all those whose lives are hard and hidden. [Pause] Let us pray to the Lord.

For all gathered here: that we may be thankful to God when life is joyful, and seek his help when it is difficult. [Pause] Let us pray to the Lord.

For our own special needs. [Longer pause] Let us pray to the Lord.

President: Almighty and ever-living God, as we journey towards the goal of your kingdom, may we experience the protection of Mary the

Mother of your Son. We ask this through the same Christ our Lord.

REFLECTION   **The stream of life**

Life could be compared to a stream.
In its journey to the sea
a stream cannot always advance by the shortest route,
but has to twist and turn,
and pause a while here and there,
without ever coming to a complete stop.
And yet in spite of all this dallying,
in spite of all these detours,
how quickly life's stream runs down to the sea.
Lord, may your gentle hand guide us,
so that in spite of doubts, difficulties and dangers,
we may keep the stream of our lives
flowing towards your kingdom.

All Saints

1 NOVEMBER

INTRODUCTION AND CONFITEOR

Today, the feast of All Saints, we concentrate on those who became saints in ordinary and hidden ways, and who will never be canonised. Let us pause to remember one genuinely holy person we have known. [Pause]

It is Christ who calls us to holiness, and who helps us to attain it.

Lord Jesus, you call us to holiness by helping us to be witnesses to truth. Lord, have mercy.

You call us to holiness by helping us to be witnesses to justice. Christ, have mercy.

You call us to holiness by helping us to be witnesses to love. Lord, have mercy.

HEADINGS FOR READINGS

First Reading (Rev 7:2-4.9-14). Here we have a vision of the victorious followers of Christ rejoicing in his presence in the heavenly Kingdom.

Second Reading (1 Jn 3:1-3). In his love for us, God has made us his children, and destined us one day to see him as he is. We should live a life that is consistent with this great hope.

Gospel (Mt 5:1-12). Here Jesus talks about the qualities he wishes to see in his disciples, qualities that are exemplified in the lives of the saints.

HOMILY 1   **The beatitudes**

In the Beatitudes we see the qualities Jesus wishes to see in his disciples, qualities that are exemplified in the lives of the saints.

A mere glance shows that they are a complete reversal of conventional standards and values.

The world says, 'Blessed are the rich, because they can have anything they want.' But Jesus says, 'Blessed are the poor in spirit.' By 'poor in spirit' he means those who put their trust in God rather than in money; those who realise that it is not the amount of money they possess that makes them rich but the kind of people they are.

The world says, 'Blessed are those who live it up.' But Jesus says, 'Blessed are those who mourn.' It is only those who love who are capable of true mourning. To open one's heart to other people is to share their burdens and sorrows. But to open one's heart is to begin to live.

The world says, 'Blessed are the strong and the tough.' But Jesus says, 'Blessed are the gentle.' Gentleness is not a form of weakness as many think. It is a form of great strength. There are many vital tasks which only gentleness can accomplish.

The world says, 'Blessed are those who hunger for power, status, and fame.' But Jesus says, 'Blessed are those who hunger for what is right.' To live rightly is what life is about. Those who rate this as important as eating and drinking will taste real happiness even here on earth.

The world says, 'Blessed are those who show no mercy and who take no prisoners.' But Jesus says, 'Blessed are the merciful.' Happy those who make allowance for the sins of others, and whose greatness lies in their ability to forgive. They will receive God's mercy for their own sins.

The world says, 'Happy those who have clean fingernails, clean teeth, and clean skins.' But Jesus says, 'Blessed are those who have clean hearts.' It is from the heart that all our thoughts, words, and deeds flow. If the heart is clean, then all that flows from it will be clean – like water flowing from an unpolluted spring.

The world says, 'Blessed are the troublemakers and war-mongers.' But Jesus says, 'Blessed are the peacemakers.' Happy those who spread understanding among people, those who welcome the stranger, and who work for a more just society. They are true children of God.

The world says, 'Blessed are those who lie and cheat and who get away with it.' But Jesus says, 'Blessed are those who make a stand for what is right.' If they suffer for their stand, the wounds they bear will be honourable wounds.

The beatitudes are the marks of a true disciple of Jesus. They are the standards by which we measure holiness. The things the beatitudes stand for are very beautiful and very precious – things such as peace, goodness, joy, love, gentleness, compassion, mercy, integrity … The beatitudes are not so much about holiness as about goodness. But there is no holiness without goodness. In fact, goodness is holiness.

A person who lives according to the beatitudes is already living in the kingdom of heaven.

HOMILY 2   **True heroes**

Nowadays we are in danger of being drowned in bad news. The newspapers and television seem to carry little else but stories of bad things that happen – murders, robberies, wars, and so on. Many find it all very depressing. It draws attention to the very worst aspects of human nature.

An evil act may cause momentary surprise or shock. But in the end evil leaves us cold, and evil people are dull. Goodness, on the other hand, inspires us. And so it is that the saints are the most interesting people of all. The saints leave a trail of light behind them.

Some time ago a woman in Cork found £4,300 in a handbag lying on the roadside, and drove to the nearest police station. When she arrived there, the son of the owner was at the desk reporting the loss. The woman was soon dubbed Ireland's woman of the year at a time when dishonesty and scams are the name of the game.

The woman to whom the handbag belonged said, 'Happiness for me is finding a passer-by with a heart and a conscience.' And the policeman on duty at the desk said, 'It restored my faith in humanity.'

All through the year the Church puts before us a series of inspiring stories – the lives of the saints. These stories show us what human beings, aided by the grace of God, have managed to accomplish – deeds of heroism, greatness of heart, and nobility of spirit. They are a celebration of human goodness. People have been inspired, motivated, energised much more by reading biographies and lives of the saints than by reading books of theology. The day Mother Teresa died a man said, 'Today I am proud to be a human being because Mother Teresa was one.'

Besides the canonised saints, there are legions of anonymous saints. The Church keeps this feast to recognise these and to celebrate their goodness. And so today we honour and rejoice in the little people, the forgotten heroes and heroines, people who in their own humble ways have followed Christ. The lives of many people are littered with great sacrifices and acts of quiet heroism.

There are on earth those whose integrity, kindness, and generosity make up for the greed and selfishness of others. Their example gives encouragement to those who are struggling, courage to those who are fearful, and comfort to those who are suffering.

Even the little saints cause the vision of a higher and a purer life to rise up before us. They inspire us to try to win back our finer, kinder and healthier selves. They provide us with a mirror. Looking at them, we see human beings at their brightest and best. The road to holiness demands courage and stamina, but for those who know where to look it is full of footprints.

> Lives of great men all remind us
> We can make our lives sublime,
> And, departing, leave behind us
> Footprints on the sands of time;
> Footprints, that perhaps another,
> Sailing o'er life's solemn main,
> A forlorn and shipwrecked brother,
> Seeing, shall take heart again.

Henry W. Longfellow

HOMILY 3   **Witnesses to love**

The saints were people who dared to live a Christian life. Their lives are an encouragement and inspiration to us. However, it's very easy to get devotion to the saints wrong. There is a tendency to turn them into objects of superstition and sterile cult. In which case devotion to them becomes more of a hindrance than a help.

Some people think that all they have to do is get a rub of a relic for the holiness of a saint to be transferred to them. It's not that easy. The saints serve as models for us in our following of Christ. They do not provide us with short-cuts and ways of evading the hard slog and the narrow road. We must not expect them to do for us what we could do for ourselves.

There is a story about a man called Peter who prided himself on having a great devotion to St Francis of Assisi. Now Peter was very friendly with a carpenter and his family. The carpenter's wife had a crippled brother who lived with them. One Sunday afternoon Peter went for a walk with the carpenter and his wife. The crippled brother said he was happy to remain behind by himself provided he had a book and a glass of water beside him. Having provided him with these, they left him, locking the door behind them.

They had a very enjoyable walk, basking in the warm autumn sunshine. As dusk fell they went to a restaurant for supper. But as he was eating Peter began to feel uneasy at the thought of the cripple sitting alone in a darkening house. If a fire were to break out he would perish.

Suddenly he thought of St Francis, and reflected: 'What's the use of studying the life of the saint, and following his footsteps in far-off Assisi, if I leave a cripple alone in a dark house, while I have it in my power to help him?'

So he abruptly rose from table, left the wine and the food there, and ran back to the house to be with the crippled man. He said later, 'I felt an invisible hand press against my heart, and was filled with such pain and shame that I began to tremble. I knew that St Francis was giving me a message.'

Here we have a fine example of what the saints are supposed to mean to us. They challenge us, perhaps even shame us into living a Christian life. The Church sets them up as models precisely because they imitated Christ. They are reminders to us of what life is about. They inspire us, guide us, and intercede for us. They are examples, teachers, friends, and advocates. But they can't do anything in our stead. Of what use would it be to boast about having a great devotion to some particular saint if that devotion had no effect on our lives?

Piety is no substitute for goodness. Perhaps there can be goodness without holiness. But I'm quite sure that there is no holiness without goodness. All of us have the capacity for goodness. In the final analysis, love is what it's all about. A loving person is a holy person. To be a saint is to be a witness to love. There is no higher vocation than this. St John of the Cross said, 'In the evening of our lives we will be examined on love.'

PRAYER OF THE FAITHFUL

President: Confident in our communion with all the saints, let us bring our needs before God, who calls us to a live a life worthy of our dignity as his children.

Response: Lord, hear us in your love.

Reader(s): For Christians: that they may strive to imitate the saints in their greatness of heart and nobility of spirit. [Pause] We pray in faith.

For all people of goodwill: that they may persevere in the path of goodness, for that is the path of holiness. [Pause] We pray in faith.

For all those who are weighed down by troubles and disappointments: that the example of the saints may give them courage and hope. [Pause] We pray in faith.

For all gathered here: that we may live our lives in such a way that we become an example for others. [Pause] We pray in faith.

For our own special needs. [Longer pause] We pray in faith.

President: Lord, you have given us many friends in heaven. Their example inspires us and their prayers help us. In your goodness, give us fellowship with them and unending joy in your kingdom. We make all our prayers through Christ our Lord.

REFLECTION   **Only one life**

Remember that you have only one soul;
that you have only one death to die;
that you have only one life to live,

which is short and has to be lived by you alone;
and that there is only one glory, which is eternal.
If you do this, there will be many things
about which you care nothing.

St Teresa of Avila

The Immaculate Conception
8 DECEMBER

INTRODUCTION AND CONFITEOR

In celebrating the feast of the Immaculate Conception, we are celebrating the radical holiness of Mary. She never belonged to the kingdom of Satan. From the first moment of her existence she belonged to the kingdom of God. We too are called to belong to the kingdom. We can count on Mary's help in our struggle against evil. [Pause]

Lord Jesus, your kingdom is a kingdom of truth and life. Lord, have mercy.

Your kingdom is a kingdom of holiness and grace. Christ, have mercy.

Your kingdom is a kingdom of justice, love and peace. Lord, have mercy.

HEADINGS FOR READINGS

First Reading (Gen 3:9-15.20). This deals with the origin and consequences of sin, and with God's promise of salvation.

Second Reading (Eph 1:3-6.11-12). Through Christ, God has adopted us as his children, and called us to holiness.

Gospel (Lk 1:26-38). In the story of the Annunciation, we see Mary's obedience to God, which opens the way for the coming of the Saviour.

SCRIPTURE NOTE

The First Reading tells the story of the origin and consequences of sin. Sin is essentially disobedience to God. The reading ends with God's promise of salvation. As we know, Mary had a major role to play in that salvation. That is why this reading is chosen for today's feast.

The Second Reading is a hymn of praise to God for the blessings he has given us in Christ. God has chosen us to live in holiness. Today we are celebrating the radical holiness of Mary.

In the story of the Annunciation (Gospel), we see how Mary cancels the disobedience of Eve – 'Let it be done to me according to your word' – thus opening the way for the coming of the Saviour. For us holiness consists in doing the word of God, just as it did for Mary.

HOMILY 1   **Twenty-four carat gold**

What makes gold so valuable? A number of things. There is its brilliant yellow colour. Thin sheets of pure gold are translucent. Then there is the fact that, when pure, it is the most malleable of all metals. However, traces of other metals reduce its malleability. Again pure gold is an ideal conductor of electricity. But once again traces of impurities affect this. Gold is rid of impurities by being put through a refinery. Pure gold is said to be 24 carat.

One day a young shepherd came into town with a large lump of yellow ore. Though its surface had traces of earth on it, when the experts cleaned and examined it they were flabbergasted. 'This is impossible!' they said. 'Everything on this earth is impure and contaminated in some way.'

'Do you mean it's pure gold?' asked the shepherd.

'Yes. We can't find a trace of impurity in it. It's 24 carat. Just look at the way it shines.'

And they showed him how to look at it, and he marvelled at what he saw. 'Where did you find it?' they asked him.

'I stumbled across it up in the mountains,' he replied.

'We can do anything we want with this,' they said. 'It has absolutely no need to be put through the refinery. If all ore was like this we'd be out of business.'

When we say that Mary was conceived without original sin, in a manner of speaking, we are saying that she was pure gold. Though made of the stuff of this earth, she had no impurities in her. From the beginning of her life she belonged totally to the kingdom of God. And all this she owed to a special act of God. In order that she might be a worthy mother for his Son, God allowed her to enjoy in advance the benefits of Christ's redemption.

This does not mean that Mary's life was sunshine all the way. If anything, the opposite is nearer the truth. Her sinlessness made her more vulnerable. But, like pure gold, she was more pliable in the hands of God. She did not resist what his grace wanted to do in her and through her. And just as pure gold is an excellent conductor of electricity, Mary was an excellent conductor of God's light and love.

Since we come from the hand of God, we too have gold in us. But it is not yet of the 24 carat variety. We have impurities mixed in with it that dim its lustre, and which make it more resistant to the hands of the Craftsman, and a more imperfect conductor of his light and love.

But Christ has made it possible for us to refine the gold in us. This process was begun at our Baptism, and will go on right throughout our lives. It will entail pain, sacrifice, and struggle. But Mary our Mother will help us. In her we see what we are called to be.

HOMILY 2   **Mary's Yes**

The idea of a call runs counter to today's culture. We're taught to keep our options open. A commitment puts an end to that. In this kind of climate it's not easy to allow oneself to be chosen.

The tendency today is to seek fulfilment and happiness through 'doing one's own thing'. It's what *I* want that matters. It is, of course, good and necessary to find and do that which deep down we feel we are called to do. Nevertheless, there can be a lot of selfishness in the 'do you own thing' approach. It often means taking the easiest path in the belief that this is where freedom and happiness lie.

But this is not necessarily the case. In fact, following one's own inclinations and desires is more likely to lead to slavery and unhappiness. Paradoxically, happiness and fulfilment are to be found not in freedom, but in the willing acceptance of duty. But it has to be a duty, not grimly accepted, but willingly accepted. The more difficult the task to which we devote ourselves out of love, the more it will exalt us.

Left to ourselves we tend to follow the line of least resistance. Hence, we need someone to challenge us, someone who has our best interests at heart, and who will not let us settle for anything less than the best that we are capable of.

Here Mary is a great example to us. When the angel asked her to become the mother of Jesus, she didn't say, 'Sorry, but I have my own plans. I want to do my own thing.' She said, 'I am the handmaid of the Lord, let what you have said be done to me.' In effect what she was saying was: 'It's not what I want, but what God wants, that matters.'

Mary made a total gift of herself to God, and accepted the task he gave her. Even though she didn't understand all the implications of it, she trusted that God would give her all the help she needed.

Life imposes a lot of duties on us. Where would the world be if everyone just thought of themselves, and insisted on seeking their own happiness and fulfilment independent of others and of God?

Those who accept duty as Mary did, will find happiness and fulfilment, maybe not in the eyes of the world, but certainly in eyes of God, and deep down they will know it.

Mary shows us what true worship of God consists in. It consists in making one's life an offering to God. 'I am the handmaid of the Lord ... ' Mary's 'yes' is an example of obedience to the will of God, which is the way to salvation and holiness.

HOMILY 3   **Sinlessness**

The feast of the Immaculate Conception underlines the radical holiness of Mary. The angel Gabriel addressed her as 'full of grace'.

Because she was chosen to become the mother of the Saviour, God enriched her with gifts appropriate for such a role. Right from the beginning of her existence she was free from any stain of original sin. And by the grace of God she remained free of every personal sin her whole life long.

Humanity tends to be identified with sinfulness rather than sinlessness. The suggestion is that unless we know sin, we are not human. The result is that it's easy to regard Mary as the fourth person of the Godhead. To put her on such an exalted pedestal that she is utterly above and beyond us. But this is the not the Mary we find in the Scriptures.

In the Gospel we meet a woman who is 'deeply disturbed', asking herself, 'what this greeting could mean.' Before she gives her *fiat* she questions the angel. We find this questioning, this wondering, this pondering again and again in the Gospels.

God has given us the freedom to choose between good and evil. In so doing he has made sin possible – sin means choosing evil. But in giving us the freedom to choose, God also made virtue possible. Unless we had to make a choice between good and evil no virtue would be possible.

Mary too had the freedom to choose evil rather than good. It wasn't that she couldn't sin, but that she chose not to sin. But we might say, 'It was easy for Mary!' It wasn't easy for her. She too had to struggle to do the will of God. She was wholly human. The fact that she didn't sin, does not imply any lack of humanness. Sin is not an intrinsic ingredient of humanness. Quite the contrary. It is a fall from humanness. Yet when someone falls you hear people say, 'Ah, sure he's only human.' Thus we use humanness as an excuse for laziness, carelessness, and selfishness.

Sin is blindness, sin is ignorance, sin is absence of love. Far from understanding more of human life because we sin, we understand less of it. Sin separates us from others, and imprisons us in our own selfishness. The sinner cannot see beyond the self.

The gift of the Immaculate Conception must not be seen as easy or cheap grace for Mary. Far from protecting her from the joys and pains of living, it leads her to experience these at a deeper level. She was not immune to suffering, or hurt, or disappointment, or temptation.

She understands our struggles and our weakness. Every day we are faced with choices: to do good or to do evil. We have in us a strain of rebelliousness, of self-centredness, of short-sightedness, which causes us to make the wrong choices. But with the grace of God we can make the right choices. Even though there is no once-and-for-all victory over evil in our lives, every right choice makes the next right choice easier.

Adam and Eve lost their original innocence. So did we: we lost our childhood innocence. However, we can regain it. The second innocence is different from the first. The first is incapable of committing sin; the second is unwilling to commit sin. No matter how old we may be, God makes it possible for us to be reborn in innocence of character.

PRAYER OF THE FAITHFUL

President: The Lord worked wonders for Mary, and works wonders for us too. Let us bring our needs to him now, knowing that Mary is praying with us.

Response: Lord, hear our prayer.

Reader(s): For the Pope and the bishops: that they may continually remind the People of God of their call to holiness. [Pause] Let us pray the Lord.

For all people: that they may see the holiness of Mary as an example of all that is best and beautiful in humanity. [Pause] Let us pray to the Lord.

For all women, and especially for mothers: that they may experience the help of Mary the Mother of Jesus. [Pause] Let us pray to the Lord.

For all of us: that Mary our Mother may help us to persevere in the struggle to overcome evil. [Pause] Let us pray to the Lord.

For our own special needs. [Longer pause] Let us pray to the Lord.

President: Lord, at the angel's message, Mary became the temple of God, and was filled with the light of the Holy Spirit. Grant that following her example, we may humbly and steadfastly seek to do your will. We make our prayer through Christ our Lord.

REFLECTION   **The Role of a Mother**

A mother is a constant source of blessing and protection.
She is our strength in weakness,
    our consolation in sorrow, and our hope is misery.
Everything in nature speaks of a mother.
The sun is the mother of the earth,
    nourishing it with light and heat.
It never leaves at night until it has put everything to sleep,
    to the songs of the birds and the brooks.
The earth, in its turn, is mother to the trees and flowers.
And the trees in their turn become mothers
    of their fruits and seeds.
And Mary is our spiritual mother.
    Holy Mary, Mother of God, pray for us now
    and at the hour of our passing from this world to the Father.

New Sunday and Holy Day Liturgies

YEAR A

Flor McCarthy SDB

Provides for Year A (the Year of Matthew) all the elements you find in **New Sunday and Holy Day Lituriges, Year B**:

- three homilies for each occasion
- all homilies very focussed
- most Sundays have an additional story as well as the three homilies
- Scripture Notes for each occasion highlight biblical teaching or a theological theme
- carefully prepared introducitons, headings, prayers of the faithful and reflections
- all changes based on fifteen years of preaching, reflecting and reading

ISBN 1-871552-66-4

372 pages   Sewn paperback   235 x 156 mm

£14.99

Dominican Publications
42 PARNELL SQUARE, DUBLIN 1

Wedding Liturgies

Flor McCarthy SDB

Contains eighteen fully worked out liturgies – including readings from the rsv text – allowing both for weddings with Mass and weddings without Mass. Also provides material for wedding anniversaries.

' ... a precious boon ... provides all that is required for the enhancement of the church function, its enrichment by well-thought-out homilies, a wide-ranging choice of biblical texts, a selection of reflective passages after the Communion. A rich treasury indeed ... Worth its weight in gold' P. J. Brophy, parish priest, in *Doctrine and Life*.

ISBN 0-907271-96-0

x + 133 pages   Sewn aperback   215 x 138 mm

£7.99

Dominican Publications
42 PARNELL SQUARE, DUBLIN 1

Funeral Liturgies

Flor McCarthy SDB

A greatly revised new edition of a work which, when it first appeared in 1987, was acclaimed as 'a real God-send ... a welcome abundance ... Every circumstance and condition is considered.'

   Among the extensive revisions and improvements is a major addition – the inclusion of Committal Services allowing for use either at the graveside or at the crematorium.

ISBN 1-871552-47-8

272 pages   Sewn paperback

£9.99

Dominican Publications
42 PARNELL SQUARE, DUBLIN 1

The Gracious Word, Year B

COMMENTARY ON SUNDAY AND HOLY DAY READINGS
Wilfrid Harrington OP

INTRODUCTION TO THE LITURGICAL SEASONS
Philip Gleeson OP

Detailed scriptural commentary on the readings for each Sunday and Holy Day in Year B, plus introduction to the Gospel of Mark (the Gospel for Year B) and shorter introductions to other major biblical books. Also includes an analysis of the Infancy Narratives and an account of the distinctive features of the various Passion Narratives.

Three artists are featured – Benedict Tutty, Michael Lydon and Seán Adamson.

1-871552-56-7

256 pages   Paperback   210 x 135 mm

£8.99

Dominican Publications
42 PARNELL SQUARE, DUBLIN 1

The Gospel of Mark
A REFLECTIVE COMMENTARY

Denis McBride CSsR

Fr McBride employs here the clarity, scholarship and awareness of present-day needs evident in his earlier books. He shows that one can only understand the full identity of Jesus in the light of suffering and death: until Jesus fulfils his true destiny on the cross, his full identity remains hidden. Because of who he is, Mark insists, Jesus was destined to suffer. Is that also true of the people for whom Mark wrote? Is it true for believers in every succeeding generation?

Denis McBride, an English Redemptorist priest, has lectured in New Testament Studies for many years at the Hawkstone Hall International Pastoral and Study Centre for priests and religious.

ISBN 1-871552-55-9

272 pages   Paperback   210 x 135 mm

£8.99

Dominican Publications
42 PARNELL SQUARE, DUBLIN 1